T0315039

A Land of Milk and Butter

Markets and Governments in Economic History
A series edited by Price Fishback

*The Public Good and the Brazilian State: Municipal Finance and Public Services
in São Paulo, 1822–1930*
by Anne G. Hanley

Clashing over Commerce: A History of US Trade Policy
by Douglas A. Irwin

Selling Power: Economics, Policy, and Electric Utilities Before 1940
by John L. Neufeld

Law and the Economy in Colonial India
by Tirthankar Roy and Anand V. Swamy

Golden Rules: The Origins of California Water Law in the Gold Rush
by Mark Kanazawa

The Pox of Liberty: How the Constitution Left Americans Rich, Free, and Prone to Infection
by Werner Troesken

Well Worth Saving: How the New Deal Safeguarded Home Ownership
by Price Fishback, Jonathan Rose, and Kenneth Snowden

The Charleston Orphan House: Children's Lives in the First Public Orphanage in America
by John E. Murray

The Institutional Revolution: Measurement and the Economic Emergence of the Modern World
by Douglas W. Allen

A Land of Milk and Butter

How Elites Created the Modern Danish Dairy Industry

MARKUS LAMPE AND PAUL SHARP

The University of Chicago Press
Chicago and London

The University of Chicago Press, Chicago 60637
The University of Chicago Press, Ltd., London
© 2018 by The University of Chicago
All rights reserved. No part of this book may be used or reproduced in any manner
whatsoever without written permission, except in the case of brief quotations in
critical articles and reviews. For more information, contact the University of Chicago
Press, 1427 E. 60th St., Chicago, IL 60637.
Published 2018
Printed and bound by CPI Group (UK) Ltd, Croydon, CR0 4YY

27 26 25 24 23 22 21 20 19 18   1 2 3 4 5

ISBN-13: 978-0-226-54950-7 (cloth)
ISBN-13: 978-0-226-54964-4 (e-book)
DOI: https://doi.org/10.7208/chicago/9780226549644.001.0001

Library of Congress Cataloging-in-Publication Data

Names: Lampe, Markus, author. | Sharp, Paul, 1977– author.
Title: A land of milk and butter : how elites created the modern Danish dairy
    industry / Markus Lampe and Paul Sharp.
Other titles: Markets and governments in economic history.
Description: Chicago ; London : The University of Chicago Press, 2018. | Series:
    Markets and governments in economic history | Includes bibliographical
    references and index.
Identifiers: LCCN 2018008656 | ISBN 9780226549507 (cloth : alk. paper) | ISBN
    9780226549644 (e-book)
Subjects: LCSH: Dairy products industry—Denmark—History. | Agriculture—
    Economic aspects—Denmark.
Classification: LCC HD9275.D42 L36 2018 | DDC 338.1/762142094891—dc23
LC record available at https://lccn.loc.gov/2018008656

♾ This paper meets the requirements of ANSI/NISO Z39.48-1992 (Permanence of
    Paper).

Contents

Contents

Acknowledgments

The present book partly draws on research carried out jointly with Ingrid Henriksen, Peter Sandholt Jensen, Ekaterina Khaustova, Eoin McLaughlin, and Christian Volmar Skovsgaard, whom we thank for allowing us to share published and unpublished ideas, data, and results. We thank the editors and publisher of the *Economic History Review* for permission to use material from our articles "Just Add Milk: A Productivity Analysis of the Revolutionary Changes in Nineteenth-Century Danish Dairying," *Economic History Review* 68, no. 4 (2015): 1132–53 (underlying part of chapter 6); and "The Strange Birth of Liberal Denmark: Danish Trade Protection and the Growth of the Dairy Industry since the Mid-nineteenth Century," *Economic History Review* 65, no. 2 (2012): 770–88 (written jointly with Ingrid Henriksen, underlying part of chapter 8). We also thank the editors and publishers of the *European Review of Economic History* for permission to use material from our articles "How the Danes Discovered Britain: The International Integration of the Danish Dairy Industry before 1880," *European Review of Economic History* 19, no. 4 (2015): 432–53 (underlying chapter 7); and "The Role of Technology and Institutions for Growth: Danish Creameries in the Late Nineteenth Century," *European Review of Economic History* 15 (2011): 475–93 (written jointly with Ingrid Henriksen, underlying part of chapter 9), both used by permission of Oxford University Press.

We would like to thank especially those colleagues who commented in detail on all of the manuscript and greatly helped to make it clearer, more focused, and better contextualized, namely Per Boje, Ingrid Henriksen, Eoin McLaughlin, and James Simpson, as well as two referees for the University of Chicago Press.

Further, we would like to thank Rob Bryer, Carsten Burhop, Juan Carmona,

Mette Ejrnæs, Giovanni Federico, Eva Fernández, Silke Hüttel, Brooks Kaiser, Jan Tore Klovland, Michael Kopsidis, Pablo Martinelli, Chris Meissner, Alan Olmstead, Kevin Hjortshøj O'Rourke, Jan Pedersen, Ramon Ramon-Muñoz, Steve Toms, Martin Uebele, and seminar, workshop, and conference participants in many places around the world for sharing data and valuable comments and suggestions on the underlying work. Hege Hauglund, Andreea-Alexandra Maerean, Ursula Nemeth, and Camilla Hedegaard Svenningsen provided valuable assistance in the research behind and the formatting of the book, and Joseph Sharp provided valuable proofreading at an early stage. Julia Dávila-Lampe and Christian Volmar Skovsgaard helped to draw the maps and figures presented in the book. We would also like to thank all those who at various stages have offered advice and encouragement. If we have not mentioned you above it is not because you were not appreciated. Last, we would like to thank our families for their patience with us during the writing of this book, if not necessarily their understanding of our fascination with Danish butter!

This book would not have come to be had we not happened to be in the same New Researchers' Session at the 2007 Annual Conference of the Economic History Society in Exeter; and had the International Committee of the Department of Economics of the University of Copenhagen, chaired by Karl Gunnar Persson, not granted a postdoc position to Markus Lampe, in a project supervised by Ingrid Henriksen; and had Paul Sharp not been granted a postdoc to work on topics relating to this book by the Carlsberg Foundation. After sharing an office in Copenhagen, we met in different places, especially at Universidad Carlos III in Getafe, the University of Southern Denmark in Odense, the Vienna University of Economics and Business, and the University of Copenhagen in order to complete parts of the book. We thank Spain's Ministerio de Ciencia e Innovación, the Danish Council for Independent Research, the Carlsberg Foundation, and Fundación Ramón Areces for financial support of the research presented in underlying papers at various stages.

Glossary of Weights and Measures

rigsdaler	Unit of currency used until the introduction of the krone (= 0.5 rigsdaler) with the Scandinavian Monetary Union from May 5, 1873
tønde land	Unit of land corresponding to 0.55162 hectares
tønde hartkorn	From 1662 to 1903 this gave the taxable value of the land and was a quality- (fertility-) adjusted unit of land of varying size. Thus, high-fertility land of 1 *tønde hartkorn* would have a small area, and low-fertility land of 1 *tønde hartkorn* would cover a larger area.
pund	Unit of weight, 500 grams
kande	Unit of volume, 1.93 liters

Map of Denmark, Schleswig, Holstein, Lauenburg, and Altona, with places discussed in the book marked

Introduction

Je inniger die Verbindungen mit England werden und je mehr der Markt dieses Artikels [Butter] sich erweitert, am Ende im ganzen schleswig-holsteinisch-dänischen Insel- und Küstengebiete ein Land erzeugen werden, in dem, wo nicht Milch und Honig, doch Milch und Butter im Ueberfluß fließen, und das sich als solches Irland und Holland rivalisirend an die Seite stellen kann.

The more intimate connections with England become, and the more the market for this article [butter] expands, a land will be created throughout Schleswig-Holstein and Denmark . . . where not milk and honey, but milk and butter is flowing in abundance, and which may rival Ireland and Holland.

—JOHANN G. KOHL, *Reisen in Dänemark und den*
Herzogthümern Schleswig und Holstein

When Senator Bernie Sanders declared in the 2016 American presidential primaries "We should look at countries like Denmark," his words started a debate that, together with, for example, the recent success of Danish TV shows, media discussions of the concept of *hygge*, and Denmark's frequent status as the world's "happiest country," served to imprint that small country in the north of Europe on the consciousness of people around the world. For the economic historian Denmark also presents an interesting story, one illustrated by figure 1.1, which maps the 1,163 cooperatives that had spread across the country by 1909 and that enabled the successful management of the competitive pressures of the first wave of economic globalization in a way that distinguished Denmark from most of continental Europe.

Given that the majority of these cooperatives were established within a decade in the 1880s and early 1890s—and that they were all relatively sophisticated and highly capital-intensive factories using steam-powered machinery to produce butter in small rural villages—this rapid spread is remarkable. Not surprisingly, therefore, especially when seen from abroad, the economic history of Denmark seems almost in total to be the story of the rise of the cooperative movement. In fact, that agricultural cooperation explains much of Denmark's economic modernization seems to be pretty much everything one needs to know about this country from the perspective of an international textbook, apart perhaps from the agrarian reforms it underwent in the 1780s (which enabled farmers to create the cooperatives), or that it sent emigrants

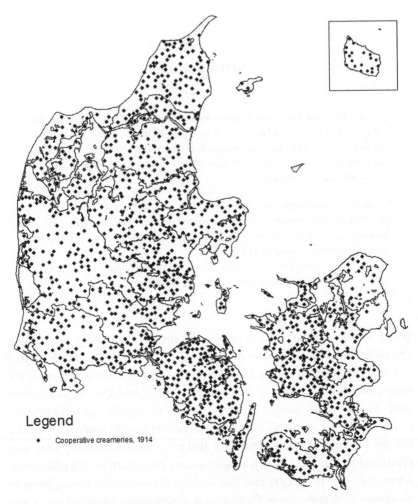

FIGURE 1.1. Location of cooperative creameries in 1914
Source: Created by the authors with the assistance of Christian Volmar Skovsgaard, based on data from Bjørn (1982a).

to the United States (some of them to set up dairy cooperatives) or that it later became a major user and exporter of wind power. And since this narrative is based on rather unlikely heroes for a modernization process—medium-sized farmers and smallholders living in the countryside—it has attracted wide attention as a reference for agricultural modernization, economic development, the origins of capitalism, change management, and even nation building (Kindleberger 1951; Johnston and Mellor 1961; preface by Jawaharlal Nehru in P. Manniche 1969; Senghaas 1986, chs. 2–5; Burnes 2009, 26–27; Trampusch and Spies 2014).

Likewise, the idea of a democratic and cooperative countryside is very much part of conventional Danish economic and national history. Often, this is seen as a reflection of a new national consciousness after the traumatic loss of the duchies of Schleswig and Holstein to Prussia in the Second Schleswig War (1864). Thus, when the Federation of Danish Cooperatives celebrated its centenary in 1999, the Danish prime minister called the cooperative movement "part of the history of the country of Denmark, which won inwardly what we lost outwardly after the catastrophe in 1864" (quoted in Mordhorst 2014, 121). Indeed, in prior research and many of the wider narratives about modern Denmark within the country and in terms of its perception by outsiders, the invention of the dairy cooperative by some Jutland farmers in 1882—and some of the events immediately preceding it—has been presented as a critical juncture in the development of modern Denmark.

When we first encountered this story, as foreigners entering Denmark and its academic world, we fully embraced it, but we soon came to ask ourselves, how was this possible? Where did Denmark's cooperatives come from so suddenly, and why did they spread so quickly? We found some answers, mainly in the works of economists and economic historians, but, as will be clear from the discussion of this literature below, research has exhibited a tendency to focus on the immediate determinants of cooperation rather than seeking to understand the institutional and technological bedrock upon which they stood. Clearly, the technology, the educational and scientific establishments, and not least the cows, all of which were to be crucial for the cooperatives, did not spring up overnight in the 1880s. Thus, looking for deeper historical answers led us on a journey that was to stretch back more than a century before the first cooperative. And the answers we present in this book suggest a rather different narrative than the above: a narrative less about the Danish peasantry and cooperatives and more focused on the role of (often German-speaking) elites who moved into Denmark, established themselves on traditional landed estates, and implemented a program of enlightened reform, which we argue laid the foundation for the later success of Danish agriculture. This interpretation does not question the importance of the cooperatives for Danish development, but it does help to explain the rapidity with which they spread throughout the countryside, and the success they enjoyed. The end result of our work might therefore seem surprising at first glance, since this is a book about Danish dairying that treats the cooperatives only very late (in chapter 9) and rather briefly. In fact, however, as the quote above from the famous German travel writer, Johann Georg Kohl, makes clear, already in the 1840s it was possible to discern the beginnings of what would become one of the backbones of Danish success—supplying agricultural products to the rapidly growing and industrializing English market—beginnings that preceded the creation of the first cooperative creamery by nearly four decades.

As our work progressed we soon noted that, of course, there had been dairying in Denmark before 1880 and that there were already established modernized practices; a good reputation in distant markets; networks of merchants, dairy tenants, administrators (enlightened farmers) and scientists; and even specialized education programs, mostly within a circle of owners of landed estates organized around the Danish Royal Agricultural Society (Landhusholdningsselskab). Since at least the 1760s, following models from Holstein, a German duchy ruled by the Danish monarch in personal union until 1864, this network had evolved into a cluster of dairy entrepreneurs within the framework of the large landed estates. In the agricultural system of these estates, a new Holstein cultivation process was implemented in which milch cows would be rented out to specialist tenants, who took care of them and the marketing of their produce. The tenants made use of the estates' pasturelands, temporary pasture in the crop rotation, and fallows for grazing and haymaking, while the cows provided manure and stable tenancy fees to the estate economy. The new methods benefited estates much more than peasant farmers, since they were subject to rather high minimum optimal sizes of production units due to the need for a specialist manager, the construction of specialized hygienic facilities, and a larger production to obtain a better price. Better-quality herds, larger output volume, and continuous contact with traders constituted additional advantages of estates. For peasant farmers, such advantages were traditionally impossible, since constant production, the hiring of specialists, and the construction of specialized facilities were not feasible for managers of smaller herds (Olsen 1957, 140–44).

This mixed farming model spread all over Denmark, and individual dairy tenants actually benefited from this spread, since it allowed for more regular and specialized market connections, gave access to a larger market beyond that within and immediately adjacent to Denmark (such as Hamburg and Norway), and created a reputation for Holstein and Danish export butter. Reputation and wider markets served to stabilize prices and diversify demand. Thus, this early cluster of dairy producers (and the merchants buying and marketing their produce) played a role in the rise of estate dairying similar to that played by cooperatives for peasant milk producers one hundred years later. The cooperatives in fact adopted the model of estate dairies on a (milk-producer-wise) smaller scale, allowing peasants to benefit from advances in modern techniques and more regular distribution channels for produce. As can be seen in figure 1.2, this led to a pronounced shift in the

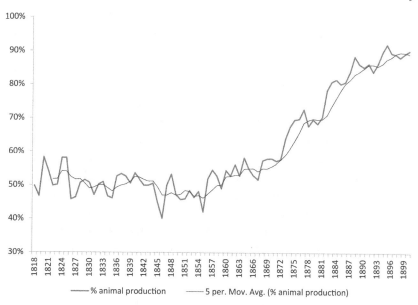

FIGURE 1.2. Percentage distribution of agricultural production value to animal products with five-year moving average, 1818–1900

Source: Henriksen, Lampe, and Sharp (2012), based on data from S. A. Hansen (1984, 233–35).

output structure of Danish agriculture from grain-based to animal-based production from at least the 1850s.

Recent studies in economics and political science have expressed conflicting views on the role of large landowners in economic development, as we will describe below, but in the case of Denmark we observe that a relatively strong central government stripped local elites of much of their power (and local government responsibilities) and launched agrarian reforms in which peasants obtained rather secure property rights (and became farmers) as well as relatively uniform access to education and other basic public goods. Large landowners then concentrated on taking part in central government or in becoming private entrepreneurs of professionally managed landed estates (cf. Kjærgaard 1994, ch. 8). Many chose the latter and used their resources to adopt modern methods that in the long run would have positive, although not necessarily intended, spillover effects on the wider agricultural population. These spillover effects emerged mostly because merchants and, to a certain degree, emerging well-to-do farmers found markets abroad for the produce of these professionalized estates and sought an additional supply of high-quality produce. They looked first to other large estates but then applied their best practices to the conditions of peasant production, a strategy that eventually led—again mostly or wholly unintentionally—to the rise of the cooperative movement.

In this process, we also observe a remarkable capacity of Danish elites in town and country to absorb and adapt foreign practices—or to integrate foreign-born innovators into their circles—although not always without tensions. Nevertheless, as we will see, a salient number of the main agricultural innovators in the eighteenth and nineteenth centuries were from northern Germany and moved to Denmark to reap the advantages of backwardness by introducing methods they had known and often practiced in their home country. This transfer of ideas and practices is most evident in the early name for estate dairies in Denmark and the duchies of Schleswig and Holstein, *hollænderier*, because the creators of the initial model had been immigrants from the Netherlands, where high-quality dairying had emerged already in the Middle Ages. But it is also reflected in the import and adaptation of crop-rotation systems, bookkeeping practices, and the general ideas of the Enlightenment and enlightened farming, as well as in the increasing orientation toward the virtually unlimited demand of foreign markets that opened up as mercantilism was dismantled in most places after the Napoleonic Wars.

Therefore, the present book is both a revision of the roots of Danish economic development and a rather peculiar case study of the role agriculture can play in economic development. Methodologically, as is common in case studies (Gerring 2004), we mostly rely on changes within Denmark over time to provide an in-depth analytic narrative of what happened there. In this, we sometimes take advantage of variation within the country—for example, in the spread of the Holstein system (chapter 4); sometimes we also discuss similar or adjacent places (especially the duchies of Holstein and Schleswig but also the Netherlands, Ireland, Prussia, and Sweden) and the main market for Danish exports, Great Britain. But our study is and remains most fundamentally a study of Denmark, not a comparative study of agricultural development or the dairy industry. Since Denmark has come to be something of a paradigmatic case in this respect, we believe that our in-depth revision is both necessary for understanding this particular case and for conceptualizing or reconceptualizing the conditions and mechanisms that underlie successful transformations in the agricultural sector. Then, based on this, comparisons can be made with other countries and paths—an analogy would be the fruitful stimulation that successive examinations of the British industrial revolution and its causes and consequences have had for our understanding of the causes and effects of modern economic growth. And much like successive reexaminations of the industrial revolution stand in close contact and build on advances in the economics of growth and development, our study only makes sense if we contextualize it within the main streams of economics and sociology that have investigated the role of agriculture in development and the conditions for successful agricultural development.

By bringing the traditionally dominant dairy producers—the large landed estates—back into the story, we therefore not only extend the existing story by more than one hundred years backward in time but also widen the picture. This widening contributes to two strands of literature that intersect only occasionally in the field of economic development: one focusing on the role of elites in development and another examining the role of agriculture in the transition to modern economic growth. Both strands ask how industrialization is brought about most effectively and thus how to escape—from a theoretical point of view—a traditional and stagnating sector like agriculture.

At the intersection of both literatures, the concentration of resources and power in the hands of traditional rural elites is often seen as leading to underinvestment in human capital and public goods such as education or health infrastructure and a lack of institutional modernization and political stability in general (Engerman and Sokoloff 2002; Lizzeri and Persico 2004; Banerjee and Iyer 2005; Galor, Moav, and Vollrath 2009; Acemoglu and Robinson 2012; Baten and Juif 2014; Cinnirella and Hornung 2016). Such negative effects would also manifest themselves in a reduced likelihood that agricultural producer cooperatives would emerge in unequal and socially fractionalized economies (Fernández 2014; O'Rourke 2007).

Clearly, there are plenty of examples of countries in which elites did not necessarily aid development in the countryside, and the spillovers we suggest above did not occur. A thorough understanding of how and why these experiences differed from the Danish case is clearly beyond the scope of the present work, since it would require detailed analyses of the developments in other countries. Nevertheless, we can discern some limiting factors, whose absence in Denmark was critical to the path described here. The first might be the inability or unwillingness of elites to invest. Elites in some countries might simply not have developed an interest in the marketing of agricultural surpluses because no suitable outlet for surpluses existed; this surely mattered to the timing of the Danish story as well. Economic elites might also have lacked capital or clearly defined property rights in relation to ruling political elites and thus lacked means and incentives to invest. A second limiting factor would have been the inability of peasants to adapt and benefit from knowledge and practices developed by elites, due to the same reasons mentioned above: capital constraints like lack of access to land or credit (e.g., because of lack of collateral or insufficient monetization) and inadequate individual property rights (including communal decision making on cultivation schemes and the limitations to the use of one's physical resources inherent in the need to perform unfree labor). In addition, the technologies used by elites might not have been reproducible at the peasant level; peasants might rationally have decided not to engage in commercialized farming if their subsistence was at constant risk; or elites might have actively blocked peasants from commercial contacts (whether directly or through restrictions on education) or prohibited the adoption of new technologies. In addition, some of these factors might have led to tensions and occasional violent confrontations between elites and the general agricultural population, increasing the social distance between them and thus the costs of information transmission and imitation. The latter might be described as a lack of "social capital" (Putnam 1995, 2001). One might think of India and many other developing countries, as well as parts of Spain and southern Italy, as examples of the first set of factors, while the second set has affected such countries as East Elbian Prussia and Russia (at least until 1906). Ireland, to which we will return repeatedly throughout the book, provides an example of a situation where conflict increases the weight of the second set of factors.

Nevertheless, a positive role for strong rural elites—as opposed to one based simply on the lack of capacity or interest of small farmers—has been argued by Melissa Dell in work on Peru and Mexico, contexts in which property rights were poorly defined and large landowners were able to shelter dependent peasants from extractive state institutions and effectively lobby for better provision of collective goods and infrastructure (Dell 2010, 2012). Recently, Squicciarini and Voigtländer (2016) have highlighted a similar context and historical setting as ours: France between 1750 and 1850. They emphasize the importance of the *type* of elite—as well as the economic context and incentives—to whether elites act as antagonists or protagonists of development. They show that knowledge elites (or what they term, following Mokyr 2005, the "upper-tail density of knowledge"), in their case proxied by the regional density of subscribers to that paragon of the Enlightenment, the *Encyclopédie ou Dictionnaire raisonné des sciences, des arts et des métiers*, led the French modernization process both before and after the French Revolution. Thus, in the spring of 1789, regions with denser knowledge elites sent more demands for mass education and other modernist programs to King Louis XVI, and they also displayed higher levels of education in the early nineteenth century (Squicciarini and Voigtländer 2016) and higher levels of development in general (Squicciarini and Voigtländer 2015). However, the authors underline explicitly that these outcomes only occurred after 1750, and materialized as a consequence of an acceleration of technological change which made elite knowledge suddenly useful for entrepreneurial activity in new sectors, while preexisting knowledge elites had previously mainly served less materialistic purposes (Squicciarini and Voigtländer 2015). Thus, together with the changed opportunities, the nature of the knowledge also can be argued to have changed to become more "useful" in the sense highlighted by Mokyr (2009) for the English enlightenment and its consequences for the industrial revolution. The focus of these existing studies is, however, in contrast to the present work on how elites facilitated a transformation out of agriculture, and, particularly in the studies by Squicciarini and Voigtländer, the focus and the proposed ways in which elites contributed to economic development are very broad and not specified in much detail.

Our work also connects with the existing, more immediate explanations suggested by economists and economic historians for why the cooperatives emerged in Denmark. O'Rourke (2006, 2007) discusses how Ireland tried rather unsuccessfully to emulate the Danish cooperative model. He traces the homogeneity, egalitarianism, and lack of conflict among the Danish population to the security of its property rights—a product of late eighteenth-century centralization and land reform. This development changed the status of the elites, reducing their powers of exploitation; it also gave more secure assets to the rest of rural society and thus, ceteris paribus, decreased the likelihood of violent conflict. This, in turn, enabled a denser network of social relations to develop among the elite, the rest of rural society, and the wider environment, thus strengthening what Putnam (1995, 2001) has termed "social capital." This can be expected to have facilitated an environment of relatively low transaction and contract-enforcement costs and the dense information-sharing network that we examine in later chapters. In comparative studies across countries (Fernández 2014), social capital has been highlighted as a main determinant of agricultural cooperation alongside low land inequality and (Protestant) religion, but it is difficult to argue for these factors as an explanation of different levels of cooperation within Denmark. Finally, and more speculatively, there might be a connection between elites and social capital formation if, as suggested by Squicciarini and Voigtländer (2016, 1), regions with a greater concentration of knowledge elites also had a denser network of mutual aid societies. Thus, the local presence of rational farming might have directly or indirectly contributed to the emergence of related emanations of social capital in the form of cattle insurance, credit pools, and so on, which in turn might have fostered cooperation.

Another factor that the existing literature attaches to dairy cooperatives is more directly related to our main argument. Henriksen (1999) in her statistical analysis of Denmark finds that preexisting cow densities are the most important predictor of the spread of the cooperative movement. In other country-commodity-specific studies, the scale of production prior to the introduction of cooperatives has also been highlighted as an important factor,[1] alongside other product-specific factors and access to transportation networks. We argue in chapter 4 that a main determinant of local cow densities before the emergence of the cooperatives is the adoption of modern dairying on the estates in the form of *hollænderier*, which led to imitation by nearby smaller farmers.

The second strand of literature we relate to articulates the traditional view of the passive role of agriculture in the process of economic modernization and economic development. Since agriculture was historically the most important sector in most economies (except those relying on fisheries, pastoralism, or hunter-gatherer activities), it was argued that economies would have to move *away* from more or less subsistence-oriented agriculture in order to advance through industrialization and achieve the development of a modern service sector within a market economy. The most extreme economic models, like the two-sector classical growth model by Arthur W. Lewis (1954), see agriculture as a sector where labor is employed very inefficiently and can be channeled into more dynamic economic activities without affecting agricultural production, as was probably the case in many developing countries just after the Second World War, with India being the model case (Tomlinson 2013, 63). While not all classical accounts take such extreme views, a general consensus emerged in the 1950s that for modern development to advance agriculture would necessarily have to shrink. Johnston and Mellor (1961, 567) described three basic reasons. First, the relative demand for agricultural products falls as income increases because the demand elasticity for agricultural produce is below one; that is, increases in income lead to less-than-proportional increases in spending on foodstuffs (although this is not necessarily true for dairying, as we will see below). Second, it is generally assumed that traditional agriculture did/does not use its resources in the best possible way, so that efficiency gains (more production with the same or fewer inputs of, for example, labor, land, and capital) would be possible. And, third, although such efficiency gains existed, the most dynamic sectors with the highest productivity gains were outside agriculture, since modern technology is biased toward industry, transport services, and energy generation.

Within such a passive framework—both in developing countries today and in the historical development of the world's richest economies—the best that agriculture could do was to not hinder the growth of more dynamic sectors and the economic and social transformations necessary for them. In this context five factors are generally highlighted as agriculture's critical contributions to economic development and growth (R. C. Allen 2004, 114–16; Johnston and Mellor 1961, 571–81). Agriculture should (a) increase food supplies, so a growing population that does not produce its own food (but works in factories) can be sustained without suffering from exorbitant food prices; (b) increase supply in a way that less manpower in agriculture is needed, and workers can be transferred to industry; (c) contribute to capital formation—that is, the use of agricultural incomes to finance the development process, either directly through investments in factories or indirectly through relatively heavy taxation used to create the infrastructure and conditions necessary for the development of modern sectors; (d) provide markets for the output of these new sectors—for instance, provide the demand for cheaper, factory-produced textiles instead of home-woven cloth or factory-made farm implements for use in agricultural production; and (e) export sufficient agricultural products to create the foreign exchange necessary to import foreign products, such as machines, when these are needed. While it has been noted that not all of these goals can easily be achieved, the classic policy recipes of the 1950s and 1960s would in general quite heavily discriminate against agriculture by establishing artificially low prices for both domestic food and exportables through marketing boards, an equivalent of taxation, and/or by imposing taxes on land (Johnston and Mellor 1961, Johnson 1993).

Much of this policy was a response to an earlier model of export-oriented growth that emerged in the nineteenth century and was based not on the potential for economic dynamism between sectors but on static considerations of the benefits of trade and international specialization. Grounded in the teachings of Adam Smith, David Ricardo, and others, this model stipulated that every country should specialize in the production of those commodities that it can produce relatively cheaply or more efficiently and then exchange these with other countries specializing in other commodities. Since modern industry emerged in Britain and soon spread to much of northwestern Europe over the early nineteenth century, soon a Great Specialization evolved on a world scale that led to a core-periphery division of labor, in which industrial products were exchanged for primary commodities—raw materials and foodstuffs. Since the prices of manufactures fell thanks to technological advances, but the prices of many agricultural products and minerals (initially) did not, the terms of trade of primary commodities improved in comparison to manufactures, allowing countries specializing in primary products to exchange their produce for ever more manufactures (Williamson 2011). In principle, this was a good thing from the consumers' perspective, but it might have been negative in the medium run since it led—as in the European countryside—to the substitution of factory production for home and artisan production. Such deindustrialization was one problem, especially if no indigenous industrialization took place, and in the long run productivity increases would not emerge in those countries specialized in primary production. Instead, the rising terms of trade would make primary production much more interesting as an investment than developing capabilities in the sectors where technological improvements were already under way on the other side of the Great Specialization.

Specialization in primary commodities would thus in the long run harm the possibility of real domestic economic growth (Matsuyama 1992). Instead of benefiting the entire population, gains would often be concentrated in the hands of a small elite—those owning the critical resources and rights—which would then try to block any diversification policies that might harm their social and economic position, leading to the negative impact of rural elites on economic development outlined above (Williamson 2011, 50–51). These negative effects would become much more pronounced if the terms of trade turned against such economies, as Raúl Prebisch (1950) and Hans Singer (1950) argued after the Second World War, when prices for primary products fell in comparison to manufactures. Recently, Jeffrey G. Williamson (2011) has added to this that, even given a boom in terms of trade for primary products in the nineteenth century, primary-product producers would have benefited relatively little because, even while prices rose, primary-product prices were much more volatile than those of industrial products. The incomes and revenues from primary products would thus be more volatile, making long-run investments in infrastructure, education, and so on more problematic. Thus, apart from the fact that economies would be less dynamic and less likely to sustain increases in levels of income, reliance on the production of primary goods for export would expose producers to commodity lotteries, the only escape from which would be industrialization.

Parting with these compellingly pessimistic views of the possibility that development can be achieved in and through agriculture, recent research has opened new paths to understanding rural development. Its main criticism of the consensus opinion regarding the passive role of agriculture is that, while admittedly in modern economic development the relative size of agriculture must decline, the way agriculture is positioned and treated in this process is critical to it being able to fulfill at least some of the five functions outlined above. Just as a cow needs to be properly fed in order to increase milk yields (see chapter 6), agriculture needs to develop in order to become more efficient—and for this simple extraction of labor and capital are not sufficient.[2] The ideal is then to achieve a balanced general development process, which otherwise might be choked off if disparities between developing urban areas and disfavored agricultural hinterlands are too great.

Already in 1961, Bruce F. Johnston and John W. Mellor argued for increased efforts to raise agricultural productivity through (1) research efforts to tailor existing advances to local contexts, (2) extension services to improve interactions between the laboratory and the farm, (3) the spread of new inputs like chemical fertilizers and improved seeds and breeds, and (4) a general increase in capabilities through education, which would aid the absorption and adoption of best practices in the countryside. Much of the technical side of this program has seen its ups and downs in practical development projects, but the focus on enhancing agricultural and rural capabilities, improving access to best practices, and increasing integration of rural areas into the economy through infrastructure development has been reinforced recently.

One important aspect of such rural development policies is to find out how to complement traditional agricultural systems with new crops and products that improve productivity. Such improvements aim not only to raise incomes but also to diversify production in order to spread risk, especially for very poor smallholders. One obvious candidate for such diversification is livestock. In recent publications, the Food and Agriculture Organization of the United Nations (FAO) has highlighted this and, in a Pro-Poor Livestock Policy Initiative, gathered evidence and summarized the advantages of livestock for poverty reduction and development (FAO 2012, 37–51). First, livestock contributes to income diversification, household food security, and a more diversified diet, even if the sector is not market oriented. For example, especially if market access is precarious, as in rural Ethiopia, cow ownership has been shown to help child nutrition and avoid stunting (Hoddinott, Headey, and Dereje 2015), something that might be behind the historically exceptional heights of Danes in the eighteenth and nineteenth centuries and inhabitants of other countries in northwestern Europe with a large livestock sector. But mixed farming with livestock provides not only meat and milk but also manure as fertilizer for the fields and potentially traction animals for plowing and transportation to increase crop production. If fed on otherwise uncultivable land or on crop residues and waste, livestock also improves the efficiency of agricultural resource use.[3]

Second, livestock is a form of capital which does not require constant additional money savings because it reproduces itself. As a form of capital, it can also serve as collateral or be sold or consumed in times of acute economic stress, thus minimizing nutritional risk while at the same time contributing to a diversification of income sources that decreases exposure to economic risk. Also, livestock is normally reared and taken care of all year long and thus smooths labor demand over the year and the seasonal cycles of crop production, as does the production of fodder crops whose harvest times do not coincide with those of food grains. Somewhat speculatively, the aforementioned Kohl (1846, 62) claimed that the regular year-round work involved in dairying became culturally engrained and led to a more steady mood—for example, in the Netherlands—in comparison to populations exclusively focused on crop growing or viticulture that involved intensive short-term efforts followed by large celebrations—a culture that is less useful for regular factory or office work as the economy develops. With some more serious backing, it has been argued that, since livestock is often taken care of by women, such a distribution of labor also might help to improve the balance of gender in agricultural households.[4] More gender equality has been shown to contribute to better nutritional and educational outcomes for children and hence to the development of capabilities for long-run economic development (Duflo 2012). As we will discuss below, however, the industrialization of dairying seems in some respects to have placed women among the biggest losers in our story.

In the field of economic history, Broadberry (2013, 4) has recently recognized the role of livestock in English agriculture as one of the main pillars of the early economic development of Britain and wider areas in northwestern Europe in the early modern period: "The first structural factor is the mixed agriculture with a large livestock component that helped to put the North Sea area on a path to high-value-added, capital-intensive, non-human-energy-intensive production."[5] Thus, the aforementioned features of the European agricultural system, of which the Danish version discussed in this book is a good example, replicate some of the central features of nonagricultural sectors. Agriculture can thus be a driver of growth in the same way as the nonagricultural sectors discussed in the classical accounts mentioned above, jointly with relatively rapid technological change and, potentially, above-average skill intensity. The production of butter and the associated by-products of cheese and bacon (skim milk, buttermilk, and whey were used as hog feed), as practiced in Denmark, was not just agricultural production with an important livestock component. It involved the processing of primary products (milk) into foods and the use of residues for by-products. Because of the perishability of milk, this process historically had to take place close to where cows and their feed were located, most likely in rural areas. There is thus a clear component of industrialization, including the accumulation of financial capital and the use of human capital, to the development of the Danish dairy industry, running from the early estate dairies to the later cooperatives in a process involving spillovers from innovative elites to rural producers in general.

What we can also see from existing studies is that butter production also represented a less volatile and relatively favorable ticket in the commodity lottery, probably because it was more similar to manufacturing than the production of most other agricultural commodities. Historically and today, the income elasticity of consumer demand for butter (i.e., the ratio of the percentage change in expenditure on butter to the percentage change in income) is much higher than that for typical agricultural products such as grains. To our knowledge, the only study of historical demand elasticities for cereals in comparison to dairy and other livestock products (meat) is that by Trevon D. Logan (2006), who uses the 1888 Cost of Living Survey, for which the United States Department of Labor interviewed thousands of households in the United States, the United Kingdom, and a much smaller section of continental western European households. Logan (2006, 539–43) finds the elasticity of expenditures on dairy products in Britain to be 0.71 with respect to household income and 0.90 with respect to household expenditure, quite similar to those for meat (0.72 and 0.93, respectively) and much higher than those for cereals (0.28 and 0.34).[6] This implies that a doubling in household income or expenditure led to an increase in the demand for livestock products of 70 to 90 percent, but an increase in spending on cereals of only some 30 percent, implying a shift in consumption patterns away from a cereal-based diet toward a more animal-based diet. In table 1.A1 in the chapter appendix, we show that recent studies of developing and developed countries confirm these results. Given the broad range of estimates, the differences between the elasticities for dairy and meat are probably not very different nowadays and might be close to 1, while the demand for cereals seems to lie between 0.2 and 0.6. This again means that demand for dairy products on average will increase much more than demand for cereals as incomes increase.

An increase in demand that is more proportional to income should also in the long run lead to more favorable price developments and more stable prices than those for grains and similar agricultural products. Figure 1.3 traces the long-run movement of the prices of butter in relation to other agricultural products from 1700 to 1900 and thus the market signals that Danish landowners and peasants were receiving during the period of our study, in this case from the British market, which both turned out to be the main outlet for Danish exports and is commonly held to reflect world market conditions before the First World War.[7] Any value higher than 100 means that the same amount of butter can be exchanged for more of the commodity in question; that is, butter prices rose by more or fell by less than the prices of alternatives. In figure 1.3 we see that butter prices in the long run evolved favorably in

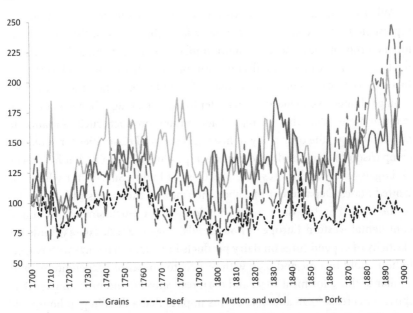

FIGURE 1.3. Relative prices of butter compared to alternative farm products in the United Kingdom, 1700–1900 (1700 = 100)

Source: British prices from Clark (2005) and Sauerbeck-Statist data set as reported by Jacks, O'Rourke, and Williamson (2011), deflated by the UK consumer price index compiled by Hills, Thomas, and Dimsdale (2010).

Note: Underlying price series for butter divided by price indices for the respective goods. In grains, wheat and barley weighted 50:50; mutton and wool weighted 50:50.

comparison to all other agricultural commodities except beef. This was especially the case from about 1850, when mercantilist protection generally ended across Europe (Tena-Junguito, Lampe, and Tâmega 2012; Federico 2012b), European and global markets integrated, and European prices of more storable commodities such as grains and wool came under pressure from new sources entering the world market (such as from the United States, Russia, Canada, Argentina, Australia, and so on; O'Rourke 1997). By 1900, the proceeds from the same amount of butter would buy 2.3 times as many grains as in 1700, 3 times as much wool, and roughly the same amount of beef and mutton.

Figure 1.4 shows that butter prices also evolved favorably in comparison to the main tropical commodity, sugar, due to the development of European substitutes in the form of beet sugar, which was subsequently used as a way to support struggling grain farmers through protection and subsidies.[8] By 1900, compared to 1700, relative prices for butter were 9 times higher than sugar prices. Butter prices also evolved more favorably than prices of bar iron, as an

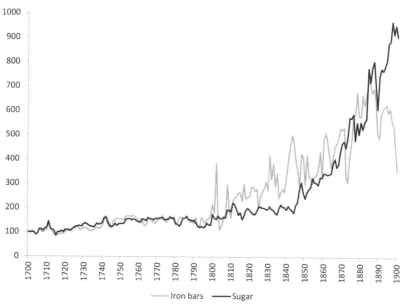

FIGURE 1.4. Relative prices of butter compared to manufactures (iron bars) and tropical agriculture (sugar), 1700–1900 (1700 = 100)

Source: British prices from Clark (2005) and Sauerbeck-Statist data set as reported by Jacks, O'Rourke, and Williamson (2011), deflated by the UK consumer price index compiled by Hills, Thomas, and Dimsdale (2010).

example for manufactured goods, of which, by 1900, 3.5 times as much could be exchanged for the same quantity of butter.[9]

Between 1700 and 1900, butter prices were also consistently less volatile than those of grains and evolved similarly to those of beef and mutton but much more favorably than those of wool (see table 1.A2 in the chapter appendix). The volatility of butter prices was also below that for manufactured products, while sugar prices exhibited surprisingly low volatility alongside their considerable fall. All this is even more remarkable since from the mid-1870s margarine appeared on European markets as a strong substitute for butter, thus checking a probably even more favorable evolution of butter prices (Lampe and Sharp 2014a). As we will see in later chapters, the often-discussed alternative specialization in raising livestock for the production of beef or mutton seemed to be as favorable in terms of price developments but was much riskier due to the imposition of health-motivated import bans in the main export markets, Britain and Germany. Beef production also probably did not entail the same benefits in terms of rural industrialization since, even in contrast to bacon production, beef cattle were generally exported live and fattened by intermediaries to be slaughtered at the destination. In general, therefore, we can conclude that butter was indeed a relatively fortunate good to specialize in, but this was probably because it combined both a relatively high income elasticity of demand and a more industrial production technology.

To better illustrate that butter production is both agricultural and industrial, a short introduction to how butter is produced will be helpful. Butter production is essentially a three-stage process: first, the milk must be produced; second, the cream must be extracted from the milk; and third, the cream must be churned to make butter. Butter is almost always made from the milk of cows since that of, for instance, sheep and goats is less suited to this purpose.

In its natural state, a cow will conceive in late spring and give birth to a calf around 280 days later, with production of milk peaking after around fifty days and declining thereafter. The quality and quantity of the milk depends most importantly on the cow's breed, its diet, and its health. As we will see in later chapters, throughout our period, important advances were being made in all aspects of dairy farming in Denmark. The technology for milking the cow did not advance, however, until the introduction of milking machines in the early twentieth century. Milking was thus performed by hand by the milkmaid, with generally around twenty cows per milkmaid in the larger estate dairy units.

As for the second stage, the extraction of the cream, unhomogenized milk contains butterfat dispersed in microscopic globules throughout the liquid (unlike most store-bought milk today, in which the fat has been more evenly distributed or, in the case of skim milk, removed completely). The traditional Danish method of separating cream from milk was called the *bøtte* (or tub) system: milk was poured into a flat container with a large surface area—the *bøtte*—after which the cream would gradually rise to the surface; it was later found that cooling the milk accelerated this process. By the 1880s, however, the *bøtte* system had been replaced by the mechanical centrifuge. Thus the main advances in mechanical technology for dairying appeared in the nineteenth century—although most of these appear only toward the end of our story.

In the final stage of butter production, the butterfat globules in the separated cream are surrounded by membranes (phospholipids) and proteins that prevent them from pooling into a single mass. The process of churning agitates the cream, damaging the membranes and allowing the milk fats to conjoin and separate from other parts of the cream. Thus, small butter grains are left floating in the watery part of the cream called buttermilk. This liquid is drained off, and the grains are worked (i.e., pressed and kneaded together) on a wooden board, releasing the remainder of the buttermilk and leaving a solid mass: the butter. This was (and still is) often mixed with salt, in order to allow the butter to keep longer before going rancid. The process of churning the cream was traditionally performed using a plunge churn, in which a staff was repeatedly plunged into a container, or a barrel churn, in which a paddle churned the butter when a handle was turned. The process of churning was only mechanized in the mid-twentieth century.

Apart from the more subjective quality criteria, there are two main measures of the efficiency with which milk is produced. First, the amount of milk produced per cow, which as we will see in chapter 6 increased rapidly over our period. Second, the quantity of butter produced per unit of milk, which we turn to in chapter 9. Moreover, the production of butter resulted in a couple of by-products: skim milk and buttermilk. Changes in the use of these by-products were also important to the success of the Danish dairy industry, as explored in chapter 8.

Thus, butter production can—and in the case of Denmark did—contain many of the elements of an industrialization process but without the huge sectoral shifts in the labor force and migrations from rural areas to cities (Carmona, Lampe, and Rosés 2017; Williamson 1994). This does not mean that the process described in this book was a substitute for industrialization and urbanization, which certainly also happened in Denmark, but that these processes were accompanied by parallel developments in the countryside that fostered a relatively balanced developmental path.

Therefore, the present book is basically three things: (1) an in-depth investigation of how an elite avant-garde established best practices whose spillover effects transformed a wider (rural) population, (2) a revision of the roots of Danish economic development, and (3) a case study of the role agriculture can play in balanced economic development. To embed our study in the existing literature and show how this work contributes to the literature, we follow an approach familiar from theory creation in the social sciences: the "bathtub" of macro-micro relations attributed to James Coleman (depicted in figure 1.5). Normally, this scheme is used to illustrate how phenomena on an aggregate macro level (e.g., openness to new ideas) relate to the attitudes or perceptions of individuals, firms, and so on (e.g., dense networks of information exchange), which have consequences for individual action (e.g., the adoption of organizational and technological innovations), which then can be collectively discerned at the macro level (e.g., in the form of technological progress). In practice, the "bathtub" often illustrates how difficult it is to trace the impact of general social and economic processes at the individual level or to verify that findings that apply to individuals in detailed historical studies

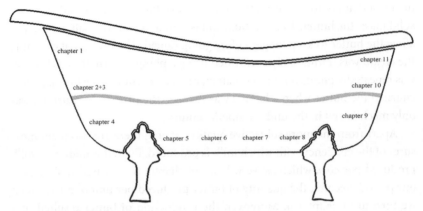

FIGURE 1.5. Plan of the book
Source: Created by the authors with the assistance of Julia Dávila-Lampe.

actually generalize. We adapt this idea somewhat liberally for the structure of our work.

After having outlined the general argument and the conceptual and methodological framework in this chapter, chapter 2 provides an overview of the most important geographical, cultural, and historical fundaments of Danish history over the period from 1660 to the early nineteenth century, thus setting the scene in which our story plays out. We put special emphasis on a series of enlightened political reforms since the 1780s. In chapter 3 we zoom in on one branch of reform that was particularly important for agriculture, the agricultural reforms that led to a large-scale transformation of most of Denmark's sixty thousand medium-sized farms from labor-burdened semi-feudal tenancy arrangements and communal cultivation to enclosure and freehold or lifetime lease. In the process, traditional estates lost much of their local economic and political power but retained their self-cultivated main farms (demesnes). Chapter 4 then moves to the level of the dairy sector and explains how the introduction of a new cultivation system, *Koppelwirtschaft*, on landed estates from the 1760s led to the rise of large dairies in a mixed farming system often adequately dubbed the Holstein system in English-language accounts. We examine how this system spread first among estates and subsequently to the surrounding peasantry, where it helped establish the competencies and assets that would enable the later spread of cooperative medium- and smallholder dairy production.

Chapters 5 to 8 examine specific developments that created opportunities for the expansion of the dairy sector through estates as well as the classes of farmers and smallholders, detailing the specific links that emerged between estate practices and peasant imitation. Chapter 5 deals with the importance of the early introduction of sophisticated measuring, record keeping, and accounting practices, which allowed for a lively public discourse on best practices and resource use. We argue that the capabilities developed in this process were instrumental to the rapid spread of smallholder dairying later on. The description of this capability-building process is complemented in chapter 6 by our analysis of the introduction of specialized agricultural schooling and apprenticeship programs; the chapter charts the introduction and development of best-practice methods and examines the incipient agricultural research and experimentation efforts that not only met international standards but in many ways established the frontier of knowledge. Chapter 7 then outlines how Danish merchants and estate owners established the marketing channels necessary for taking advantage of the rapidly growing markets abroad, especially in industrializing Britain, and how they actively stimulated quality improvements to obtain more marketable produce. Chapter 8 analyzes the role of the Danish government in the development of the dairy industry, which is normally presented as a liberal hands-off attitude. We show that, apart from providing a development-friendly environment by sponsoring general education and related research, the Danish government through the structure of the tariff laws in the nineteenth century also helped to shift relative prices in favor of dairying and thus (initially inadvertently) encouraged diversification of commercial produce toward livestock production, most notably through a high tariff on (skim-milk) cheese, an important by-product of butter production under traditional methods.

In chapter 9 we finally describe how these developments, which were largely confined to a cluster of landed estates and their dairy units until the second half of the nineteenth century, spread to medium-sized farms and smallholders, initially through a model of privately owned community creameries, which then evolved into and were spread by the dairy cooperatives from 1882. Chapter 10 returns to the aggregate level of the Danish economy and examines the posthistory of these developments on a national scale, linking the development of agriculture and dairying in Denmark to the overall economy and society. In joining the early to the late nineteenth century through the evolution of the dairy sector in this book, we of course do not intend to argue that these were the only links that mattered to the general process of Danish economic development: industrialization and the development of transport, banking, and so on occurred in parallel and might reveal further links worthy of deeper exploration; here they are summarized as potential connections between chapters 2 and 10. Finally, chapter 11 reexamines current and past general strategies and prescriptions for agricultural development and considers the transplantability of the Danish experience to other contexts; we conclude by presenting the implications of our historical case study for fostering agricultural and general development in today's developing countries.

Appendix

TABLE 1.A1. Recent estimates of income elasticities of demand for dairy products, meat, and cereals

Country	Period	I/E	Cereals	Dairy	Meat	Excess dairy over cereal	Source
India	1983–2005	E	0.187 (cereals); 0.050 (mean wheat, rice)	1.640/0.429 (milk)	n/a; 0.669 (meat, fish, eggs)	141.3/61.9	Kumar et al. (2011, 11), QUAIDs model/FCDS model
China (urban)	2001	E	0.9575 (mean rice, other grain)	1.004	1.192 (mean beef, pork, poultry)	4.7	Gould and Villarreal (2006, 11)
China	2002–5	E	0.116	1.002	0.438	88.6	Huang and Gale (2009, 403), means of low, middle and high elasticities
Brazil	1987/88 and 1995/96	I	0.237 (wheat)	0.721 (milk)	0.743 (mean meat, ham)	48.4	Menezes, Azzoni, and Silveira (2008, 2565)
Mexico	2006	I	0.065 (tortilla); 0.818 (cereals)	0.905	0.939	84.0 (tortilla); 8.7 (cereals)	Wood, Nelson, and Nogueira (2012, 82), average of all four reported coefficients
Italy	1952–2003	E		0.663			Bouamra-Mechemache et al. (2008, 649)
France	1960–2004	E		0.704			Bouamra-Mechemache et al. (2008, 649)
USA	1982–2000	I	1.351 (cereals and bakery)	2.246	1.810	89.5	Reed, Levedahl, and Hallahan (2005, 35)
Average			0.537	1.035	0.965	63.2	
Median			0.212	0.905	0.841	73.2	

Note: Observations ranked from low to high by average income per capita in given period according to Maddison data set (Bolt and van Zanden 2014). "I/E" indicates income or expenditure elasticity. "Excess dairy over cereal" calculates for a 100 percent increase in income by how many percentage points dairy demand increase exceeds cereal demand increase. "n/a" means no estimate available. "Average" takes mean for cells with multiple elasticities. "Median" takes all elasticities into account individually. "China (urban)" comprises urban parts of the provinces of Jiangsu, Shandong, Guangdong, Henan, and Heilongjiang only.

TABLE 1.A2. Price volatility for selected products, 1700–1900

	1700–1750	1750–92	1816–50	1850–1900	Whole period
Butter	0.142	0.074	0.154	0.081	0.116
Barley	0.181	0.191	0.240	0.116	0.181
Wheat	0.239	0.193	0.217	0.174	0.206
Cheese	0.159	0.080	0.141	0.115	0.127
Beef	0.094	0.071	0.165	0.082	0.105
Pork	0.149	0.098	0.230	(0.134)	0.154
Mutton	0.101	0.081	0.164	0.093	0.110
Wool	0.108	0.147	0.221	0.136	0.152
Iron bars	(0.096)	(0.104)	0.260	0.163	(0.161)
Sugar	0.096	0.080	0.100	0.107	0.097

Source: See figure 1.3.

Note: Price volatility defined as in Jacks, O'Rourke, and Williamson (2011) as standard deviation of $(\ln(P_t) - \ln(P_{t-1}))$. French Revolutionary and Napoleonic Wars (1793–1815) excluded. Parentheses denote that in more than 10 percent of years covered nominal prices are not changing from one year to the next, which might be an indication of data problems.

The Economic and Political Context for Danish Agricultural Development, ca. 1660–1850

Today, Denmark is a small state in northwestern Europe, with a highly developed welfare state, high living standards, and a relatively homogeneous population with a pronounced national identity, high levels of education, and unrivaled levels of life satisfaction and income equality. For much of the period studied in this book and the preceding centuries, however, Denmark was somewhat different: a conglomerate monarchy[1] comprising Norway (until 1814), provinces in southern Sweden (until 1659), the duchies of Slesvig/ Schleswig, Holsten/Holstein, and (from 1814) Lauenburg in northern Germany (until 1864), as well as Iceland (until 1944), Greenland, the Faroe Islands (both still affiliated with Denmark), and colonies in the Caribbean,[2] Africa,[3] and India,[4] which were all sold to the United States and Britain between 1845 and 1916. From 1660 to 1849, the changing Danish territory was ruled by absolutist monarchs, and during much of the eighteenth century severe, semifeudalist laws in Denmark proper restricted the movement of the population, as we will discuss below.[5]

In economic terms, relatively little can be said about GDP per capita and rural or urban wages before 1800. Recently, Ekaterina Khaustova and Paul Sharp (2015) reconstructed real wages for Copenhagen and Copenhagen County from 1731 to 1913 in a manner comparable to Robert C. Allen's (2001, 2009a) figures for a variety of cities across Europe and the rest of the world. Allen's method compares nominal wages for comparable professions (e.g., urban and rural unskilled laborers) to the cost of a consumption basket that adjusts for price differences across time and space. If we divide wages by the cost of the basket, we get what Allen calls "subsistence ratios" or "welfare ratios," which express how many times a male wage can purchase the basket

TABLE 2.1. Welfare ratios (nominal wages/respectability basket), 1750–1840

	Copenhagen	Copenhagen (rural)	London	Amsterdam	Antwerp	Leipzig	Madrid	Milan	Paris
1750	0.58	...	1.76	1.46	1.28	0.70	0.75	0.48	0.73
1770	0.57	...	1.38	1.34	1.24	0.55	0.61	0.53	0.61
1790	0.51	0.52	1.21	1.22	1.16	0.54	0.56	0.42	...
1820	0.55	0.55	1.27	1.02	1.22	0.66	...	0.35	...
1840	0.71	0.71	1.31	0.99	1.21	0.64	0.82	0.39	0.96

Source: Khaustova and Sharp (2015) and R. C. Allen (2001).

for a family with the consumption needs of three adult-equivalent members. Allen constructs a "bare-bones subsistence basket"[6] and a "respectability basket," which contains more and higher-value foodstuffs (such as cheese, eggs, and beer) as well as more fuel and candles and, in absolute terms, covers higher housing expenses. In the case of Copenhagen, the respectability basket is on average 2.65 times as expensive as the subsistence basket.

Table 2.1 presents these welfare ratios for male workers in Copenhagen (urban), Copenhagen County (rural), and leading European and north Atlantic cities: London, Amsterdam, Antwerp, Leipzig, Madrid, Milan, and Paris. We concentrate on welfare ratios calculated with the respectability basket, although before the 1840s Danish worker families could barely afford it, at least when relying on the labor of a single family member, as can be seen from ratios below one.

Before 1820, real wages in and around Copenhagen were rather stationary (with some annual fluctuations not reflected in the table); they were lower than in the leading parts of the European economy during that period (London, Amsterdam, Antwerp) but catching up with Paris and Leipzig and clearly higher than in southern Europe. So we can assume that, before 1820, in all likelihood the majority of the increase in production went as rents to small urban and rural elites and, more importantly, served to enable substantial population growth without falling standards of living.

This finding is supported by preliminary work by Cristina Radu (2016), who makes use of a vast and detailed database of prices and wages collected by the Danish Price History Project (see Andersen and Pedersen 2004). These data cover the period 1660 to 1800 and provide 21,528 wage observations for eighteen manors. She constructs a representative nominal wage series using the method described by Gregory Clark (2005) and deflates this in a number of ways inspired both by Robert C. Allen (2001, 2009a) and by Kim Abildgren (2010), who has constructed a consumer price index that covers this period.

Radu finds that real wages were surprisingly constant during the eighteenth century, with the standard of living in rural Denmark similar to or below that in poorer European cities.

In this context, it would be desirable to include rents to capital and land in the picture to show the evolution of Danish GDP per capita and its distribution. However, the evidence available before 1850 or 1870 is sketchy and the data inconclusive. For example, David Landes (1999, 232) features a table based on data assembled by Paul Bairoch (1981, 10), which situates Denmark as one of the poorest countries for which there is data in 1830, on par with Norway and with only Russia and Japan behind it.[7] However, in the latest version of the Maddison data set of global GDP per capita comparisons (Bolt and Van Zanden 2014), Denmark was already one of the richest countries in Europe in 1820, surpassed only by the United Kingdom, the Netherlands, north-central Italy, and the United States, and ahead of the other Scandinavian countries as well as France and much of southern Europe. A third source, the indirect GDP estimates by Prados de la Escosura (2000), situates Denmark in 1820 at the end of a six-country sample (behind Australia, the United States, the United Kingdom, the Netherlands, and France) with real GDP per capita at 51.3 percent of the US level.

While revised estimates of historical GDP per capita for Denmark (and many other countries) are still under construction, we can tentatively conclude that Denmark by 1750 or 1820 in terms of wages and productivity was behind the most productive economies of the time (the United Kingdom, the Netherlands, modern-day Belgium, the United States, and maybe northern Italy) but ahead of most of the rest of the world. As we will demonstrate in chapter 10, however, Danish wages and GDP increased considerably over the nineteenth century, and, most notably, this growth began not at the typical moments of modernization after 1870 or 1880 but earlier, maybe from the 1840s or 1850s, although the timing remains unclear. This growth also saw Denmark catch up to the leading economies of the period, first Britain and the Netherlands and then the United States. This is important for our narrative since a key point of this book is that the roots of Denmark's economic transformation, at least in terms of agriculture, can be traced back to before the Napoleonic Wars, although Danish growth was certainly interrupted by that event.

In the rest of this chapter we start by providing a short overview of economic theories relevant to understanding and contextualizing Denmark's economic performance over this period, specifically theories relating to geography, demography and the disease environment, institutions and politics, human capital, and culture. These collectively formed the preconditions that to differing degrees allowed Denmark, or at least Danish agriculture, to embark on the development path we describe in the remainder of this book. With this theoretical framework in mind, we then present an overview of the Danish experience. One important institutional development with clear relevance for our story—land reform—we will return to in the next chapter.

Theories of Economic Development

If we believe accounts of global economic development such as Landes (1999), Denmark's catch-up to the world's leading economies requires little explanation. Landes concluded (248) that "this impressive performance owes everything to cultural preparation"—namely high-level literacy and first-class education at higher levels as well as early political order and stability: "Property rights were secure; the peasantry was largely free [in Scandinavia], and life was a long stretch of somber hard work broken intermittently by huge bouts of drinking and seasonal sunshine." Upon deeper inspection, Landes's argument exhibits not only a distinct scent of prejudice but also melds a rather idiosyncratic mix of factors including individual freedom, property rights, work attitudes, and education. It also leaves the reader puzzled as to why catch-up was necessary at all and why modern economic growth did not actually start in Scandinavia instead of nearby Britain. We propose, inspired by recent works on economic growth, to distinguish four factors that might be called root causes of economic growth (or the lack thereof): geography and the physical environment; demography and the relative abundance of labor and resources; the political and institutional environment and the security of property rights; and the interplay between culture, religion, and education of elites and the general population.[8] As will become clear, these also broaden the specific arguments given for the role of elites and agriculture in economic development surveyed in chapter 1.

Jared Diamond (1997) has highlighted geography as *the* main determinant of economic development: the shape and location of Africa, Eurasia, and the Americas conditioned the existence and diffusion of domesticable species of plants and animals, which in turn determined the viability of agriculture and animal husbandry and hence settlement patterns, population densities, and technological and economic progress. Within this framework, further research has proposed that particular features of geography and climate had more specific implications: such as shaping access to markets and openness to new ideas (Dalgaard 2010); determining the viability of advanced agricultural techniques and tools (Gallup, Sachs, and Mellinger 1999; Andersen, Jensen, and Skovsgaard 2016); shaping the disease environment (Gallup and Sachs

2001); and, potentially, fostering the cultural traits highlighted by Landes, which apparently contradict Montesquieu's famous conjecture ([1748] 1989) that ready availability of food in the tropics led to laziness and the absence of hard work in agriculture.

Demography, especially population growth, acts as an important barrier to sustained economic development in classical accounts of the "poverty of nations," such as that of Rev. Thomas Robert Malthus (1766–1834). Malthus's pessimistic view posits that any increase in living standards almost inevitably leads humans to increase their fertility and life expectancy, and thus to expand the population as a whole. Since this larger population uses more resources, especially cultivable land, this diminishes the sustainability of the increase in living standards, giving rise to a "Malthusian trap" and economic stagnation in the long run (Clark 2007, 19–32). In contrast, however, Boserup (1965) argued that human societies can and actually do adapt to population growth by adopting more labor-intensive cultivation techniques, so that the backlash of population growth can at least partly be avoided. Others, following Adam Smith, have elaborated on this by pointing out that higher population densities also facilitate market integration, specialization, and the exchange of ideas, and thus enable learning by doing and hence technological progress, making it possible to sustain growing populations at higher standards of living (Persson and Sharp 2015, 52–56, 67–69; Galor and Weil 2000).

Institutions, and especially the accountability of central government by stakeholders, represent one of the most popular fundamental explanations of economic growth. Daron Acemoglu and James A. Robinson (2012) succinctly posit this as a difference between societies with extractive political institutions, which enable powerful elites to economically exploit their subjects, and societies with inclusive political institutions, in which subjects control the government, thus ensuring institutional actions that align the interests of all parties, especially through the establishment of property rights and their impartial enforcement. In this account (Acemoglu and Robinson 2012, 216), absolutism is a clear recipe for economic stagnation as observed in the Russian and the Ottoman Empires into the twentieth century, as well as in Denmark until 1849: "Absolutism is rule unconstrained by law or the wishes of others, though in reality absolutists rule with the support of some small group or elite." Such unconstrained elites can and will use centralized power to ban innovations and entrepreneurship since they might endanger the economic and political status quo from which elites benefit. Douglass C. North, John Joseph Wallis, and Barry Weingast (2009) explain that external threats and wars often triggered transitions from extractive to inclusive political and social orders. Especially after the European military revolution of the sixteenth and seventeenth centuries, wars and defense required increased state capacity and huge amounts of human and financial resources (Tilly 1992; Bogart et al. 2010). Mobilizing these resources turns out to be easier if rights are granted to potential creditors and the general population to enhance their commitment to the cause.

Finally, the role of culture, religion, and education has been highlighted not only by Landes (1999) but also in *The Protestant Ethic and the Spirit of Capitalism*, the famous work by Max Weber (1930) that influenced Landes's focus on work ethic but has been assessed critically by economic historians at least since Tawney (1926). More recently, studies on Prussia have shown that protestants had higher literacy rates and better education in general (Becker and Woessmann 2009). Better education in turn generally led to lower fertility and hence contributed to escaping the Malthusian trap (Galor and Weil 2000; Becker, Cinnirella, and Woessmann 2012). Moreover, education contributes to technological progress and its spread and, hence, to higher incomes, as discussed in chapter 1. In addition, Oded Galor and Omer Moav (2006) argued that the actual transition from a setting with extractive institutions to one with inclusive institutions was not the consequence of political decisions but brought about by the need of elites for more educated subjects to advance their dominant production model. Religion and shared beliefs in general have also been argued to be the basis for differences in institutional quality (Greif 1994) and the dense social exchange labeled as "social capital" (Putnam 1995) mentioned in chapter 1.

This short and by no means comprehensive overview illustrates that in the long run all these factors condition and reinforce each other. Even the natural environment requires institutions and technology to make it useful to societies that experience economic development.[9] The review also makes clear that the connections between these factors become more understandable if we first examine them separately. We do so in the following.

Geography, Infrastructure, and Openness

The territory of Denmark proper is characterized by a coincidence of particularly fortunate geographic conditions. It embodies the perfect combination of temperate climate, universal access to the sea, and proximity to the most dynamic centers of the early modern economy—Great Britain and the Netherlands. Regarding climate, the combination of temperate summers and relatively mild winters, together with plentiful rainfall, makes the country suitable for both agriculture and cattle raising. Climate and geography taken together, all of Denmark lies in the "temperate ecozones proximate to [within

100 km of] the sea" which account for only 8 percent of the inhabited area of
the earth but contain 23 percent of its population and produce 53 percent of
its GDP (Mellinger, Sachs, and Gallup 2000, 169; cf. O'Rourke 2006, 160). In
terms of physical geography, no place in Denmark lies more than fifty kilometers from the coast (Henriksen 2006), which is abundant in natural harbors,
and the terrain is flat with an average altitude of thirty-one meters.[10] With its
continental part (Jutland) marked by fjords and 443 islands, Denmark has
the second largest coastline-to-area ratio of any independent country with
more than one million inhabitants, surpassed only by Singapore (Dalgaard
2010, 129).[11]

Flat terrain and plenty of coast aided a natural export orientation and the
early emergence of an integrated market. Apart from early endeavors of the
Vikings and other Norsemen, Denmark and the whole of the Danish monarchy was integrated into the trade of northern Germany (Hanse), the Low
Countries, and Great Britain since the Middle Ages. Nevertheless, the special
advantage of a long coastline still required investment to exploit it. Thus, the
natural conditions of the port of Copenhagen were rather benign, but the
larger ships that evolved with the transatlantic and Asian trade in the seventeenth and eighteenth centuries required a greater depth of water, especially if
unloading was to be made at quayside. In this sense, until the late eighteenth
century this port was rather shallow and large transoceanic vessels approach-
ing it had to offload to smaller ships. Although the depth of the harbor was
increased to six meters in the late eighteenth century, allowing ships to enter,
special barges were still often needed for loading and unloading by the East
and West Indies trading companies. Most other harbors were even less developed (Boje 2014, 80–82).

Since distances to the sea were rather short, roads were of relatively minor
importance and saw little improvement until the late eighteenth century,
when Denmark's first turnpike roads appeared (1773), after which a tax was
introduced (1793) to finance road construction according to the French-
German *chaussée* example. Many of these projects, however, were only finished in the 1850s (87–88). Canal construction was also relatively unimportant in Denmark proper, although when the Eider Canal between Kiel and
Rendsburg on the border of Schleswig and Holstein opened in 1784 this was a
major achievement, since it constituted a new navigable gateway between the
North and Baltic Seas.[12]

It was in particular the improvement of harbors and the construction of
railways from the 1840s, together with the improvement of the postal service
and the coach system during the late eighteenth century, which integrated the
country more and more, especially during the middle decades of the nine-

teenth century. Per Boje (2014, 90–94) highlights that effective communication was improved after a reorganization of the postal service in 1694, but the true integration of the country and the larger realm required steamships, which only appeared in the late 1810s. Thus, in the late eighteenth century, post coaches took six to seven days from Copenhagen to Altona/Hamburg, and express riders made the distance in about fifty hours (92), a time that was much reduced by steamships. British travel writer Samuel Laing noted in an 1852 publication that "[s]team power has made the most disjointed kingdom in Europe the most compact" (Laing 1852, 291). At the same time, the postal service also improved, with the 1840s seeing a reduction in postal rates and a related spread of newspapers beyond the rather elitist (but nevertheless impressive) circulation they enjoyed in the second half of the eighteenth century (Boje 2014, 94; Kjærgaard 1989). Then, in 1854, the telegraph arrived, connecting first Copenhagen with Altona/Hamburg.

All these advances in transport and communication would help deepen the integration of Denmark into international markets, a phenomenon observed since very early times. Since the Danish soils lacked large coal and ore deposits, necessary both for metallurgy and to drive steam engines, the inhabitants of Denmark relied on imports from a very early stage (Randsborg 2009; cf. Dalgaard 2010, 130–31) and kept their markets relatively open into the nineteenth century (Henriksen 2006, O'Rourke 2006). These long-term economic links not only brought trade and commerce but also fomented the spread of ideas, such as the Lutheran Protestant Reformation, which the Danes embraced in 1536 (Henriksen 2006), and a religious movement of pietism and more worldly enlightenment, which both became very influential in Denmark during the (early) eighteenth century and has been argued to have facilitated late eighteenth-century social transformations including the agricultural reforms, as we will return to below (Kayser Nielsen 2012, 71–75).

Population and Demography

Around 1600, the territory of Denmark proper had a population of around 500,000 to 600,000, some 85 percent of which lived in rural parishes (Johansen 2002, 13). In the 1640s and 1650s a mortality crisis took place, from which Denmark slowly recovered, so that, according to different backward projections, around 1670 the population of Denmark was somewhere between 500,000 and 550,000. The considerable fluctuations during the seventeenth and early eighteenth centuries affected the workings of agriculture and the stocking of farms (Johansen 2002, 22–23, 44; Kjærgaard 1994, 12; A. Lassen 1965, 11, 530). It has been estimated that probably 30 percent of the farms on the major islands of Zealand and Funen were tenantless after the war with Sweden (1657–60) and famine and a plague epidemic in some parts of the territory around 1659. The share of deserted farms on Jutland was probably lower, maybe around 10 percent (Skrubbeltrang 1978, 98–103; based on Olsen 1957). After the 1660s, despite the Scanian War of 1675–79 (when Denmark tried to reconquer its former southern Swedish provinces lost in 1659), population recovered and grew slowly until about 1710 (to somewhere between 625,000 and 700,000; Johansen 2002, 44; Dombernowsky 1988, 275) but then was reduced again due to an outbreak of plague in Copenhagen and Helsingør in 1710–11 (Johansen 2002, 61–63) and Danish-Norwegian participation in the Great Northern War of 1710–21.

By 1735, Denmark probably had a population of about 715,000 inhabitants and from there experienced first moderate and then accelerating population growth. On average, between the 1650s and the 1780s, population grew at a rate of 0.3 to 0.4 percent per year, with 841,000 inhabitants recorded in 1787, and then at 1 percent per year until 1820, when population is estimated to have been just below 1.1 million (Johansen 2002, 80). During the crisis after the Napoleonic Wars, demographic growth slowed somewhat only to take off again from the 1840s. From 1840 to 1913, population grew at slightly over 1 percent per year, so that in 1880 there were close to 2 million inhabitants and in 1911 some 2.75 million people within the borders of modern-day Denmark (cf. Johansen 2002, 125, 173; Skrubbeltrang 1978, 392–93; Kjærgaard 1994, 13; A. Lassen 1965; Maddison 2006).

Continuous population growth from around 1750 was not a specifically Danish phenomenon but characterized all of northern and western Europe. It can be described within the pattern of the first phases of a demographic transition and thus potentially escapes the kind of Malthusian trap described above, with first declines in mortality, especially child mortality (Johansen 2002). More important than the relative peace after the wars with Sweden in the seventeenth and early eighteenth centuries was probably the reduction in the frequency and severity of epidemics thanks to better housing[13] together with increased immunity against contagious diseases from natural adaptation and smallpox inoculation (from 1750) and vaccination (after 1800). The improved education of midwives was probably also a factor (Henriksen 2006, citing Banggård 2004; cf. Kjærgaard 1994, 191–92). Finally, Henriksen (2006) mentions the positive influence of the agrarian reforms described in the following chapter in terms of reducing contagion, since enclosures led to a new, more dispersed settlement pattern as more and more farmers moved out of the villages to new farmsteads on formerly outlying areas.

Despite evolving economic development and partially thanks to the land reforms which are the subject of chapter 3, the Danish population remained on average rather rural: in the 1787, 1801, and 1840 censuses, between 79.1 and 79.4 percent lived in rural parishes, with this share declining only slowly to 76.6 percent in 1860 and 72.0 percent in 1880, and then somewhat faster to 61.5 percent in 1901 and 57.0 percent in 1911 (Johansen 2002, 82, 125, 173). The relatively sparse—at least during the seventeenth and eighteenth centuries—population density led to a relatively high land to labor ratio (Henriksen 2006), which made Danish peasants first tenants and then owners of relatively large farms, which allowed them to be relatively well-off. This was despite the reintroduction in 1733 of restrictions to the movement of men in the countryside in the form of adscription (*stavnsbånd*, see below) motivated by the problem of deserted farms after the aforementioned outbreak of plague, the Great Northern War, and the concomitant difficulties in finding suitable tenants and securing recruitment for a new rural militia, which estate owners had to administrate and guarantee (see Dombernowsky 1988, 267, and references given there).

While the land to labor ratio deteriorated with the growth of population and labor force especially from the 1780s, the size distribution of farms remained rather constant over the period of the land reforms, and a rural proletariat of smallholders (cotters), landless workers, and servants grew alongside the more and more established class of tenants and, increasingly, owners of medium-sized farms. This rural lower class on the one hand allowed for more intensive agricultural production[14] and on the other hand fueled the moderate urbanization process from the early nineteenth century. By the 1850s, the Danish land to labor ratio was still higher than those of the western European core countries (United Kingdom, Netherlands, Belgium, Switzerland, and the western part of the German lands), similar to that of Sweden but clearly below that of France, the southern and eastern European periphery (Italy, Spain, Russia, eastern Prussia, and much of the Habsburg Empire), and areas of European settlement in North America.[15] Especially in southern Europe, however, the quality of much of the arable land was often lower than in Denmark. The Danish position in the middle of this distribution, together with its favorable location, would in terms of international specialization hint at a potential role as provider of agricultural goods to the center; these goods, however, would be increasingly labor intensive in comparison to those produced in and exported by more peripheral countries, especially those with equally fertile soils.

We would expect, however, in the seventeenth and eighteenth centuries, when the population was considerably smaller and international integration and specialization much more limited, less intensive cultivation or intensive cultivation to be limited to a relatively small share of the land with wider areas being only extensively (or occasionally) used. This is exactly what the land-use studies of Karl-Erik Frandsen (1977, 1983) found for the seventeenth century: in 1662, admittedly a time of crisis, only 20 to 30 percent of the land classified as arable was actually cultivated. The rest was used extensively, with especially the outfields used only extensively for animal husbandry, which meant that for example an important share of dung that could be used as fertilizer was unlikely to be recovered and applied to the cultivated fields (see also Skrubbeltrang 1978, 276–77). This changed, however, especially during the latter part of the eighteenth century, when the arable land was used in more intensive crop rotations and some of the former pastureland and woods were reconverted into arable land, involving substantial investments in work and money by peasants, to make way for more intensive techniques and more and more efficiently used livestock, as we will discuss in chapter 4 (Dombernowsky 1988; Kjærgaard 1994, 25–27 and ch. 3; Skrubbeltrang 1978, 98–100, 242–44, 406–7).

Institutions and Politics

After defeat in the 1657–60 war against Sweden, which had temporarily reduced Denmark to "Copenhagen inside the walls,"[16] an assembly of the estates of the realm agreed in 1660 to centralize many rights and powers previously shared with the nobility, to abolish elective monarchy, and to transfer absolutist power to the Danish king Frederik III. The rights of the king were fixed in the *lex regia* of November 14, 1665, published in 1709, converting Denmark into "the most extreme absolutist state in Christendom" (Kjærgaard 1994, 203; cf. Horstbøll and Østergård 1990, 157–58). This might on the face of it be seen as a sort of mirror image of the story described by North, Wallis, and Weingast (2009), although as will be explained below the goal of centralization was never really achieved.

At the same time, feudalism and local bondage systems characterized the countryside in many parts of the realm. Although formal servitude existed only in the duchy of Holstein (until 1805), in other parts of the monarchy some form of feudalism was present, most notably the local bondage system called *vornedskab* on Zealand, Lolland, Falster, and the surrounding islands, which since the thirteenth century had bound men to their birth manor, whose owner could force them to become tenant of a deserted farm.[17] While *vornedskab* was phased out from 1702 as part of the unification of law under absolutism, already in 1733 a similar adscription system (*stavnsbånd*) was reintroduced for the whole of Denmark proper, formally to guarantee military recruitment but effectively again binding men to farms.

Thus, for much of the country, with a small interruption in the early eighteenth century, the institutional conditions were set for economic disaster in terms of the sort of framework outlined above by Acemoglu and Robinson (2012): centralizing, formally unlimited absolutism combined with quasi-feudalist limitations on the movement of men born in rural areas (where, as we have noted, 80 percent of the population lived) and severe restrictions on their choice of occupations and entrepreneurship. This system benefited a small elite—the local estate owners, the central administration, the king, the church, and the local priest—ensuring soldiers for the war and laborers for estate demesne cultivation as well as tax and tithe payments.[18]

For more than a century after 1660, Danish absolute monarchs and their central bureaucracy still had to share power and administration with the traditional elite, noble estate owners who collected taxes, administered military service (and kept a proto civil registry for males), organized access to arable land, and oversaw rural schools and minor courts. Many estate owners were also owners of the village churches. The fact that centralization in practice fell behind theoretical ambitions can be explained in technical terms by the relatively weak physical and communication infrastructure of the time and in terms of power by the large amount of resources under the control of estate owners, something that was undermined only gradually by a growing and more powerful central administration (Løgstrup 1984; Kjærgaard 1994, 203–16) and by changes in the ownership of landed estates, many of which after 1660 were acquired by members of the ascendant merchant class, bourgeois government executives, and even sons of tenant farmers. It has also been highlighted that increased market integration and commercialization in the second half of the eighteenth century led many estate owners to focus on economic and cultural aspirations and to retreat from power politics or at least from active opposition to the reform projects of the central government that would reduce decentralized power and administration (Kjærgaard 1994, 230–37).

When absolutism was formally introduced in 1660, the newly empowered central government undertook many steps to centralize power and unify all aspects relating to the governance of the realm. The central administration, which previously had consisted mostly of the court and Danish and German chancelleries (in charge, respectively of the Danish-Norwegian- and German-speaking areas of the realm), was reorganized according to the Swedish-European system into colleges: a mixed form of specialized councils and ministries, to which burghers were appointed alongside members of the nobility. The most salient changes were the reorganization of the administration of the navy and the army, which were the largest and most expensive in per capita terms in Europe (Kjærgaard 1994, 15), and of government finances in the Finance College (from 1679 Rentekammer), as well as the conversion of the German chancellery into something like a ministry of foreign affairs. A State Council, including the heads of the different colleges, was introduced to guide government policy, although remnants of the old court system and royal advisors remained (Horstbøll and Østergård 1990, 160; Østergård 2006, 59–60).

A new tax system and army were set up and the many different provincial law codes were unified into the proto civil codes of the Danish Law of 1683 and the Norwegian Law of 1687 (Horstbøll and Østergård 1990, 159–60; Østergård 2006, 67). Territorial administration and judicial administration were unified in the form of districts (*herred*) and counties (*amt*) with government-appointed law courts and bailiffs in every district and a county governor (*amtmand*) as the formal supervisor of the private administrative functions of the estate owners, who retained considerable power on their demesnes and subordinate farms leased out to peasants (Løgstrup 1984, 288, 302).[19] The Danish Law also underlined that contracts, even oral agreements, were binding and codified further security of property rights (Boje 2014, 64).

The aristocratic privilege of estate ownership was abolished with the introduction of absolutism, and an increasing share of estates became the property of nonaristocrats and a new aristocracy created by the absolutist kings (Løgstrup 1984, 300; Linvald 1912). The latter groups, importantly, were among those who acquired crown lands sold to cover the expenses of the lost war against Sweden. Thus, while at the time of the 1688 tax assessment 25 percent of the land (weighted by assessed productive capacity) belonged to the crown (down from about 50 percent in 1660), 47 percent was in the hands of old and post-1660 ennobled aristocrats; 10 percent belonged to churches, schools, and universities;[20] 17 percent to burghers; and 1 to 2 percent to a small group of freehold peasants (Løgstrup 1984, 285; Skrubbeltrang 1978, 111–12). By 1766, the crown share had declined to about 10 percent, while private estate owners (including institutions) owned about 86 percent, with the rest falling to local churches (2.5 percent) and cities and freeholders (1.2 percent each; calculated from Linvald 1912, 147–48).

In 1912 Axel Linvald published a study in which he tried to contrast the relative importance of bourgeois and aristocratic estate owners over time. Because the status of owners could not always be determined and institutions (e.g., the University of Copenhagen) were not included, his sample covers about 80 percent of the land belonging to private estates. He distinguishes

TABLE 2.2. Axel Linvald's estimate of the composition of private estate owners (%)

	Bourgeoisie	Old aristocracy	New aristocracy	Non-Danish aristocracy	Total hartkorn covered
1730	22.9	35.9	21.7	19.5	253,451
1746	29.2	29.3	21.4	20.1	258,273
1766	30.9	27.8	19.9	21.4	262,349

Source: Linvald (1912, 154–55).

Note: Total hartkorn for Denmark proper was around 360,000 tønde, excluding the off-lying island of Bornholm, where after 1744 all farmers were freeholders, and no estates existed (Skrubbeltrang 1978, 111–12).

three groups of nobles: old (pre-1660), new (post-1660), and foreign (aristocracy ennobled not in Denmark but abroad). Distinctions between these three groups are sometimes problematic, since, for example, foreign nobility includes both nobles from Holstein (which belonged to the Danish monarchy) and nobles from outside Denmark (often from German-speaking areas like Mecklenburg) who resided in Denmark despite being of foreign descent (for example, Count Adam Gottlob Moltke—probably the largest landowner in Denmark in the 1760s and an important figure we will return to in chapter 4—would be of non-Danish aristocracy since he came from a German noble family from Mecklenburg, although he became a Danish count in 1750). Danish nobles include only those who at the time of being ennobled belonged to Danish families. Table 2.2 shows that, although things moved slowly, both the bourgeoisie and the non-Danish aristocracy gained in relative and absolute importance, while the old aristocracy, despite retaining large possessions, lost ground. With the new wave of privatization of crown estates from the 1760s (see chapter 4), this process speeded up, and even some fortunate nonbourgeois sons of tenant farmers managed to become estate owners (Dombernowsky 1988, 216–20, 253–57)—for instance, with the benefits earned on newly enclosed freehold farms.

That landownership can be traced quite well and can be weighted by the productivity of the land owes to one of the major achievements of early Danish absolutism: the introduction of a unified tax system. This system abolished several individual and regionally idiosyncratic taxes and introduced a tax on the productive capacity of agricultural land valued by volume in tønde (barrels) of hartkorn (hard grain, i.e., grain for baking bread). Together with sales of crown estates, the system was adopted as a source of revenue to consolidate government finances. The basic idea of the new tax, based on a Swedish example and initially adopted in 1662, was to establish a land register, assess the production capacity of the land in a unified system, and tax each unit equally. A first register based on reported in-kind rent receipts was established ad hoc in 1662 with modifications in 1664 and 1681. In the 1680s a comprehensive land survey was undertaken in all parts of Denmark proper, and all land was classified into different classes according to a unified quality scale differentiating, roughly, between arable land, pastures, woodlands, and less useful land like heathland. These classes were than aggregated by their estimated value in terms of *tønde hartkorn* (see Skrubbeltrang 1978, 107–12 for details).

The introduction of the *hartkorn* assessment after 1660 contributed in practice to a transformation of government finance away from traditional sources such as crown land revenues toward a tax state with a nationally uniform tax base, although taxes had to be raised with the help of private estate owners (cf. Horstbøll and Østergård 1990, 160). In exchange, the demesne itself was exempted from taxation if the estate administered and guaranteed the tax payments of subordinate farms of at least 200 *tønde hartkorn* within a two-Danish-mile radius (about 15 km), a point which was to be important for the process of enclosure, as will be discussed in the next chapter. The tax burden on peasant land increased significantly, from an equivalent of maybe a little more than 0.5 rigsdaler per *tønde hartkorn* (thus about 3 rigsdaler for the average peasant farm) in the first half of the seventeenth century (Ladewig Petersen 2002, 57) before the *hartkorn* assessment, to a variety of taxes linked to the *hartkorn* valuation, which increased over time but should of course be viewed relative to changes in the value of the land and especially grain prices and productivity. According to Rafner (1986), the real tax burden for an average peasant farm (taking account of the increased prices of grain) increased from 17.7 rigsdaler in the 1660s to 28.8 rigsdaler in the 1670s, a level near which it fluctuated throughout the eighteenth century with a slight decline before the land tax was reformed in 1802 (see also Skrubbeltrang 1978, 168–69, 234–35, and Dombernowsky 1988, 280–82).

A second aspect of absolutist reform on which estate owners and central administration had to collaborate was military recruitment, which started with compulsory military service in 1663 (Kjærgaard 1994, 204–5) that used a *hartkorn*-value-based recruitment system. The system applied first to soldiers (knights) for the national regiments, and after 1701 it applied to regular recruits for a rural militia of around fifteen thousand soldiers, who would be trained on Sundays after church.[21] The rural militia was suspended in 1730, but, when it was reintroduced in 1733, recruitment came with an important new advantage for landowners.[22] All males between fourteen and thirty-six years old who entered conscription rolls administered by the estate now needed the permission of the estate owner to leave the estate. This new form of bondage, termed adscription (*stavnsbånd*) was extended to nine-to-forty-year-olds in 1742 and to four-to-forty-year-olds in 1764. Men could be released from adscription or exempted from military service under one of four conditions: first, if they were older than the maximum age; second, if they had finished military service (but restrictions to this condition were introduced in 1739, 1746, and 1774); third, if they obtained (against a fee) a free pass from the landowner; and, fourth, if the landowner used his right to exempt a young man from military service because he had taken over a tenant farm (Løgstrup 1984, 306–7).

After 1660, many estate owners also bought their corresponding churches from the crown and with this obtained a say in the appointment of priests, parish clerks, and school teachers, who had important influence over the rural population (Kjærgaard 1994, 205). Purchase of churches was often an investment,[23] but it also included the *jus patronatus* of appointing the local priest, a somewhat limited right given that since 1690 the central government (the king) had to confirm the appointed priest and since 1704 only candidates who had passed the University of Copenhagen's theology examinations could be appointed (Løgstrup 1984, 293–95). Probably more important was the influence of estate owners on schools in their villages both directly as landlords and as owners of the *jus patronatus* of the church, an issue we turn to below. Since the Reformation in 1536, the parish clerk, financed by church tithe and offertory, had to teach the members of his parish to read and understand Luther's catechism, and rural schools were often established around this religious instruction.

While estate owners thus retained important local power amid a still only partially integrated polity and economy and effectively operated a private bureaucracy outside the control of the central public administration, the center of power was also under the effective control of aristocratic large estate owners of old and new nobility during much of the first century of Danish absolutism, especially during the reigns of Christian VI (1730–46) and Frederik V (1746–66), as forcefully argued by Thorkild Kjærgaard (1994, 213). However, this rule ended after the accession of the (psychologically unstable) Christian VII to the throne, who dismissed the former de facto prime minister, Lord Chamberlain Count Adam Gottlob Moltke. The king soon became influenced by outsiders to the traditional circles of power, especially court physician Johann Friedrich Struensee, son of a famous pietistic theologian, who in 1770 dissolved the Council of State. As a dictator of sorts, Struensee started a comprehensive "enlightened" reform program with the help of academic advisors like the botanist Georg Christian Oeder.[24] This program, however, suffered a serious backlash after Struensee was overthrown by conservative forces in 1772 and beheaded for diverse acts of high treason that included his reforms, his liaison with the queen (who was exiled to Celle in Germany), and

a document—forged by his enemies—that supposedly revealed a coup d'état
against the king. Conservative forces took over again, and reforms were fore-
stalled and partly repealed, but central administrative capacity was preserved,
and some of the more moderate and politically powerful advisors to the king
remained in office. One of the main aims of the conservative forces was to
create a more Danish-Norwegian government. A decree that reserved government jobs for those born in the realm of the Danish king was issued in 1776 to
roll back German influence in central administration (such as that of Moltke
and Count J. H. E. Bernstorff, both from Mecklenburg, and later Struensee[25])
and to encourage Danish-Norwegian patriotism (Østergård 2006, 62).

These politics—and the personnel decisions of the conservative government, including the dismissal of Count A. P. Bernstorff as minister of foreign
affairs in 1780—encouraged Crown Prince Frederik in 1784, when he had
turned sixteen and was nominated to the State Council, to persuade his father
to dismiss the conservative cabinet and grant executive competences to the
crown prince himself. With a group of advisors that included the previously
dismissed Count A. P. Bernstorff and Count Ernst Schimmelmann, as well
as Count Christian Ditlev Reventlow and the Norwegian lawyer Christian
Colbiørnsen, Crown Prince Frederik would resume and reinforce a liberal-
enlightened reform program that would decisively modernize the monarchy
(Østergård 2006, 62–63; Kjærgaard 1994, 240).

In the following thirty years, between 1784 and 1814, this group of enlightened estate owners, intellectuals, and administrators strengthened the power
of central government and, via the improved infrastructure and communications described above, used it to reinforce and advance reforms, guided on
the one hand by liberal ideas of individual freedom and responsibility and on
the other by a specific state paternalism directed especially toward the farmer
class. They established and followed a concept of absolutism that defined absolutist power of the king as a guarantee for law and order and, in the words
of Colbiørnsen, "the general good," which in their eyes was based on a sort of
social contract enacted via a consensus within elite public opinion that was
unaffected by immature mass agitations (Horstbøll and Østergård 1990, esp.
170–72). This liberal-paternalistic version of absolutism had its roots in a discourse based on Grotius developed by Pontoppidan during the centenary of
the introduction of absolutism in 1760, when Pontoppidan was prochancellor
of the University of Copenhagen (Horstbøll and Østergård 1990, 158, 162, 171).
Contrary to but contemporaneous with the demise of the original textbook
absolutism in France, its Danish version achieved a peaceful transition[26] from
the old, quasi-feudalist, and effectively decentralized state to a modernized
and more liberal social and political order on its way toward full-fledged capi-

talism and, eventually, democracy (Horstbøll and Østergård 1990; Østergård 2006, 2012). It failed, however, in converting the conglomerate monarchy into a joint nation state, as evidenced by the much smaller Denmark we know since 1864 (with few but polemic changes during the early twentieth century) (Kayser Nielsen 2012).

A number of examples will serve to illustrate the reforms that were put in place. In 1770, Struensee had declared press freedom and the end of censorship, a measure that survived the conservative backlash, during which only criminal liability for publications was intensified. Liberalization increased in 1784, although in 1799 an ordinance issued under pressure from the Russian Tsar made it illegal to publish anonymously and subjected writers condemned under the criminal liability provision to censorship (Horstbøll and Østergård 1990, 175). In 1797 many mercantilist measures were repealed in a new customs tariff (Boje 2014, 160–66; Kjærgaard 1994, 223; Rasch 1955), and in 1792 Denmark became the first imperial power to prohibit the slave trade (Røge 2014), although slavery was to stay in the Danish West Indies until 1848. Other aspects of public life, such as poor relief (Skrubbeltrang 1978, 418–21), the health system (Løkke 2007), and schooling (see below) were also reformed and reorganized.

As for the estates owners, little by little their role as middlemen between central administration and most of the population was dismantled, as administrative capacity and communications improved (see Kjærgaard 1994, 228–30). Thus, in 1788 the monopolistic privilege of estate owners and market towns to fatten oxen in stalls was abolished, as were many of the privileges of merchant and trade associations and guilds in market towns during the 1790s. In 1791, the parish bailiff's role was strengthened, and in 1795 a comprehensive system of local justices of the peace and conciliation boards was established (Kjærgaard 1994, 227). Tax exemptions to demesnes were ended in 1802. These measures came with other restrictions on estate owners and the abolition of their traditional rights to appoint manorial courts and local priests in 1807.

The Napoleonic Wars and their aftermath caused an economic crisis in Denmark that affected its government, which had defended a policy of armed neutrality that since the end of the Great Northern War in 1720 had led to important wartime trading profits. This time, however, from 1801 the British Royal Navy repeatedly attacked Copenhagen and the Danish-Norwegian fleet, which was almost completely destroyed as a consequence of the so-called Gunboat War of 1807–14. After the war, Denmark had to accept the loss of Norway, which first declared independence and then was joined in personal union to Sweden (until 1905) by the Congress of Vienna. Denmark obtained the much smaller German duchy of Lauenburg south of Holstein in compensation.[27] The economic reform process was largely paralyzed after 1814 and especially after state bankruptcy and a currency crisis in 1813 that led to the abandonment of the old specie rigsdaler and the introduction of a paper currency, the rigsbankdaler, pegged to Hamburg's accounting currency, the mark banco (S. A. Hansen 1984, 112–16).

As in other European countries, in Denmark the 1830s brought demands from a (rather small) urban bourgeoisie for more participation and political rights for a wider population. In the following two decades, absolutism little by little gave way to democratization, first through regional consultative assemblies in Denmark (Jutland and the islands), Schleswig, and Holstein in the 1830s. These reforms were prompted less by internal demands of religious and political opposition to absolutism in Danish towns and countryside than by demands from Holstein, which belonged to the German Confederation and, following the July Revolution in Paris in 1830, had instructed the election of consultative assemblies in 1831. The Danish government granted this mandate and held elections for consultative assemblies, which first met in 1834 not in the regional capitals but in the provincial towns of Viborg, Roskilde, Schleswig, and Itzehoe to avoid the danger of political turmoil among major urban populations (Horstbøll and Østergård 1990, 176–78). In Denmark proper, only male estate owners and freeholders that owned more than 4 *tønde hartkorn* and farm tenants that had leased at least 5 *tønde hartkorn* were entitled to vote if they were at least twenty-five years old. In market towns and in Copenhagen minimum wealth requirements applied, so that less than 3 percent of the population was entitled to vote; also, the electorate was divided by classes and between towns and rural areas, and each vote did not have the same weight. This was a cautious step toward democratization, since none of the principles of Danish absolutism was affected by the assemblies, which had no legislative or budget authority; nevertheless, they "did become national political laboratories which played an important part in training a political class" (Horstbøll and Østergård 1990, 179). The new constitution of 1849 represented a more decisive step toward democracy, since it ended absolutism and personal privileges of the nobility and introduced separation of powers and an elected two-chamber parliament as well as civil rights such as freedom of assembly.

However, in the first decades of the nineteenth century, among liberals in the bureaucracy as well as officials and intellectuals in the capital cities of Denmark and Holstein, two different national liberal movements evolved, one oriented toward Germany and the other toward a "Danish" Denmark or

Scandinavianism. They eventually clashed in two civil wars in 1848–51 and 1863–64 after especially Holsteiners (increasingly backed by other Germans, particularly Prussia) questioned the rearrangement of the rule of succession for Holstein in 1846, which favored the unity of the realm over prior arrangements. In 1848, the assembly of Holstein decided to send a delegation to Copenhagen to demand a new constitution for the duchies and the admission of Schleswig to the German Confederation. Tensions about the status of Schleswig became virulent and eventually led to the loss of the duchies (see, e.g., Østergård 2012, 54–57). In the process, the peasant movement in Denmark became an ally of the Danish National Liberals, who established first an informal party called Peasant Friends and then after the constitution of 1849 a formal political party known from 1870 as the Left (*Venstre*), as opposed to the estate-owner- and merchant-dominated conservative party the Right (*Højre*). Due to more restrictive election rules in the 1866 constitution, the conservatives and Copenhagen dominated government through their majority in the upper house of the new Danish parliament until the 1890s. Afterward, the Left first gained a say in coalition governments and became, together with the Social Democrats, the leading political force of early twentieth-century Denmark.

On a lower level, peasants (that is, freeholders and copyholders of medium-sized farms) became important actors in parish-level politics: in church parish councils from 1856, in the political parish councils established by law in 1867[28] (Kayser Nielsen 2012, 81–83), and through various associations based on religious and cultural revival movements in the Church of Denmark, including the conservative Inner Mission and the liberal Grundtvig movement tied to the free schools and folk high schools discussed in the next section. The teachings of the Rev. Nikolaj Frederik Severin Grundtvig especially—with his combination of religious revivalism, culture- and language-based nationalism, a strong orientation toward the rural population, and political liberalism—left a deep imprint both on Danish politics in the late nineteenth and early twentieth centuries (Korsgaard 2006) and on the period's political, economic, social, and even educational historiography, which highlighted the teleological triumph after 1788 of central government and peasants over exploitative estate owners (Kjærgaard 1985; Østergård 1992; Korsgaard and Wiborg 2006). Recent historiography, however, has rectified this picture and aimed to bring the poorer parts of the rural population, cotters, other smallholders, and landless laborers back into the picture (see, e.g., Bjørn 1977a; Skrubbeltrang 1978; Kjærgaard 1985; Raaschou-Nielsen 1990; Østergård 1992, 2006, 2012; and Kayser Nielsen 2012).

Religion and Education

Education and religion were intertwined in early modern Denmark as in many other countries, and to a certain extent the relationship between Protestantism and human capital formation highlighted by Becker and Woessmann (2009) can be observed here. Thus, as early as 1721 the central government started a program that created in the crown estates' cavalry districts some 240 new schools, which were intended to be models for private estate owners (Skrubbeltrang 1978, 258–59; Løgstrup 1984, 259) and which would teach the catechism and basic literacy. Then, at the two-hundredth anniversary of the Reformation in 1736, confirmation was introduced by the Danish church, and a new pietistic catechism elaborated under the direction of court preacher Erik Pontoppidan, who later became bishop of Bergen (in Norway) for some years and then prochancellor of the University of Copenhagen. He was also editor of a monumental description of Denmark, the *Danske Atlas*, and a precocious and influential economics journal, *Danmarks og Norges økonomiske Magazin*, which was published from 1757 to 1764, the year of Pontoppidan's death. To be confirmed, candidates had to pass a literacy test, and this probably encouraged a certain learning culture among the rural population, since without confirmation priests would not administer the sacrament of marriage (Skrubbeltrang 1978, 257–61; Løgstrup 1984, 295).

Pontoppidan and his pietistic circle had important influence on the central government, which tried to implement comprehensive schooling with universal access and uniform curricula and teaching quality throughout Denmark in 1739. As for confirmation, catechism and reading were to be at the center of instruction, with writing and basic numeracy as optional extensions. More than one thousand new schools would have to be constructed to make universal access possible, financed by the local church and the largest local landowner at locations selected by the county governor (Skrubbeltrang 1978, 258–59). The owner of *jus patronatus* and the largest landowner (which could be the same person) were to take turns in appointing the teacher, whose competence was to be assessed by the local priest. Estate owners and parts of the rural population protested vehemently against this centralized imposition, and in 1740 the reform was attenuated: estate owners would determine where schools were to be built but still had to finance them, although they could count on work obligations from the villagers. Curricula and teacher salaries were no longer required to be uniform, and district governors and parish clerks were now only to serve as supervisors of the schools. Although this weakened universal standards of teaching content and quality, a large number of schools were nevertheless built in the following years. Birgit Løgstrup (1984,

297) mentions that seventeen hundred schools existed in Denmark proper at the middle of the eighteenth century, a number that Kjærgaard (1994, 207) calls "undoubtedly . . . sufficient . . . to give practically all children a satisfactory basic education," although school attendance in the early years seems to have been piecemeal due to initial lack of parental faith in the usefulness of formal schooling—although the requirements of confirmation seem to have provided an important incentive for, at least, minimum attendance (Løgstrup 1984, 295–97; Skrubbeltrang 1978, 259). Fridlev Skrubbeltrang (1978, 259–61) mentions that signatures by tenants on their tenancy letters and protocols, which had become mandatory written proof of tenancy conditions in 1719, became less led by the landlord's scribe and more personal, that is, resembling actual signatures and not just shakily written initials, between 1720 and 1760.[29]

In terms of teacher training, in the 1780s and 1790s, C. D. Reventlow and his brother Ludvig worked together with the priest (later bishop) P. O. Boisen on plans for a teacher seminar to specially train teachers for small village schools. In 1801 it opened its doors at Vesterborg on the island of Lolland, where Boisen was the local priest and Reventlow held *jus patronatus* (Skrubbeltrang 1978, 422). The government-financed Blågaard teacher seminar in Copenhagen had been established in 1790; it moved to larger premises in a former privileged factory for military uniforms in Jonstrup west of Copenhagen in 1808 (Skrubbeltrang 1978, 422–23).

Thus, one outstanding characteristic of the Danish population, even before the imposition of compulsory education, was the large share of Danes who knew how to read and write despite relatively poor living conditions; an influential article on Sweden by Lars Sandberg (1979) highlighted the "impoverished sophisticate" as a main driver of catch-up economic growth over the nineteenth century.[30] We have seen above that this was the case even despite the failed attempt to introduce a unified and uniform schooling system in 1739, a step that was delayed until 1814 when the Village School Act established a comprehensive centralized school system and institutions for the evening instruction of adults were founded (Kayser Nielsen 2012, 77; Løgstrup 1984; Kjærgaard 1994, 226). After the Napoleonic Wars (or the Gunboat War in the Danish case) the evolution of the educational system quickly resumed in two distinct directions: the government and economic elites continued to found teacher seminars and specialized schools, and from the 1840s an anticentralization movement established the free schools and the folk high schools inspired by and directed through the followers of N. F. S. Grundtvig.

Following English precedents, the government in 1742 helped to form the Royal Danish Academy of Sciences and Letters to promote science and technology; in 1769 it backed the foundation of the Royal Agricultural Society as an official Patriotic Prize Society,[31] which handed out awards for outstanding technical, organizational, and social-improvement writings and actions that advanced agricultural interests. The society was inspired by the Royal Danish Agricultural Academy, which had been founded in Schleswig in 1762 but had to be closed in 1767 because the superintendent of the church in Copenhagen (and father of Johann Friedrich Struensee) deemed it inappropriate for priests to be involved in the creation and activities of the academy (Boje 2014, 150; Skrubbeltrang 1978, 275–76; Hertel 1920). The society and several of its members—estate owners and others of the political and economic elite— would be important pioneers especially in technological issues in the future. The prizes helped to establish incentives for modernization, both for elite thinkers and practical peasants (see examples in Kjærgaard 1994, 38, 47–48, 52–53, 57, 101–2, 105, 121, 248, 255; and the list of contributions in Slottved 2014). The importance of the Royal Agricultural Society to the early stages of development in dairying in Denmark will be reflected by the numerous references to it in the subsequent chapters. Its members more than anyone represent the elite of Denmark, as discussed in the previous chapter.

As early as 1768, the government had planned to establish agricultural schools, a plan also discussed by the Royal Agricultural Society. Nevertheless, these plans did not become reality until in 1792 the merchant and estate owner Major General Johan Frederik Classen left his inheritance to establish a charitable foundation dedicated to education and the promotion of industriousness and entrepreneurship. From these funds, an agricultural school was planned, and land surveyor Oluf Christian Olufsen was trained—during a three-year journey through Europe—to become its founding professor. However, after opening its doors in a village on the island of Falster around 1800, the school had to be closed soon after due to a lack of prospective students. Olufsen claimed that Danish peasants did not understand why their children should learn agriculture without being paid for their work and blamed this for the school's failure (Boje 2014, 151–52). In 1804 the foundation funded a new agricultural institute in Copenhagen, where Olufsen gave lectures until his death in 1827. In 1799 Gregers Begtrup also started lecturing on agriculture at the University of Copenhagen, where he became a professor in 1801 (Boje 2014, 152), and where he completed an important series of books on Danish agriculture which we will return to in chapter 4. Prior to this, in 1773, Peter Christian Abildgaard had opened a veterinary school that was first subsidized and then taken over by the government. In 1856, it would be expanded and renamed the Royal Veterinary and Agricultural College—an important institution that we will discuss more in subsequent chapters. Together with the University of Copenhagen, the Academy of Arts (founded in 1754), and the

Technical University (founded in 1829 by the government at the initiative of Hans Christian Ørsted), Denmark had a solid tertiary education sector by mid-nineteenth-century standards (Boje 2014, 119).

Apart from this official track of educational institutions, a grassroots movement of Grundtvigian free schools and folk high schools as well as agricultural schools (to which we return in chapter 6) emerged in the countryside after 1844 (Østergård 1992, 12–13; Skrubbeltrang 1952, 17–28). After 1814, and especially from the 1840s, N. F. S. Grundtvig became probably the most influential person in Denmark. His revivalist theological ideas (a more optimistic update of pietism that is said to have suited the emerging farmer class well)—which had earned him a preaching prohibition in the late 1820s and early 1830s—and especially his interpretation of what it meant to be Danish in the historical, cultural, and linguistic sense created a form of nationalism that became hugely influential in the struggles over Schleswig and Holstein and especially after the loss of the duchies in 1864. Grundtvig's ideas remain influential in the present day. In educational matters, he underlined the importance of the living (i.e., spoken) word and, together with many followers, promoted a meeting movement outside the official channels of church and government, which he largely rejected.[32] His followers promoted an alternative, nongovernmental educational system through free schools, folk high schools (see figure 2.1), and agricultural colleges. Since initially it of course

FIGURE 2.1. Niels Bjerre (1864–1942), *From the Lecture Hall of the Folk High School in Sorø*, 1890
Source: Courtesy of the Hirschsprung Collection, Copenhagen.
Note: Many educational establishments, such as those from the folk high school movement, were independent of the government.

lacked government funding, the schools were rather small and expensive to attend, and their principals had to be real enthusiasts, as their pay was about half the salary of public school elementary teachers in the 1850s and 1860s (Skrubbeltrang 1952, 17–18). Politically, the Grundtvigian movement later aligned with the Left in parliament, which, despite as noted above being in permanent opposition until the end of the century, managed to secure some funds, recognition, freedom from interference, and sensible supervision for the free schools over the following decades (Skrubbeltrang 1952, 26–29).

Especially the folk high schools are said to have served to form a Grundtvigian farmer elite, which first became important at the local level and acquired importance in many parish councils and later established a larger political discourse and power that transformed the newly defined peasant-farmer identity into a general definition of what it meant to be Danish (Kayser Nielsen 2012, 82–83; Østergård 1992). The association culture that grew during the nineteenth century is also said to have marked a departure from a previous tendency toward individualization. This had started with the spread of pietism into Denmark in the second quarter of the seventeenth century and found its culmination in the enclosures, the abolishment of open fields and commons, and the physical dissolution of village communities with the relocation of farms onto newly consolidated properties between the 1760s and the 1800s. This, it has been argued (see, e.g., Stråth 2012, 32; and especially the internationally influential account by Kindleberger 1951, 36–37; which in turn is influenced by Jensen 1937), facilitated the spread of cooperatives after 1882, although agricultural historians have struggled to establish direct links, especially between folk high schools and the cooperative movement (Bjørn 1971).[33] Also, although folk high schools existed some forty years before the first cooperative, their spread is largely contemporaneous with the surge of the dairy industry, presumably because farmers with higher incomes had more means to dedicate to the education of their children.

To sum up, Denmark in the early decades of the nineteenth century was a poor country battered by war that nevertheless enjoyed a fortuitous geography and was already witnessing an institutional transformation. This transformation operated in parallel with the developments we discuss in the following chapters. Previous authors have stressed the importance of Denmark's land reforms to its subsequent agricultural development, and we turn to these in the following chapter.

3

The Agricultural Reforms, 1750s–1800s

No discussion of Danish agriculture in the eighteenth and nineteenth centuries is complete without a discussion of the agricultural reforms that preceded and to a certain extent took place alongside the evolution of the dairy sector. The popular view (although not the state of historical research[1]) sees the 1788 repeal of adscription as the "critical juncture" between the old, quasi-feudal regime and the start of modernity; it is the Danish version of the historical watershed between feudalism and peasant emancipation that plays an important role in the national histories of neighboring countries, especially Prussia. The Adscription Law of June 20, 1788, began a process that by 1800 completely suspended the bondage of men in rural areas to their birth estate. Bondage for the purpose of military recruitment through estate owners was abolished in favor of national conscription by the central government.[2] This also abolished the possibility of forced tenancies and transferred conscription and reserve rolls as well as authorization to leave the conscription area to local government officials, who had no economic interest in binding workers to the countryside or forcing them to accept tenancies.[3] This surely improved the bargaining position of young potential tenants, but the end of adscription alone would hardly have changed the face of Danish agriculture.

In fact, the Adscription Law was part of a much more comprehensive reform program implemented in the years between 1784 and 1807. This program converted a rural economy based on old-regime, communal cultivation, and landlord-tenant relationships (characterized by peasants' labor services and limited property rights regarding land and labor) to an institutional framework based on free individual property rights over labor, clearly defined ownership of land, and the abolition of communal patterns of cultivation and animal husbandry. The way in which the agricultural reforms accomplished this is the subject of this chapter. As we will see, many of the actors involved in both implementing and legislating the land reforms were the same elites who were also setting in motion the changes in estate agricultural practices that are the subject of the next chapter, although the management of the demesnes themselves was impacted to only a limited extent. The ultimate importance of the land reforms, however, was that a free peasantry had greater incentive and more freedom to benefit from knowledge and other spillovers from the estates. The reforms, of course, also made possible the eventual establishment of the cooperatives. We stress, in contrast to other accounts (both for Denmark and abroad), that land reforms were as such not in themselves a precondition for later economic success except in as much as they were part and parcel of a general enlightenment of the elites in the countryside.

Before the transformation of the countryside could be completed, the Danish agricultural reforms had to achieve at least six different objectives:

1. Consolidate shared grazing rights between villages
2. Disentangle open fields and enclose the lands of individual tenant farms
3. Repeal any rights, especially regarding grazing, which other farmers and smallholding and nonlandholding peasants (cotters) might enjoy under village bylaws
4. Reorganize the distribution of farmsteads according to the newly enclosed village
5. Update the old tenancy remuneration system so that it became a more liberal, capitalistically oriented system, thus abandoning
   a. Flexible entry fines (*indfæstning*), a one-time lease purchase payment upon taking over the tenancy, adjustable with each new tenant
   b. Nominally constant in-kind rent (*landgilde*)
   c. Nominally limitless labor services (*hoveri*: boon work, corvée)
6. Convert tenants (leaseholders) into freeholders—that is, privatize tenant farms

The ultimate outcome was that approximately sixty thousand subordinate farms—farms that had existed since the Middle Ages as a result of the fall in population after 1340 (Porskrog Rasmussen 2003, 8) and that had partly been rearranged in the first decades after 1660[4]—were converted into a virtually identical number of enclosed tenant farms, of which by the first decades of the nineteenth century some forty thousand were freehold property with the rest mainly held with inheritable tenancy (Dombernowsky 1988, 359). In the 1688 *hartkorn* assessment, privately owned peasant farmers accounted for perhaps just 1 or 2 percent of the land, corresponding to maybe two thousand or twenty-five hundred farms (Munck 1977, 39–42).[5] The Danish reforms thus basically cemented the existing property structure at the expense of the rights (but not the demesnes) of estate owners as well as the social and economic position of smallholders and landless agricultural laborers: as we will return to below, cotters were often left with farms that were not self-sufficient. The main beneficiaries were the tenant-owners of the sixty thousand medium-sized (approximately 5.5 *tønde hartkorn* with little variation[6]) family farms. Contrary to prior centuries, tenant-owners in the late seventeenth century managed to establish themselves as a stable rural middle class, thanks both to secure and inheritable property rights and to the rapid growth of the rural lower classes as population increased, mortality decreased, and access to tenant farms—whose desertion only fifty years before had been a reason to introduce adscription—became more and more difficult.

Figure 3.1 illustrates the changes which the reforms brought about. The top image shows the pre-reform situation, in this case for the small village of Årslev in the Sønderup parish north of Slagelse, in the west of Zealand, in 1768. It follows the original map drawn by land surveyor Christian Conrad Gercken for the sales of crown estates and their subordinate farms in the Antvorskov district. The village—consisting of fourteen farms, several houses (for cotters, etc.), and a watermill to the north—is surrounded by three large open fields for the traditional, communal three-field crop rotation, in which each farm cultivated a myriad of strips. The figure shows the 108 strips belonging to just one farm (Feldbæk 1990, 73). By contrast, the bottom image shows Årslev after enclosure in 1795. Now the village has thirteen farms, seven of which have been moved outside the village, while six remain on land distributed around the original nucleus. One farm with its consolidated 47 *tønde land* (26 hectares; not *hartkorn*) is highlighted as an example. Cotters have been assigned land in one corner of each of the farms: just 3 *tønde land* (1.65 hectares) on average.[7] To connect farms, cottages, and the village, new roads were constructed (Feldbæk 1990, 271).

Such a fundamental transformation from subsistence, security-oriented, "inefficient" agriculture toward an (in principle) liberal, market-oriented, and more entrepreneurial agriculture took place in most countries of the world between the sixteenth and the twentieth centuries, although the particulars of the process, the context in which they occurred, and the outcomes in terms of efficiency and distribution differed widely from country to country (Federico 2005, 172). This context specificity introduces a certain danger of oversimplification when comparing the Danish case to other countries, although a few words on potential paths not taken provide some perspective. In principle, for

FIGURE 3.1. Map of the village of Årslev before (*top*) and after (*bottom*) enclosures
Source: Drawn by Alice Rosenstand after the original map by C. C. Gercken (1769) and further materials in the land register archives under the supervision of Ole Feldbæk; Feldbæk (1990, 73, 271).

example, and as occurred in other countries, the property rights that ended up in the hands of peasant farmers could have been acquired by/granted to the landlord, to peasants as a community, or to all members of rural society, including cotters, whether individually or communally. Also, there were a variety of options for the terms of compensation—for instance, monetary or in kind—for the rights (grazing, etc.) of landlords and cotters. Thus, we describe below how, after some experimentation and a few false starts, Denmark reached a sort of equilibrium.

The Danish approach and outcome was certainly very different from the English case, where most land was merged with the estate demesnes into large farms owned by landlords and frequently operated by capitalist tenants employing landless labor (and shepherds), thus forcing former tenants to become agricultural laborers or to leave the countryside (see R. C. Allen 1992). It was slightly more similar to the Prussian experience of reform between 1799 and 1816, in which a similar conversion of peasants into independent farmers was achieved, but in Prussia peasants received only half of the land and had to pay considerable compensation to the landlords for their loss of boon work and related duties (Federico 2005, 148). It also differed from the Russian case, where peasants received the largest parts of their holdings after emancipation in 1861 but had to cultivate holdings as a commune (*mir*), until the 1906 Stolypin reforms made enclosures and the division of communal property possible (147–48). Irish tenancy reform through the Irish Land Law Act of 1881 was probably the most immediately comparable. The landlords' relative position had already been reduced to simple rent receivers by rent ceilings established by the Landlord and Tenant Act of 1870, when the state incentivized the purchase of full property rights by offering advances raised through publicly traded government land bonds (Foley-Fisher and McLaughlin 2016; Federico 2005, 151). These tenancy reforms did not, however, involve enclosures, the emancipation of peasants, the compensation of cotters' rights, or the commutation of labor services, and they occurred in the very different economic environment of the late nineteenth century (McLaughlin 2015).

Before 1750

At the time of the imposition of absolutist rule in 1660, a situation wherein the vast majority of land was divided between the crown and the nobility was already giving way. In a process that was largely complete by the 1680s, new groups became estate owners, a market for land developed, and owners consolidated their demesnes into a single demarcated holding (making the organization of farming and boon work from peasant tenants much easier) (Skrubbeltrang 1978, 276–77; Dombernowsky 1988, 214). Thus the precondition for the development that was to take place on the estates was in a sense already in place at an early date.

A major source of discontent with the prevailing agricultural regime, apart from common cultivation and collective grazing, was the system of rent payments and services fixed in the Danish Law but modified (especially regarding labor services) over the eighteenth century. Rent consisted of three components: first, an entry fine (or lease purchase price) that was paid at the beginning of the tenancy, which was normally defined as life tenancy and in practice took about twenty to twenty-five years on average (cf. Skrubbeltrang 1978, 159, 225); second, a fixed annual rent in kind (*landgilde*), which would also be fixed in monetary value (according to local tradition) but not be updated (until 1792); and, third, labor services on the demesne (both with and without horses) of an (in principle) unlimited extent. All these services were to be fixed in the *jordbog* (soil register; see chapter 5) of the estates and, at least from 1719, in the tenancy letters and protocols issued to the tenants (Skrubbeltrang 1978, 163–66, 229–33; Henriksen 2003, 24–25; Dombernowsky 1988, 282–86, 330–50).

While the annual rent could not be adjusted to market conditions, and entry fines could only be charged with tenant changes, the general impression of especially the classical literature is that labor services increased over time, thus making tenancy conditions worse and worse and causing labor to be used less and less effectively due to principal-agent problems in demesne cultivation (Henriksen 2003, 28) and the corresponding opportunity costs for tenants (28–29): Peasants aimed to minimize effective physical work effort when working on the demesne to save their resources for their own cultivation, which in turn suffered from the loss of time due to the increase in days spent on the demesnes. The argument concerning shirking in demesne vs. own cultivation might actually not fully apply, since many of the labor services were actually performed by servants and cotters and not by the tenant farmers themselves (Henriksen 2003, 24; Kjærgaard 1985, 110; Skrubbeltrang 1978, 432). The opportunity costs of the work performed on demesnes was however economically more important for peasant farmers as prices rose and agriculture became more labor intensive, both through the introduction of new cultivation systems like the Holstein system (*Koppelwirtschaft*) and through intensified cultivation and better preparation of the fields in general (Skrubbeltrang 1978, 241; Dombernowsky 1988, 215–16). Demesne labor services also arguably led to an overpopulation of horses required for boon work in relation to other animals (cows, for example) on peasant farms, a situation that was aggravated by the outflow of tithe and in-kind rent from these farms that might otherwise have served as winter fodder. Estates, by contrast, could count on relatively abundant fodder and had little need to keep horses for plowing and transport (Henriksen 2003, 27; Skrubbeltrang 1978, 353).

As noted in the previous chapter, the requirement that a certain concentration of subordinate farms was needed to achieve tax exemptions meant that farms already clustered around the demesnes, but these farms themselves were still extremely fragmented under the traditional open-field system. In terms of property rights, over the eighteenth century, especially in Funen and Jutland, which had not been subject to local bondage before 1702, an increasing security of tenure has been attested by Danish historians. This came first in the form of so-called family tenure (a halfway copyhold), meaning that tenancy letters and protocols stipulated that tenancy would be guaranteed both for the actual tenant and a specified member of the family, such as a son, son-in-law, and so on. For tenants, this created security (especially regarding the organization of their provision in old age) since they could then renounce their tenancy in favor of a family member who, presumably, could be trusted more than a nonfamily successor with the formal obligation of maintaining retired former tenants. For estate owners, especially in times of crisis, this also ensured that an experienced and motivated new tenant would take over the farm, which is why estate owners often exempted specific tenant sons from conscription or families and estate owners arranged early transitions as a signal of commitment to avoid conscription. Since tenancy letters and protocols exist only in fragmentary form from around 1690 and did not become mandatory until 1719, it is difficult to follow a long-run tendency here, although historians have highlighted that family tenancies became more and more frequent over the eighteenth century once "leasehold for life" had become the norm on farms (but not necessarily for cottages) and sanctioned by the Danish Law.[8] This also of course had the consequence, however, that the estate owner could exert considerable pressure on tenants through the (implicit or explicit) threat of conscription.

1757–1783: Early Attempts at Reform and Backlash

The first decisive attempts at reform came with the establishment of an official Agricultural Commission, set up and presided over by Moltke himself from 1757. Their main concern was what might be seen as the logical next step after the consolidation of the estates: the enclosure of the land of subordinate farms or, at least, the disentangling of grazing rights between villages. This commission created a large amount of (largely ineffective) legislation and published even more reports on other issues, but in terms of enclosures and the consolidation of outfields for grazing, it passed legislation rather quickly.

Hence, provision 3-13-13 of the Danish Law had previously prohibited the enclosure of arable land, meadows, or any other soil by ditches or hedges without consent from *all* affected landowners, but this was now repealed since it prevented owners from doing, in the words of the commission, "their own thing as usefully as they best knew and could" (cited in Skrubbeltrang 1978, 279). In other words, it restricted the freedom to adopt best practice. The corresponding laws on the reduction of common cultivation were passed in 1758 for Zealand and the surrounding islands, in 1759 for Funen, and in 1760 for Jutland. They also contained a provision for extending the effectively cultivated area, which, if it had a *hartkorn* rating lower than that for arable land was not to be reclassified or taxed at higher rates (280). Even if this legislation was mostly directed at the consolidation of lands at the village level between estate owners, especially outfields, it served as a basis for future enclosures, and, by the initiative of estate owners, it further "equalized" the size/*hartkorn* value of the peasant farms in their villages (Skrubbeltrang 1978, 285).

In the following years, an enclosure movement—led by elites operating on their own estates and through the government—emerged throughout the country. The elites' motivation relates of course generally to the rise of enlightenment thought in this period; but, at least as much, it shows a desire to increase the productivity of the land, potentially allowing the possibility both to extract higher rents and to exploit favorable opportunities for agricultural exports. The most famous were the enclosures organized by Torkel Baden (1765–77) of forty-two of foreign minister Count J. H. E. von Bernstorff's peasant farms in Gentofte, Vangede, and Ordrup, just north of Copenhagen. There were many more examples, including in Jutland (Kayser Nielsen 2012, 73, citing Gregersen 1981, 406; see also Skrubbeltrang 1978, 272–73, 295–99; and Dombernowsky 1988, 311–21). The commission also wanted to set an example in the crown domains that it administered by creating new model estates using Holstein cultivation systems (see the next chapter) and enclosing all subordinate tenant farms in these—for instance, in the Vordingborg and Antvorskov districts in southern Zealand (Skrubbeltrang 1978, 284; Dombernowsky 1988, 256). Although these domains soon had to be sold off for lack of government funds, enclosures were at least partially undertaken (233–34).

Parallel to this, on some estates during the 1750s and 1760s, more secure forms of tenancy evolved within the existing legal framework. Thus, after 1757, several estates of crown cavalry districts in Skanderborg and Koldinghus in Jutland were parceled out and sold in pieces, some of them acquired by former tenant farmers (Skrubbeltrang 1978, 272–73; Bjørn 1977b, 119–20).[9]

Formal copyhold, "inheritable tenancy," was introduced on the crown lands in Hørsholm county (northwestern Zealand) in 1761, on the newly enclosed farms of Count Bernstorff's estates north of Copenhagen in 1767, and on Bistrup Manor near Roskilde (west of Copenhagen), which the king had transferred to the magistrate of Copenhagen in 1661 in recognition of the city's services during the previous war. In 1764, copyhold had been introduced on two estates of the influential Scheel-Plessen family, and their owner, Christian Ludvig Scheel von Plessen, was to be a member of a new General College for Agriculture (from 1769 to 1770) and its successor, the General Commission for Agriculture (from 1770 to 1773) (Skrubbeltrang 1978, 272–73; Dombernowsky 1988, 311–12). This early granting of copyhold and purchase of freehold (in Jutland) is said to have facilitated the enclosure movement from below, since copyhold tenants could initiate enclosures themselves (Bjørn 1977b, 120–21).

The new General College for Agriculture (Generallandvæsenskollegiet) replaced the old Agricultural Commission in 1768. One of its main tasks was to prepare a new decree on owner-occupier farmers, which was eventually issued in 1769 and formally introduced new legal ways to make tenancy more secure for the peasants and encouraged estate owners to sell farms to their current tenants. The main incentive was that, even if the estate owner sold the farm, he would retain the right to count it as a subordinate farm in order to maintain the tax exemption for his demesne. In exchange, the estate owner would also remain liable for the new owner-occupier farmer's tax payments (Skrubbeltrang 1978, 322–24). It also became possible to incorporate peasant farmlands into the main demesne for some period after 1769. This did not, however, lead to a large wave of farm dissolutions (Skrubbeltrang 1978, 295–99), and neither did it trigger a large wave of conversions into freehold, at least in part because after 1769 crown land and crown estates were mainly sold off en bloc to investors with sufficient liquidity and not to tenant farmers (Henriksen 2003, 32).

The recently founded General College for Agriculture was replaced in 1770 by Struensee with a new General Commission for Agriculture (Generallandvæsenskommission) with Oeder as the main driving force for further technical and social reforms. The General Commission was then dissolved after Struensee's fall in 1773, but even the conservative government maintained the pro-enclosure legislation, clarifying existing legislation in a new decree in 1776, when Count Moltke's son Joachim Godske Moltke, a pro-reformer, became president of the Treasury (*Rentekammer*).

Turning to boon work, this was, despite popular misconception, not part of adscription, but the most significant part of the aforementioned dysfunctional rent payment system. Reforming the system, however, proved to be difficult. How to regulate boon work and to adapt the rent system to the increasing commercialization of agriculture was discussed, with little practical result, by the first Agricultural Commission between 1757 and 1767 (Skrubbeltrang 1978, 321). In 1769, a decree was issued that required estate owners to document and send their boon-work arrangements to the central government. About five hundred estates did so,[10] but nevertheless the decree had little effect on actual boon work, since the estate owners were free to fix the number of days without consultation of their tenants or interference by other authorities (Skrubbeltrang 1941; 1978, 359–62). Under Struensee, Oeder issued a new decree, which was to be repealed after the fall of that government, which established maximum workloads (in work and horse days of different sorts) for a model farm of 6 *tønde hartkorn*, with specific formulas for larger and smaller farms. Løgstrup (1974) has assessed for one estate (Løvenborg Manor near Holbæk on Zealand) that this decree, if it had ever become effective, would have reduced labor services to about 55 percent of that which the estate owner had reported under the 1769 decree. Finally, in 1773 and 1774, new rules were issued, according to which the county governor and two men experienced in agriculture were to assess the labor services of each estate, with the result that boon work was now on many estates officially documented as "unspecified," that is, explicitly not fixed or subject to any constraint (Skrubbeltrang 1978, 367–70).

Thus, although important initiatives were taken in this period, the fall of Struensee and the conservative backlash meant that the reforms were largely incomplete before the 1780s. It is clear that the elites understood the inefficiencies within the system and recognized what needed to be reformed, but there was a general reluctance or disagreement about what should be done and the extent to which it was necessary or desirable (seen from their perspective). Nevertheless, the various commissions collected valuable evidence as well as practical experience in the introduction of enclosure through their experiments on both crown and other estates.

1784–1802: The Completion of the Reforms

With political change and favorable conditions for agriculture in the 1780s and 1790s the process of land reform gained new momentum. In 1784 the obligation to collect tax payments from freehold farms was transferred from estate owners to the county governor, although freehold farms could still be counted to qualify for tax exemptions for the demesne if they had been sold to their current tenant (Henriksen 2003, 29, 32; Løgstrup 1984, 304; Skrubbeltrang 1978, 417); this provision was only abolished with the tax reform of 1802, after much privatization had already taken place (Kjærgaard 1994, 217–19). This provision encouraged conversion to freehold but also improved the bargaining position of the tenants, who generally enjoyed leasehold for life, a right that was confirmed and clarified in decrees in 1790.

Financing the acquisition of freehold was not straightforward. Under the tenancy system, in which large parts of the rent were labor services, peasant households were monetized to a relatively small extent and hence in most cases did not hold large savings, thus constraining the ability to obtain credit in the countryside (Skrubbeltrang 1978, 417). Available sources of credit were municipality administrations and their endowments (e.g., for poor relief), which gave loans against the security of land and farms, as well as private lenders in market towns such as local notables and, occasionally, priests (417–18).

The government aimed to provide additional credit as well. In 1786, the Treasury set up the Kongelige Kreditkasse as an institution to provide loans to businesses in Denmark, Norway, and the duchies. It was also supposed to use its funds to help nonowner peasants finance longer and more secure tenancies and full ownership, granting loans for twenty-eight years at an interest rate somewhat above the market level, thus reflecting the longer repayment and greater uncertainty. The Kreditkasse was however rather cautious in its lending to tenant farmers and conducted detailed background checks of not only the assets of the farm but also the farming abilities of the potential borrowers (Skrubbeltrang 1978, 416; Dombernowsky 1988, 357–58). Its loans, which started in earnest by 1793, were an important source of finance for peasants in the first year but became less and less so, especially after 1797, when another government institution, Den almindelige Enkekasse (the General Widows' Fund) became the main official credit provider. Skrubbeltrang (1978, 416) reports that some eight hundred peasants, mostly from Jutland, obtained loans from the Kreditkasse for purchase of their farms.

The General Widows' Fund, set up in 1775, provided pensions mainly to soldiers' widows but was open to other citizens as well. It became the main source of government finance for peasants in the context of the agricultural reforms when in 1797 C. D. Reventlow joined its board and steered the fund toward agricultural loans. At first, some 10 percent of funds were lent to agriculture, but from 1800 this increased rapidly to more than half, and during some years in the early 1800s all loans the fund made were to finance freehold purchases (Skrubbeltrang 1978, 416–17). According to figures collected by F. A. Bergsøe, the Widows' Fund provided loans totaling 3.163 million rigsdaler to 4,019 peasants. About 80 percent of the loans were again to peasants in Jutland, although the average loan there (640 rigsdaler) was less than half that on the islands of Zealand, Funen, and Lolland (1400 rigsdaler) (Skrubbeltrang 1978, 417). Since as stated above a total of forty thousand farms were turned into freehold, most former tenants must have found financing outside these two official institutions, including seller financing via annualized payments or mortgages on the property.

The development of the crown estates was taken up again after the change of government in 1784 with a new commission for the crown lands in Frederiksborg and Kronborg counties in northern Zealand known as the Small Agricultural Commission—to distinguish it from the Large Agricultural Commission set up in 1786, which prepared the legislation for the comprehensive national agricultural reforms.[11] The Small Commission collected valuable practical experience in its organization of the enclosures of the crown lands, for example regarding which farms and farmers were to be settled on new farmsteads outside the villages (out-settlers should not be drinkers and should preferably be younger), how out-settlement was to be financed (out-settlers were to be compensated by those farmers who remained in the village), as well as how to motivate tenants to participate in and make possible the considerable investments necessary for the new roads, hedges, and ditches (capital outlays were to be incentivized with initial tax exemptions and reduced labor service requirements). We will return to these issues below, but for now it suffices to mention that the participation of peasants and the positive attitude toward this process in general was aided by the favorable impressions that Bernstorff's earlier enclosures relatively nearby had given rise to (Skrubbeltrang 1978, 291–94).

The Large Commission in turn prepared new rules and clarified older ones on the organization of enclosures, particularly regarding the practical issues regarding tenancy, the out-settling of farms from the village, and the allocation of land to cotters. Laws passed in 1787 and 1791 created an even more solid basis for the private enclosure process, which by then was already well under way. The most important features of these concerned the organization and compensation of those who moved out of the village onto new outlying farmsteads and the rights of cotters and smallholders, more on which below. Finally, repeated clarifications were published of points on which the enclosure process was or seemed inconsistent with the 1683 Danish Law (Skrubbeltrang 1978, 260, 301–3).

As touched on above, a central question was the organization and financing of the relocation of peasants to new farms on enclosed land outside the village center. According to the 1776 decree every landowner was entitled to consolidate and enclose his or her holdings in a village, and the remaining inhabitants and landowners in the village would have to take part in the costs of the physical restructuring and planting of hedges and so on. County governors and newly appointed agricultural commissioners (of which seven existed for the whole country) were available to assist and guide the process.

In 1781, the Treasury promised subventions of 50 to 150 rigsdaler per farm that was moved to new holdings, but just 1,000 rigsdaler per year was budgeted for this purpose (Skrubbeltrang 1978, 285; Dombernowsky 1988, 321–23, 327–29). The 1787 decrees contained the provision that peasant farmers could not effectively oppose relocation and that all peasants (even freeholders) had to take part in the transport of the material necessary for relocation (for example, timber from the estate's forests); a clarification in 1795 gave estate owners the right to divide the expenses and workload between all peasants under the estate's influence. Finally, further clarifications during the 1790s stipulated the tax exemptions related to enclosures, especially for relocated peasants, and set limits on the redeemable expenses for new farmsteads and cottages (Skrubbeltrang 1978, 301–2, 396).

In terms of boon work, the government conducted a large inquiry based on a memorandum by Reventlow (Skrubbeltrang 1978, 372–79; Kjærgaard 1980), but initially did not enact new legislation apart from the commutation rules for enclosed lands in 1792 and a public order decree in 1791 that regulated fines and corporal punishment for servants and cotters who failed to show up or did not satisfactorily carry out their service obligations (Skrubbeltrang 1978, 379–80, 415; Horstbøll and Østergård 1990, 163). Although boon work commissions were set up for each county in 1795–97, change was slow because many estates were leased to professional tenants with long contracts which were to last for the duration of the new seven-to-eleven-year crop-rotation system of *Koppelwirtschaft* (Skrubbeltrang 1978, 385). In fact, one of the reasons why boon work might have been so difficult to reform was that, as we will discuss in the next chapter, the labor was used to make the improvements to the land necessary to implement this new system. We do not wish to imply that forced labor was necessary to modernize the estates, since, if the process of reform had not been so slow, they could in principle offset the cost of hiring day laborers by the prospect of increased rents.

The final steps to the reform process came in the 1790s, when the remaining boon work was abolished and capitalized in order to pay for the rest of the reform process. First, a 1792 decree on the distribution of enclosure and relocation costs among tenants modified the prevailing system in a way that allowed for the conversion of previous in-kind payments and labor services into *flexible* monetary rents under certain conditions (Henriksen 2003, 25). Then, in 1799, a boon-work decree was finally issued by Reventlow (Skrubbeltrang 1978, 388–91). Limitless or insufficiently specified boon work was to be abolished, and tenant farmers were to be able to work their own land and to pay their other taxes and obligations. The central idea was that each tenant and estate owner should conclude an agreement, and that the Rentekammer should supervise the process and outcome. Rights and obligations were also defined much more clearly than in previous legislation. But this, again, failed to deliver the desired results, partly because a common practice was to commute boon work into monetary payments during the 1790s, thus locking in much of the relatively high levels achieved during these years (Skrubbeltrang 1978, 435–36) but also, more importantly, due to the mass conversion of leasehold and copyhold into freehold property.

Cotters and Laborers

Another main concern raised by the enclosures was the role of cotters (which included rural artisans, craftsmen, and other nonagricultural secondary occupations) and less fortunate members of rural society such as servants, whose access to communal resources was abolished as a consequence of the new simplified property rights for enclosed farm properties. The main issue was the terms of the compensation they should receive for their rights to benefit from communal resources. Both farmers and estate owners needed these growing rural lower classes as workers in times of rising prices and intensified farming, but clearly both, and especially the tenant farmers, did not want to lose too much cultivable land to them in the enclosure process. Thus, some kind of remuneration had to be given to them to avoid a problem of rural poverty, which would have increased the need for poverty relief. Relief had been provided by estate owners before the 1780s and by estate owners and peasants afterward, with the consequential risk of rural exodus and/or a need to increase wages.

Initially, the official target was to have two cottages per medium-sized farm, each of which should have around 0.17 hectares of arable land per cottage and/or an equivalent in pasture. A regulation in 1778 increased this to 0.5 *tønde land*. This was followed by a new decree in 1781 intended to allow cotters to sustain their houses and farms so as to retain them as workers on the land. This stipulated that "cotters with enclosures had for certain either the possibility for grazing *or* their own arable land." Skrubbeltrang (1978, 285–87) highlights that in practice it remained unclear whether these were *rights* (which could be compensated for by money) or whether this should actually lead to land assignments (especially regarding grazing). In the end, the lawmakers' intention became that the cotters should receive circa 3 *tønde land* (ca. 1.65 hectares), of which about 0.5 *tønde* should be arable and the rest pasture. This would in general support one cow and four sheep, but in some places it was only sufficient for one cow *or* four sheep. Moreover, this land was not required to be in the proximity of the cottages, with its exact location to be coordinated by estate owners and government officials (288–89). Finally, the Soil Law of 1787 stipulated that cotters should receive 3–4 *tønder* (1.65–2.2 hectares) of medium-quality land (301).

The labor services and tax payments to be delivered by these new small-holders also remained unclear and subject to local variation for a long time; seen in relation to the land they held, smallholders' obligations were in practice normally much higher than those of tenant farmers. In 1805 it was decided that cotters' labor services did not fall under the legal definition of labor services (*hoveri*); instead labor services were to be fixed in cotters' tenancy contracts or in separate agreements, a provision that according to the literature did not assist in lowering the disproportionate burden that fell onto the smallholders and landless laborers (Skrubbeltrang 1978, 390–91, see also 366–67). In many villages, not only did economic and social class divisions become more pronounced with these provisions and the underlying market processes but also the geographic separation between farmers and cotters increased (Skrubbeltrang 1978, 410–15, 432–33; Kjærgaard 1985, 117).

Epilogue

After 1766, and increasingly after 1784, Danish absolutism created the legal framework for a conversion of most prior relationships, especially but not only in the countryside, from older forms of bondage and subordination to estates to more capitalist and market-oriented relations. Initially, estate owners, such as Moltke, both on their private initiative and through the government, enabled the legislation and set precedents (by example) for a process which was to take the best part of half a century to complete, partly due to the backlash after the fall of Struensee but also due to conflicting ideas and interests among the elites themselves.

Nevertheless, by the early 1800s the transformation was more or less complete. The elites sought to change and improve the countryside both on their estates (a topic for the next chapter) and more generally, although far from everyone gained in the process. In so doing, they were relieved of some obligations and lost some of their rights. This fact, together with the much earlier enclosures of their demesnes, laid the ground for their transformation into the commercially oriented rational farmers which will form a large part of our story. As a by-product of their reforms, however, elites also created a new class of owner-occupier farmers outside the demesnes, who were in time to attempt to emulate the improvements on the estates we discuss in subsequent chapters and eventually to eclipse them with the birth of centralized village production and finally the cooperatives.

A final question remains as to why a coincidence of wants between peasants and estate owners emerged from the 1780s and allowed this process to be completed. Henriksen (2003) provides a sophisticated explanation of this at the micro level based on the incentives of peasants and estate owners. She argues from contemporary sources that principal-agent problems and the difficulties of monitoring the labor services performed by tenants' servants on the demesnes created a considerable wedge between the (opportunity) cost of this labor to tenant farmers and the benefit that estate owners derived from it, for example in terms of marketable grain production. This difference led to differential valuation when the value of these services was capitalized by tenants and estate owners, and a sales price had to be fixed. The maximum price at which peasants would buy their farms and hence eliminate labor services on the demesne would be considerably higher than the minimum that estate owners would expect, especially where labor services made up a large share of the rent payments. To estate owners, additional incentives to accept a relatively low price would be the government provision (from 1784) to transfer the costs of tax collection upon sale from estate owners to the government and the provision that tax privileges for estates would continue if sale was to be to the current tenant and not to other potential market participants.

As a consequence, the sale price of the farm would be significantly below the maximum price the tenant would be willing to pay for being able to use his servants (and horses and implements) on his own farm instead of the demesne. Henriksen argues that the actual future value of the farm to the tenant under freehold would be even higher, since under tenancy potential improvements and productivity increases available with more intensive labor would be concealed from the estate owner. She backs her reasoning with observations (collected by Gregers Begtrup around 1800) of sales of peasant farms to tenants and their later resales by these same tenants, which show a price increase of on average 170 percent across different available samples during calculation periods of less than ten years (Henriksen 2003, 31, table 3). She also mentions that purchases were often at least partially financed by the resale of small plots to cotters at much higher unit values, since for cotters no comparable purchasing privilege existed (see also Kjærgaard 1985, 117).

The Spread of the Holstein System

As we touched on in earlier chapters, the developments that the elites on the landed estates promoted in the country as a whole took place alongside a considerable improvement of their main farmlands, the demesnes, in particular the adoption of a new, more productive crop rotation, which we will argue sowed the seeds for the emergence of the modern Danish dairy industry. As we previously noted, the demesnes, which together comprised only around 10 percent of all arable land in the country (Feldbæk 1990, 246), had been consolidated long before the enclosures and privatization of peasant lands and were not subject to restrictions on property rights from common cultivation. Moreover, for most of the eighteenth century, the estate owners and their administrators could rely on, and even increase, the boon work delivered by farmers and smallholders, thus enabling them to implement an intensified crop-rotation system with larger livestock densities. Thus, from the 1750s, a pioneering group of estate owners was able to import a particular set of best practices from abroad, which then spread among Danish estates and were developed further in the process. These practices were eventually imitated by the peasantry as well and thereby created the environment in which the dairy industry would flourish after around 1850.

In fact, the origins of the Danish dairy industry can be directly traced to over a century earlier in the duchy of Holstein (and to a lesser extent the neighboring duchy of Schleswig). Building on advances made by the Dutch, this duchy was already a leading center of dairying in the eighteenth century (Iversen 1992; Riis 2009, 213–15).[1] Early on, a system developed here on the large manorial estates known as *Koppelwirtschaft* in German, or *kobbelbrug* in Danish, which, combined with a dairy unit, is often called the Holstein system in English. This consisted, in comparison to the traditional three-field crop rotation, of a new layout and more intensive usage of the fields through crop rotation, but, since it still comprised a large amount of land temporarily left aside for pasture, it also soon came to be associated with dairying. The unprecedentedly large herds of milch cows these estates kept, commonly running into the hundreds, allowed for professionalization in the handling of cattle and dairy products and most importantly for our story the development of a new system of butter production, the *hollænderi* (German: *Holländerei*). *Koppelwirtschaft* became the dominant field system in the duchies in the 1700s, although its spread is poorly understood. It is not clear whether it came about through enclosure of estate demesnes with an increased focus on cattle rearing in the 1500s, or whether it was connected to the spread of dairying (Porskrog Rasmussen 2003, 455–56). Nevertheless, as we will soon see, these advances spread to Denmark proper from the 1750s, and imitation and adaptation there formed the basis of dairying in Denmark. In fact, in 1846 (some three and a half decades before the first cooperative), as noted in the introduction, the German travel writer J. G. Kohl was already predicting that the composite monarchy of Denmark would soon become a land not of milk and honey but of milk and butter. While the composite monarchy soon fell apart, the legacy of Holstein dairying for Denmark was here to stay and would be a cornerstone of the Danish dairy industry as it became famous in subsequent decades.

In the following, we first describe the Holstein system and its transmission to Denmark and then demonstrate that the spread of cooperatives after 1880 followed the introduction of protomodern dairies on estate farms more than a century earlier, most clearly through increasing cow densities in parishes where early Holstein dairies could be found. We interpret this as a trickle-down process by which the newly independent medium-sized farmers and at least a share of the cotters imitated practices and production choices of local estates to take advantage of knowledge and marketing and distribution contacts that emerged based on the larger production units. This pre-preparation in and appreciation of dairying then greatly facilitated the spread of modern cooperative creameries from 1882.

Koppelwirtschaft and Centralized Dairy Facilities in Schleswig and Holstein

Koppelwirtschaft was a collective invention by estate owners and their administrators in sixteenth-century Schleswig and Holstein, the German part of the Danish monarchy, intended to overcome the fundamental problem of intensified organic agriculture—that is, how to sustain production and yields in the long run by obtaining sufficient fertilizer from animal husbandry. It consisted of changing the traditional three-field rotation with outlying pasture areas into an eleven-field rotation, thus alternating the use of individual fields between pasture and grain cultivation over eleven years. This was important both for sustaining grain yields and obtaining sufficient fodder for the animals, normally in the form of summer pasture and winter hay—all this as production surpluses were exported from rural areas in order to sustain growing urban populations.[2]

In modern times, this problem arose first in the coastal provinces of the Netherlands and modern-day Belgium, where early population growth had led to much higher population densities than elsewhere, thus providing incentives to develop more intensive and commercialized agriculture. It was from here that approaches were diffused and adapted to local conditions in other places, such as "convertible husbandry" in England (Mokyr 2009, 173). The basic solution, also in Holstein, consisted in reducing outlying grazing areas (pastures) which were only used extensively and converting them into part of the crop rotation by changing the traditional design of fields and the crop rotation itself.

In parallel to this, the use of clover and other perennial forage legumes like alfalfa/lucerne made its way into northwestern European agriculture, where clover was gradually introduced into the intensified crop-rotation systems both to obtain feed for animals and because the many grain crops had a tendency to impoverish the earth, weakening the animals which grazed on it. The advantage of clover and related root crops lies in their nitrogen-fixing properties, which form an important part of the replenishment of soils, although it took modern soil chemistry to fully understand the process. The use of clover to replenish the soil has deep historical roots in the agricultural systems of the Mediterranean during the Roman Empire. These were rediscovered in northern Italy in the late Middle Ages and saw a resurgence during the Renaissance and subsequent episodes of agricultural improvement and rational farming in most of western Europe, including the British Isles (Ambrosoli 1997).[3] From around 1800, the use of clover spread throughout Denmark (Dall, Jensen, and Naz 2014; Kjærgaard 1994, 72–87).

In theory, there were many ways of combining animals and bread, fodder and cash crops in different land-management systems. *Koppelwirtschaft*, even if it involved the improvements outlined above, meant that a large proportion of the fields was left as fallow (between one-seventh and one-eleventh) and did not give a return. Thus, Albrecht D. Thaer in Germany promoted New Husbandry (in Danish *vekselbrug* or *vekseldrift*) based on English-Flemish practices (see, e.g., Thaer 1801–4). This involved the introduction of more clover, other legumes, and oil plants to replenish the soil; the use of the fallow to grow fallow fruits—potatoes, linen, root vegetables, and so on; and the introduction of summer stable feeding for cattle, which meant less land was needed for grazing and a more efficient use of the manure.

Despite the enthusiastic promotion of New Husbandry in Denmark in the early 1800s, it did not become widely adopted because it appears to have been unsuitable for Danish conditions, except for in its most fertile areas. Also, as discussed in chapter 2, even after considerable population growth from the mid-1700s, land was still relatively abundant in Denmark in comparison to labor, indicating that a relatively more land-intensive version of intensified agriculture seemed more appropriate. Similar reasoning applied to Schleswig and Holstein, where Thaer himself was informed by a leading practitioner that barn feeding in summer led to quality risks for milk and butter production for large herds—as well as a risk to the reputation of the farmer—and it was therefore to be avoided in an agricultural system in which dairy output played a central role (Thaer 1799, 197–203; see also Rixen 1800, 362–64). *Koppelwirtschaft* was thus to become the advanced agricultural system of choice in Schleswig, Holstein, and Denmark (S. P. Jensen 1998, 43–47).

Koppelwirtschaft was introduced on large manors because they were the most commercially oriented agricultural units, the most likely to be able to sustain capital investments and labor efforts (via boon work or hired labor), and had the most freedom to act under the institutional framework of the time. It should be highlighted that everywhere *Koppelwirtschaft* was introduced, it was mainly used by estates in their directly controlled production on the demesne. Many of these, managed by relatively professional staff, exhibited a much higher market orientation than the average farmer (Porskrog Rasmussen 2010b, 182), and required more complex decision-making and control tools, for both arable farming and animal husbandry. Hence, they were also at the forefront of other innovations such as the detailed accounts kept on farms and big dairies that we discuss in the following chapter, which allowed for the rationalization of decision making, especially in the more nontraditional economic activities like dairying.

By contrast, as we have seen in chapter 3, before the 1790s almost all peasant cultivation took place within village-level, communal, open-field cultivation schemes, which in principle could be—and sometimes were—reorganized into a communal *Koppelwirtschaft* scheme, although these were never widely adopted. This was, among other factors, due to the considerable labor and capital costs involved in rearranging and enclosing the fields and the uncertainty of the benefits that might come from a more commercially oriented cultivation in comparison to the risk-minimizing traditional three-field rotation (S. P. Jensen 1987, 109; Jespersen 2004, 131–32).[4] Only with the enclosures of individual farms could modern crop rotations be adopted by individual farmers, which they were after some time, as described in more detail below. Thus, with the advances in cultivation and animal husbandry on the estates, a gap emerged between estate and peasant producers in terms of grain yields and, for example, butter quality (Bjørn 1988a, 159; S. P. Jensen 1987, 110; see also chapter 6 below).

The system invented in Holstein and Schleswig prioritized the quality of pastures over agricultural land. With its soils particularly suited for fertile grasslands, the region had in the sixteenth century focused on oxen fattening and horse breeding, and during the seventeenth and eighteenth centuries, partly under the influence of specialized immigrants from the Netherlands, it had developed a strong dairy sector. This focus on dairying in the duchies seems largely to have been promoted by changes in the relative prices of grain and oxen versus dairy products (Porskrog Rasmussen 2003, 447; 2010a, 180).[5] Since the original innovators were immigrants from Holland, the tenants involved in dairying became known as *hollænder* or Dutchmen (and their dairies *hollænderier*), even if they were not of Dutch descent.[6] The lease contracts were awarded in auctions and based on fixed rents per cow of up to 10 to 12 rigsdaler/reichsthaler per milch cow (Schröder-Lembke 1978, 63).[7]

In fact, these leases seem to have been one reason the dairies were so productive, since they entailed that the business of the dairy was leased from the estate owner to a specialist dairy tenant with a well-specified contract.[8] Drejer (1925–33, 181–82) gives a full description of the typical contents of these.[9] In general they specified the *hollænder*'s legal situation and how the business should be run. Tenants were usually provided with specially adapted dairy rooms, stables, and so on, but they had the responsibility to look after them. Likewise, they were provided with good and well-fed milch cows and bulls, for which the tenant was responsible and forbidden to sell, slaughter, or rent out; if cattle became injured or no longer provided good milk, tenants were required to replace them. Finally, the tenant was given a large inventory of implements. In terms of running the business, tenants were told where and how to feed the cattle and where to milk them. During the winter, tenants were told what they would be supplied, what they could take for themselves (typically hay from the fields), and how much grain would be provided for the household. Tenants were responsible for providing firewood, wood for tools, and so on. Lastly, tenants were usually told to be careful with fire, candles, tobacco pipes, and so on; not to keep loose dogs; and that fishing and hunting were not permitted on the estate.

Although these contracts are valuable as a source of information about what was expected of tenants by estate owners, Carsten Porskrog Rasmussen (1987, 63–65) warns that contracts are by their very nature normative; they of course do not tell us whether these conditions were met or, indeed, whether they were (economically) favorable for the tenant. In terms of contract theory (Hayami and Otsuka 1993), we can highlight that fixed rent payments for the contract duration implied that the dairy tenant would receive the full marginal return on his efforts while also being in general the bearer of the risk, while the estate owner (or the estate tenant if it was rented out) would receive a fixed rent and thus some fixed income while he bore the risk for the rest of the exploitation of the estate—principally grain production. From the estate owner's point of view, these tenancy contracts thus contributed to mitigating risk, especially the risk of operating one of the more skill-intensive parts of his exploitation, where direct operation would potentially be difficult without specific knowledge of production processes and marketing.

While these arrangements, apart from being historically path-dependent, thus seemed to be economically sensible in a world of incomplete information and difficult monitoring, they were surely not without costs. Karl von Treskow (1810) mentions some of the potential conflicts.[10] For example, if the dairy tenant is entitled to a certain amount of grain for winter feeding of the cows, it might be difficult for him to force the granary administrator to give him good grain that could be sold on the market more profitably, if the estate was not entitled to any gains from better-fed cows. On the other hand, the maintenance of cows might also give rise to disputes, especially in cases of serious disease and epidemics or in years of bad grazing, when some cows might stay dry and not produce milk. Such disputes might have led to inefficiencies, but these were probably no bigger than the inefficiencies that would have arisen in other contractual arrangements, such as the employment of a steward to manage the dairy directly. However, as we will see in the next chapter, in the 1850s and 1860s in Denmark, some tenants seem to have become discontented with their arrangements, and some estate owners seem to have been successful with direct management of their dairy units. Whether this reflects general efficiency advantages of one contractual arrangement over another, however, is difficult to say given the intensive confrontation and thus the probable high degree of bias in the contributions.

Many estates came to have very large herds of cows, even by the standards of the late twentieth century. By 1715, of forty-six manors in Schleswig, there were ninety-one dairy units with a total of 11,696 cows, much larger than the units in Holland, from where the system had been imported and adapted (Porskrog Rasmussen 2010b, 181–82). The professionalized dairy units were superior and innovative compared to traditional methods in many ways; in

FIGURE 4.1. Michael Ancher (1849–1927), *Cows Being Driven across the Moor*, 1902
Source: Courtesy of the National Art Gallery of Denmark.
Note: Although this painting is from a rather late date, it illustrates very well the traditional gender division in agriculture.

particular, they included the following advantages: (1) practical, often independent, rooms (the *hollænderi*), where a reasonably constant temperature was maintained throughout the year; (2) practical tools, which were easy to clean; (3) a very strong focus on hygiene; (4) regular milking times and milking standards that ensured the last drops of cream-rich milk were collected; (5) temperature control of the cream, so that it could be skimmed and churned at the optimal time; and, finally, (6) carefulness at all times from milking to packaging (Bjørn 1988a, 158–59).

The actual dairy work, milking and processing the milk into butter and cheese, would be done by a woman, often the dairy tenant's wife, who was also in charge of supervising the (also female) milkmaids, keeping the premises clean, and training new dairywomen for an apprenticeship fee. The tenant or dairy manager himself would be mainly in charge of feeding and supervising the cows and organizing the transport of milk from the milking places (often on outlying fields) to the dairy unit itself. In this, milk processing under the Holstein system followed traditional gender roles (as illustrated in figure 4.1), which were also followed in peasant households under much different conditions (Fink 2009, 455–56; B. K. Hansen 2006, 179–81; cf. Sommestad and McMurry 1998, 149–52, for the case of Sweden). The estates also continued to innovate outside the dairy itself, for example by providing strong feeding with hay and grain through the winter, so that cows could be productive as soon as they went onto grass (H. S. Hansen 1994, 59).

Before the Holstein system, combining *Koppelwirtschaft* and *hollænde-rier*, spread to Denmark, it arrived at the beginning of the eighteenth century, via estate owner Joachim Friedrich von der Lühe, at the Panzow estate in neighboring Mecklenburg, where soils were not so favorable to grass, and productive specialization focused on grains. He nevertheless also introduced a relatively large herd of cattle, constructed a dairy unit, and leased it to a specialized dairy tenant (Schröder-Lembke 1978, 65–67).

The Spread of the Holstein System to Denmark

In the Kingdom of Denmark itself, from the Middle Ages until the seventeenth century, estates as well as peasant farms typically only had as many cows as they needed to feed the household, and more sophisticated dairy products were imported from Holland (Appel and Bredkjær 1924–32, 279–80). This began to change from the second half of the eighteenth century as herds increased, and the word *hollænderi* entered the language (Drejer 1925–33, 138). However, although we can find some examples of *hollænderi* in the seventeenth century (see, e.g., Drejer 1925–33, 140–43; Skrubbeltrang 1978, 120), some of which had large herds and were sometimes run by Dutchmen, it was not until the late eighteenth century that dairying in Denmark was revolutionized following the Holstein model. Actually, for the latter half of the 1700s, authors often highlight the low proportion of cows (and bulls) relative to horses in the use of pasture in Denmark. Hans Hertel (1920, 149–51), for example, estimates the cattle to horse ratio at only 1.4:1 in the 1770s,[11] when the tenants of subordinate farms and cotters still had to hold a significant number of horses to perform boon work on the estates' demesnes (see chapter 3). By 1914, the ratio of cattle to horses was 4:1, and this was in no small amount due to the continuous increase in the number of milch cows: in 1760 there were maybe 270,000 in Denmark, increasing to 335,000 in 1774, and to 450,000 in 1810 (Drejer 1962, 22; S. P. Jensen 2007, 140). The first (surviving) livestock census of 1836–37 gives 578,000 milch cows in 1837. In 1861, a new census recorded 756,834 milch cows, and by 1881, the year before the first cooperative creamery was founded, there were 898,790.

An important prerequisite for the spread of the Holstein system into Denmark was the redistribution of land throughout the late seventeenth and eighteenth centuries—for example, the sale during the eighteenth century of most of the crown estates, which until the 1600s had been under the direct administration of the monarch. The 1600s saw some advances in agriculture, including the improvement of pastureland through drainage and a better understanding of the way in which to use manure. Much of this came under the guidance of entrepreneurial aristocrats—for example, Christian Rantzau, owner of the Demstrup estate near Randers in east Jutland from 1627 to 1663, who used his serfs to improve his land and possibly to introduce a version of *Koppelwirtschaft* (Frandsen 2005, 46–47). As mentioned in chapter 2, the precarious financial situation of the crown, largely as a result of continuous wars and other military obligations, meant that the kings were forced to sell off more and more estates between the 1660s and the 1760s, until almost all the crown estates were privatized. Many of these were purchased by buyers with little knowledge of agriculture (Frandsen 2005, 58, and 74–76), and a debate ensued about how to take advantage of this situation to introduce reforms and a general modernization of agriculture (S. P. Jensen 1998, 37–38; Feldbæk 1988, 19).

The introduction of *Koppelwirtschaft* was at least in part a result of this development, although most saw it simply as a means to increase grain yields. This is best illustrated by a famous quote by Adam Gottlob Moltke, who is generally credited with introducing *Koppelwirtschaft* into Denmark (S. P. Jensen 1998, 92), from a plan devised in 1746 for King Frederik V: "Agriculture in these lands seems to be still very backward. I keep myself assured that, if the soil here would be worked as is custom in other countries, especially in Holstein, the land could yield twice as much as it has produced hitherto."[12] In the context of his ascent to Lord Chamberlain for Frederik V in 1746, Moltke received the large estate of Bregentved in southern Zealand, and before 1751 bought four more nearby estates: Turebyholm, Juellinge, Tryggevælden, and Aslev (Porskrog Rasmussen 2010a, 11).[13]

Moltke, who was born in Mecklenburg, became page to the Danish crown prince in 1722 at the age of twelve and then, when the crown prince became King Christian VI in 1730, became page-in-waiting to the new crown prince and administrator of his household from 1743. When his master became King Frederik V in 1746, he named Moltke Lord Chamberlain (Feldbæk 1990, 216–17). In 1759, Moltke came to own, under fortuitous circumstances, the estate of Niendorf near Lübeck, on which *Koppelwirtschaft* was firmly established, and sold it two years later for a large profit (Porskrog Rasmussen 2010a, 19–21). Moltke brought the former leaseholder of Niendorf, Johann Matthias Völckers, to his estates on Zealand to become his administrator and agricultural reorganizer there. He started on the newly established farm of Stenkelstrup (later named Sofiendal after Moltke's second wife Sophie Hedevig Raben), where Völckers by 1766 established an exact copy of Holstein *Koppelwirtschaft* with the layout of the eleven fields (see figure 4.2), the original crop rotation, and a *hollænderi*. Under the supervision of Völckers, who in many cases also acted as leaseholder of the transformed estates, Alslev, Turebyholm,

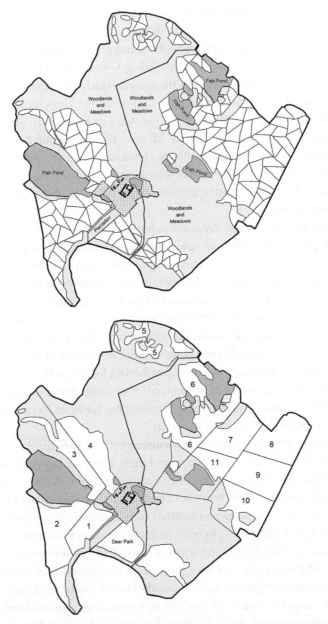

FIGURE 4.2. Field layouts of Moltke's Bregentved estate before (*top*) and after (*bottom*) the introduction of *Koppelwirtschaft*

Source: Created by the authors with the assistance of Julia Dávila-Lampe, based on a 1760s map published in Løgstrup (2015, 18) and preserved in the private Bregentved Manor Archive in Haslev.

Note: The top map shows numerous individual fields under the traditional three-field rotation system; the botttom map shows the plan—originally drawn into the upper map—of how these were to be reorganized into the eleven fields of the new rotation system. See also Porskrog Rasmussen (2010b, 29).

and the Bregentved main estate were also reorganized by 1767, with Juellinge following in the early 1770s. Most of Moltke's reorganized estates were then, as before, leased in auctions to interested leaseholders (see also S. P. Jensen 1998, 49–51).

In reports he wrote in the 1780s for the king, and for the reform-minded governing crown prince (to highlight his role as a reformer), Moltke claimed that the value of his lease contracts by 1787 had increased more than 200 percent since the introduction of *Koppelwirtschaft* in the 1740s. Porskrog Rasmussen (2010a, 26–27) has remarked that although this increase should be qualified since cattle plagues had decreased the value of estates in the late 1740s, it was still far beyond the increase in prices[14] over the same period, which measured about 30–40 percent. For the estate of Turebyholm he quotes increases in the leasing fee from 2,700 rigsdaler before 1767 to 5,000 in 1792, the year of Moltke's death. The number of cows had also increased on Moltke's estates, although only by 18 percent, from 670 to 790. Thus, Moltke's reorganization certainly increased the capitalized value of his estates and probably the efficiency in the use of resources, especially cows, as well.

The restructuring of the estates involved substantial expenses on improvements and infrastructure, as well as lots of hard work, which again fell largely on the unfortunate peasants who were subject to traditional boon-work obligations and mobility restrictions under the adscription system, both of which, as noted in chapter 2, were gradually extended throughout the eighteenth century until the final abolition of adscription, the increasing regulation of boon work, and the rapid transformation of subordinate into freehold farms toward the end of the eighteenth century (see chapter 3 and Olsen 1957, 148). Increasing prices of agricultural goods from the 1760s meant that there was an incentive for estates to do this. But as we have seen in the previous chapter, as time progressed, a new model for the estates emerged where the peasants had partial or full rights to own their farms, and estate owners (and well-to-do farmers) hired their labor from the growing servant and cotter class and acted more and more as commercial entrepreneurs. This became attractive for estate owners, since real wages were stationary or even falling at least from the 1750s (see chapter 2). Then, as land prices increased, estates became sought-after investment objects. Their owners took advantage of this by selling off their tenant farms and even by parceling out their demesnes in some cases (Frandsen 2005, 74–76).

Moltke was imitated by his neighbors. For example, the Løvenborg estate of Severin Løvenskjold was reorganized in 1767 with Völckers as expert, and the Gisselfeld estate, adjacent to Bregentved and owned by Frederik Christian Danneskiold-Samsøe, in 1768 (Porskrog Rasmussen 2010a, 27; S. P. Jensen

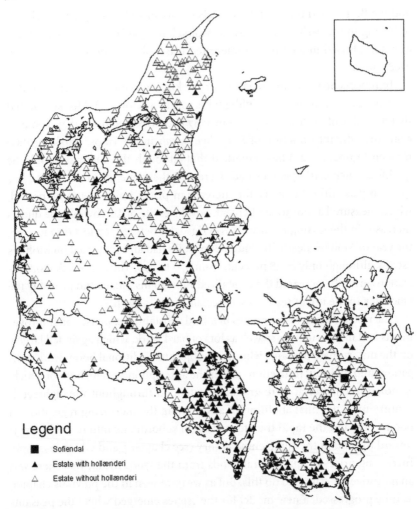

Legend

■   Sofiendal

▲   Estate with hollænderi

△   Estate without hollænderi

FIGURE 4.3. Location of *hollænderier* among all estates in the Kingdom of Denmark in 1782
Source: Created by the authors with the assistance of Christian Volmar Skovsgaard, using data from B. S.
Andersen (1963), C. Christensen (1886–91), and Roholt (2012).

1998, 52). In 1769 the estate of the Vemmetofte Jomfruekloster was reorganized, with Völckers as consultant to its administrator, Christian Friedrich
Westerholdt (Linvald 1905–8, 250; Prange 1971, 552). Gradually Moltke's example was followed in other parts of Denmark.[15] Figure 4.3 gives an overview
of the location of estates that in an official document compiled in 1782 appear
as operating a *hollænderi*.

Actually, by 1800 most demesnes were using *Koppelwirtschaft*, and it was
accepted as the ideal, while peasant agriculture on the other hand largely still

used the medieval three-field system (F. Hansen 1889, 10; Bjørn 1988a, 35; Frandsen 2005, 90). Within the operation of *Koppelwirtschaft*, however, there was some regional variation: not all estates had taken the path of establishing *hollænderier*, with cattle fattening as the main alternative still in use. The islands of Denmark were seeing an expanding dairy industry (Skrubbeltrang 1978, 242, 401). Some of the estates were reaching Holstein proportions—for example, Antvorskov, where they had three hundred milch cows.[16] Jutland, on the other hand, was still focused on supplying cattle and horses for export to Germany (Drejer 1962, 20–21; Appel and Bredkjær 1924–32, 293).[17] As can be seen from figure 4.3, the proportion of estates in Denmark with *hollænderier* was just 11 percent in 1782. The true decline in meat cattle relative to dairy cattle would come about only during the first third of the nineteenth century (Appel and Bredkjær 1924–32, 284).

The state of Danish agriculture around 1800 is summed up in a series of books by Begtrup (1803, 1806, 1808). He particularly stressed the favorable state of dairying on the island of Funen, where even peasants, who had more cows and received better prices than elsewhere, produced dairy mostly to supply the Copenhagen market. The quality of the cattle was good, for both the estates and peasants—in comparison, of course, to the rest of Denmark at the time—and red was the favored color.[18] He was, however, particularly impressed by the estate production, of which he wrote that the dairies seemed to have been built "for a higher purpose" (Begtrup 1806, 96–98). On Zealand he seemed to have been much more taken with the estate production than that of peasants and noted that estates had attempted to imitate the Holstein system with herds of up to five hundred cows (Begtrup 1803, 404–8). Jutland was the most backward region due to the historical importance of the trade in live cattle, but even there cattle fattening had become less important, and half the estates had introduced dairying (Begtrup 1808, vol. 5, xxvii–iii). The largest dairy farms were in Borglum and Breilev Kloster, the second largest of which was owned by a Holsteiner (Begtrup 1808, vol. 6, 499).

A systematic assessment of the further spread of dairying can be obtained from a series of reports on the state of agriculture in each county commissioned by the Royal Agricultural Society and published between 1826 and 1844; figure 4.4 provides a map of the counties. These *amtsbeskrivelser* (county descriptions) were to answer twenty-nine set questions (see the appendix to chapter 5), including some specifically about animal husbandry—for instance, one asked whether dairying or steer fattening gave the best return. Since different locations were described at different points in time, these provide a valuable source for understanding the spread of modern dairying across the country. The earliest reports are somewhat colored by the agricultural crisis

FIGURE 4.4. Map of the counties (*amter*) of Denmark as they existed in 1803
Source: Created by the authors with the assistance of Christian Volmar Skovsgaard.

that followed the Napoleonic Wars and continued until around 1830. These
five early reports focus exclusively on counties in Jutland and reflect the concerns of farmers about the decline in the trade in live cattle. Dairying is little
mentioned, except in the case of Aarhus County in the mideast of the peninsula.

Three reports were published in the early 1830s, one from the island of
Zealand, emphasizing that dairying was a dominant activity, and two from
north and central Jutland, which reveal that the estates were mostly fattening
steers for export. Between 1837 and 1840, six more reports were published.

FIGURE 4.5. Johan Thomas Lundbye (1818–1848), *A Cowshed on a Farm at Vejby, Zealand*, ca. 1844
Source: Courtesy of the National Art Gallery of Denmark.
Note: By the 1840s, good dairy practices were even spreading to the peasantry in Zealand, although the stable presented is more representative of an earlier state.

The reports for the islands of Funen and Zealand describe estate production as being heavily dominated by dairying, with lively local discussions about dairy science. In Præstø County, in the south of the island of Zealand close to where Moltke first introduced the Holstein system in 1766, it is also stated that good dairy practices were even spreading to the peasantry. Figure 4.5 illustrates practices further away, in a village in Frederiksborg Amt in the north of Zealand, and shows the presence of dairy cows, but in an old-fashioned and rather untidy peasant stable. Viborg County in midwest Jutland is described as undergoing a transformation: dairies had been rare, but this was changing.

Between 1842 and 1844 the final five reports were published. These cover all parts of the country and give an interesting snapshot of the extent to which modern dairying had spread. Furthest to the north and west of Jutland, in Thisted County, mostly steers were kept. South and east of that in the center of Jutland, in Skanderborg County, steer production is described as being in freefall, with most estates having moved to dairying. Odense County on Funen and Holbæk County in the north and west of Zealand were dominated by dairying, but peasant dairying was very poor. Finally, Maribo County, covering the islands of Lolland and Falster to the south of Zealand, again neighboring the area where the Holstein system was first introduced, was also dominated by dairying, but important inroads had been made into peasant production, where some peasants had introduced clean dairy parlors, comparable in quality to the estates.

A Second Wave of Entrepreneurs from Schleswig
and Holstein Come to Denmark

Thus, by the 1840s the transformation of Denmark was already well under way. As noted above, travel writer J. G. Kohl observed that the Holstein system had spread throughout the country, even to northern Jutland, where he noted that many farms had already switched from oxen raising to dairying. He was impressed by the scientific nature of this progress and noted that important articles on dairying from the duchies were reprinted all over Denmark. In conclusion, as quoted in the introduction to this book, Kohl stated his belief that Denmark would eventually converge on the duchies (1846, 58–60). In this process, a second wave of Holstein practices swept into Denmark as entrepreneurs from the duchies of Schleswig and Holstein acquired estates in Denmark in the 1820s and 1830s (Bjørn 1988a, 24) and took part in the development of a renewed cluster of progressive estate owners oriented toward commercial dairying.

One of the most famous examples in this respect was the Valentiner family. Heinrich Christian Valentiner purchased the Gjeddesdal estate in Greve, close to Copenhagen, in 1822.[19] The estate was in poor condition and losing money, but he introduced the system he knew from home. It has been suggested that he emigrated because in Zealand estates could still be purchased that were less advanced and cheaper than in Holstein (Andresen 1992, 1–4), despite Zealand being the Danish center of the Holstein system. Although the estate began by exporting salted meat to England and France in the 1820s, H. C. Valentiner soon began to replace steers with cows; he opened a dairy in 1831, and when his son Adolph took over in the same year, the estate kept only cows (Andresen 1992, 5–7). Adolph Valentiner proved a great innovator and contributor to dairy science, publishing the first of many articles in the Danish agricultural journal *Tidsskrift for Landøkonomi* (henceforth *TfL*) in 1837; in the article he highlighted, among other things, the primacy of profit motives and published his own accounts (Andresen 1992, 7–8), to which we will return in chapter 5. The success of Gjeddesdal, where a program was established in 1853, made it an attractive place for young farmers to visit and learn their trade, and from the 1860s it was the site of numerous experiments by the Royal Agricultural Society, the members of which were mainly estate owners (Andresen 1992, 8–10) From 1868 Gjeddesdal continued to play an important innovative role under Adolph's son, Heinrich Nicolai Valentiner. Between 1837 and 1875, when the role of formal agricultural education passed to the agricultural colleges, the Royal Agricultural Society organized (subsidized) apprenticeships for dairywomen on its members' estates, including Gjeddesdal. At its height, around three hundred apprentices were placed through the program, thus again demonstrating the importance of the estates for spreading modern dairying across the country (Hertel 1920, 358).

Another energetic promoter of dairying was yet another Holsteiner,[20] Edward Tesdorpf, who took over Orupgaard on the island of Falster in 1839 and additional estates in the area in the following years. He brought in angler cattle from eastern Schleswig in 1841, and his whole herd changed in 1845 (Bjørn 1988a, 152–53). Despite the fact that he promoted, as we will see in subsequent chapters, many valuable innovations, his importance to the spread of the Holstein system has certainly been overemphasized by writers such as Hertel (1920, 274) who, in a history of the Royal Agricultural Society, of which Tesdorpf was a president from 1860 until 1888, goes so far as to date the birth of modern dairying to his move to Denmark: something which can be clearly disproved by the narrative presented above.

The Trickle-Down from the Estates

As we discuss more in detail in the following chapters, the resulting radical reorientation of Danish agriculture toward export dairying developed first on estates and built on the preexistence of the *hollænderier*. In this process, estate owners, dairy administrators, and tenants developed an empirically minded discourse oriented toward recognizing and arguing for best-practice solutions in decision making and specialization based on extensive record keeping and accounting, and promoted the dissemination of accounting knowledge. This practical discussion, for example in the *TfL*, also blended directly with the rapid advances in the nascent scientific agriculture and dairy sciences, which thus were made available to a larger group of farmers. This scientific rationalization, however, came at the expense of the traditional female predominance in dairy work on the estates and in peasant households. Together with merchants and shipping entrepreneurs, estate owners organized direct exports to the main market, Britain, and thus contributed to overcome the convenient but expensive (and soon politically inconvenient) use of the trade hub of Hamburg and Altona. As important as this, the proponents of export-oriented dairying in Denmark promoted the wide spread of good practices and high standards, following the Holstein example, which built a favorable reputation for Danish butter in times of relatively high transaction costs and information asymmetries.

Over time, the pioneer efforts on larger estates thus trickled down to a larger agricultural population, a process aided by the generally good education of the Danish population and the foundation and extension of the Royal Veterinary and Agricultural College and the agricultural schools. The well-defined property rights that had emerged from the reforms of the late eighteenth and early nineteenth centuries and the investments in enclosures had led to improvements in land quality such as the drainage of marshes and swamps. As a consequence, the intensity of land use also increased significantly on the more than 90 percent of the land that did not belong to estate demesnes. Abildgren (2010, 15, fig. 5) has shown that already by 1845, when comparable statistics were first collected, 62 percent of Denmark's land area was under cultivation, a share that increased rapidly from the late 1850s to a maximum of 74 percent and marked a clear difference with the low cultivation intensity in the 1600s and early 1700s described in chapter 2.[21]

Thus, just prior to the emergence of the cooperatives, so-called community creameries, which allowed for the centralized production of butter using milk from local peasants, were promoted in the 1860s by merchants and the agricultural societies in order to increase the availability of high-quality butter for export (McLaughlin and Sharp 2015). The emergence of the co-ops themselves relied largely on the invention of the automatic cream separator in the late 1870s. Peasant producers owned just a few cows, and their milk production could not easily be transported to a central production facility that used traditional methods.[22] This was not a limitation for separation using centrifugal force. Thus the cream separator finally allowed peasants to enjoy the benefits of the *hollænderier* more than a century after they were introduced to Denmark.

In ongoing work, we have found that it is possible to show that parishes served by the first wave of cooperatives, those established between 1882 and 1890, were relatively more likely to be closer to estates that had had a *hollænderi* by 1782, one hundred years before. This relationship is illustrated in figure 4.6. It held true even when taking into account, in a multivariate regression framework, that other factors, such as general location,[23] distance to the coast (a communication advantage), soil quality, population density, and the presence of market towns might increase an inclination toward dairying. Moreover, this result becomes stronger if we use a technique that models, in an instrumental variable approach, the spread of modern dairying as a concentric geographical diffusion process originating in Sofiendal, where Moltke first introduced *Koppelwirtschaft* and the Holstein system (see our ongoing work first outlined in P. S. Jensen et al. 2017 for details).

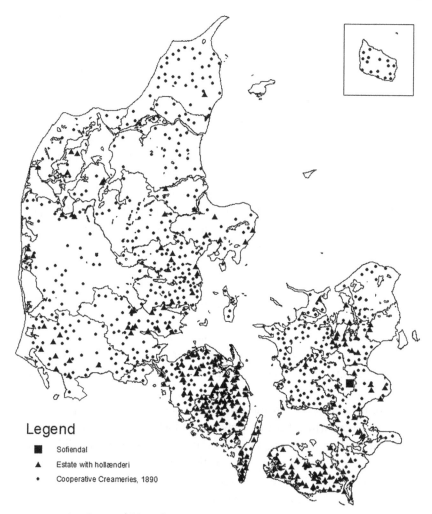

Legend

■ Sofiendal
▲ Estate with hollænderi
• Cooperative Creameries, 1890

FIGURE 4.6. 1782 estate dairies and 1890 cooperatives
Source: Created by the authors with the assistance of Christian Volmar Skovsgaard, using data from B. S. Andersen (1963), C. Christensen (1886–91), Roholt (2012), and Bjørn (1982a, 1988b).

These preliminary results are consistent with our argument that ideas and practices spread from the pioneering estates to the surrounding peasant-farmer population. We can show that this had tangible effects since cow densities were higher in parishes closer to early *hollænderier* in all livestock censuses since the first surviving census of 1837, while the overall geographical dispersion of cows remained stable over time. Unfortunately, we do not have detailed data on livestock before 1782. A census was undertaken in 1774, but the detailed results seem to have perished in a 1795 fire in Copenhagen (Holck 1901, 95).[24] There is also no detailed or comprehensive data on peasant production for our period.

Our claim that estate creameries facilitated the spread of cooperatives diverges from what prior literature has argued, but it is not inconsistent with it. As mentioned in chapter 1, Henriksen (1999, inspired by Ó Gráda 1977) has attributed the rapid diffusion of the cooperative dairy movement in Denmark mostly to preexisting cow densities, which we, at least in part, attribute to the prior existence of *hollænderier*. She also highlights that in some parts of the country there were fewer cooperatives because estate dairies were particularly large and dominant, a finding that we could not directly corroborate. In P. S. Jensen et al. (2017) we show, however, (in further econometric specifications) that parishes closer to estate demesnes, independent of whether these operated a dairy unit or not, were on average less likely to be served by a cooperative in 1890, so that only those estates with *hollænderier* brought positive spillover effects. The importance of prior existence of a high density of producers for the emergence of cooperatives has also been shown in other contexts (Garrido 2014). But our main contribution is to have linked this to the prior existence (and the introduction from abroad) of a more modern production system operated by elite producers, who were, however, not in any sense directly promoting the cooperatives, as we will see in subsequent chapters.

As for the duchies, where our story began, they became in 1864 part of the German market, which became increasingly sheltered from competition on the world market after Bismarck's protectionist turn of 1879 and did not develop as fast, although in many respects they seem to have developed in parallel with Denmark. Nevertheless, the direction of technology transfer now changed: innovations came largely from or via Denmark; dairy consultants were hired from there, and the first cooperative creamery was founded in 1884, only two years after the first opened just north of the post-1864 border (see H. S. Hansen 1994 and 1996 for a full account).

From Bullshit to Butter:
Accounting and Production Decisions

So far we have established that there was a trickle-down effect from elites to individual farmers over the one hundred year period from the 1780s to the 1880s. In this and the following chapters we will add to this by showing in detail how the basis for modern dairying was put in place between circa 1820 and 1880, starting with the role of the systematic recording of information on production, input, and output.

Bookkeeping and accounting have long been recognized to be basic ingredients of capitalist economies in the sense that they supply the raw material (data) and the cognitive framework (the idea of capital and return on capital employed) for decisions that compare different outcomes and opportunity costs, thereby making the rational, acquisitive entrepreneur possible (see Sombart 1916; Carruthers and Espeland 1991; Chiapello 2007). An example is the introduction of double-entry bookkeeping and the structure it imposes on business records. Much of this literature, however, investigates the practices of merchants and merchant bankers and manuals written for them. While this literature has important merits, the use of accounting methods for the modernization, systematization, and rationalization of agriculture has potentially far greater effects since, in terms of economic weight, agriculture was the main sector in all premodern societies, and its transformation was key for the onset of modern economic development and growth (Dennison and Simpson 2010).

In our case, Danish estate owners, administrators, and an increasing circle of tenants and freehold farmers were pioneers in adopting high-quality record keeping and accounting and in using these accounts to make and justify economic decisions and to publicize productive choices in the context of what became known as rational (or enlightened) farming in the late eighteenth and early nineteenth centuries. In this, they built on the work of early local pioneers who adapted double-entry bookkeeping to agriculture around 1800 and publicized its use in the construction of a broad epistemological base for agriculture. By following the specific Danish debate outlined below, whereby Danish farmers shared information on their accounts and sought thereby to improve on them as well as to learn from them, we are able to gain a much clearer picture of what the idea of the capitalist rationalization of the farm (Depecker and Joly 2015) actually implied.

The use of bookkeeping and accounting for rational specialization is also related to the question of whether (and from when) peasants became farmers with a capitalist outlook on their activities, and from when (and how) capitalist attitudes can be observed in estate owners and their stewards. In this context, Rob Bryer (2000a, 2000b, 2006) recently renewed an old debate by arguing that the explicit calculation of return on invested capital (ROIC) reveals the calculative mentality of capitalist farmers in contrast with—in a Marxist-oriented theory of stages—feudalist or precapitalist capitalistic accounting signatures regarding the assessment of returns on feudal rents alone.

While the sources surveyed in the following clearly show the market-oriented outlook of Danish estate owners and administrators from an early stage, our sources—like sources for other countries—seldom enable us to trace whether ROIC was calculated or not. We are, however, convinced that another aspect of bookkeeping and accounting is much more important in economic reality, if not in the history of accounting itself: the use of accounting figures as empirical evidence in a public debate about the future of agriculture, with the aim of establishing and diffusing best practices and setting the ground for informed decisions about what to do and what not to do, what to produce, what to use as inputs, and so on. As Danish agriculture became more specialized, this increased demands on accounts and records and provided additional incentives to improve best practices and to spread the general knowledge of accounting, again contributing to a better information basis for decision making.

We thus conceive the use of accounting and bookkeeping not just as manifestations of users' mental framework or mirrors of actual practice on estates. We also think it is more than a mere rhetorical tool of persuasion. It is something like a general-purpose technology that allows for the systematization of information in a way that answers existing questions—for example, whether milk or beef should be produced. With these answers, it raises new questions about both the method itself and the implications of its results. A virtuous circle was thus set in motion in Denmark around 1850, leading to the refinement and wide diffusion of a technology that enabled an ever-wider group of estate owners, farmers, and even smallholders to make smart decisions and understand and benchmark their own results against those of others. Accounting and bookkeeping was thus, at different stages, a tool for understanding, a catalyst for modernization, and (at least partially) a cause for rationalization and smart specialization. In other words, accounting enabled the relative price information we discussed in chapter 1 to be interpreted so that farmers knew both what was most profitable to specialize in and the most efficient way of doing so.

Each individual decision, with its sustaining evidence, might seem trivial, since decisions dealt with such basic choices as how much weight animal production should have in the total output of a farm; whether that production should be sheep holding or dairying; what to produce (beef, butter, pork); the choice of inputs (grazing on grass, grains, or concentrates); technologies (so-called ice dairies or modern separators); and eventually organizational forms beyond the individual production unit (private or cooperative creameries). But together these decisions constructed the specific method of dairying that would constitute Denmark's main comparative advantage for decades, a comparative advantage that defined the distinct means of development that concern the present book.

We thus combine the analysis of accounting and bookkeeping practices with a specific and source-based study of the self-discovery of the Danish agricultural sector as high-quality dairy producers over the nineteenth century. We provide a specific case of how accounting can work as a tool for facilitating the economic progress of developing countries, creating knowledge spillovers from elite pioneer producers to a much wider group of farmers.[1] To do this, we first outline the different theoretical contributions we build on. Then we go back to the roots of the use of agricultural accounting in Denmark, followed by a discussion of particularly salient accounting-based contributions in the lively Danish agricultural press, with pioneer estate owners and administrators as initial contributors. Finally we demonstrate how the extension of record keeping and accounting to a wider base of farmers and dairy professionals set the base for widespread application of best practice when large and small non-estate farmers became the main protagonists of agricultural modernization through the simultaneous introduction of cooperative creameries and large-scale automatic cream separators, which enabled the peasantry to finally reap the full benefits of adopting dairying and techniques developed in the realm of the estates.

Accounting and Self-Discovery

In a seminal contribution, Ricardo Hausmann and Dani Rodrik (2003) have highlighted that under real-world conditions, in developing countries there are large uncertainties regarding which specific activities to focus on to take advantage of export-led growth in a growing world economy. While it is easy to argue that poor, densely populated countries should focus on labor-intensive goods, there is little guidance as to which specific industries entrepreneurs should invest in: "Knowing that Bangladesh's comparative advantage lies in labor-intensive manufactures and not in high-tech machinery is useful for sure, but that leaves hundreds, if not thousands, of different types of activity up for grabs.[2] The six-digit Harmonized Schedule (HS), which most countries use to assess customs duties, comprises around 5,000 different commodity groups" (616). Their basic observation, validated by a theoretical model, is that there are disparities between the private and social benefits of discovering which activities are useful to specialize in. Thus, there is too little ex ante investment and entrepreneurship involved in discovering which new activities will help exploit basic comparative advantages, and too much diversification ex post. That is, since entrepreneurs cannot guarantee that they can keep a successful market niche discovery for themselves, they will not invest, and the considerable social returns resulting from successful specialization will never materialize. Taking this approach back two hundred years, it also illustrates the problems of agricultural economies in a period of a connecting and integrating world economy. While the integration of national and international markets for agricultural goods potentially offered large gains for farmers tailoring their production to rising market demands, discovering how to take advantage of this potential in the real world implied large uncertainties and the potential waste of sunk costs for those who were unsuccessful.

In our early modern or premodern setting, such uncertainties regarding potential success and appropriability of profits were reinforced by the path dependency and inertia of traditional ways of doing things in a world short of insights into precise cause-effect relationships and what Douglas W. Allen (2012) has summarized as the basis of many apparently inefficient premodern institutional arrangements: "These conditions create a situation where any outcome is a 'noisy signal' of the various inputs, and the individual contributions of nature and people cannot be separated with certainty. With noise, measurement itself might have little meaning even when done correctly" (11). Although Allen's claim that this is the key to a new unified understanding of the premodern world has been emphatically criticized (Mokyr and Espín-Sánchez 2013), the general point that the quality of information conditions the understanding of causality and informed decision making is not new. It ties in well with a literature that precisely highlights the role of accounting, especially double-entry bookkeeping, and the change in world view that authors have argued it either causes or reflects.

The well-known Sombart thesis—that is, "that the system of double-entry bookkeeping . . . was an active catalyst in the economic expansion that occurred in Europe . . . , both as an instrument for the ordering of economic data, and in the role that it played in transforming medieval man's attitude" (Winjum 1971, 353)—is subject to a wide debate among accounting historians (Yamey 1964; Winjum 1971; Funnell and Robertson 2011). Thus Bruce G. Carruthers and Wendy Nelson Espeland (1991) highlight that the rhetorical impact of double-entry bookkeeping was of much more importance than its substantive contributions, while Nathan Rosenberg and L. E. Birdzell Jr. (1986, 126–27) single out double-entry bookkeeping as the possible source of the idea of continuing an enterprise as an entity separate from its owners.

As mentioned above, Bryer (2000a, 2000b, 2006) gave a new twist to this literature by arguing that not the use of double-entry bookkeeping but rather the explicit calculation of ROIC reveals the difference between capitalist and precapitalist mindsets of farmers. Bryer traces these changing mentalities through available accounting records for the early modern period, in particular those of a select group of British farmers, notably the precocious 1610–20 accounting records and calculations by Robert Loder (Bryer 2000b, 370–78; Fussell 1936). However, Bryer's agenda and evidence has received some criticism by, most notably, Steve Toms (2010), who finds that the evidence that Loder calculated ROIC for his farm is rather ambiguous. This reflects one major problem with this agenda, which is that little of the available early accounting information from British agricultural institutions fits the framework of modern balance sheets. Especially the surviving records of large traditional manors have been generally deemed inappropriate for an integral assessment of profitability, return on invested capital, productive specialization, or market orientation of farmers (Turner, Beckett, and Afton 2001; R. C. Allen 1992), something they share with similar institutions in other countries (see, e.g., Carmona 1995; or Bracht and Scholten 2015, and the following section). While such accounts have nevertheless been used to reconstruct, for example, agricultural production in a national accounting framework (Apostolides et al. 2008), much of the research on accounting standards and the use of accounts and bookkeeping is based on normative or secondary literature, such as accounting guides (see, e.g., Parker 1997; Scorgie 1997) or the data collected by contemporary agricultural experts like Arthur Young (Allen and Ó Gráda 1988).

Recently, two new strands in the interpretation of agricultural accounts have been opened: Eric Schneider (2014) has used information from medieval manorial accounts from Winchester (1325–70) to estimate the elasticity of supply in price changes to gauge the market orientation of production (and found them to be rather low, hinting at a lack of manorial responsiveness to market price changes). Closer to our period, Caitlin C. Rosenthal (2013) explores the world of accounting on slave plantations on the British West Indies and in the American South to trace the evolution of "commercial numeracy" and the use of more and more standardized account books as a "repository of insight" to manage slave labor more efficiently—for example, by establishing very demanding target rates for cotton pickers based on previous experience or information exchanged between plantation owners and managers. Thus, "calculation enabled the expansion and modernization of slave economies" (735) especially through the development of standardized productivity measures, often at the expense of the working conditions of slaves, as well as the reallocation of slave labor to the most productive tasks in the plantation system at any point in time.[3]

While Rosenthal focuses on the use of accounting for monitoring and control, a techno-organizational response under very specific conditions to the uncertainties highlighted by Douglas W. Allen (2012), the main point of our research emphasizes the contribution of accounting to the mitigation of Hausmann-Rodrik uncertainties on productive self-discovery and productive specialization. We stress that accounts can be used to develop viable insights into useful specialization and, more importantly, to communicate these insights to others. The latter function, although potentially plagued by the problems of free copying and nonappropriable social benefits, nevertheless brought, above all, high reputation, increased information, and, if acted upon, transaction density to the enlightened estate owners, administrators, and farmers surveyed below.

We thus argue for a purely selfish economic motivation for the sharing of information we describe below, although this is not to deny the importance of other possibly underlying reasons, such as patriotism or high levels of social capital. Nevertheless, to be able to reap the benefits of specialization in dairying, regular market contacts and reputation for quality were necessary. Since internal economies of scale in dairy production were negligible (apart from a minimum size for professionalized regular production),[4] what really mattered was to establish a group of good-quality producers of sufficient size to allow the establishment of a good reputation for regional production, which could only be sustained if production was sent from the farms to the market regularly. So, a dense cluster of specialized professional dairy producers would benefit each individual estate producer. This phenomenon, similar to that solved by cooperatives for small peasant producers at the end of the nineteenth century (Henriksen 1999), might well have provided a sufficient incentive for the diffusion of information on good practices as widely as possible, above and beyond the reputational and patriotic considerations of individual contributors to the debates surveyed below.[5]

The literature on Danish dairying, such as by the noted historian Claus Bjørn (see Bjørn 1982a), has also mentioned the importance of the development of modern accounting practices to make informed, rational choices about specialization in crops and animal husbandry, but this has not yet been investigated in depth. We therefore use information from a large body of historical primary sources to close this gap. We trace the evolution of record keeping, bookkeeping, and accounting best practice (through discussion in agricultural science journals), its diffusion (through popular journals and teaching materials), and the use of the resulting information to assess the possibilities and opportunity costs of decisions for individual production units (estates).

The Early Development of Accounting in Agriculture

The early history both of professional dairying and of accounting in Denmark are largely the history of developments on the traditional landed estates. This might partly reflect a survivor bias since, until the early nineteenth century, estates were an integral part of the bureaucracy of the Danish state.[6] The surviving estate accounts from this early period, which can be found in relative abundance in the Danish national and regional archives, reflect this. Most simply recorded current receipts and expenses and controlled the tenants' payments of rents, tithes, and taxes, thus solving what Carruthers and Espeland (1991) call the principal-agent mission of accounting. Such accounts sometimes remained almost unchanged in format well into the twentieth century.

But in parallel, from the late eighteenth century, an increasing literature dedicated itself to the most profitable employment of agricultural resources in a quest for rational farming. This quest was embodied in Germany by the figure of Thaer, who showed himself to be inspired by English practices, especially those of Arthur Young and his contemporaries. As outlined in chapter 4, this context emphasized two objectives: to discover the optimal crop rotation for the soil, climate, and market conditions of each region; and to collect solid data to understand profitability, mostly in terms of grain yields and the necessary manure production in order to sustain them (Depecker and Joly

2015, 78–80; Lampe and Sharp 2017). To enable the collection of such data and with it an empirical basis for agricultural science and practical decision making, Thaer (1806b) developed and presented his personal system of agricultural double-entry bookkeeping, which was widely praised in Germany as well as in Denmark but also critically scrutinized.[7]

One of the most comprehensive contributions to this debate came from Denmark, where the colorful, though often overlooked, character of Carl Frederik Gyllembourg (1767–1815) had developed his own system of accounting in parallel to Thaer (see Thaer 1806a), for which he received praise and prizes from the agricultural elites of the Royal Agricultural Society (D. C. Christensen 1996, 598). In his published but unfinished *Forsøg til et Landbrugs-Bogholderie* (Attempt at an agricultural bookkeeping; Gyllembourg 1808), he presented a comprehensive system of tables to record material and monetary flows of estates. His most important contribution probably lay in highlighting the importance of calculating profits and, since, as he put it in his second volume, "accounting has two aims: the scientific and the mercantile" (55). While Thaer seemed to be most interested in separating the long-run real production increases from the fluctuation of market prices, and therefore used imputed "natural cost prices" in many of his accounts (see the discussion in Lampe and Sharp 2017), Gyllembourg argued that without monetary calculations it was impossible to know which form of production was optimal. Unlike Thaer, he did not use his schemes to make prescriptions regarding which practices to adopt.

In this sense, Gyllembourg's work was complemented by Begtrup's (1803–12) monumental study of agriculture in Denmark (see chapter 4), in which Begtrup repeatedly discussed which crop rotation was most adequate in different parts of Denmark. This found Thaer's critical acclaim and was translated in extracts in Thaer's house periodical, *Annalen des Ackerbaus* (Begtrup 1810). A particularly salient example of Begtrup's reasoning can be found in the first volume on northern Jutland (a traditional cattle-raising region) from 1808, where he considers the relative merits of keeping one hundred cows as opposed to one hundred steers, finding a profit of 1,004 rigsdaler from the former as opposed to 360 rigsdaler from the latter (Begtrup 1808, vol. 5, xxxi–xxxii). It is a very simple calculation, and it is not clear whether it was based on actual accounts or was simply a thought experiment. Nevertheless, he deducts the interest expenses on the capital investment, as well as expenses such as wages for the dairymaids and fodder for the steers (apparently feed for the cows cost nothing, since presumably they simply ate grass and hay).

Some of the knowledge developed in such studies (Lampe and Sharp 2017) might have become dormant during the agricultural crisis after the Napoleonic Wars, when publications on agricultural accounting became very rare (Degn 2010). One exception came in 1846, when Hans Frederik Hellesen (1846) published his *Bogholderi for Landmænd* (Accounting for farmers). He starts with the usual complaint that most farmers do not keep good accounts but that accounting is important in order to know which activities make profits or losses. He therefore presents a quick and simple system based on single-entry bookkeeping (not double-entry) with a considerable focus on dairying. Although he provides guidelines for pricing items not priced by the market (3), his work is otherwise unremarkable, as is his importance in the context of the agricultural development of Denmark.[8]

Improvements in Accounting Practice after the Napoleonic Wars

Much of the later secondary literature (see, e.g., Drejer 1925–33, 289–90; Hertel 1891, 434) identifies not Gyllembourg or Begtrup (much less Hellesen) as the introducers of scientific agriculture and advanced record keeping into Denmark but rather Johannes Friis, owner of the small Lillerup Manor near Horsens. Nevertheless, it seems more likely that Friis only gave a new boost to existing good practices. Friis had traveled widely in Europe in order to educate himself and had visited Thaer's Agricultural Academy in Möglin among other agricultural schools, as highlighted in the university lectures of his old friend Thomas Riise Segelcke at the Royal Veterinary and Agricultural College (Segelcke 1891, 64–65, 117; see also Hertel 1891), which are discussed below. According to these lectures, in the first decades of the 1800s, farmers did not keep good accounts, but this changed in 1859 when Friis acquired Lillerup Manor and introduced scales and Italian double-entry bookkeeping. Friis, born in 1832, was too young to have met Thaer personally, but his visit to Möglin, as well as contact with some of Thaer's former students in Denmark, such as Niels Erik Hofman Bang of Hofmansgave, where Friis taught in 1855, probably had important influences on Friis.[9]

That in practical discourse accounting and evidence-based decision making had not been abandoned after the Napoleonic Wars is best illustrated again by the most comprehensive source on early nineteenth-century Danish agriculture, the so-called *amtsbeskrivelser* discussed in the previous chapter. The fixed set of twenty-nine questions (reproduced in an appendix below) was often framed in a way that asked local respondents for the relative suitability and profitability of alternative uses of similar agricultural resources. The most salient example in our context is question 18, which asked whether milch cows or cattle for fattening were more advantageous. (In the previous chapter, we drew on these results to trace the expansion of dairying in Denmark.) This question has to be seen in context with questions 5 and 6, which ask for the prevalent crop rotation, the extension of grassland in comparison to arable, and the local conditions regarding barn feeding of cows (with fodder crops). Such questions were central to the identification of later specialization patterns and served as long-established "focusing devices" (Rosenberg 1976; Mokyr 2002, 83).

In fact, since the traditional Jutland oxen trade had entered into crisis during the eighteenth century due to protectionist policies as well as serious outbreaks of cattle plague (see chapter 7), this question was amply discussed especially in Jutland (Drejer 1925–33, 158–63). We argue based on Hausmann and Rodrik (2003) that seeing the advantage of one choice over the other is difficult for those involved in the process, although the social benefits of the right choice would be large. Thus, the existence of competent experts and a sufficiently large number of informed receptors with a common pool of propositional knowledge becomes decisive (Mokyr 2002).

To make such enlightened discussions possible, the scientific press in Denmark was highly important. The main forum for what follows was the journal of the estate-owner-dominated Royal Agricultural Society, TfL (Kærgård 2007; Lampe and Sharp 2014b), first published in 1814. Much of the debate about production decisions on estates played out in its pages in parallel with discussions on the development of sophisticated accounting methods. Another important journal, which reached farmers outside the elite ranks of the Royal Agricultural Society, was Ugeskrift for Landmænd (Farmer's weekly, henceforth UfL), first published in 1855;[10] the majority of the works referred to below can be found in TfL and UfL. Bjørn discusses in detail some of the contributions made by early contributors to TfL (Bjørn 1982a, 1982b), among them Gyllembourg himself, whose last work was published there posthumously in 1816 (Krusius-Ahrenberg 1947, 356–58).[11] Of course, not all articles in TfL and UfL were of the kind surveyed below. Both publications also reported on agricultural meetings and exhibitions (often organized by the Royal Agricultural Society and its local branches), surveyed the situation of agriculture in Denmark, and were also important for spreading information to Denmark from overseas both by translating or reviewing important work in foreign languages and by transmitting advice from merchants about what it was precisely foreign markets (particularly, of course, the British) were demanding. But from around 1855, discussions on dairy accounts and lessons to be learned from them occupied an increasing share of the pages of both periodicals.[12]

What renewed the lively discussion was probably a speech by Edward Tesdorpf (1856) at the annual meeting of the regional Maribo (Agricultural) Eco-

Meieriproductionen paa Broholm i Aaret 1857.

FIGURE 5.1. Sehested's 1857 dairy accounts for Broholm, published in *TfL*
Source: Sehested (1858).

nomic Society in 1856, in which he underlined, using data from his dairies, that early calving and feeding cows through the winter was profitable in part because the by-products from dairying could be fed to pigs, thus increasing pork production. This speech was published by the editors of *UfL*, who invited Tesdorpf to give further details. This drew a response from another estate owner, Adolph Valentiner (1856), who published results from his dairy and comprehensive comments. However, two articles published by Frederik Sehested (1857, 1858) in *TfL* took this discussion to a new level (in terms of data and comprehensiveness), presenting detailed accounting information for his estate, Stamhuset Broholm near Svendborg, for 1856 and 1857. Figure 5.1 reproduces a key table of his article on 1857.[13]

Sehested's main question was whether quantities of milk produced could profitably be increased by changing the composition of feed, particularly in favor of beets. As such, it is a contribution to the discussion on "strong feeding"—that is, the use of grains, oilcakes, and so on to improve milk yields and the production of pork as a by-product. On the one hand, Sehested (1857) presents a very detailed account of the use of the 95,542 *kander* (ca. 183,500 liters) of milk that his 128 cows had produced in 1856, in the form of self-consumed and sold full milk, cream, butter, buttermilk and skim milk (by-products of butter production), full-fat cheese, whey (by-product of cheese production), pork and fattened beef and future milk-production cattle (fed with milk, skim milk, buttermilk, and whey). He thus showed that the detailed recording of each step in the sophisticated production chain allowed producers to trace and control the use of milk and by-products and to benchmark the amount of milk used per unit of butter or cheese. Thus, of every 100 *kander* milk, on average 3 pounds of butter, 9 pounds of skim-milk cheese, 9 pounds of buttermilk and 75 pounds of whey (the latter two as feed for pigs and calves) would result (with 4 pounds of liquid lost in evaporation, etc.). On the other hand, his methods offered a way to assess the value of milk, which was only very occasionally sold as such, since at that time it was usually made into butter and its by-products. He did this using his detailed production matrix and the calculated values of and obtained revenue from butter, cheese, pork (net of other feed for pigs, also meticulously recorded), and other products. Of the 100 pounds of milk, the butter would produce a little more than 5 rigsdaler of income, the cheese 1.68 rigsdaler, and the buttermilk, skim milk, and the whey fed to pork and calves close to 1 rigsdaler, giving a total revenue of 7.7 rigsdaler per 100 *kander* milk.[14]

From this Sehested calculates profits (deducting from income actual expenses for wages, energy, basic wear and tear, and calculatory expenses for self-produced feedstuffs and grassland), arriving at a "net earnings" figure per *tønde land*. In the end, all was summarized by the fertilizer value of the cow—a practice common then due to the contemporary agricultural focus on keeping livestock primarily for their value in terms of fertilizing arable land. This way of calculating implies that minimizing the deficit of the cow (and the price of manure) could be achieved by maximizing the value of other outputs of cows, on which the subsequent discussion is centered.[15]

This is taken up again in a reply by A. Valentiner (1858), who argues that Sehested's contributions are useful, especially his way of obtaining calculatory values for products whose prices could not be observed, but that his interest in quantities of output should not lead Danish farmers to forget that, apart from maximizing production, their produce needed to be suitable for sale at the best possible price. In *UfL*, a contributor writing under the pseudonym m-e- (1859) provided additional calculations on the value of milk via its marketable products.

This initial round was accompanied and followed by a boom of published accounts, in part to provide comparisons and in part to provide further substantial input for the discussion. For example, Sophus Bjørnsen (1857) included accounts of his forester residence farm Valdemarslund near Helsingør with a relatively small herd of forty to fifty cows, for 1846 to 1856; additional information composed a complementary article published posthumously by the editors of *TfL* (Bjørnsen 1859). Tesdorpf's administrator N. P. J. Buus (1858) provided some of the in-depth information requested by the editors of

UfL in 1856, reporting information on Tesdorpf's estate Gedsergaard for 1857–58. Tesdorpf (1861) extended these to the year 1859–60 for two of his estates, Gedsergaard and Orupgaard.[16] Theodor Hasle (1858) reported a time series of basic production figures for the dairy at Rosenlund, Lolland, based on data facilitated by its tenant for 1841 to 1857. Peter B. Feilberg (1861, 1862) transmitted accounts from a dairy in Holstein from 1854 to 1859 and again from 1861. Then, in 1863, Baron Zytphen-Adeler (1863) published about twenty years of accounts for his estate of Adelersborg (now Dragsholm Castle) in northwestern Zealand. Buus (1865, 1866b) presented a survey of a small number of dairy farms on the island of Falster in 1864 and 1865, ranging from Tesdorpf's Gedsergaard estate with 109 cows to a farm in Skjelby with four cows, enabling comparison of small and large farms. Further publications of dairy accounts by ordinary farmers (K. H. 1865; H— 1869) increased the scope for comparability in all directions.

Tesdorpf, who in 1860 had become one of the presidents of the Royal Agricultural Society, also entered the discussion with major contributions over the following decade (1861, 1867, 1868, 1871). He reported data going back for the 1850s, mainly for his estates Orupgaard and Gedsergaard on Falster. In Tesdorpf (1866), he presented a comprehensive account of five years of using "artificial fertilizers" (guano and calcium phosphate from Chile saltpeter or crushed bones) on his estates, especially Orupgaard; the work discusses the (beneficial) results on output of grain and the resulting higher milk and pork yields from the much-increased grain feed for cows and pigs.

The accounts of his estates were also used by his administrators in key articles on other economic decisions, especially regarding the relative productivity of milk/butter production and cattle fattening/beef production in those years. Moreover, Tesdorpf also contributed to a debate, which began before 1860 as the relative prices of dairy products and bacon rose relative to that of wool, concerning whether to keep sheep or cows and concluding in favor of the latter (Larsen 1924–32, 611–14)—an important first step on the road toward specialization in dairying. Thus, much like Begtrup (1808), Buus (1866c) contrasted two one-hundred-animal herds, one specialized in dairying and the other in beef production, modeled respectively on Tesdorpf's estates Gedsergaard and Frisenfeldt. He made various improvements to Sehested's early methodology: accounting for an "amortization" of 6 percent per year on the inventory, including stables for pigs and dairy equipment, and calculating an annualized value of the grassland. He also assumed that dairy cows are only "in production" for approximately four years, requiring that each year capital reinvestment in cows be made to keep the herd size constant. Converting everything into fertilizer value, he found that fertilizers from beef production were much more expensive than from dairy production. In 1873, Hans Frederik Fenger returned to this issue, updating Buus's data but again confirming that, at least on Falster, beef production was much less cost-effective than dairying.

Finally, it was again Tesdorpf himself (1874, 1875) who used his accounts to justify the choice between the (then traditional) *bøtte* system for cream separation in butter making and the emerging water- or ice-dairy system (later superseded by the cream separator), clearly favoring the new system. Thus, the publication of articles in *TfL* meant that farmers could understand that dairying was more profitable than meat production, and that modern methods of cream separation were superior to the traditional forms.

As we have seen, many of these debates involved both *TfL* and *UfL* and hence reached a rather large audience. One of the most lively and telling discussions in *UfL* involved an exchange between several estate and dairy tenants and leading experts in 1861. The starting point was a piece by Niels Erik Hofman Bang (1861) on the conditions of tenants in Denmark that contributed to a more general discussion of the issue. Hofman Bang claimed that, while estate owners could generate net earnings of about 70 rigsdaler per cow, tenants often had to content themselves with much less, 20–25 rigsdaler per cow, even in years with sufficient rain (and hence abundant grass). The published results of estate owners could thus, for different reasons discussed by Hofman Bang, not serve as the basis for rents payable by tenants.[17] In response to Hofman Bang, an anonymous Forpagter K (Tenant K) (1861) claimed that he had obtained more than 42 rigsdaler per cow and was convinced that one could do even better, in the same way that grain yields were increasing constantly with best practice. One of the things the author highlighted, apart from the dairy installations and the quality of the herd, was the positive impact of early calving on milk yields, an insight gained from his careful weekly records on milk yields. This triggered a series of short responses, some anonymous, some of which questioned the accuracy of K's results and requested clarifications, which K quickly provided (W. 1862; m-e- 1862a, 1862b; Dalgas 1862; En gammel Meierimand [An Old Dairyman] 1862; Forpagter K 1862).

In a longer piece, Hofman Bang (1862) put the discussion into perspective. Although he expressed his approval of using accounting information to discuss fundamental social and economic issues, he was not convinced that K's data disproved his initial claim. He countered by giving his own accounts from different leases of large dairy units (more than 180 cows) from 1842 to 1849 and for some years in the 1850s; they showed average net earnings of 10.60 rigsdaler per cow in the 1840s and between 19 and 20 rigsdaler in the mid-1850s (224–25). His accounting practice, however, deviated somewhat from K's rudimentary accounts in that Hofman Bang explicitly included changes in the appraisal value of the herd over the year. He blamed his low results in the 1840s on bad grazing, loss of cows, a bad barn, a warm milk cellar, and "very simple" milch cows. He then compared these numbers to the good conditions underlined by K (1861) and brought them into the general discussion of the situation of dairy tenants. Outstanding profitability, even if revised downward, he emphasized, did not disprove his point, since K seemed to have been enjoying many of the favorable conditions whose general absence Hofman Bang (1861) aimed to address. He also underlined that the accounting information presented in the current discussion was highly biased, since few dairy tenants would go through the pains of consolidating their records into publishable summaries (Hofman Bang 1862, 227). This would lead to a double bias: records were probably better for more able tenants, and good results would be overrepresented. He thus called for more data. He also compared the average situation in Denmark to that in Mecklenburg, where often no tenants could be found due to unprofitability, and in England, where long-term leases had created much better average conditions, which should serve as a model for Denmark.

Although the discussion remains inconclusive and highlights certain institutional problems in the estate dairy sector, it illustrates very well how not just leading dairymen but wider circles took part passively or actively in the discussion, which also resonated in *TfL* and the Swedish *Tidskrift för svenska landtbruket* (see notes to Dalgas 1862, 268) and thus transcended the pages of *UfL*. While the discussion centers on the profitability of dairy leases, many authors give at least equal weight to other questions on individual aspects such as the profitability of pigs (m-e- 1862b) or the question of whether an additional amount of feed grain is better given to cows to increase milk yields or to pigs to enhance the quantity of by-products (Dalgas 1862). The shape of the discussion also reflects an increasing interest in comparisons to systematically assess the sources of high and low net earnings based on use of feed and grazing, length of leases, cow breeds, complementarity with other animals (mainly pigs and sheep), and beef production (Hofman Bang 1862). In this sense, the exchange helped shape the discussion of acceptable ways of calculating net earnings, renewing the call for the publication of accounts of dairy units of various sizes applying diverse practices under different institutional and geographical circumstances.

As can be expected, the discussion intensified and ramified even more in later years, both in *UfL* (Wassard 1864; C. I. 1864; Buus 1866a; Den Alsiske Landboforening 1866; Friis 1869, with data for his Lillerup estate from 1859 to 1865) and *TfL*. For example, a discussion in 1868–69, based on another intensive exchange of accounting results, focused on feed (Ræder 1868a, 1868b, 1869a, 1869b, 1870; L. 1868; 33, 1868; Forpagter 1868a, 1868b; Friis 1869; Schroll 1869; Fenger 1869), and a follow-up exchange directly addressed the role of accounting in agriculture and how to establish best practice (Ræder 1875a, 1875b; Schroll 1875; Forpagter 1875).

The Institutionalization of Accounting:
Standardized Accounts and Education

The usefulness of such accounts for production decisions together with the rapid spread of modern dairying in Denmark, as well as calls like that of Hofman Bang (1862) for more representative variation, seem to have motivated *TfL* to publish a regular series of accounts from 1876. Regional accounts were gathered and separately published for 1876 and 1877 for the regions of Zealand (H. N. Valentiner 1876b; ten farms), Funen (Schroll 1876; 1878; twelve and seventeen farms), Lolland-Falster (Bokelmann 1877; sixteen farms), Jutland (Winkel 1877; 1878; fifteen and twenty-four farms) and northwest Jutland (Leegaard 1878; nine farms). From 1879, this work became standardized and summarized for all of Denmark; a regular series of articles called Mejeribruget i Danmark began with Janus Henrik Winkel's (1880) survey of the accounts of twenty-eight farms for the 1878–79 production year. Winkel also edited the report for 1880, after which Christian Sonne took over until the 1884 report published in 1885. From then, the well-known dairy consultant and later professor Bernhard Bøggild edited the report until well into the twentieth century. Figure 5.2 illustrates some of the data presented in Sonne's report for 1881.

These reports allowed farmers to make informed production and marketing decisions and to use their own accounts to benchmark their performance against others' results. For example, from 1878–79 we find printed tables in the archives of the Basnæs estate (located in western Zealand), which serve to preserve and consolidate annual records on dairying and assess productivity and efficiency in milk, butter, cheese, and pork production in a way that is compatible with the published tables in *TfL*.[18]

Parallel to the widening of the circle of participants in public discussions on accounting, there was an increasing recognition in the agricultural schools of the importance of bookkeeping. At the Royal Veterinary and Agricultural College the central figure in this respect was the aforementioned Thomas Riise Segelcke (figure 5.3), who is often seen as the father of modern dairy science in Denmark. He was a lecturer at the college from 1874, where he be-

Tab. VI. Mejeriernes Aarsregnskab.

Mejeriernes Nr.	Koholdets Størrelse	Antal Dage	Opfodret pr. Ko til Køer og Svin, alt reduceret til Pd. Kraftfoder							Produceret pr. Ko						Produktionens Værdi pr. Ko			Produktionsværdien med Fradrag af Foderets Værdi	Kvægrace	Mejerisystem.	Tillagt og fødet Antal Kalve	Smørrets Art
			Køerne				Svin		Ialt Værdi	Mælk Pd.	Smør Pd.	Ost Pd.	Pd. sk. Mælk		Svin Pd.	Smør Kr. Ø.	Svin, Ost og skummet Mælk Kr. Ø.	Ialt Værdi					
			Kraftfoder Pd.	Hø, Roer etc. Pd.	Ialt Pd.	Ialt Kr. Ø.	Kraftfoder Pd.	Værdi Kr. Ø.					Salg	Kalve og Husholdn.									
1	125	360	530	1128	1658	99.18	271	16.28	115.44	3398	109.9	121.0	152	877	120.2	129.17	76.36	205.53	90.09	Jydsk.	Blikfade. Om Sommeren forelobig Afkøling.	2	Surt Smør.
2	112	369	1369	481	1850	111.07	549	32.24	143.24	4161	138.3	164.9	54	905	227.5	155.56	126.17	281.73	137.79	Jydsk samt blandet Nordslesvigsk og Angler.		21	do.
3	110	360	1457	626	2083	124.94	572	34.32	159.30	4085	139.3	114.0	84	806	265.5	165.95	127.93	293.88	134.58	Jydsk og Ayrshire.	Ismejeri.	20	do.
4	79	368	1289	894	2183	130.96	621	37.26	168.24	4098	135.1	159.0	144	528	211.0	160.89	112.32	278.62	105.38	Nordslesvigsk.	Vand og Is.	14	do.
5	70	370	1699	252	1951	117.06	730	43.30	160.39	4159	140.8	134.0	76	1036	214.5	163.88	119.51	283.39	122.83	do.	Ismejeri.	11	do.
6	31	379	744	644	1388	83.26	345	20.70	103.96	3446	111.6	73.4	103	ca. 1200	142.0	121.96	81.41	203.36	99.38	Korthornsblanding og Jydsk.	?	11	do.
7	72	378	1151	821	1972	118.32	119	7.14	125.46	3237	111.3	37.7	100	1036	109.0	131.47	57.74	189.21	63.75	Blandet Jydsk.	Vand og Is.	18	do.
9	37	367	1412	365	1777	106.02	273	16.28	128.40	4064	139.5	146.0	82	1226	77.7	154.43	74.37	229.32	106.33	Angler, Jydsk og Fynsk.	Bøtter.	6	do.
10	62	360	2016	332	2348	140.88	123	7.38	148.26	5038	181.5	213.3	201	470	166.7	228.24	113.66	336.34	188.58	Blandet Fynsk og Angler.	Centrifuge.	10	do.
11	70	375	1040	705	1745	104.70	500	30.00	134.70	4128	185.7	141.1	92	955	128.8	160.09	89.69	249.40	114.70	Fynsk og Jydsk.		18	do.
12	56	374	1164	1961	3125	187.50	662	39.72	227.22	3778	134.2	97.5	187	860	120.0	168.94	94.52	258.18	31.26	Angler og Fynsk.	Bøtter og Is.	14	do.
13	90	374	1408	898	2306	138.36	400	24.00	162.36	4575	142.9	230.4	66	510	214.5	165.74	129.33	294.07	132.61	Blandet Angler.	Ismejeri.	32	do.
14	87	367	1140	1774	2914	174.74	275	16.80	191.54	4144	153.7	86.0	127	1012	105.0	173.22	65.69	239.01	47.87	Angler.	Vandmejeri.	11	do.
15	143	377	1355	638	1993	119.48	715	42.90	162.48	4825	150.1	166.6	257	902	205.9	175.95	128.77	299.88	137.45	Angler og Fynsk.	Bøtter til Nytaar, herefter Ismejeri.	35	do.
16	61	373	576	954	1530	91.80	500	30.00	121.80	3888	127.3	160.7	75	876	180.6	146.65	114.43	261.08	139.28	Jydsk.	Vand og Is.	15	do.
17	119	368	841	886	1727	103.42	353	21.18	124.60	4293	149.4	127.7	27	984	157.0	180.42	92.22	272.64	147.84	do.	Bøtter og Is.	32	do.
18	80	377	1375	187	1562	93.72	»	»	»	3977	138.9	191.8	44	959	168.2	165.54	107.06	272.60	—	Angler.	Centrifuge.	34	do.
19	44	365	1745	457	2202	132.12	375	22.50	154.62	5055	182.2	120.8	16	1366	166.0	204.99	108.64	313.63	158.41	Blandet Fynsk og Angler.		9	do.
20	85	355	1910	161	2071	124.26	642	38.52	162.78	4835	173.9	170.3	90	824	255.4	198.60	137.15	335.75	172.97	Nordslesvigsk.	Bøtter.	13	do.
21	115	368	1406	762	2168	130.08	206	12.36	142.44	4172	136.7	156.0	130	1065	116.8	176.24	98.98	275.22	132.88	Nordslesvigsk.	Ismejeri.	26	Sødt Smør.
22	19	365	1883	1008	2891	173.46	1000	60.00	233.46	5609	180.2	205.1	41	1496	256.8	206.44	149.66	356.10	122.64	Fynsk.	Ismejeri.	5	Surt Smør.
23	65	369	1652	384	2036	122.16	424	25.44	147.60	5080	167.0	221.7	402	724	166.0	207.12	121.84	328.96	181.36	Rød dansk.	Is og Bøtter.	10	do.

FIGURE 5.2. *TfL*'s dairy report for 1881
Source: Sonne (1882).

came its first permanent lecturer in dairying and agricultural accounting in 1880 and professor of the same from 1892 (see the following chapter).

Segelcke was trained in Denmark, graduating in applied science in 1855 from the College of Advanced Technology (Den Polytekniske Læreanstalt, founded in 1828; now the Technical University of Denmark). Subsequently, Segelcke spent 1857–59 traveling around Europe and the United Kingdom, where he visited the famous Rothamsted Experimental Station. Back in Denmark, he was employed by the Royal Agricultural Society as a dairy consultant from 1860 until 1880; he worked on experiments in dairying, particularly concerning the chemical properties of milk and its durability, and feeding. Segelcke was an enthusiastic supporter of the scientific approach to agriculture, which he promoted in a series of articles in *TfL* between 1862 and 1866 on how to produce good-quality butter (Bjørn 1982a, 32). The most salient of these is probably his *3. meddelelse om Mejerivæsenet* (Third communication on dairying), published in 1865, in which Segelcke argued for a reform of work practice in dairying. Like Friis, he stressed the importance of the use of scales and thermometers, and of keeping accurate records (Drejer 1925–33, 289–90).

Nevertheless, Bodil Hansen (2006) and other historians have stressed that Segelcke's program and actions exhibited distinctly conservative thinking (somewhat contrary to Friis), as Segelcke linked traditional practices in dairying, which he argued had to be overcome, with gender characteristics of the

FIGURE 5.3. Thomas Riise Segelcke lecturing on the utilization of milk in butter making at the Royal
Veterinary and Agricultural School
Source: Courtesy of the Copenhagen University Library, Frederiksberg.

women who were traditionally responsible for dairy work. He perceived that
women relied too much on practical skills and tradition and were incapable
of bookkeeping and scientific reasoning in general and, therefore, unable to
be protagonists of the analytic form of farming he envisioned (Bjørn 1982a,
28; B. K. Hansen 2006, 187–208; Fink 2009, 459–61). The fact that men, as
dairy managers, contributed to the discussions outlined above, while women
were mostly absent from them, also reflects the male dominance of the public
sphere at the time, although some dairywomen active at estates did publish
indications as to how the dairy practices on large estates could be made useful and profitable on farms with as few as three cows. B. K. Hansen lists seven
guides published by Danish dairywomen on their trade between 1872 and
1886, two of which appeared in at least two editions (B. K. Hansen 2006, 212–
14; see also Fink 2009, 462).[19]

Thanks to the efforts of one meticulous student, Niels Larsen, the lectures
of Segelcke (1891) have survived in the library of the former Royal Agricultural and Veterinary College. These extend to 143 pages of beautifully hand-
written notes, covering all aspects of accounting for agriculture, including
its history (abroad and in Denmark), theory, and practice (Segelcke 1891).[20]

In particular, Segelcke highlighted the practical importance of pre-prepared blank accounting books for the ordinary farmer, which they simply had to fill in, especially the *Prøvemælkningsbog* (Sample milking book) published in 1864 by Kammeraad Andersen, which contained one page for each cow per month (60). Segelcke had himself published several of these blank books from the 1860s, for example Tesdorpf and Segelcke (1862), which reproduced weekly accounting tables used on Tesdorpf's estates, and the *Mejeridagbog* (Dairy journal) and *Mejeritavler* (Dairy tables) he published jointly with Friis (Friis and Segelcke 1866; 1870–74), as well as Segelcke's *Meierilærlingen* and *Optegnelsesbog*, a record book for dairy apprentices with introductory explanations (Segelcke 1872; Friis and Segelcke 1870). Other shorter versions were published by other authors (Segelcke 1891, 64–65), and we found many of these reviewed in *UfL*, alongside more extensive accounting guides.[21]

Thus, by the time of the emergence of the first cooperative creamery in 1882, its members were able to draw on the accumulated wisdom of almost eight decades of work on improving agricultural, and specifically dairy, accounting in Denmark. Somewhat ironically the operators' meticulous record keeping was initially used against them, when the chairman of the dairy committee of the United Jutland Agricultural Associations commissioned a report (M. C. Pedersen [1855] 1981) to demonstrate the cooperative's inferiority to its proprietary rivals; although the chairman concluded the opposite, as we will return to briefly in chapter 9.

Nevertheless, the cooperatives' weekly journal, *Mælkeritidende*, continued the tradition of publishing accounts, and, under the guidance of Segelcke, the Royal Agricultural Society's new dairy consultant from 1886, Bernhard Bøggild, was to publish a series of books explaining to cooperative farmers how to apply this knowledge—including accounting—to their activities (Bøggild 1886, 1887a, 1889b, 1891). After Segelcke's death, Bøggild became the new professor of dairying and agricultural accounting. His advice regarding bookkeeping as a necessary part of an agricultural education became more specific over time, starting with a general statement that "record keeping and accounting must of course be practiced from the beginning of the apprenticeship" (Bøggild 1886, 23). Dairymen, he stressed, must be competent not simply in making butter but also in bookkeeping (1887a, 57) with apprentices taught accounting for two years (i.e., throughout the apprenticeship). Bøggild himself provided specific details as to how accounts should be kept (e.g., 1889b, 1899).

The focus on accounting also spread to other agricultural schools, such as Ladelund, founded in 1879, which began educating dairymen in Denmark in 1887. Over 25 percent of the teaching was initially devoted to accounting, although this fell to around 14 percent in the early twentieth century (Bjørn 1982a, 182–83). We will discuss more generally the role of agricultural schooling in the following chapter.

International Recognition

The care with which accounts were kept in Denmark was recognized by foreign observers as early as 1866, when John Wilson, professor of agriculture at the University of Edinburgh, reported on agriculture in Denmark at the Agricultural Exhibition held in Aarhus that year (Wilson 1867). He praised the accounts of Valentiner's Gjeddesdal estate as "kept with scrupulous exactitude, even to the smallest details" (63). "Mr. Tesdorpf, like Mr. Valentin[er], believes in the importance and value of strictly-kept 'Farm Accounts,' and can turn to his 'ledger' and give the debtor and creditor statement in produce as well as in cash returns, of every department of his farming since he came into possession of the property" (65). "[His] statement of the dairy returns . . . not only testifies to the care and exactitude with which the 'Farm Accounts' have been kept, but also gives an analysis of the dairy returns of a farm for a longer period, upon a large scale and with a greater minuteness of detail than has ever before been published" (67).

Moreover, he poured scorn on the rule of thumb, that is, the experience but non-science-based practices, used in the United Kingdom, comparing it with Denmark where "a philosophic treatment, based on sound scientific principles, is the rule and not the exception." Wilson recounted an episode when Friis showed him his accounts, and he explained how he doubted dairymaids would be able to implement such a system in his country. Friis replied:

> On first showing it to his own head dairymaid she burst into tears, and continued in a very distressed state of mind for a full week afterwards. As she regained her composure, a few figures were seen chalked on the board; these rapidly increased, until they reached the last column, when she acknowledged freely the value of the daily details, which testified to her own skill while recording her dairy returns, and declared that she would never take the management of any other dairy unless she had the comfort and protection of a similar arrangement. From that day the success of Messrs. Friis and Segelcke's "Dairy Register" was assured, and it is now finding its way into all the best dairies of the country. (Wilson 1867, 75–76)

Later, a series of reports by Henry Michael Jenkins, the head of the Royal College of Agriculture in Cirencester, heaped similar praise on the standards of Danish dairy accounting—for example, that "[Tesdorpf's] books have been kept with scrupulous care and minuteness" (Jenkins 1876) and that the "dairy records kept on three farms in the Island of Fyen . . . [illustrate] the care and accuracy with which the accounts are kept on Danish farms, and especially Danish dairies" (Jenkins 1882, 29). He also notes that it was common for the farmer's wife to keep the books, rather than paying clerks, as was apparently the norm in the United Kingdom (Jenkins 1882, 34), although his example was the rather remarkable Hanne Nielsen of Havarthigaard, who was in fact more the entrepreneur in an enterprise that invented many new types of cheese (still popular today), which found a ready market in her little, royally endorsed shop in Copenhagen.[22]

Thus, by the end of the 1880s, based on the knowledge gained from accurate record keeping, Danish agriculture was almost uniformly producing butter (and pork from the by-products of butter production) for the British market, using milk produced all year round by Danish red cattle kept in stables and fed on concentrates, with the final product produced in modern steam-powered creameries using automatic cream separators. This process relied, however, on the transmission and implementation of the lessons learned from accounting, which we turn to next.

Appendix

Translation of the standardized questions in the Danish county descriptions, from the index of Dalgas 1826, vol. 1, on the county of Vejle.

1. *Hvorledes ere Jorderne deskafne, saavel Jordsmon som Underlag? høie eller side? Jevne eller bakkede? Lide Jorderne af skadeligt Vand? Kunde Vandingsenge anlægges?* [How is the land formed, both above and below? High or low? Flat or hilly? Does the land suffer from damaging water? Could drainage be laid?]
2. *Findes der Kilder, Indføer? Er Vandmasken i disse i de senere Aar betydligen aftagen? Hvad menes Aarsagerne dertil at være? Har man udtørret Søer eller Moser?* [Are there springs, wells? Has the quantity of water in these fallen considerably in recent years? What are thought to be the reasons? Have lakes and bogs been drained?]
3. *Hvorledes er Klimatet? Tørt, fugtigt, koldt, luunt, etc.?* [How is the climate? Dry, wet, cold, warm, etc.?]
4. *Hvorledes er Udskiftningen? Ere Jorderne meget udparcellerede? Hvilke Følger har det havt? I henseende til Folkemængde, Dyrkning, Tillæg af Kreaturer, etc. etc.?* [How is the agricultural reform going? Is the land very much divided? What consequences has

it had? With reference to population, cultivation, animal raising, etc., etc.?]

5. *Hvilken er den almindelige og meest gjængse Dyrkningsmaade? Hvilke Afvigelser gives derfra? Bruger man Kobbeldrift med reen Brak, eller Vexeldrift med Brakfrugter? Hvad dømmes herom? Er no-gen betydelig Deel af Jorder udlagt til varigt Græsland?* [What is the common and most widespread method of cultivation? What devia-tions are there from this? Is *Koppelwirtschaft* with pure fallow used, or crop rotation with fallow crops? What is the judgment on this? Is any significant part of the land given to permanent grassland?]

6. *Gjør Sommerstaldfodring Fremgang? Hvilke Indvendinger gjøres der-imod?* [Is summer stable feeding spreading? What objections are there against it?]

7. *Anvendes Kalk, Dynd, Mergel eller kunstife Gjødningsmidler? Har man gjort Forsøg med at brænde Grønsværen, saavel paa Agre, som Enge? Virkningerne deraf? Hvorledes var det Jordsmon, hvorpaa Brændingen fandt Sted? Leret, Mergelagtigt, sandet eller tørvagtigt?* [Is chalk, marl, or artificial fertilizer used? Have people tried burn-ing the turf, as well as fields and meadows? What have been the effects of this? How was the surface of the earth where the burning took place? Claylike, marl-like, sandy, or peaty?]

8. *Bruges ogsaa Stude til Markarbeide?* [Are steers also used for field-work?]

9. *Hvorledes ere Agerdyrkningsredskaberne? Erkjendes Svingplovenes (de saakaldte engelske Ploves) Fortrinlighed? Ere de nyere arbeidspa-rende Redskaber bekjendte og benytede?* [How are the arable tools? Is the superiority of the swing plow (the so-called English plow) acknowledged? Are newer labor-saving tools known of and used?]

10. *Er der raae eller uopdyrkede Jorder? Optages disse til Dyrkning? Paa hvad Maade? Under hvilken Sædfølge? Og med hvad held? Har man, forsaavidt Opdyrkninger have været foretagne, uder at staae i Forbindelse med allerede organiserede Avlsbrug, brugt Heste eller Stude som Arbeidsdyr? Og har man til Besætning fornemmelig valgt Hornqvæg eller Faar?* [Is there barren or uncultivated land? Will this be used for cultivation? In what way? Under what crop? And with what success? Have people, insofar as cultivation has taken place, done this in connection with previously organized animal husbandry, used horses or steers as working animals? And have people mostly chosen cattle or sheep for the herd?]

11. *Sørge Agerdyrkerne for at skaffe sig god Saaesæd?* [Do arable farmers make sure they get good seed for sowing?]

12. *Dyrkes mindre almindelige Sædarter, Foder- og Handelsplanter?* [Are smaller common types of grain, feed, and plants for sale grown?]

13. *Spores Sygdomme hos Kornet? Rust? Brand? Har man paalidelige Erfaringer om Aarsagerne dertil?* [Are there traces of disease in the grain? Rust? Burn? Are there reliable lessons regarding the causes?]

14. *Har man nogen bestemt Regel om den Grad af Modenhed, Sæden bør have, naar den skal høstes, for at blive bedst Handelsvare?* [Is there a particular rule about the degree of maturity the grain should have when it is harvested so that it can be the best market good?]

15. *Hvorledes ere Kornvarerne beskafne? Sørges der for deres Rensning? Er de paatænkt nogen Foranstaltning til deres Tørring? Til deres videre Forædling?* [What are the grains composed of? Is it ensured that they are cleaned? Have any arrangements been made for drying them? For their further processing?]

16. *Er Producternes Afsætning forbunden med Vanskelighed, saasom af Mangel paa gode Torve eller Udskiftningssteder?* [Is it difficult to sell the products, due to lack of good markets or trading places?]

17. *Opgive Bønderen endnu Ævret? Eller holdes der over Markfred? Reises nyt Hegn, og vedligeholdes det gamle?* [Do peasants still remove fencing around the fields? Or is there enclosure? Are new fences put up, and are the old ones maintained?]

18. *I hvad Tilstand er Qvægavlen? Saavel i Henseende til Qvægets Beskaffenhed, som Antal, efter Gaardens Areal? Give Mælkekøer eller Fedeqvæg størst fordeel?* [In what condition is cattle raising—with reference to quality as well as quantity—by farm area? Do milch cows or beef cattle give the best return?]

19. *Er Hesteavlen i Til- eller Aftagende? Aarsagerne dertil?* [Is horse breeding increasing or declining? What are the reasons?]

20. *Udbreder den fiinuldede Faareavl sig? Er Faarefoldning i Brug? Staldfodres Faarene nogetsteds? Er den indenlandske Faarestamme i Til- eller Aftagende?* [Is the breeding of fine-wool sheep spreading? Is sheep penning used? Are the sheep barn-fed anywhere? Are the domestic breeds of sheep increasing or decreasing?]

21. *Udbreder Havedyrkningen sig? Hvor store ere de haver, Bønderne i Almindelighed anlægge eller have anlagt?* [Is horticulture spreading? How large are the gardens the peasants usually lay out or have laid out?]

22. *Gives der i Egnen Skov, som kan afgive Brændeveed og Gavntræ? El-*
ler nye Skovanlæg? Tørveskjær til egen Forbrug eller til Salg? Tænkes
der paa Plantninger af vilde Træer, saavel til Hegn, som i sluttede
Plantninger paa 2, 3 til 4 Skjepper Land, til Gavntræ og Brændsel?
[Does the region have forest which can give fuel and timber? Or
new forestry areas? Peat cutting for own use or for sale? Has it been
thought to plant wild trees as well as hedges (as borders on 2, 3, to
4 Skjepper Land) for timber and fuel?]

23. *Er Huusfliden i god Fremgang? Ere dens Frembringelser kun til egen*
Brug eller ogsaa til Salg? Hvorledes kunde Huusfliden opmuntres,
for at Varerne kunde gaae mere i Handelen? [Is cottage industry
making advances? Are its products only for own use or also for
sale? How could cottage industry be promoted so that the products
could do better in trade?]

24. *Findes der udmærkede Agerdyrkere i Egnen? Baade af de større*
Godseiere og mindre Gaardeiere, i og udenfor Bondestanden? Hvad
have de udrettet? [Are there good arable farmers in the region?
Both among the large estate owners and the smaller estate owners,
within and outside of the peasantry? What have they achieved?]

25. *Er der noget oekonomisk Selskab i Egnen? Hvad virker dette?* [Is
there an economic society in the region? What does it do?]

26. *Er Eiendommenes Priis i Stigen eller Falden? Findesarbeidsløse*
Mennesker? Hvor stor er Arbeideslønnen? Kunne Beboerne have Bi-
Næringsveie udenfor Agerbruget, f.Ex. ved Kalkbrud, ved Bearbeid-
ning af gode Leersorter til brændte Varer, eller beslige? [Is the price of
property increasing or falling? Are there unemployed people? How
high is the wage? Could the residents have secondary employment
outside agriculture, e.g., in lime pits, with the processing of good
types of clay for earthenware or the like?]

27. *Hvilke Dele af Landbruget fortjene, efter Local- og Tidsomstændig-*
heder, især Anbefaling? Fortjener den animalske eller vegetabilske
Production Fortrinet? Af den første igjen enten Qvæg- eller Faareavl,
eller hesteopdræt? Hvilke Væxter, enten til Sæd, Foder eller Handel,
kunne med meest Fordeel dyrkes? [What parts of agriculture earn,
according to local and present conditions, special recommenda-
tion? Does animal or vegetable production give the best return?
Considering the former is it either cattle or sheep breeding or horse
rearing? What crops, either as seed, feed, or for trade, could be
cultivated with the best return?]

28. *Gives der i Districtet noget særegent, som for andre Egne kunde gavne til Efterfølgelse eller Advarsel?* [Is there anything distinctive in the district which might be of use to other areas, either in terms of imitation or warning?]

29. *Hvad ansees i Almindelighed for, at kunne gavne Egnen med fortrinligt hensyn til dens Localitet?* [What is generally seen to be of benefit to the region especially regarding its locality?]

6

Science, Innovation, and the Dissemination of Knowledge

As we have seen, by the 1870s Danish dairying on the estates had been transformed by the introduction of the Holstein system with modern, centralized dairy facilities. The development of modern accounting methods had revealed the advantages of this move into dairy production, leading estates to abandon for example the traditional livestock trade in favor of an increasing specialization in butter for export. Improved record keeping also meant a new scientific approach to agriculture, which allowed for the determination of, for example, the optimum way to feed cows, to process the milk, and other important advances.

This chapter considers specifically the contributions of Danish agriculture and scientists to dairy science, which included the import of best practice from Germany (including Holstein and Schleswig), the Netherlands, and the United Kingdom. As we will see, innovations continued to flow from abroad, but increasingly Danish dairy science was to lead the world. In particular we will discuss the role of the Royal Agricultural Society (and other agricultural organizations), which conducted experiments on estates, organized meetings and competitions and awarded prizes, and helped promote the expanding scientific press, whose articles laid the basis for much of the discussion in chapter 5. Agricultural schooling, and the work of dairywomen and scientists at these institutions, is another important component of this story, and here the government also played a role. Education, together with a program of apprenticeships, allowed the knowledge generated by the elites on their estates and at the new research institutions to spread to a wider population.

The ultimate outcome of all this was of course productivity increases, which, together with the rapid increase in the number of cows in Denmark (discussed in chapter 4), formed the basis of the rise of the country as a dairy exporter. Many accounts of Danish agriculture have focused mostly on the productivity gains in the second stage of dairy production—that is, separating the cream for the butter from milk, which came with the spread of the automatic cream separator; this happened in the 1880s, largely through the cooperatives, which we will return to in chapter 9. Before this, however, the most important improvement was in the productivity of the cows themselves—that is, how many liters of milk they produced per unit of time—the determinants of which we analyzed econometrically in Lampe and Sharp (2015a), and we will discuss more below. We start by documenting that productivity first increased on the estates and later diffused to the wider population of farmers; we then discuss what enabled this.

Productivity of Cows

We know very little about milk yields in Denmark for the first half of the nineteenth century. We know, however, that around 1860 Denmark had a large concentration of cows, but they were far less productive than just a few decades later. One thorough study of an aspect of the improvements in milk production is by Henriksen and O'Rourke (2005), who examine the effect of the introduction of winter dairying to Denmark (which we discuss in more detail below). As they document, and as table 6.1 reports in a wider context, Denmark rapidly closed on the leading dairy producers measured in milk yields per cow. As can be seen, milk yields in the highly commercialized and urbanized economies of Britain and the Netherlands were initially higher than in Denmark, but the structural transformations experienced in Denmark happened much faster and went beyond what seems to have been achieved before 1880 in these countries, where both milk yields and agricultural TFP (total factor productivity) grew little during our period of study (Smits 2008; Van Zanden 1988). Advanced intensive dairy systems using commercial foodstuffs and winter feeding had been developed in the Netherlands since the seventeenth century but advanced relatively slowly during the long nineteenth century (Van Zanden 1988, 216, 224; Smits 2008, 98–106; Henriksen and O'Rourke 2005, 546–47); in consequence, some of the modern practices adopted in Denmark during this period came to define the best-practice frontier at the turn of the century.

Thus, a cow typically produced 1.1 tons of milk per year in 1860; this increased to 2.5 tons annually by 1900; that is, the production per cow increased by almost 3 percent per year. These advances came through better breeding, feeding, and general care and paralleled the growing importance of dairying for the Danish economy. Danish cows eventually became as productive as

TABLE 6.1. Milk yields in tons per cow

	1850	1860	1870	1880	1900
Denmark		1.1	1.5	1.8	2.5
Netherlands	2.3	2.4	2.5	2.5	2.6
Britain			1.9	2.2	2.2
France			1.2	1.6	1.8
Switzerland			2.1	2.2	2.6
Austria			1.0	1.0	1.4
United States	1.1	1.2	1.2	1.3	1.5
Danish estates	1.3	1.7	1.8	2.0	2.5

Source: E. Jensen (1937, 396; Denmark); Van Zanden (1985, 106, table 5.14; Netherlands 1850, 1880; 1860 = average 1850/1870); Bieleman (2010, 291, table 4.10; Netherlands 1900); Van Zanden (1988, 7, table 2; Netherlands 1870; Britain 1870; Austria 1870; France 1870); Federico (2005, 71, table 5.1; index numbers to reconstruct Britain and Austria 1880, 1900); Wade (1981, 340, table F-9; France 1880; 1900 extrapolated with average 1880–90 growth rate); Brugger (1978, 228; Switzerland 1870 = average 1866/1876; 1880 = average 1876–86; 1900 = 1901); Olmstead and Rhode (2008, 333, table 11.1; United States, taken from original estimates by Bateman 1968). "Danish estates" represent a sample reported to *TfL* (see chapters 5 and 8) from 1880. Before this date, we have calculated weighted averages of the estate dairies for which data was available from the bookkeeping discussions surveyed in chapters 4 and 7 or from archival sources. The sample consists of two estate dairies in 1850, three in 1860, and three in 1870 (actually, 1869–73). Orupgaard, as a clear outlier, has been excluded (see figure 6.1).

Dutch cows, which for a long time had been the leaders. Importantly for our story, these data also illustrate well the whole industry's achievement of the levels attained on the estates.

The early milk yield estimates for the whole of Denmark given by Einar Jensen (1937, 395–96) for 1860 are actually based on data reported by Tesdorpf, who might be suspected of selecting estates that were performing relatively well, given the considerably above average performance of his Orupgaard estate, as illustrated in figure 6.1. The suspected bias, however, does not seem to affect the national estimate since the yields reported for all of Denmark are much lower than those for Orupgaard or those reported by Buus (1865, 1866b) for farms around Tesdorpf's Gedsergaard on Falster, which despite having fewer than ten cows used winter feeding and other modern practices. We therefore assume that the yields are representative of Denmark as a whole and are not too biased.

A comparison of the national average with the estate sample and Orupgaard illustrates that cows on estates were on average about ten to fifteen years ahead of the national average until the 1880s, from which point the average cow in Denmark and on the estates gave equal yields. Orupgaard, as one of the most productive farms and where modern practices were first adopted and developed, obtained in the 1850s milk yields that equaled the national average

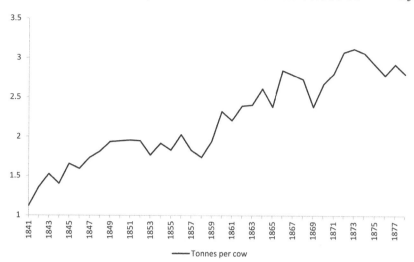

FIGURE 6.1. Milk yields on Orupgaard, tonnes per cow
Source: Authors' calculations based on data for milk production per cow given in PA Zealand, QA-257 Orupgård Gods, Statistik over høst, mejeridrift og fårehold 1849–1904.

in 1880, and by the 1860s its cows were as productive as the average Danish cow in 1900. We see this as an indicator that the productivity-enhancing advances described below spread from the very frontier of the estate sector to a wider section of estates and then, largely after 1880, to the peasant farms.[1] However, as illustrated by Buus's survey of farms around Gedsergaard in the 1860s, in some places best practices spread to the peasantry even before that.

In addition to higher milk yields, the butterfat content of the milk also increased from around 3.3 percent to 3.5 percent over the second half of the nineteenth century, which, together with more advanced cream separation technologies from the 1880s in particular, meant that more butter could be produced per liter of milk. Thus milk to butter ratios fell from 32.4 in 1861 to 30.7 in 1871 and 29.6 in 1881 on the eve of the widespread introduction of the automatic cream separator, after which it fell to 27.0 in 1893 and 25.5 in 1903 (calculated based on data given by Jensen 1937, 396).

Early Technological Change

Data which might point to the increasing sophistication of Danish dairying before 1880 is hard to come by; for example, there is no reliable information on the capital investments of Danish agriculture before 1876. Cohn (1957, 302–3; 1958, 545–46) provides some on maintenance and depreciation from 1835

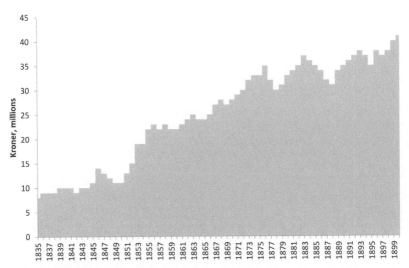

FIGURE 6.2. Maintenance and depreciation in agriculture, 1835-1900
Source: Data from Cohn (1957, 302–3; 1958, 545–46).

but offers little information on how he constructed his data. Nevertheless, this data, presented in figure 6.2, provides some indication of the growing importance of capital investments in agriculture from the 1850s and 1860s.

The innovations themselves are however very well documented, and the following draws heavily on A. Christensen (1925–33, 240–49, 258–92, 339–42), Bjørn (1982a, 25–47), and S. P. Jensen (1982, 1988b). Besides minor improvements in utensils and the dairy buildings themselves, most innovations concerned the main capital good, the cows themselves, and can be divided roughly into those relating to feeding and breeding. As we have seen, the leading dairy producers were initially certain large landholders producing high-quality "estate butter" based on the Holstein system; until around 1860, the main development concerned the continued spread around the country of the system's focus on hygiene, general care, and attention.

In relation to utensils, the traditional wooden milk pails and other containers began to be replaced with glazed clay and eventually iron. Toward the end of the 1850s, it also became more common to use horses to power butter churns or to make use of threshing machines. Increasing attention was also paid to the layout of the dairy itself, making use of model dairies both home and abroad. As for separating the cream from the milk, the greatest advance came with the invention of the Destinon system, named after von Destinon, owner of the Grönwohld estate in Holstein, who first worked with it in 1843. The traditional separation method involved placing milk in large flat containers, from which the cream was subsequently skimmed from the top after the milk had settled. The new system made use of large rectangular iron dishes, cooled with water, and the cream was skimmed from the top using a specially designed rod, the same length as the breadth of the dish, resting on two wheels, which was used to pull the cream into a container. This innovation however did not spread widely in Denmark, partly because it required much space and partly because the productivity gains were not considered sufficient for the investment.

Experimentation and Schooling

The Royal Agricultural Society was again instrumental in encouraging and sponsoring innovation and experimentation, initially mostly on the estates of members. Just one year after its foundation in 1769, the society had 210 members, twenty of whom were estate owners, thirty-nine correspondents, and most of the rest priests or holders of government office (Hertel 1920, 39–40). The society published research, awarded prizes, and performed experiments on the estates of its members. Very little attention was paid to dairying in the first decades of the society's existence, with more focus given to enclosures (82–83), hedgerows (104–10), the cultivation of bogs and meadows (110–17), and the introduction of clover (124–30). The little attention that was given to cattle focused mostly on meat production, with that on dairying mainly directed toward the production of cheese, with prizes offered for the production of Dutch and English cheeses in particular—perhaps not surprisingly, given the inspiration for the society (153–55). Then, the decades after the French and Napoleonic Wars marked something of a crisis for the society, related no doubt to the crisis in the economy generally and agriculture in particular; prices reached their lowest point in the nineteenth century during the 1830s, and the number of prizes awarded was reduced drastically after 1830 (302).

By 1854, the society only had forty paying members (296), but this situation reversed itself in the 1860s: by 1860 membership had grown to 226 members, increasing to 449 in 1869 (446). With the Holstein system already well established on many estates (see chapter 4), the society turned to trying to improve practice on smaller farms, offering for example a prize in 1856 for an essay on how cattle farming should best be managed for a farm with 100 to 150 cattle, and for one with just 20 to 50, although no entries were judged to be of sufficient quality (309–10). Similar prizes were offered in subsequent years.

This period also witnessed the beginnings of a greater interest in experimentation, with the contemporary literature full of various calls for greater control of the milking abilities of cows (with reference to both volume and fat content), as well as increased interest in how to produce cheese (including panels to judge produce)—at the time considered to be potentially the most profitable branch of dairying. It was, however, mostly from the 1860s that changes in relative prices meant that more systematic attention was paid to dairying—and to butter production in particular—by members of the Royal Agricultural Society. From 1846, local agricultural societies—particularly after their merger into regional societies (Jutland in 1872 and Zealand in 1880)—also encouraged and promoted best practice through organizing dairy exhibitions and lectures and awarding prizes, such as for the best butter.

We have already highlighted in the previous chapter the importance of the agricultural and scientific press, and of course the activities of the societies were supported greatly by this (*TfL* being initially the organ of the Royal Agricultural Society itself). By the 1830s there were no fewer than seven agricultural journals, many supported by the society, and this number expanded after the constitution of 1849 guaranteed press freedom. One of the most important was *UfL*, founded in 1856, which by the 1870s was hosting lively debates about dairy systems, both for and against centralization of butter production for a wider audience outside the traditional estates.

Human capital formation was more generally supported for an ever-wider share of the population through formal education.[2] Early attempts to start agricultural schools failed due to the Napoleonic Wars and the subsequent depression (Hertel 1920, 275–76). Then in 1835, Jens Christensen, a farmer from Jutland, contacted the Royal Agricultural Society with a request that his daughter should be educated in "the improved dairying." Conventional channels for such an education involved an apprenticeship at an estate dairy, where the apprentice would learn the skills from the dairywoman in charge of dairy production and be charged an apprenticeship fee for it. The society then discussed the question of a more general dairy education and in 1837 took upon itself the responsibility for educating girls in dairying—that is, it placed the apprentices in selected dairy units and covered the fees for the training. In the first year, four girls were placed in apprenticeships on various dairy farms (most famously Hanne Nielsen's Havarthigaard) for a one-and-a-half- to two-year education, and during the following decade around twenty girls were being educated each year (Fink 2009, 458; B. K. Hansen 2006, 190–91, 215–19). This continued until 1875, by which time around three hundred had been educated, and the society's support was no longer considered necessary. As we have touched on before, Segelcke's program of promoting scientific agriculture involved a considerable push to bring men into dairying, although initial attempts were relatively unsuccessful, at least in terms of numbers. Thus, boys were educated by the society as *hollændere*, starting in 1853, in a two-year program where they learned how to milk and care for the cows and pigs; the society's support continued until 1891—that is, much longer than the comparable program for girls (B. K. Hansen 2006, 202–4). Especially the girls and women trained from an early age by experienced dairywomen at modern dairies helped to spread good practices not only in the estate sector but also to a wider segment of farming. They did so by, for example, acting as traveling consultants for local agricultural societies and occasionally publishing advice on how to make Holstein practices work at a smaller scale. Some of the trained dairywomen also married farmers and introduced best practice on their farms with local spillover effects (B. K. Hansen 2006, 212–14, 225–29, 237–39; Fink 2009).

In his report for the UK Royal Commission on Technical Instruction in 1884, Henry Michael Jenkins noted the "remarkable" amount of time that peasant students were under education: from ages seven to fourteen at a village school, from fourteen to eighteen at a secondary school (while gaining practical experience on a farm), from eighteen to twenty-one as an apprentice, and finally one or two years at an agricultural school. Jenkins provides a concise survey of the typical path of agricultural education in Denmark at the time (Jenkins 1884, 163–64). Agricultural apprenticeships lasting two years were supported by the Royal Agricultural Society (mostly for the practical education of dairymen, dairywomen, and managers of drainage and irrigation works). Anybody eighteen years or older and of good character could apply for such an apprenticeship, during which they would be placed on a number of farms, receiving a small amount of money from the farmer as well as board and lodging. They received books from the society and were to keep a diary of what took place on the farm. When this was completed, they would receive a certificate. More theoretical instruction could follow; they might spend five to six months at one of the agricultural schools attached to a primary school (*folkeskole*); they might enter a more complete course for nine to ten months at a *folkeskole* or a specialized agricultural school (*landboskole*); or they might spend twenty-one to twenty-seven months at the Royal Veterinary and Agricultural College in Copenhagen (about which more below).

An important figure became that of Thomas Riise Segelcke (see also the previous chapter), who authored the series Communications on the Dairy Sector in *TfL*, the first instalment of which, from 1862, laid out his aims to implement a scientific approach to agriculture, focusing particularly on the fat content of milk, the layout of the milk cellar, and methods for separating the cream, particularly the Destinon system. His second communication, from 1864, reported on a journey he had made in England and Holland. But it was Segelcke's third instalment, from 1865, that stressed the importance of what was to become the basis for the spread of the modern scientific approach: bookkeeping, proper care and attention, and accurate measurement using scales and thermometers. His final communication, from 1866, focused on the importance of the treatment of milk before skimming, emphasizing artificial cooling, which was to be the first major breakthrough in the second stage of production before the centrifuge itself.

Segelcke, markedly conservative in his views on gender roles and his skepticism regarding the analytical capabilities of women, sought explicitly to promote the education of men in butter production. From 1867 the Royal Agricultural Society established an education for dairy managers, but by the time it was closed down only thirty men had been educated, largely due to difficulties in finding dairies willing to offer men an apprenticeship in an environment where dairying was an overwhelmingly female occupation. More successful was his introduction, in 1869, of dairy consultants educated by him and employed by the agricultural associations, particularly to assist smaller farms improve their butter. Several folk high schools from the 1860s introduced education in dairying for girls (Fink 2009, 463), and Tune Agricultural School established the first dairy school for girls in 1873 (B. K. Hansen 2006, 219–22). Modern dairies were established at Tune, where one of Segelcke's assistants taught how to make butter. Niels Petersen's school at Ladelundgaard, founded in 1879, again with its own dairy, was to have particular importance (see chapter 9) as one of the first to offer education in the use of the centrifuge (see Klitmøller 2008).

Figures 6.3 and 6.4 illustrate the number of students enrolled at high schools and agricultural schools from 1844 to 1900: here it should be noted again that high schools (Danish: højskole) refer to institutions for the education of adults and not for children. These figures unfortunately do not provide much information about education in dairying specifically, but they give some measure of the growing importance of formal education for adults, particularly from the 1860s. Thus, for example, while the general population increased by around 10 percent between 1870 and 1880, the number of students enrolled at high schools increased by 54 percent, and those at agricultural schools by 78 percent.

The most important educational establishment was founded with government support in Frederiksberg, near Copenhagen, in 1856: the Royal Veterinary and Agricultural College.[3] Unlike other agricultural schools, which received some government funding but were generally established through charitable bequests (Jenkins 1884, 163, 166), the Royal Veterinary and Agricultural College was an entirely state-run institution. Here, it was Niels Johannes Fjord, who became docent in 1858, who was to have particular importance.

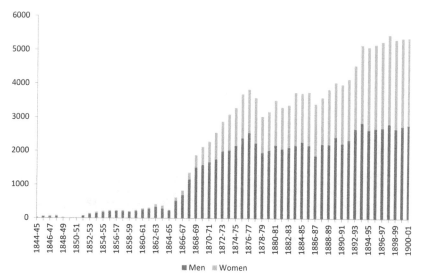

FIGURE 6.3. Number of students enrolled at high schools, 1844–1900
Source: Data from Borup and Nørgaard (1939–40, vol. 1, 468–69).

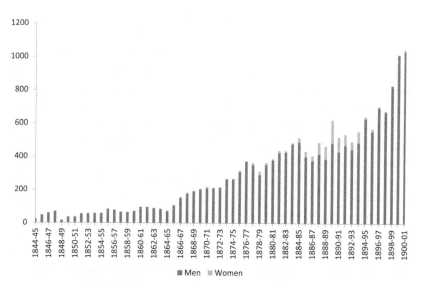

FIGURE 6.4. Number of students enrolled at agricultural schools, 1844–1900
Source: Data from Borup and Nørgaard (1939–40, vol. 1, 468–69).

FIGURE 6.5. The statue erected in honor of N. J. Fjord in front of his Agricultural Economic Experimental Laboratory
Source: Courtesy of Copenhagen University Library, Frederiksberg.

From the late 1870s there was increasing critique of Segelcke, who many considered not to be focusing on the central issues, and Fjord gained his position as the leading authority on dairying. He was initially employed by the Royal Agricultural Society, but from 1875–76 his work was supported by government funding. In 1879 he presented the first results of his work with centrifuges and in 1882 received funding for his Agricultural Economic Experimental Laboratory, which he established in 1883 (see figure 6.5). His work led to a gradual understanding of the optimum level and mixture of feed to ensure the cows' good health and greatest productive capacity. This marked a point of transition from scientifically minded trial-and-error investigations at the level of the farm to specifically designed laboratory experiments in a dedicated environment. Many of Fjord's experimental techniques were completely without precedent and led to great advances in dairy science. Experimentation elsewhere in Denmark and abroad led to healthier cows, less prone to previously widespread illnesses such as tuberculosis and other infectious diseases, for example those that caused cows to spontaneously abort.

Feeding and Breeding

As mentioned above, perhaps the major advance was the understanding of how to get cows to produce milk during winter through early calving and winter stable feeding. This method was proved in 1887 but was understood prior to that date and widely practiced in estate dairies by the 1860s (the first exhibition of winter butter was in Aarhus in 1868, initiated by Hans Broge, who we will discuss more in subsequent chapters). It greatly increased the productive capacity of a cow and allowed year-round butter exports from Denmark. Danish butter accordingly increased from around 10 percent of British winter butter imports in 1881 to over 40 percent in 1900, with much of the rest coming from Australia (Henriksen and O'Rourke 2005, 537).

Feeding and breeding of the cows also saw considerable progress. In relation to feed, advances focused on two areas: the nutritional value of individual foodstuffs and the individual animal's requirement for the production of milk or meat. At the beginning of the nineteenth century, Thaer had formulated the concept of the value of hay as a common unit for accounting for the nutritional content of various types of feed, but as this was confronted with increasing understanding of the chemical basis for nutrition through the nineteenth century, in particular by German scientists, there was a demand for a more scientific unit. This was met in Denmark in 1880 by the tenant farmer Janus Winkel who invented the concept of *kraftfoderenhed* (literally unit of concentrate) later shortened to *foderenhed* (literally unit of feed) which expressed the nutritional value of any foodstuff in relation to 1 kilogram of a mixture of 50 percent barley and 50 percent oats (Statistics Denmark 1911, 122). Prior to this there was however lively debate in Denmark and elsewhere on the best way to feed a cow. Although much of this research was later found to be worthless (for example in terms of increasing the fat content of the milk), other work demonstrated the importance of giving cows more feed than was strictly necessary to survive, particularly through the use of concentrates; the concept of "strong feeding" formed the basis of an extensive discussion in the agricultural press from the mid-1870s, although concentrates had been used on the most advanced dairy farms as early as the 1850s (Sehested 1857, 1858; see discussion in chapter 5).

In terms of breeding, one of the great contributions was the new breed of Danish red milch cow (see figure 6.6). Although designated for the first time in 1878, the Danish red was the result of earlier successful attempts and had already received recognition at an agricultural meeting in Odense in 1863. Statistics on the proportion of cows of this breed for the whole country are not available for the nineteenth century, but the number of red bulls used for mating had increased to 14,281 (53 percent of the total) by 1893 according to the official statistics (Statistics Denmark 1911, 122). In the sample of estates given by *TfL*, although no estates had Danish red cows from 1880 through 1886, 7 percent had them in 1887, increasing to 48 percent in 1890, and 69 percent in 1900. Danish red cows had excellent milk-producing quali-

FIGURE 6.6. Theodor Philipsen (1840–1920), *Grazing Cows on the Island of Saltholm*, 1892
Source: Courtesy of the National Art Gallery of Denmark.
Note: The painting illustrates well the variety in traditional breeds of cow that could be found in the Danish countryside through most of the second half of the nineteenth century. The important Danish red milch cow can be seen standing on the right-hand side of the picture.

ties and gradually replaced the more traditional breeds (mostly Jutland and Angler). Shorthorn cattle, introduced from England, were used primarily for meat production.[4] Then, after Fjord's invention of a control centrifuge for determining the butterfat content of milk in 1887, it became clear that it was not feed that, as had previously been assumed, determined the butterfat content of milk or even so much the breed of cow, but rather the individual cow itself. This led to attempts to find the good butter cows and use them for breeding, and various (partly government-funded) breeding associations sprang up to support such initiatives.

Finally, the process of separating cream from milk was accelerated and improved by the practice of cooling the milk, using initially cold water and later ice. This both accelerated the separation of the cream from the milk and also allowed for the use of taller, narrower containers, as opposed to the wide *bøtte* which had previously been used, thus allowing for the processing of more milk in the creamery. As was noted by Segelcke in his Communications on the Dairy Sector in *TfL*, this was already common practice in parts of Holland, Sweden, and the United States, and Danish dairies based on the Holstein system began to make the required changes. An agricultural meeting in Copenhagen in 1869 displayed the first domestic results, with the first water dairy in Denmark established at Gjeddesdal and Lerchenfeldt on Zealand. Ice dairies were a natural improvement on water dairying, with the first established at Glibing Mølle near Horsens in 1873, and Tesdorpf himself converted to ice dairying in 1874. Much of Fjord's experiments in the following years thus concerned how to preserve snow and ice from the winter for use in the ice dairies.

This combination of research, education, and the spread of best practice through the agricultural press and exhibitions was certainly in no small part the reason that, in 1879, Danish butter produced by Mrs. Casperine de Lichtenberg from the Hessel estate near Grenaa (northeast of Aarhus) won the Champion Prize at the International Agricultural Exhibition in London. Her participation owed much to the encouragement of Tesdorpf and Segelcke (who was responsible for the Danish dairy display), and the result was that, even before the cooperatives and before the predominance of male dairy engineers, Danish butter had received world renown.

A Quantitative Analysis of the Determinants of
Productivity Increases in Danish Dairying

The fact that Danish estate owners and dairy managers argued that scientific progress and rational economic decisions could only be made based on accurate measurement and record keeping, as we discussed in chapter 5, allowed us (Lampe and Sharp 2015a) to use the popular tool of modern agricultural economists, stochastic frontier analysis (SFA), to estimate production functions for milk and thus identify how productivity and efficiency advanced with the introduction of new practices. The data underlying that study were the result of the aforementioned annual survey of Danish estates published by *TfL* over a number of years from 1880. Although this is toward the end of the period of interest to the present work, the *TfL* data allow us to assess the importance of earlier changes, since their survey deliberately included backward estates using outdated technologies and practices.

Although there is a large body of literature on the estimation of production functions for milk, particularly using SFA, none to our knowledge has focused on historical time periods. More importantly, none has concentrated on periods when great changes were made to the organization of the dairy industry. With this unique data source, we investigated far more radical changes and demonstrated the productivity and efficiency implications of a large number of factors, such as feeding, breeding, the modernity of the farm (as a proxy for the farmer's education or general outlook), scale, and more.

In layman's terms, SFA allowed us to estimate the best-practice production possibility frontier (PPF)[5] and then to calculate the gap between each estate's production given its inputs and the theoretical maximum at the frontier. Our data gathered an unbalanced panel of fifty-five estates and a total of 377 observations. These returns were anonymized, so we unfortunately do not know the location of the individual estates, but assigning unique identification numbers allowed us to link observations from individual estates over time. Using our preferred specification of the model, the average inefficiency is 16.8 percent, ranging from 0.9 percent to 61.9 percent.[6] The fact that this is relatively efficient compared to findings from modern studies no doubt reflects the productivity lead of Danish agriculture at this time.

In order to understand better the features of the more and less efficient farms, table 6.2 illustrates the mean values of our variables for the first quartile of the distribution of inefficiencies (the least inefficient farms), and for the fourth quartile (the most inefficient farms). *Milk* is the amount of milk produced per year in Danish *pund* (500 g). *Cows* is the number of cows on the estate (an average of the number of cows reported for the winter and for the summer seasons, which were reported separately).[7] *Feed* is the amount of feed in *pund* given to the cows (expressed in Winkel's *kraftfoderenheder*).[8] *Red* takes the value 1 if the herd is of Danish red cows, and 0 otherwise. This measures the use of a more productive, biologically innovated, version of the capital good cow. In contrast, *shorthorn* is a dummy taking the value 1 if the herd is of the shorthorn (Danish: *korthorn*) variety and, thus, dual-purpose cattle used at least as much for beef as for milk production (hence it was a technologically more vintage and less specialized cow). We assumed that Danish red shift the production frontier upward, while dual-purpose shorthorns shift it downward. *Graze* is the amount of grassland used per cow in *tønde land*. While above the nutritional value of grass consumed from grassland is transformed into *feed*, we also used it independently to explain inefficiency: in traditional pasture farming, the amount of pastureland limits the number of cows and the nutrition for the latter, while stable feeding and the use of commercial feedstuffs overcomes these limits. We therefore assumed that farms that use much grassland per cow are more traditional, using stable feeding potentially more for the survival of summer grazing cows in winter than to maximize their production possibilities. Related to the use of winter dairying, *calved* gives the percentage of cows that have calved before January 1 and, thus, are able to produce milk during the winter.

System is a dummy taking the value 1 if the estate is modern—that is, owns and operates an automatic cream separator.[9] We believe this last to proxy the modernity of the estate since the cream separator was of no use for the production of milk (only for the extraction of cream from milk to make butter),

TABLE 6.2. Characteristics of farms at different levels of efficiency

	1st quartile (least inefficient)	4th quartile (most inefficient)	Mean
Milk	524,839	331,696	451,711
Cows	97.5	87.0	96.6
Feed	353,222	275,982	326,274
Red	0.51	0.14	0.38
Shorthorn	0.00	0.06	0.02
Inefficiency	0.04	0.33	0.17
Cows	97.5	87.0	96.6
Graze	0.806	1.191	0.942
System	0.649	0.340	0.501
Calved	53.1	43.2	46.8
Year	1890.4	1890.3	1890.0

Source: Lampe and Sharp (2015a, 1146, table 10).

Note: Cows appear twice, once as a factor of production and once to measure the size of the estate and see if larger dairy units are more or less efficient than smaller ones. See text.

so any effect of this variable on the production of milk is not a direct effect of the technology per se. It is expected to measure education, professional management, and adoption of best practices in a broader sense. It remains to be seen whether this modernity also reflects a shift from female to male dominance of the estate dairy unit—and thus a socially conservative backlash—or how these processes were negotiated at the level of individual estates.

As suggested by the econometrics, the size of the farm and the year do not have a substantial impact on efficiency, although clearly larger farms were generally more efficient—but this was due to the practices they employed rather than their size per se. Less efficient farms made more use of summer grazing, less use of stable production in the winter,[10] and were less likely to own a cream separator. Our findings support to a large extent those from modern studies which describe how technical efficiency is usually explained by "farmer education and experience, contacts with extension, access to credit, and farm size," and that all but the latter usually have a positive and significant impact on efficiency.[11]

This chapter focused on the advances in dairy production before the rise of the cooperatives and summarized our quantitative assessment of some of the main forces behind Denmark's lead in agricultural productivity in a period when the basis for modern dairying was developed and diffused in that country. Danish farmers were apparently well educated,[12] and our results show that that education and the disposition to use modern methods (like automatic cream separators in the second stage of production) contributed to increasing efficiency of production. In fact, in his report for the British

Parliament in 1884, Jenkins stated that the fact that "Danish butter . . . has practically no rival on the London market" was "directly traceable to technical instruction" (Jenkins 1884, 179). Another important factor was the adoption of practices leading to more efficient use of the capital good cow, here exemplified by calving in the fall and stable feeding in the winter, which allowed for year-round production. Finally, biological innovation, although at first on unstable scientific grounds, led to the improvement of the capital good cow and hence to higher milk yields and increasing efficiency. This improvement happened from a comparatively early stage, since the Danish estates in our data set had focused on milk instead of beef production from an early date, which can be seen from the few observations on the use of multipurpose beef-milk cows of the shorthorn variety in our sample; this observation is backed by articles in the leading agricultural journal of that time such as Fenger (1873), who, based on actual accounting data from individual farms, showed that beef production was less lucrative than milk production under the circumstances of the 1870s.

Additionally, by increasing the importance of commercial and imported feedstuffs (grains, oilseed, and palm-kernel cakes) relative to pasture area and using these effectively to increase milk production (e.g., via stable feeding), Danish farmers overcame the constraints of their own lands,[13] took advantage of declining prices for grains in Europe during the late nineteenth century, and committed to a market-oriented export agriculture.

As we will discuss in chapter 9, the innovation that changed the industry for good—and allowed best practice to flow to the peasant farmers—was the automatic cream separator, a centrifuge. Experiments on the estates took place throughout the 1870s (after German precedents in the 1860s), and Fjord investigated the technology from 1878. The first centrifuge dairy was established in 1880, and by 1881 ninety centrifuges were in use. In terms of butter production, however, the increases in milk production were at least as important. Between 1880 and 1900 annual milk yields in Denmark increased by 700 liters per cow—that is, an increase of 33.7 percent. For the second stage of production, Henriksen, Lampe, and Sharp (2011) have shown that the amount of butter produced from a constant amount of milk increased with the introduction of cream separators by between 9.2 and 25 percent, depending on the amount of milk processed (since previous technologies had decreasing returns to scale). As we will discuss, the introduction of cooperatives increased efficiency by an additional 5.3 percent, giving a grand total of between 14.9 and 31.6 percent more butter produced from the same amount of milk.[14] Hence, the contribution of improvements in milk yields per cow to increases in total butter production per cow between 1880 and 1900 were at least as great as the contribution of more efficient transformation of this milk into butter.[15]

Appendix

In Lampe and Sharp (2015a) we started our formal analysis by estimating a series of baseline models for the production functions using the tools of SFA (see Kumbhakar and Lovell 2000). These models have the general form for panel data

(1) $y_{it} = \beta' x_{it} + v_{it} - u_{it}$

here y is the output of firm i, and x is a vector of inputs. The important contribution of these models is the separation of the error term into a standard stochastic error, v_{it}, and an inefficiency term, u_{it}. The form of the production function—the productivity frontier for our sample—is thus given by the relationship between the inputs and the outputs, while the inefficiency term tells us how far away from that frontier an individual unit is at any point in time.

For our purposes, y_{it} obviously corresponds to the (log) output of milk. The variable x_{it} is defined as follows:

$$x_{it} = \begin{pmatrix} lcows_{it} \\ lfeed_{it} \\ \vdots \end{pmatrix}.$$

In x_{it} we also include either a trend, t, to capture technological and/or especially breeding progress over time or direct measures of breed. A trend in the functional form we specify in most of our regressions below, a Cobb-Douglas-type production function, can be interpreted as Hicks-neutral, disembodied technical change. This might seem odd at first sight, since breeding progress manifested itself in the bodies of cows. However, it could be argued that what the Danish red cows achieve is to enable an increase in output from a constant bundle of inputs—in our case, with the same amount of cows and feed. This is the classical definition of the productivity effect of Hicks-neutral technical change (Mundlak 2000, 134).

Table 6.A1 reports the estimation results for the baseline models. Models (1a)–(1c) are simple pooled regressions using various formulations of the log-likelihood: half normal, exponential, and truncated normal respectively.[16] For models (2) and (3) we estimated a production function using the stochastic frontier model with a time-varying technical efficiency term formulated by George E. Battese and Timothy J. Coelli (1995). In these models, the inefficiency term, u, is given by $u_{it} = \exp[-\eta(t - T)]|U_i|$. In all specifications bar

TABLE 6.A1. Estimation results, baseline models, dependent variable *lmilk*

	(1a)	*(1b)*	*(1c)*	*(2)*	*(3)*
Constant	6.261***	6.239***	6.262***	7.361***	15.165
	(0.326)	(0.331)	(0.326)	(0.309)	(12.939)
lcows	0.601***	0.612***	0.602***	0.760***	1.853
	(0.042)	(0.043)	(0.043)	(0.039)	(3.125)
lfeed	0.324***	0.316***	0.323***	0.181***	−1.456
	(0.040)	(0.041)	(0.041)	(0.037)	(3.132)
lcows^2	n/a	n/a	n/a	n/a	0.061
					(0.215)
lfeed^2	n/a	n/a	n/a	n/a	0.088
					(0.192)
lcows*lfeed	n/a	n/a	n/a	n/a	−0.130
					(0.393)
Wald test of constant returns to scale (χ^2)	256.03	247.56	256.80	430.02	0.23†
Trend	0.006***	0.007***	0.006***	0.004***	0.005***
	(0.001)	(0.001)	(0.001)	(0.002)	(0.001)
μ	n/a	n/a	−0.031	n/a	n/a
			(0.173)		
λ	3.218***	n/a	3.247***	2.563***	2.472***
	(0.619)		(0.634)	(0.050)	(0.055)
σ	0.216***	n/a	0.224***	0.191***	0.184***
	(0.011)		(0.046)	(0.001)	(0.001)
θ $(= 1/\sigma_u)$	n/a	8.871***	n/a	n/a	n/a
		(1.019)			
σ_v	n/a	0.087***	n/a	n/a	n/a
		(0.008)			
η	n/a	n/a	n/a	0.019*	0.019*
				(0.011)	(0.011)
Average inefficiency	0.159	0.113	0.155	0.167	0.161
Period covered	1880–1900	1880–1900	1880–1900	1880–1900	1880–1900
No. of cross-sections	n/a	n/a	n/a	55	55
No. of observations	377	377	377	377	377
Log-likelihood	224.497	222.808	224.514	371.739	372.649

Note: $\hat{\mu}/\sigma_u = 0$; $\lambda = \sigma_u/\sigma_v$; $\sigma = \sqrt{\sigma_u^2 + \sigma_v^2}$; stochastic frontier, $e = v - u$; for models (2) and (3), $u_{it} = \exp[-\eta(t - T)]|U_i|$.

*/*** = significant difference from 0 at 10%/1% level.

† = The test for joint significance of the three extra coefficients in the translog specification.

one we assume a Cobb-Douglas production function; although in (3) we experiment with a translog function. This latter leads to insignificance of both factors of production, but clearly this is due to multicollinearity of the *lcows* and *lfeed* variables with their interactions. A joint test of the significance of the three extra variables in the translog specification cannot reject that they should be omitted. All other estimation results are both qualitatively and quantitatively very similar.

Having determined that the baseline model for the production frontier and the estimated firm specific inefficiencies seem relatively robust to the specification of the model, we extended the analysis by modeling the inefficiency terms as $g(z_{it}) = \exp(\eta' z_{it})$, where z is a vector of variables which might explain inefficiency.[17] The results are presented in table 6.A2. In the ineffi-

TABLE 6.A2. Estimation results, technical inefficiency effects models, dependent variable *lmilk*

	(4)	(5)	(6)
Constant	7.073***	7.154***	7.136***
	(0.361)	(0.417)	(0.369)
lcows	0.732***	0.717***	0.734***
	(0.051)	(0.054)	(0.051)
lfeed	0.212***	0.216***	0.208***
	(0.045)	(0.050)	(0.046)
Wald test of constant returns to scale (χ^2)	280.17	220.32	274.48
Trend	0.007***	n/a	0.005***
	(0.001)		(0.001)
Red	n/a	0.040***	n/a
		(0.012)	
Shorthorn	n/a	−0.150***	n/a
		(0.050)	
Inefficiency			
Cows	0.001	0.001	0.001
	(0.003)	(0.003)	(0.003)
Graze	0.308***	0.395***	0.296***
	(0.081)	(0.129)	(0.082)
System	−0.201***	−0.359***	−0.181***
	(0.091)	(0.071)	(0.089)
Calved	−0.010***	−0.009***	−0.011***
	(0.003)	(0.003)	(0.003)
Trend	n/a	n/a	−0.011
			(0.011)
λ	3.215***	2.932***	3.878***
	(0.102)	(0.123)	(0.096)
σ	0.230***	0.217***	0.277***
	(0.005)	(0.005)	(0.009)
Average inefficiency	0.168	0.167	0.169
Period covered	1880–1900	1880–1900	1880–1900
No. of cross-sections	55	55	55
No. of observations	377	377	377
Log-likelihood	388.338	378.893	388.843

Note: $\lambda = \sigma_u/\sigma_v$; $\sigma = \sqrt{\sigma_u^2 + \sigma_v^2}$; stochastic frontier, $e = v - u$; $u_{it} = \exp(\eta' z_{it})|U_i|$.

*** = significant difference from 0 at 1% level.

TABLE 6.A3. The distribution of the estimated farm-level inefficiencies for models (1a)–(6)

Estimation	Mean	SD	Minimum	Maximum
(1a)	0.159	0.098	0.025	0.360
(1b)	0.113	0.090	0.027	0.582
(1c)	0.155	0.098	0.025	0.371
(2)	0.167	0.119	0.012	0.617
(3)	0.161	0.117	0.013	0.605
(4)	0.168	0.120	0.010	0.619
(5)	0.167	0.113	0.014	0.586
(6)	0.169	0.120	0.010	0.614

ciency term, z_{it}, we included the variables *cows* (as a control for the size of the farm), *graze*, *system*, and *calved*. In model (6) we also include a trend.

In model (5) we examined the impact of improved breeding, which we believe largely drove technological progress in milk production, by replacing the trend in the production function with dummies for two types of breed of cow: the Danish red, and the shorthorn. As explained above, the former is considered instrumental for the productivity gains seen by Danish agriculture over this period. The latter was a dual-purpose cow used both for milk and meat production. The control group of cows is thus all other breeds, who were by and large traditional breeds from which the Danish red was eventually bred. Our motivation for placing them in the production function was that superior (for milking) breeds of cow would correspond to an outward shift of the production possibility frontier.

Note again the robustness of the estimation to the different specifications. Table 6.A3 gives some idea of the similarity of the distribution of the farm-specific inefficiencies for the nine models we estimate. This is especially notable in the light of the fact that these types of model are considered to be very sensitive and prone to give extreme results in the case of misspecification or poor data.[18]

How the Danes Discovered Britain

The previous three chapters emphasized the developments within Denmark in terms of agricultural advances and specialization. The discovery of comparative advantage we described in chapter 5 also requires, however, the discovery of new markets outside the domestic market and the establishment of connections to those outside established marketing channels if these do not already sufficiently communicate consumer demand and market prices on one side of the relationship and product characteristics and availability on the other. New products in the export portfolio often need special attention and care to be able to unfold their full potential for long-run economic development. Although the elites we earlier discussed were not necessarily thinking about the long run, it was certainly in their interests to establish a market for their goods, and the way in which they did so will form a large part of this chapter. Moreover, here we introduce a new set of elites: the merchants who helped establish the connections with first Hamburg and then the United Kingdom. These were to prove of vital importance as producers outside the estates also sought to find a market for their produce. Moreover, as we will discuss in chapter 9, butter traders provided much of the initial push to centralize peasant butter production in a process that would eventually give birth to the cooperatives.

As we touched on in the introduction, conventional Danish economic and national history emphasizes that the later breakthrough of Danish exports reflected a new national consciousness. In fact, the prime minister's words in 1999 were taken from a commemorative medal for the 1872 Copenhagen exhibition of industry and art, which bore the famous expression by the poet H. P. Holst: "*Hvad udad tabes, skal indad vindes*" (What outside is lost, must inside be won). With the loss of the duchies of Holstein and Schleswig to Prussia in the Second Schleswig War (1864), this became a potent national symbol of strength in times of adversity. As another former prime minister expressed it in 2014 when marking the 150th anniversary of the war, "Out of the defeat in 1864 grew the modern Denmark. With democracy. With a well-educated population. With equality between the sexes. Freedom for the individual. And the whole of our welfare society based on solidarity."[1] This idea runs through both Danish literature (Westergaard 1922, 19–20) and international literature on Denmark based on it, such as the internationally influential paper by Charles P. Kindleberger (1951, 35–36, 40–41, 44–45). Seemingly as proof of this, within a couple of decades of 1864, the Danish economy, led by Danish agriculture (particularly dairying, which became the envy of the world), was rapidly catching up to the world's leading economies. In this literature, Kindleberger, based on E. Jensen's (1937) English-language account of the evolution of Danish agriculture since 1870, stressed the role of the cooperative movement—and behind it the evolving national peasant self-consciousness embodied in folk high schools and the Grundtvig movement—as the protagonists of this reorientation, which signaled a decisive new phase in the political, economic, and social history of Denmark. Jensen's account, in turn, reflected much of the general view in Denmark by that time, a view that since then has been nuanced in Danish historiography[2] but stands in general unchallenged, as reflected by the words of the prime minister in the twenty-first century. The reorientation of exports away from Germany and toward the United Kingdom, tangible in the establishment of direct shipping connections with the United Kingdom, plays an important symbolic role in this story as pars pro toto of a renewed national cultural sovereignty and new role models in culture and politics.

We nuance the story about the importance of 1864 by again examining the factors that enabled such sudden trade reorientation. We take the story of the butter trade back to the eighteenth century and gather all available relevant information from before 1864, and we show that, in terms of direct exports to Britain, 1864 did indeed mark a sudden break. We then, however, turn to price records to demonstrate that markets were integrated between Copenhagen and London even before this date but via Hamburg. In fact, until the 1860s, Denmark was very dependent on this hub, particularly for exports to Britain. But then she rapidly developed her own infrastructure, in particular direct trading routes with Britain, and these were to be of vital importance for expanding agricultural exports. So, while the 1864 war made trade via Hamburg if not impossible then at least politically unacceptable, trading directly with Britain independently reduced costs considerably by cutting out the Hamburg middlemen. The important question then is why Denmark ever traded via Hamburg, and how such a sudden reorientation was possible.

Our answer considers the literature on service clusters and export hubs, and asks how less-developed countries can escape path dependencies in traditional trading patterns and bring home the high-value-added parts of their export trade. This connection between market integration and path dependency is a relevant topic in economic history and has recently been formally modeled by the economist Thomas Chaney (2014) as a combination of informational frictions for exporters and the role of geography and distance in explaining trade flows. Chaney formalizes what business historians have known for a long time: exporters depend on a network of contacts to find trade partners, and this network is geographically biased and conditioned by previous contacts. Gaining reliable information on foreign markets and establishing functioning distribution networks is far from trivial. In preindustrial times, substantial specific investments in networks and in the protection of business abroad had to be made (Greif 2000; Grafe and Gelderblom 2010), and it took large shocks, such as wars and revolutions, to reorient existing networks (Schulte Beerbühl 2013).

For nineteenth-century markets in sophisticated agricultural products, where asymmetric information, quality uncertainty, and cheating prevailed, the problems of establishing reliable distribution channels abroad have been highlighted (Simpson 2004, Stanziani 2010). Under these circumstances, clusters of agents with more contacts, deeper information on foreign demand patterns and business practices as well as better credit availability, more frequent connections, and better storage are at a clear advantage over peripheral trading locations. Theoretically, a model by Paul Krugman (1993) demonstrates that such hubs are favorable locations for industries subject to increasing returns and that the location of a hub can be self-sustaining, reinforcing historical accident through subsequent path dependency.

We reinterpret the Danish case in this light as the weakening of the historical advantages of a trade hub and a considerable shock jointly dismantling existing path dependency. In our interpretation, the Second Schleswig War certainly provoked the sudden change, but this was not simply a reflection of national consciousness after 1864. Initially Hamburg provided services that Denmark could not, but as the first era of globalization moved on the use of this hub entailed larger opportunity costs as the Danish economy developed its own capabilities.

At the same time, the Danish case is representative of late nineteenth-century agricultural globalization: both the Great Specialization between countries' industrialized urban regions and agricultural hinterlands and the formation of a core-periphery model with industrialized countries at the center (and the United Kingdom centermost). In a process resembling von Thünen's rings of specialization (Kopsidis 2014; Peet 1972), the perishability of individual commodities, relative factor endowments, and absolute geographical advantages marked the potential extent of this specialization. This fueled international trade in agricultural commodities, which grew at annual rates above 3 percent from (at least) 1850 until the First World War (Aparicio, Pinilla, and Serrano 2009). As such, the Danish case is typical and atypical at the same time: in the late nineteenth century, many smaller and/or poorer countries followed export-oriented development strategies based on a narrow selection of commodities.[3] What is less typical is the medium- and long-term development that this strategy earned Denmark, a point we will come back to in later chapters when we put the Danish case into perspective.

The Anglo-Danish Butter Trade

We start our inquiry into the Anglo-Danish butter trade collecting evidence from trade statistics, which however reveal an unexpected barrier in the early nineteenth century: Exports of butter[4] were considered a state secret until 1820 (Drejer 1962, 21), and if statistics were kept they have not been preserved, which makes it less than straightforward to trace the evolution of Danish butter exports or any other exports before this point. The first meaningful trade statistics, the *Eksportstatistiske Tabeller* (Export statistical tables), start only in 1820; they included information on grain exports, adding tables on butter and cheese in 1821 (Boje 1977, 57–60). From these series, which are preserved in the Danish National Archives and run to 1834, we can assess the total exports per product of the Danish monarchy (henceforth Greater Denmark)—including the duchies of Schleswig and Holstein but not the free port of Altona, which is listed as a destination—and the distribution of export destinations. We can also assess each entity's share of the total (and that of the different regions of Denmark proper—the continental peninsula of Jutland and the islands of Funen, Zealand, and Lolland-Falster), as well as a breakdown by customs districts. Unfortunately, it is not possible to know the destinations of exports from each of the constituent parts of Greater Denmark. However, it is the reorientation of trade by the kingdom—that is, Denmark proper—that interests us here.

Nevertheless, for the whole of Greater Denmark we can see a clear pattern in this early period, as illustrated in table 7.1. More than 70 percent of all butter exports went to Hamburg and the adjacent Danish free port of Altona (which is today a district of Hamburg), and, together with the Baltic Hanse-

TABLE 7.1. Butter export destinations (%) and total exports (*tønder*) for Denmark and the duchies of Schleswig and Holstein, 1821–34

Abstract	Altona	Hamburg	Lübeck	Other Germany	Britain	Norway	Sweden	Other	Total
1821–24	23.0	50.4	6.7	10.2	0.8	7.9	0.1	0.9	42,782
1825–29	22.5	49.2	3.5	9.5	6.4	7.8	0.1	1.0	51,863
1830–34	27.5	44.3	3.4	8.0	9.1	4.9	0.0	2.8	48,682
1821–34	24.4	47.8	4.4	9.2	5.7	6.8	0.1	1.6	48,132

Source: Danish National Archive (Rigsarkivet), Generaltoldkammeret, Toldkammerkancelli og Sekretariat. Eksportstatistiske Tabeller 1820–1834 (Nr. 22.298).

Note: "Other Germany" includes returns for Germany, Bremen, Hannover, Mecklenburg, Oldenburg (incl. Eutin), Prussia, and the ports of Rostock, Stettin, Stralsund, and Wismar; it does not include Helgoland and destinations given as "North Sea" or "Baltic." 1 *tønde* of butter = 112 kg.

atic port of Lübeck, more than 75 percent went to port cities. For the rest, we can see an increasing share of direct exports to England and Scotland and a decreasing share of exports to Norway, which had been ruled by the king of Denmark until 1814.

However, as figure 7.1 shows, the exports of butter from Denmark proper accounted for a relatively small fraction of total exports from Greater Denmark in this period, 28.8 percent on average. More importantly, Danish economic historians (especially Boje 1977, 66–72) have highlighted that the distribution of export destinations was probably somewhat different for the Kingdom of Denmark than for the duchies. In the former the importance of the traditional market of Norway was much higher than in the aggregate, and Altona would have taken a larger share than Hamburg, although much of the latter was simply passing through the Danish free port to the Hanseatic city.

This can be confirmed for the period 1838 to 1852,[5] for which we have, from the first published Danish trade statistics, an overview of the destinations of butter exports from Denmark proper, which we have aggregated in the same way as before in table 7.2.[6] For the period before the First Schleswig War (1848–51), 38.4 percent of exports went to Norway, and another 44.8 percent to Altona; the shares to Hamburg and Germany are much smaller than those reported for Greater Denmark in table 7.1. "Other" destinations are also slightly more important, among which the Danish possessions of Iceland, Greenland, and the Faroe Islands dominate alongside the Danish West Indies. The shares to Lübeck and direct exports to Britain are similar to the Denmark and duchies aggregate before the war.

During the First Schleswig War, we observe increasing direct exports to both the Hanseatic towns of Hamburg and Lübeck but especially to Britain

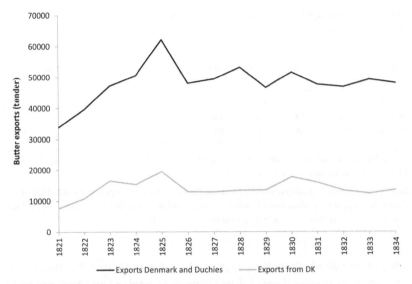

FIGURE 7.1. Total exports of butter from Greater Denmark, 1821–34
Source: Exports Denmark and Duchies: Danish National Archive (Rigsarkivet), Generaltoldkammeret, Toldkammerkancelli og Sekretariat. Eksportstatistiske Tabeller 1820–1834 (Nr. 22.298); Exports from DK: Boje (1977, 316).
Note: One tønde of butter = 112 kg.

TABLE 7.2. Shares of exports of butter from Denmark by destination (%) and total exports (tønder), 1838–52

	Altona	Hamburg	Lübeck	Other Germany	Britain	Norway and Sweden	Other	Total
1838–42	47.2	0.6	3.5	0.3	13.7	31.1	3.6	16,941
1843–47	42.4	0.4	0.9	0.3	5.4	45.7	4.9	11,589
1848–51	12.0	5.0	8.6	0.5	21.2	47.6	5.2	13,659
1852	21.9	0.7	2.5	1.3	11.3	60.0	2.5	21,351
1838–52	34.5	1.7	3.9	0.4	12.8	42.3	4.4	14,576

Source: Statistisk Tabelværk.
Note: Altona includes the small neighboring port of Wandsbek. 1 tønde of butter = 112 kg.

and Norway. In part, this seems to reflect the reversal of a former trend away from butter exports to Britain (sometimes linked to the repeal of the British Corn Laws which fostered grain exports; see Boje 1977, 62–68). At the same time, the importance of Altona shows a marked decline. Note that there is no overall decline in the volume of butter exports from Denmark during the war. The notable trade diversion from Altona toward Norway, Britain, Hamburg, and Lübeck might be an effect of the war that cut trade routes to Altona and through the duchies; it might also reflect some of the efforts to establish direct trade connections to Britain described below. However, even in 1852, we see a marked reorientation back toward Altona (again taking 21.9 percent of exports) and a reduction in the British share to 11.3 percent,[7] while the share of exports to Norway is still rising.

Unfortunately, it is difficult to assess whether these changes and reversals persisted, since in 1853 the Danish government ceased to publish accounts of the destinations of the exports from the different parts of Greater Denmark. Thus, destinations are given in the trade statistics only for the sum of Denmark and the duchies until 1861 and for Denmark and Schleswig (excluding Holstein and Lauenburg) for 1862 and 1863.

Of course, after the Second Schleswig War and the loss of the duchies in 1864, Danish trade statistics and their accounts of destinations of exports refer to Denmark only (see table 7.3). For the first years after the war (1864–68), we observe an almost complete reorientation of trade, with more than two-thirds of butter exports going to Britain, a much-reduced orientation toward Norway, and a clear loss of importance of both Altona (now probably included under duchies), Hamburg, and Lübeck. Also, and importantly, total exports doubled between 1848–52 and 1864–67, and from there continued to increase at a fast pace. These patterns would remain and be reinforced after the 1880s, until finally in 1900 around 90 percent of Danish butter exports would go to Britain.

This leaves the important question of what happened between 1852 and 1864. Was the Danish reorientation a gradual process already starting with the First Schleswig War, or were trade patterns reversed again toward Altona and indirect exports via Hamburg? There are three ways to assess this, none of them perfect. The first is to look at the distribution of the exports of Den-

TABLE 7.3. Shares of exports of butter from Denmark by destination (%) and total exports (*tønder*), 1865–72

	Duchies	Altona	Hamburg	Lübeck	Other Germany	Britain	Norway and Sweden	Other	Total
1864	7.7	—	1.4	0.9	0.0	64.2	23.2	3.6	39,939
1865–67	11.9	—	0.7	0.7	0.1	64.0	20.5	3.3	42,805
1868–72	9.7	—	0.1	0.3	0.1	81.9	6.8	1.4	62,487
1873–77	8.3	—	0.3	0.5	0.2	83.7	6.2	0.7	123,081
1878–81	7.2	—	0.4	0.4	0.0	84.8	6.4	0.8	106,898
1864–81	9.0	—	0.4	0.5	0.1	79.1	9.7	1.5	84,421

Source: *Statistisk Tabelværk.*

Note: Altona is now included in "Duchies," which refers to Schleswig, Holstein, and Lauenburg. 1864 refers to the 1864/65 fiscal year (after the war). 1 *tønde* of butter = 112 kg.

TABLE 7.4. Shares of exports of butter from Denmark and the duchies by destination (%) and total exports (*tønder*), 1838–62

	Altona	Hamburg	Lübeck	Other Germany	Britain	Norway	Sweden	Other	Total
1838–42	22.5	54.7	1.8	0.6	8.2	7.6	0.1	4.5	75,064
1843–47	27.9	56.4	1.9	1.1	1.3	8.1	—	2.8	72,054
1848–51	n/a	n/a	n/a	n/a	n/a	n/a	n/a	n/a	n/a
1852	17.7	83.2	4.4	1.8	5.1	26.1	0.2	2.0	52,680
1853–57	16.4	64.7	2.1	0.3	4.7	9.7	0.3	1.7	75,187
1858–62	13.3	65.6	2.0	0.8	6.0	10.8	0.7	0.8	76,420

Source: Statistisk Tabelværk.

Note: "Altona" includes the neighboring small port of Wandsbek. "Other Germany" after 1852 also includes the duchy of Lauenburg. In 1843–47 "Sweden" is included under "Norway." 1 *tønde* of butter = 112 kg.

mark and the duchies during this period to see if there is a more general trend toward Britain. Then, we can also look at British import statistics to see if Denmark is gaining a larger share. And, finally, we can look at the import and export statistics of Hamburg.[8]

While data for the period of the 1848–51 war is missing for Greater Denmark, table 7.4 suggests that no important changes in trade patterns can be discerned before 1863. At most, we can see the increasing trend of exports to Norway (especially in 1852), probably from Denmark, and a shift from trading via Altona to trading via Hamburg. The share of direct exports to Britain in 1858–62 is no larger than in 1838–42. However, it might be possible that an increased share of exports from the duchies to and via Hamburg concealed a different trend from the Kingdom of Denmark regarding direct exports to Britain.

To shed light on this possibility, figure 7.2 compares total Danish butter exports, Danish (direct) exports to Britain, and British (direct) imports from Denmark as reflected in British statistics, from 1836 to 1881, the critical period of our study. If we believe the British statistics, in the period from 1853 to 1862, direct exports from Denmark were gradually increasing in absolute terms, although their growth was smaller than that of overall British butter imports before 1863.[9] We can see that from the late 1860s the figures for exports to Britain, imports into Britain, and Danish total exports become very similar. From the mid-1850s to the mid-1860s, we observe increasing comovement between total Danish exports and imports into Britain. Before the 1850s, comovement between Danish export totals and trade to Britain is difficult to discern. So, either trade between Britain and Denmark was small and unim-

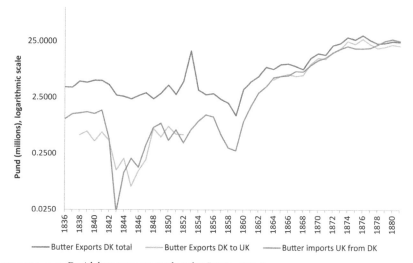

FIGURE 7.2. Danish butter exports, totals and to Britain, 1836–81
Sources: Data for the years 1836–40 and 1851–52 from *Statistisk Tabelværk* and *Tables of the Revenue . . .* (1835–43, 1854); for the years 1841–50, BPP (1854–55, 7); for the years 1853–82, *Annual Statement of the Trade . . .* (1855–98). Data for 1854 interpolated between 1853 and 1855.
Note: Years 1875–81 corrected for margarine imports into Britain (Lampe and Sharp 2014a).

portant before the late 1860s or it was routed through Denmark's main visible export destination, the Altona/Hamburg trade hub.

It remains difficult to assess how much of Danish butter was actually traded to Britain via Altona and Hamburg in the period before 1864 due to the lack of trade statistics for Altona.[10] We can, however, have a look at the sources of Hamburg's imports since 1850 (see table 7.5) and check whether at least the assumption that there was substantial exchange between the Hanse city and its smaller Danish neighbor is correct.[11] Furthermore, since it is unlikely that much butter was produced in Hamburg itself we can assume that—apart from consumption by its inhabitants—the structure of the sources of Hamburg's butter imports resembles quite closely the proximate (Altona, Lübeck) and ultimate countries of origin of the butter that was exported from Hamburg to Britain.

We see that effectively 46 percent of Hamburg's butter imports arrived from or via Altona, and almost another 20 percent arrived from places or routes that might originate in the duchies. Direct imports from Denmark are negligible, except for the war year of 1850, where they account for 3.2 percent of imports.

Unfortunately, the practice of crediting overland imports with the rail-

TABLE 7.5. The sources of Hamburg's imports, 1850–72 (%) and total imports (*zentner* of 50 kg)

	Denmark by sea	From and via Altona	From and via Lübeck	Duchies (excl. Altona)	Other Germany possibly duchies	Other Germany not duchies	Other	Total imports
1850–51	1.6	40.6	8.1	0.0	28.2	20.1	1.3	159,669
1852	0.0	55.6	1.7	0.0	25.7	16.7	0.3	142,436
1853–57	0.1	53.0	2.3	0.0	17.3	26.8	0.5	169,035
1858–62	0.0	38.8	3.9	0.0	17.7	35.1	4.5	136,917
1863–64	0.0	46.9	1.9	0.0	14.1	27.8	9.3	164,492
1865–67	0.0	41.9	7.6	1.0	13.5	34.2	1.7	168,644
1868–70	0.0	38.0	21.5	0.6	11.7	26.8	1.4	221,434
1871–72	0.0	41.5	31.9	0.0	13.2	9.7	3.6	239,977

Source: *Tabellarische Übersichten des Hamburgischen Handels* (1851–73).

Note: Data for 1864 not entered; corresponding averages refer to years with data only. "From and via Altona" comprises items "From and via Altona" and "Altona-Kiel railway." "From and via Lübeck" comprises items "From and via Lübeck," "Lübeck by cartload," "Lübeck by railway," and "Lübeck-Hamburg railway." "Duchies (excl. Altona)" refers to "Holstein by Lübeck-Hamburg railway" (listed from 1865 only, before probably included under Lübeck). "Other Germany possibly duchies" refers to places north and east of Hamburg, i.e., Harburg and Lüneburg as well as Lower Elbe and unidentified landward imports "by cartload." "Other Germany not duchies" refers to places and routes that do not require crossing Schleswig or Holstein, i.e., Upper Elbe, Hamburg-Berlin railway, East Frisia, Oldenburg, Bremen, and the Weser River and Prussian ports at the Baltic Sea. The high share of "Other" in the 1860s is due to a short-lived increase in butter imports from the United States.

road, waterway, or river port from where or on which they were consigned makes it impossible to trace the sources of imports any further. It is, however, very likely that much of the butter exported from Denmark to Altona recorded in table 7.2 ended up in Hamburg. From there, more than 75 percent of all seaward exports were shipped to Britain in the period 1845–56 for which we have export data (see table 7.6).

This exhaustive look at the available information on trade flows between Denmark, the duchies, Hamburg, and the United Kingdom presents a picture which is consistent with the traditional story of Danish trade. There was indeed a sudden shift after 1864, and butter exports before this date largely went to or through Hamburg. Whether this means that trade between Denmark and Britain before 1864 was of little importance cannot dependably be inferred from the trade statistics, however.

Nevertheless, economic historians have a second source of information to investigate whether markets were integrated or not, a source that is often more abundant than reliable trade statistics in earlier periods: commodity prices. Commodity prices are commonly used to investigate the extent of integration between distant markets, employing statistical methods ranging

TABLE 7.6. Destinations of Hamburg's seaward exports, 1845–56/1873 (%) and total seaward exports (tønder)

	Britain	Iberia	America	Other	Total
1845	69.0	21.7	7.5	1.9	29,977
1846	75.8	14.4	8.4	1.4	26,695
1847	81.9	11.7	4.8	1.7	41,020
1848	79.1	14.7	5.7	0.5	25,616
...					
1850	79.5	11.8	7.0	1.7	30,073
1851	86.0	7.0	7.0	0.0	32,952
1852	80.4	11.0	8.3	0.3	30,815
1853	85.6	6.7	7.1	0.7	36,561
1854	87.7	5.7	4.7	1.8	42,895
1855	86.1	3.8	6.8	3.2	47,160
1856	89.4	3.5	5.4	1.7	49,337
...					
1873	85.8	0.6	7.2	6.3	64,634

Source: See table 7.5.

from the calculation of coefficients of variation (to see if prices become more similar over time) to sophisticated econometric methods that decompose price variations into local (idiosyncratic), national, and international components to make price convergence at different levels visible.[12] One branch of this literature is especially suited to our question at hand: Mette Ejrnæs and Karl Gunnar Persson (2000, 2010) have introduced cointegrated vector auto-regressive models (Juselius 2006) into economic history. The idea behind this is the law of one price, which assumes that, in the absence of trade barriers, prices should be the same everywhere, and, if trade barriers exist, levels of prices might differ, but long-run equilibrium relationships should still exist to which short-run fluctuations in individual markets would revert eventually. In this sense, Ejrnæs and Persson (2000, 2010) use cointegrated VAR models to investigate the existence of long-run equilibrium relationships between time series of prices in different markets, measure the extent and speed of price adjustment between them, and, more importantly in our context, assess which market sets the prices for the other market, or, in technical terms, from where to where shocks to prices are transmitted principally. In a more technical contribution (Lampe and Sharp 2015b), we adapted this method to the three-marketplace relationship between Denmark, Hamburg, and the United Kingdom (London) and tested whether the London, Hamburg, and Copenhagen butter prices were integrated between the mid-eighteenth and the late nineteenth century. We also test which markets determined price movements

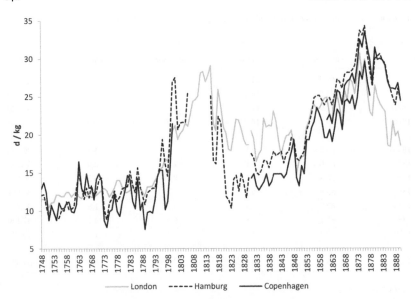

FIGURE 7.3. Prices of butter in Copenhagen, Hamburg, and London, 1748–1890
Source: See table 7.A1.

in the other markets and, to be more specific, whether prices in Copenhagen were influenced by prices in London directly or through Hamburg.

To do this, we divide our analysis into three periods determined to some extent by the availability and consistency of series of annual butter prices. The series used and their sources are detailed in appendix table 7.A1, and the raw data is illustrated in figure 7.3. Our first period is from 1748 to 1800, followed by a second period from 1831–60. Given the war, the years between 1861 and 1864 were very noisy and had a large impact on the estimation results we calculate below. This is consistent with there being a structural break at this time and implies that we cannot analyze the two periods at once, since the model we employ assumes constant parameters. We chose to start our last period in 1865, the year after the loss of the duchies, and extend it to 1890. While these three time periods allow for more appropriate econometric model specifications, the relatively short time series employed unfortunately also imply that we have relatively few observations and thus the results should be considered merely indicative. Clearly, more frequent data would solve this problem, but none are available.

What is clearly visible from figure 7.3 is the apparent synchronization, at least in levels, of the prices not only in Hamburg and Copenhagen but also in London already before 1800, although this impression might be exaggerated by the joint price increase during the Napoleonic Wars. The similar level of prices can have two basic reasons: (1) actual market integration and (2) similar productivity in all places, which even without trade would lead to similar prices. Since all three cities are in northwestern Europe, even joint short-run (yearly) fluctuations might have their origin in similar weather or in the actual arbitrage between markets with differential development of prices. After the Napoleonic Wars, prices seem to decrease much faster in Hamburg and in Copenhagen (although the Hamburg and London price series from different sources before and after 1830 also show different levels, and no usable price data exists for Copenhagen between 1800 and 1830) than in London before a resynchronization of levels and trends occurs from some point after 1840. However, since the British and the Danish series do not strictly refer to the same product (only in the very late 1870s did Danish butter become regularly quoted in the London Provisions Market reports; see Lampe and Sharp 2014a) and given that none of our series is consistent over the whole period, visual inspection is not the most reliable way of assessing market integration. Fortunately, we can go beyond visually observing general trends and conduct a more formal analysis through simple multivariate error correction models using the annual prices as described above, the results of which can be found in an appendix to this chapter. Such an analysis also allows us to assess the direction of influence between prices if it exists in a consistent way, something that would not be systematically observable if similarity in prices was caused by similar productivity and weather.

In a nutshell, these results present three sets of findings. The first is that markets were systematically integrated in all three periods—that is, already in the eighteenth century, in the period between 1830 and 1860, and from 1865 to 1890. About the periods in between, especially 1800 to 1830, which looks like market disintegration in figure 7.3, little can be said due to the lack of continuous series for Copenhagen and Hamburg. The period 1860 to 1864, as mentioned above, turned out to be problematic because adding it to the period before or to the period after affected the precision of estimates. It clearly was a period of change.

This leads to our second result, which is that our assumption that the London prices are exogenous to Hamburg and Copenhagen prices—that is, that Britain is in macroeconomic terms a large economy, whereas Hamburg and Copenhagen are (relatively) small (and price takers)—is confirmed by our econometric analysis. Furthermore, we find that in both periods before 1860, London prices drove Hamburg prices, which drove Copenhagen prices—that is, price transmission was directly from London to Hamburg but only indirectly from London to Copenhagen *via* Hamburg. The results for both 1750 to 1800 and 1830 to 1860 are strikingly similar in both periods, which suggests strongly to us that trade from Denmark went to England via Hamburg, as the literature suggests, and that this mattered for price formation in Denmark. For the period from 1865, however, the transmission was now directly from London to *both* Hamburg and Copenhagen, with no link between Copenhagen and Hamburg.[13]

A third result is that, for the last period, our analysis indicates that Danish butter prices were systematically higher than those in London (something that can also be guessed from figure 7.3), so that the export of Danish butter to Britain (and not that of cheaper British or Irish butter to Denmark) would only make sense if Danish butter enjoyed a significant premium over the Irish butter, whose prices we use as London prices. Since consistent series of actual prices of Danish butter in London are difficult to obtain before the late 1870s, this makes it difficult to assess, in terms of lower transaction costs, how much was gained by Danish producers by trading directly compared to trading via Hamburg. If prices for the same variety in different markets are used in the analysis, changes in the systematic price difference would be informative of changes in transaction costs if there is market integration and the law of one price holds, as our first result indicates. We thus must take a different approach to gauge the reduction in transaction costs. For this, we use two London and Copenhagen price series that are consistent between 1831 and 1870 (but in case of the Copenhagen series do not exist for later years) as illustrated in figure 7.4.

Although the prices follow similar short-run fluctuations, consistent with market integration over the whole period, there is a clear break in the gap between London and Copenhagen prices before and after the early 1860s (the very end of the period depicted in figure 7.4). Between 1856 and 1860, butter was on average 2.1 British pence per kilogram more expensive in London than in Copenhagen, while in 1865–69 the difference decreased to 1.0 pence per kilogram. As a proportion of the London butter price, this meant a decrease in the price gap from 8.5 percent to 4.0 percent. Note that, since we are not comparing like with like, the decline of the price gap by more than 50 percent is rather more informative than the absolute values. We do not find it reasonable, given the shaky data, to attempt to calculate deadweight losses in the style of Federico (2008) and Federico and Sharp (2013). Nevertheless, the potential savings from such a massive fall in the price gap, when accumulated over years and decades, would no doubt be huge.

All in all, we feel that the available information from both quantities and prices strongly supports the story that Danish markets were initially inte-

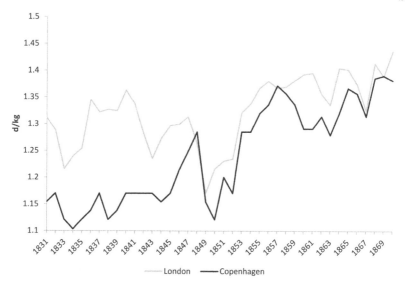

FIGURE 7.4. Copenhagen market prices and Irish prices in London for butter, 1831–70
Source: Data from Drejer (1925–33) and Klovland and Solar (2011).

grated with Britain through Hamburg prior to 1864 but integrated directly subsequently. Having demonstrated this, we now proceed to attempt to answer the two main questions posed in the introduction: Why did Denmark initially trade through Hamburg? And when and how did this move toward a direct trade with the UK?

To answer these questions, it is necessary to gain insight into three key aspects of the butter trade: the supply of dairy products, especially butter, in Denmark; demand for these products in Britain; and the services of buying, transporting, financing, and distribution between both points. Before turning to the link between Britain and Denmark, and the dependency on the Altona/Hamburg hub, we therefore look briefly at the demand in Britain and then turn to the early development of the Danish dairy industry.

The Demand Side

The industrial revolution had a huge impact on the demand for foodstuffs in Britain and thus also on the demand for butter. On the one hand, between 1760 and around 1840, the population of Britain (excluding Ireland) grew from about 5.7 to 14.9 million, at an annual rate of about 1.2 percent (Wrigley 2004, 64). Most of this population growth fueled the increasing urbaniza-

TABLE 7.7. Duties on Danish produce, 1825–97

	Butter	Cheese	Beef	Pork	Live oxen and bulls
1825–42	£1 / cwt	10.5s. / cwt	Prohibited*	Prohibited*	Prohibited
1842–46	£1 / cwt	10.5s. / cwt	8s. / cwt	8s. / cwt; bacon & ham: 14s. / cwt	£1 / head
1846–53	10s. / cwt	5s. / cwt	Free	Free	Free
1853–60	5s. / cwt	2.5s. / cwt	Free	Free	Free
1860–97	Free	Free	Free	Free	Free

Source: BPP (1897).

Note: cwt = 50.8 kg.

* Prohibition lifted for heavily salted beef and pork from 1827.

tion rate of the country and especially the growth of the industrial centers in northern England. On the other hand, real wages grew very little over this same period (R. C. Allen 2007, 2009b).[14] After 1840, population growth continued, but important improvements in living standards are also observed, which led to an increased per capita demand for luxury fats, like those contained in butter.[15] This, in turn, led to a long-term increase in both absolute and relative prices (in comparison to other foodstuffs like grains) of butter and related dairy products in Britain, as illustrated in chapter 1.

As shown in table 7.7, this price trend was reinforced by relatively high specific tariffs for butter and related products in Britain, one pound sterling per hundredweight (cwt) between 1825 and 1846, reduced to ten shillings in 1846, five shillings in 1853, and finally abolished in 1860. In ad valorem terms, this was equivalent to a 20–25 percent tariff before 1846, based on Clark's butter prices described above, falling to 8–9 percent just before the repeal of the butter tariff. As a consequence of this relatively high tariff rate, the British market was largely reserved for Irish produce, which originated within the United Kingdom and was therefore duty-free. As can be seen in figure 7.5, its share was above 60 percent in all years until 1854, in many years even higher than 75 percent. As we have already seen above, Danish produce (identified as such in the trade statistics) played virtually no role until the mid-1860s. But remember that this graph does not account for trade via Altona/Hamburg.

As with the repeal of the Corn Laws, the sequence of reductions in the butter duties after 1846 can probably be seen as a consequence of the increase in demand for butter, especially in the growing industrial centers, and an increase in prices due to the protection of producers who could not cope with the increasing demand. Hence, at least in part, the opening of the British market after 1846 and the related access to its burgeoning demand should explain

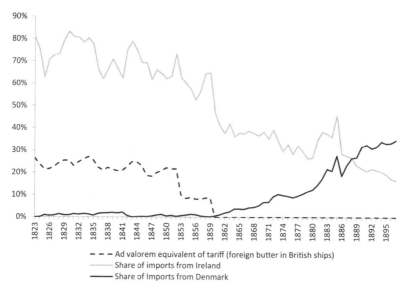

FIGURE 7.5. Shares of imports to Britain from Denmark and Ireland, and ad valorem equivalents of the British tariff on foreign butter, 1823–97
Source: Data on tariff duties from BPP (1897); data on prices from Clark (2004); for data on trade shares, see table 7.4 and Lampe and Sharp (2014a).

the relatively low exports of Danish produce to the United Kingdom prior to the reduction of UK duties on imported butter, even if the real numbers were disguised by the trade via Hamburg.[16]

The Supply Side

On the other side of the North Sea, Denmark had a long history of cattle exports, mainly from Jutland to Holland on the famous Ox Road connecting Viborg via Flensburg to Hamburg. This trade was important since the sixteenth century and came to be dominated by Dutch traders from the second half of the seventeenth century (Ladewig Petersen 1970, 84). Its importance was gradually reduced at the end of the eighteenth century, however, due to the protectionist policies of the Dutch and Danish authorities, as well as serious outbreaks of cattle plague (Appel and Bredkjær 1924–32, 250–69; Hünniger 2010, 79). From then, the Danish oxen trade became more centered on the duchies of Schleswig and Holstein, but cattle raising and fattening seems to have shown a declining trend into the 1800s (Appel and Bredkjær 1924–32, 270–71, 284; Graugaard 2006), as discussed in previous chapters.

Despite our finding of market integration from the 1750s, in the 1700s export dairying is in general not considered to have been an important activity for Danish agriculture. According to the literature, Danish estates remained reluctant to follow the conversion to dairying long under way in the Netherlands (Appel and Bredkjær 1924–32, 279–80; Ladewig Petersen 1970, 84–85). The only trade in butter at this time mentioned in the literature was imports from Holland to Copenhagen, and in the late eighteenth century occasional imports from Britain (Appel and Bredkjær 1924–32, 565; Drejer 1962, 20–21, citing Pontoppidan 1763–81).[17] However, as we have seen in previous chapters, a steady increase in the interest in dairy production has been observed over the eighteenth century (Appel and Bredkjær 1924–32, 284). Even before Moltke's introduction of *Koppelwirtschaft* at Sofiendal, for example, an early report on the advanced Schleswig and Holstein dairy sector was translated into Danish from German in the periodical *Oeconomisk Journal* in 1757 under the title "Underretning om Hollænderierne udi Hertugdømmerne Slesvig og Holsteen" (Report on the *hollænderier* in the duchies of Schleswig and Holstein; Appel and Bredkjær 1924–32, 281). On the islands of Zealand, Funen, and Langeland, apparently butter production was important on some estates but only very occasionally export-oriented, with a focus on the Copenhagen market.[18] As we have shown in chapter 4, however, from the 1760s, the Holstein system spread into Denmark and with it a rather quick diffusion of dairying on large estates took place. Dairying remained in competition with cattle fattening as an alternative use of the same resources, although estate privileges and receipts of labor and in-kind rents (to use as fodder) decreased as the agricultural reforms progressed (see chapter 3).

That Danish dairying—not only in production arrangements but also in marketing—followed the standards set by the duchies becomes once again evident from the travel accounts of Johann Georg Kohl (1846). He observed that export production of butter, very much adapted to the English market in product characteristics and packaging, had emerged since about 1820 in the duchies and was already (and probably once again) spreading toward northern Jutland and the islands of Denmark. His prediction that Denmark and the duchies would eventually integrate as a land not of milk and honey but of milk and butter is particularly interesting in the context of the supposed 1864 discontinuity. More important in the context of trade, however, is his description of how trade connections from the 1820s had promoted quality improvements in the butter of Holstein so that it could compete with Irish and Dutch butter and that these improvements in production and hygiene were undertaken explicitly to satisfy English tastes—the English being a "peculiar people who want everything according to their mind and according to whose command and impulse in our national economies of Continental

Europe more things are being reformed and changed than we generally notice." Kohl explains that the firkins used for transporting the butter mimicked Irish standards in size and shape, although certain larger estates added their own mark to the firkins and already had a "very good" reputation in Britain (63–69).[19]

Kohl highlighted the (renewed) rapid diffusion of the related practices into Denmark, largely through hiring (female) dairy workers from the duchies. He stressed, in consonance with our account in chapter 4 based on the Danish county descriptions, that by then many farms in Jutland had switched from oxen raising to dairying. Important articles on dairying from the duchies were reprinted all over Denmark (58–60). Danish accounts looking back at this period from the late nineteenth and early twentieth centuries stress that some Danish estates already produced high-quality Holstein/Kiel butter by the 1840s (Hollmann 1906, 3). For example, Edward Tesdorpf recalled in 1887 that he acquired Orupgaard in 1840 and started to export butter from the island of Falster to Hamburg soon afterward, assisted by his father, who was a merchant. He remarked that his butter was mixed with Holstein and Schleswig butter at that time, entering the marketing channels for that produce (Rützou 1887, 293).

For this early period, butter traders mostly made long-term contracts, buying the whole production for fixed prices and distinguishing between summer and winter produce (Rützou 1887, 283–84). Danish merchant houses, especially the provincial merchants Boje (1977) studied for the period 1815–47, showed some concentration among a selected group of traders on certain commodities, mostly grains, but without the emergence of fully specialized grocers (96–100). He discusses the cases of individual merchants, the most interesting of which for us is probably Samuel Cohn from Ringkøbing in Jutland, whose exports were concentrated on butter (53.7 percent), wool (22.7 percent), and hides and skins (18.7 percent) (96). Cohn had important business contacts in Amsterdam, where most of his wool went, and in Altona, on which much of his other trade, including butter, was centered. Both in Amsterdam and Altona, larger merchant houses—Siepmann Peltersen and C. H. Donner, respectively—were acting as Cohn's commission agents and effectively financing his export trade. C. H. Donner was the only Altona-based merchant house among the leading Hamburg merchant bankers, its owner Conrad Hinrich Donner being a banker and personal friend of Danish king Christian VIII (Böhme 1968, 80; Marchtaler 1959). These merchants then acted as wholesale traders and reexporters to their counterparts in other markets and provided Cohn with the commodities he imported into Denmark (Boje 1977, 88–95). From the Netherlands this was mostly tobacco, while from Altona/Hamburg Cohn imported all sorts of industrial and colonial goods, especially tobacco, coffee, sugar, and manufactured commodities like cotton yarn, clothes, and (linen) canvas (119). The Danish shipping firm A. Berthelsen served as the link between Cohn and the foreign markets (88–95). Within Denmark, Cohn was a large provincial merchant who obtained his export commodities from a series of local merchants (142–46), producers, and peddlers who bought up local peasant production and mixed it to make transportation into the market towns profitable (155–60).

Thus, in total, for the export of Danish butter to Britain, we would observe at least six or seven middlemen between producer and consumer (see also Hollmann 1906). Together with the cost of transportation via Hamburg and Altona, this might help explain the large price differentials between butter in London and Copenhagen we observed above, and thus motivates the return to one of our central questions: why did Denmark trade via Altona and Hamburg?

Hamburg as a Trading Hub

To answer the above question we can note, in the first place, that transportation routes were geared toward Hamburg. The main routes Danish butter would have taken would be through the Baltic Sea or via the North Sea. On the Baltic Sea, exports were mainly by ship to Kiel and from there to Hamburg via the Eider Canal or overland on roads; in 1844, the first railway in Greater Denmark was opened between Kiel and Altona. On the North Sea, direct shipping from ports in western Jutland would be the main choice. As to the relative use of these means, relatively little can be said due to the absence of trade statistics for the free port of Altona. However, a glimpse is given in a pamphlet by J. Eduard Weber (1853) that contains a collection of Altona shipping and trade statistics for 1852. Among these, the reception of a total of 3,858 tons (about 287 metric tons), 10,400 packages, 7 barrels, and 9 collies of butter is mentioned (app. 2, iv). Of the tons, two-thirds entered by sea, and one-third via the Altona-Kiel railway.[20] In a different table (41), the seaward transport from Danish ports into Altona of butter, thirty ships with a total load of 286.5 *last* (load, so relatively unspecific), is mentioned. Of this total load, 211 (73.6 percent) had arrived from Denmark proper and most of the rest from Schleswig. After "diverse commodities," butter was in quantity terms the most salient import from Denmark proper via sea, twice as large as imports of barley. While it is difficult to extract precise weights from these numbers, it seems that Danish butter exports to Altona in 1852 were mostly by ship, but the railroads might also have transported a substantial share.[21]

As a second aspect, reaching beyond the specific marketing channels for butter, Hamburg's relatively beneficial financial and economic situation after the Napoleonic Wars needs to be considered. Hamburg had also been severely hit by the continental blockade, but, contrary to the Danish experience, British merchants relatively quickly invested in the city when trade recovered after the war in order to revive their main distribution hub for northern and central European markets (via the Elbe River). At this time, both Copenhagen and Danish provincial merchants became dependent on credit and financing from Hamburg's merchant bankers to the extent that the new Danish currency, the rigsbankdaler, which emerged from the state bankruptcy and currency crisis in 1813, was pegged to Hamburg's mark banco. Thus, the triangular relationship Denmark-Hamburg/Altona-Britain, exemplified by merchant Cohn above, was typical in Danish trade in the 1810s to 1840s (S. A. Hansen 1984, 112–16). Also, the Danish merchant fleet and its shipping activity, particularly for Copenhagen, had declined very much as a consequence of the Napoleonic Wars. From a shipping point of view, contemporaries also stressed the pernicious effects of the Sound Toll on the development of Denmark's most important port, Copenhagen, which gave an additional advantage to the Hamburg/Altona hub on the North Sea (C. K. Hansen 1956, 9–10).

Summing up, in a time of economic crisis in Denmark, from which the country only slowly recovered over the 1820s and 1830s, Hamburg and Altona provided the services of a hub that offered regular shipping connections, finance, and volume of transactions with Britain in a period when, due to the protection of both grain and butter, access to the British market was relatively uncertain and costly.

Changing Incentives to Establish a Direct Trade with the United Kingdom

This situation seems to have changed gradually when British grain and butter tariffs were lowered and import prohibitions on live cattle were lifted from the mid-1840s. At this time, the Danish economy was also recovering from the war, the currency had stabilized, credit constraints were overcome, and the spread of modern dairying was under way. In this context, the Danish merchant fleet and direct shipping to and from England increased rapidly. Until the 1830s, this mostly involved exports of Danish grain, especially barley, and imports of coal from Britain (A. M. Møller 1998, 63–65).[22] Then, the lifting of the British cattle import ban in 1842 produced occasional direct trade—for example, when the English steamer *Tønning* collected a hundred steers for London (93)—although private initiative was not sufficient to sustain a direct connection from Jutland in those years (Poulsen 1851a, 1851b), in part due to a transportation infrastructure that was still in development in this relatively sparsely populated part of Denmark.[23]

Nevertheless, when the British writer Laing traveled around the duchies and into Denmark proper in 1851, he noted how steamships from Glasgow united the duchies and the kingdom, so that, for example, "the passage from Kiel to Copenhagen, which was formerly a voyage of six or seven days, is now performed regularly in twelve hours" (Laing 1852, 291). However, as we have seen above, the First Schleswig War (1848–51), which blocked the connection to Altona and much of the internal transport integration highlighted by Laing, inaugurated further initiatives for direct trade with Britain, among which direct trade in live cattle from Jutland (which usually traveled to slaughterhouses in Hamburg for reexport to the United Kingdom) was a main concern that found backing by the Danish government. Thus, in the 1848–51 period the Danish government helped to establish a steamship connection between Hjerting (near Esbjerg in southwest Jutland) and London (Appel and Bredkjær 1924–32, 566; Drejer 1962, 26). In the following years, the steamship *Jylland* connected several points on the Jutland peninsula to London. However, the initiative was stopped in 1855 and the steamship sold. The main problems seem to have been the difficulty of loading cattle without specialized harbor facilities, the lack of cargo for the return voyage from London, and possibly adaptation costs to British demand and distribution structures. The government therefore decided to leave the business to private entrepreneurs (Appel and Bredkjær 1924–32, 566; K. C. Lassen 1883, 384–85).[24]

Although we cannot say with certainty that butter was ever transported on this route, it is evident that by the late 1840s the technical and organizational means to establish direct trade with Britain were in place. However, our trade data suggest that the sudden reorientation of 1848–51 had entailed transaction costs that in peacetime exceeded those of the continued use of the Altona/Hamburg hub, leading to a certain return to the old pattern in the immediate postwar years. However, as the development of Danish production, shipping, and trading continued through the 1850s, new, private initiatives surfaced; these would be later reinforced—although certainly not initiated—by the Second Schleswig War.

As much as the Second Schleswig War (1864) is seen as a defining moment in Danish history, the traditional account of the rise of the dairy industry focuses very much on the visible increase in exports after 1864. The standard textbook account by Svend Aage Hansen (1984, 187) attributes the breakthrough of Danish exports of butter and pork in the 1860s to the expansion of transportation facilities, especially the decision in 1868 to establish a major harbor in Esbjerg on the west coast of Jutland to obviate the use of Altona and

Hamburg. However, this harbor was fully operational only in 1874. We argue that a number of events that coincided and cumulated over a longer period before and after 1864 were instrumental in making the Hamburg trade less attractive and favored the establishment of direct trade. The visible outcome was the opening of new direct steamship routes and the increasing involvement of both Danish and British merchants, who supplied the services previously provided by those in Hamburg. Besides the increase in Danish supply and British demand for dairy products stressed above, we see four major factors that enabled more effective private initiative in the 1850s and 1860s.

First, the Sound Toll, which for centuries had been a mainstay of Danish government finances, was capitalized and abolished in 1857 after pressure from the United States. This instantly made access to Copenhagen less expensive for ships sailing from the North Sea and through the Kattegat, thus changing its attractiveness relative to Hamburg for exports to Britain (C. K. Hansen 1956, 10). This reinforced the increase in trade and transportation between England and Scotland and the Baltic and the role of Copenhagen as a stop-off point. In 1857 three steamers (the *L. N. Hvidt*, *Thor*, and *Odin*) were circulating between England (Grimsby) and the Baltic, carrying coal and other cargo from Britain, products from the Baltic Sea, as well as passengers (emigrants) for Cornelius Peter August Koch's General Danish Steamship Company of Copenhagen (see Vestberg 1933, 22–23), one of the constituent companies of the later shipping giant DFDS (A. M. Møller 1998, 94). Other initiatives were in preparation, for example C. K. Hansen's negotiations with the Leith Hull & Hamborg Steam Packet Company for a regular connection to Leith in Scotland. These failed at first but were successful in the early 1860s, after James Currie took over the Scottish company in 1862 (C. K. Hansen 1956, 24). This would become central to the story, as detailed below.

Second, as can be seen above, the British import tariffs on butter and other agricultural and livestock commodities fell considerably during the 1850s and were finally abolished in 1860, although imports of livestock were later banned under the Contagious Disease (Animals) Act of 1869.

Third, the commercial and credit crisis of 1857 hit Hamburg and Altona merchant bankers particularly hard. After spreading through the United States and to London, in November it had reached Hamburg—at that time the trade and finance hub between London, the German hinterland, Denmark, and Sweden, (Ahrens 1978, 6–8; Böhme 1968, 88–89). In Hamburg, due to the lack of public paper money, a partly dubious chain of bills of exchange had led to a strong increase in credit and money in circulation, which suffered a sudden stop in liquidity and interbank transactions when the crisis arrived. Several private and public-private joint incentives to guarantee bills of exchange and stabilize the central merchant-banking houses failed (Ahrens 1978, 10–22; Böhme 1968, 86–98) before a loan of 100 million mark banco in silver from the Vienna Staatsbank, provided via the Austrian government, was used to back and recapitalize five key merchant houses, among them C. H. Donner of Altona (Böhme 1968, 94, 99–101; Ahrens 1978, 22–26). Although the crisis was mostly solved by late December 1857, international trust in the Hamburg currency and the functioning of the Hamburg credit market was considerably reduced, and, in consequence, Hamburg lost a large part of its role as trading and financial hub to London (Böhme 1968, 102–4). As Danish connections with the United Kingdom increased, merchants could thus increasingly look to London for services which had previously been provided by Hamburg.

Fourth, other trading costs were of course also falling as the first era of globalization proceeded. In particular, the telegraph made information much more readily available. In the Danish case, the first international connection was to Hamburg/Altona and opened in 1854. In 1855 Denmark was connected to Norway and in 1860 to England. Although the war of 1864 meant that the telegraph connection to England fell into the hands of Prussia, the Danish government soon granted a concession for a new connection to the Danish financier, C. F. Tietgen, who went on to found the Great Northern Telegraph Company (Jacobsen 2003, 201–2). This reduced information costs considerably and freed the flow of information from the flow of physical transport, whose density in the 1860s was still higher in Hamburg than anywhere in Denmark. Moreover, we have already emphasized the importance of steam shipping, which was gradually replacing sail technology over this period. As is also apparent from the quote by Laing above, over shorter routes steam shipping offered advantages in terms of cost and reliability, particularly early on (Harley 1971; Hornby and Nilsson 1980).

At this time, both foreign observers and Danish entrepreneurs had taken note of the potential of the butter trade to Britain. British vice-consul Rainals summarized the situation in a report in 1860. He described how "Denmark cannot lay claim to be considered a commercial country as the term is usually understood." Tellingly, however, he noted that Denmark was well positioned to enjoy a trade with England and suggested making a harbor for direct export, thus avoiding the Hamburg middlemen (Rainals 1860, 273–74), a point also made by another contemporary British commentator, John Wilson (1867, 81–82). At the same time, Rainals's report clearly shows that the vast majority of Danish dairy produce still needed to achieve a higher quality to be ready for exportation.[25] He stressed the "inferior quality" of most peasant produce and described their butter as "execrably bad . . . strongly salted with the commonest salt, whilst in its preparation so little regard is paid to the proper extraction of the whey or even to cleanliness that it appears strange that such produce can find a sale." Other foreign observers like the Italian Pietrocòla-Rossetti and the Frenchman Tisserand, both writing in the mid-1860s, noted similar things, also stressing that Denmark consumed and produced much butter (Tisserand 1865, 15–16) and that there was "very good milk and excellent butter" available (Pietrocòla-Rossetti 1864, 256).

The Final Push for Regular Connections to the United Kingdom

A group of Danish merchants, shipping entrepreneurs, and estate owners like Edward Tesdorpf focused on producing high-quality Danish butter, working simultaneously and sometimes jointly on its improvement, marketability, and export. They thereby provided the incentives for quality improvement of the majority of butter produced. They also created the possibility to earn profits by selling butter outside Denmark by reducing transaction costs and the number of middlemen and their share in the value added. Here we mention a few of the most important.

Philip Wulff Heyman (1837–93),[26] who later cofounded the Tuborg brewery in 1873, started his business career with a firm selling butter to Britain a couple of years after its foundation in 1858. In 1864 he was the first to pack butter in cans for export, and in 1866 he cofounded Københavns Svineslagteri (Copenhagen's Pig Slaughterhouse) (Meyer 1916). His butter export firm was pathbreaking for exports to the United Kingdom and primarily supplied canned butter to troops. He was followed by Johan Martin Christoffer Ankerstjerne in Randers and Hans Broge in Aarhus, and these merchants were key in promoting the sort of quality improvements in dairying which later were to allow the cooperative movement such a successful entrance to the market in the 1880s (S. A. Hansen 1984, 190). Broge was particularly involved in promoting butter exhibitions in Danish provincial towns, including, as we mentioned in the previous chapter, the first exhibition of winter butter (Dybdahl 1946–47, 73). Valentiner, the owner of the Gjeddesdal estate near Copenhagen, appeared in this context as an enthusiastic advocate of the establishment of centralized *fællesmejerier* (proprietary creameries, which we will return to in chapter 9) in every village. The *fællesmejerier* would promote uniform-quality butter production and packing, raising the quality of peasant butter beyond the taste and smell described by Vice-Consul Rainals (Dybdahl 1946–47, 87; Andresen 1992, 15).

Another pioneering merchant in Denmark was Gunni Busck Jr. (see Hertel 1889, 264–65), who entered the tinned-butter trade in the early 1870s and established the Scandinavian Preserved Butter Company in 1874, exporting canned butter, again primarily to troops (Brix 1924, 22). He founded the first private creamery in Denmark, Slagelse Mejeri, in 1875, and he also helped found *Københavns mælkeforsyning* (Copenhagen Milk Supply) in 1877 to supply the city with fresh milk for drinking (Brix 1924, 24–27).

A final important figure in this story of increasing Danish competence in foreign trade and shipping was the merchant Christian Kjellerup Hansen, who had started his own trading company in 1856. He first dealt in salt and coal for British steamships on their return voyage from the Baltic (C. K. Hansen 1956, 15). With the increasing shipping activity, he soon provided those same ships with Danish and Swedish agricultural produce that included grains, flour, feedstuffs, spirits, and butter (17, 20).

As we have seen before, in 1859 C. K. Hansen tried unsuccessfully to establish a regular steamship connection between Copenhagen and Leith in Scotland. Also, in 1859, he acquired the steamship *El Ole*, built in Newcastle, to establish a regular steamship connection to that port. However, this initiative also seems to have been unsuccessful. Hansen tried to sell the ship soon afterward, although it took until 1872 to finish the sale. The ship was then mostly used for passenger traffic between Copenhagen and northern Zealand (C. K. Hansen 1956, 18, 37). In 1863, just before the Second Schleswig War, Hansen finally reached agreement with the James Currie and Company steamship company for a connection to Leith; he established the first regular steamship connection to Newcastle in the same year and, in 1872, to Hull (18).[27] The new routes from Copenhagen to Leith, negotiated by Hansen personally, started on July 15, 1863, from Leith. The trips were made by two steamships, *Snowdoun* and *Gnome*, and were announced in the Danish press every day (C. K. Hansen 1956, 22–26, 35).

Based on this account, it is difficult to argue that the war was the only reason for the refocus away from Hamburg. The loss of the duchies did, however, reinforce the interest in the direct connection to Britain among Danish farmers (Bech 1865) and brought back to memory the experiences with the connection from Jutland in the early 1850s (Boye 1865). Thus, in the spring of 1865, C. K. Hansen and Tesdorpf, as president of the Royal Agricultural Society, agreed on conditions for live cattle transports starting the same year from Copenhagen, which subsequently were extended to Aarhus and to Nyborg on Funen (C. K. Hansen 1956, 24, 27).

In subsequent accounts, this was presented as the real start of commercial reorientation, for which Tesdorpf and the Royal Agricultural Society took and received large credit, although their main contribution had been to negotiate and promote live cattle exports (Rützou 1887, 283–84; K. C. Lassen 1883, 386; Appel and Bredkjær 1924–32, 567–68). This promotion involved a widely publicized speech by Tesdorpf (1856) at the Royal Agricultural Society in spring 1865, which highlighted that this new connection presented a general change for Danish agriculture in which the large farmers should forge ahead despite considerable potential sunk costs of market exploration. The discussion following Tesdorpf's speech (244–50) exhibits an increased awareness among leading Danish farmers and agricultural experts of the link between the quality and exportability of produce to the British market. The Royal Agricultural Society also contributed to decrease uncertainty by deploying observers on every single voyage until the fall of 1866; observers' short reports on the trip and market conditions in Leith were published in agricultural periodicals (Westring 1866). Hansen's company continued to publish weekly market reports from Leith and other destinations in Britain in the leading Danish newspapers *Berlingske Tidende* and *Dagstelegrafen* through the late 1860s (C. K. Hansen 1956, 27), and the weekly *UfL* contained regular reports from Leith into the 1870s.

As a consequence, by 1870 export merchants had an important presence on the Copenhagen market and demanded high-quality butter—not only for the aforementioned trade in tinned butter (Schmidt 1870, 533–35). The focus on direct butter exports to Britain had also rapidly spread to Jutland, to Odense on Funen (where a Scottish merchant had established a business), to Lolland-Falster, and thus the whole Kingdom of Denmark (Schmidt 1870, 535–36). Most of the exports continued to go to Scotland and northern England, but in winter, when Ireland and the Netherlands produced little butter, Danish exports reached the London market as well. This provided a clear indication of the early spread of winter production of high-quality butter in Denmark (Schmidt 1870), one of the factors identified as the basis for Danish success in later years (Henriksen and O'Rourke 2005). These early developments meant that Danish butter was already well known in the United Kingdom long before the cooperatives came onto the scene to exploit this in the 1880s (Dybdahl 1946–47, 100).

In conclusion, in this chapter we have quantified as far as possible what we can know about the early Danish trade in butter. We have disputed the traditional story of how Denmark saw new horizons after 1864, and we have demonstrated that—although the pattern of trade shifted decisively after this date—the origins go back further.

The importance of the British market was established from the early nineteenth century, and markets were integrated even before this. Initially this trade went primarily through the Hamburg hub because it paid to do so. Changes in the viability of the port of Copenhagen, UK tariff policy, and falling transportation and information costs began to change this already in the 1850s, when direct steamship connections with Britain were established. These were in part promoted by the same elites we have discussed until now, but they were joined by a growing merchant class looking for new markets and high-quality produce with which to supply them.

Certainly the war provided an extra stimulus to these developments, but they were already well under way. As we will see in future chapters, once the importance of the British market became established, Danish producers and authorities would continue to react—for example, by improving hygiene standards after criticism by British observers and by clearly and favorably distinguishing butter from the emerging substitute, margarine. This reconsideration and continuity might be a blow to the Danish national story, but a positive view might be that it was the hard work and vision of many great Danes—not sudden soul searching after defeat in war—that brought about the transformation of the economy that was to lead to the rapid and successful development of Denmark.

This example demonstrates the potential benefits for developing countries of escaping established dependency on a strong trade hub to bring home the high-value-added part of the export trade. However, it also provides a warning: path dependency and established networks can make the costs of such a shift very high indeed; in the present case it required a war to take the decisive leap. The policy implication might then be that foreign aid could be directed toward establishing adequate credit and trading institutions and facilities in developing countries, even though this might be at the expense of developed-world hubs and clusters. We expect the real relevance to lie principally not in transport and port infrastructure but in augmented domestic capacities for direct market discovery, in the facilitation of contacts and networks that enable the dissemination of relevant information on specific demand in foreign markets, and in the creation of direct links that join domestic producers and distributors with potential foreign importers.

Appendix A: Sources for Annual Price Series

TABLE 7.A1. Sources for annual price series

Period	Denmark	Hamburg	London
1748–1800	Copenhagen Price Current, July 1 (Friis and Glamann 1958, 261–78), Funen butter	Hamburg Price Current (Gerhard, Kaufhold, and Engel 2001, 56–57); mainly Holstein butter	Homogenized series by Clark (2004)
1831–60	Københavns Torvepriser (Copenhagen Market prices; Drejer 1925–33, 323)	(Jakobs and Richter 1935), benchmarked to 1904 Hamburg top quotation from Fick (1907, 21)	London Provisions Market (Klovland and Solar 2011), Limerick and Waterford butter
1865–90	Berlingske Tidende quotation (Drejer 1925–33, 326); manor top quotation (1865–78); Copenhagen Brokers' Current (Henriksen and O'Rourke 2005); Finest/Prima Manor (1879–90)	As previous period	As previous period

Note: We always use the highest price if a range is given; when weekly or monthly prices are available, we average the first quotation in June, August, October, and December as yearly average, following Klovland and Solar (2011). All prices converted to British pence per kg, with exchange rates from Friis and Glamann (1958, 78–103) and Denzel (2010, 191–94, 207–13) for the eighteenth century, and mint parities—18.16 Danish kroner and 20.43 German marks per pound sterling—for the nineteenth century. More detailed comments on the Danish series 1831–90 available in Lampe and Sharp (2014b).

Appendix B: Econometric Estimates

For the periods 1748–1800 and 1831–60, we estimate the following vector error correction model by maximum likelihood using PcGive 13 (Doornik and Hendry 2009):

$$
(1) \quad \begin{pmatrix} \Delta p_t^1 \\ \Delta p_t^2 \\ \Delta p_t^3 \end{pmatrix} = \begin{pmatrix} \alpha^1 & 0 \\ 0 & \alpha^2 \\ 0 & 0 \end{pmatrix} + \begin{pmatrix} 1 - \beta^a p_{t-1}^2 - t - \lambda \\ 1 - \beta^b p_{t-1}^3 - t - \lambda \end{pmatrix} + \begin{pmatrix} \varepsilon_t^1 \\ \varepsilon_t^2 \\ \varepsilon_t^3 \end{pmatrix}
$$

where p_t^1, p_t^2, and p_t^3 are the logarithms to the prices of Copenhagen, Hamburg, and London butter respectively, $\alpha 1$ and $\alpha 2$ describe the speed of adjustment (error correction) to the cointegrating relationships $(1 - \beta^a p_{t-1}^2 - t - \lambda)$ and $(1 - \beta^b p_{t-1}^3 - t - \lambda)$, the β-coefficients give the elasticities, t is a trend, and λ is a constant. The residuals ε_t^1, ε_t^2, and ε_t^3 are assumed to be iid normally distributed (the misspecification tests are reported in the appendix to Lampe and Sharp 2014c). In each case we included two lags, which were the minimum found necessary to avoid autocorrelation in the residuals. The results are given in

TABLE 7.A2. Error correction estimates, 1748–1800 and 1831–60

	(1a) 1748–1800 Danish (Funen in Cph) [P_1] Hamburg [P_2] London (Clark) [P_3]			(1b) 1831–60 Danish (Copenhagen) [P_1] Hamburg [P_2] London (K&S) [P_3]		
	ΔP_1	ΔP_2	ΔP_3	ΔP_1	ΔP_2	ΔP_3
α_a	−1.01***	0	0	−1.05***	0	0
	(0.16)	—	—	(0.22)	—	—
α_b	0	−0.57***	0	0	−0.59***	0
	—	(0.09)	—	—	(0.11)	—
	[a] (Hamburg → Denmark)	[b] (London → Hamburg)		[a] (Hamburg → Denmark)	[b] (London → Hamburg)	
β	−0.60***	−0.93***		−0.79***	−0.56***	
	(0.13)	(0.28)		(0.12)	(0.09)	
Constant	−0.43***	−0.00		0.01	0.09	
	(0.12)	(0.28)		(0.10)	(0.13)	
Trend	0.00	−0.00**		−0.00**	−0.01***	
	(0.00)	(0.00)		(0.00)	(0.00)	
Log-likelihood		304.32			206.33	
H_0: $r = 1$ (p-value)		0.126			0.738	
H_0: $r = 2$ (p-value)		0.632			0.862	
Test of restrictions (p-value)		0.50			0.28	
N		51			28	

Note: Standard errors in parentheses.

/* = significant at 5%/1% level.

table 7.A2. Here we have also reported the Johansen test for cointegration (H_0: $r = 1$ or 2), which suggested in both cases most strongly a rank of 2, and we thus allow for the less restrictive assumption of two cointegrating relationships.[28] The error correction (adjustment) coefficient, α, must be negative and significant to indicate error correction (i.e., that one variable adjusts to the other). β describes the equilibrium relationship and is expected to be negative (meaning a positive relationship).

The alpha coefficients indicate the speed of adjustment of one price to the other. Thus, since we expect to find that London prices are exogenous—that is, that Britain is in macroeconomic terms a large economy, whereas Hamburg and Copenhagen are (relatively) small—this motivates the imposition of the zeroes on the last row of the alpha matrix, which describes how London prices adjust to the other prices. We also expect the London price to be determining the Hamburg price, which in turn should be determining the

Copenhagen price, and this motivates the other zero restrictions (Hamburg prices should not be adjusting to Copenhagen prices, and Copenhagen prices should not adjust directly to London prices).

Thus, α^1 measures the speed of adjustment of Copenhagen prices (p_t^1) to changes in Hamburg prices (p_t^2) with the long-run relationship described by the elasticity β^a, and α^2 measures the speed of adjustment of Hamburg prices (p_t^2) to changes in London prices (p_t^3) with the long-run relationship described by the elasticity β^b. Since we impose overidentifying restrictions, we also get a test of these, which accepts the restrictions.[29] The (Granger) causality thus runs as expected, from London to Hamburg and then from Hamburg to Copenhagen. Moreover, the coefficients are strikingly similar in both periods, which suggests strongly to us that trade from Denmark went to England via Hamburg, as the literature suggests.

Finally, we estimate the following by maximum likelihood for the period 1865–90:

$$
(2) \quad
\begin{pmatrix} \Delta p_t^1 \\ \Delta p_t^2 \\ \Delta p_t^3 \end{pmatrix}
=
\begin{pmatrix} \alpha^1 & 0 \\ 0 & \alpha^2 \\ 0 & 0 \end{pmatrix}
+
\begin{pmatrix} 1 - \beta^a p_{t-1}^3 - t - \lambda \\ 1 - \beta^b p_{t-1}^3 - t - \lambda \end{pmatrix}
+
\begin{pmatrix} \varepsilon_t^1 \\ \varepsilon_t^2 \\ \varepsilon_t^3 \end{pmatrix}
$$

where p_t^1, p_t^2, and p_t^3 are as above, α^1 and α^2 again describe the speed of adjustment to the cointegrating relationships $(1 - \beta^a p_{t-1}^3 - t - \lambda)$ and $(1 - \beta^b p_{t-1}^3 - t - \lambda)$, the β-coefficients give the elasticities, and other parameters are defined as above. We again included two lags. Note that the difference is that in the first equation we now have p_{t-1}^3 rather than p_{t-1}^2.

The results are given in table 7.A3. Here we have also reported the Johansen test for cointegration, which suggested in both cases most strongly a rank of 2, and we thus allow for the less restrictive assumption of two cointegrating relationships.

The interpretation follows that above. For equation (2), we again expect to find that London prices are exogenous, which motivates the imposition of the zeroes on the last row of the alpha matrix. Now, however, we also expect London prices to be determining both the Hamburg and Copenhagen prices, since the direct link from Copenhagen to Hamburg has been severed, and this motivates the other zero restrictions: α^1 then measures the speed of adjustment of Copenhagen prices (p_t^1) to changes in London prices (p_t^3) with the long-run relationship described by the elasticity β^a, and α^2 measures the speed of adjustment of Hamburg prices (p_t^2) to changes in London prices (p_t^3) with the long-run relationship described by the elasticity β^b. Since we impose overidentifying restrictions, we also get a test of these, which accepts the re-

TABLE 7.A3. Error correction estimates, 1865–90

| | (2) Danish (estate) [P_1] Hamburg [P_2] London (K&S) [P_3] | | |
	ΔP_1	ΔP_2	ΔP_3
α_a	−0.55***	0	0
	(0.09)	—	—
α_b	0	−0.80***	0
	—	(0.11)	—

	[a] (London → Denmark)	[b] (London → Hamburg)
β	−1.06***	−0.86***
	(0.12)	(0.09)
Constant	0.58**	0.01
	(0.25)	(0.18)
Trend	−0.00***	−0.00***
	(0.00)	(0.00)
Log-likelihood	199.88	
H_0: $r = 1$ (p-value)	0.113	
H_0: $r = 2$ (p-value)	0.542	
Test of restrictions (p-value)	0.57	
N	24	

Note: Standard errors in parentheses.

/* = significant at 5%/1% level.

strictions. The (Granger) causality runs again as we expect: London is now determining both Hamburg and Copenhagen prices directly.

We can test more formally for the hypothesized structural break around 1864 by imposing the model for the previous period, where London drives Hamburg, which in turn drives Copenhagen (equation 1), on the post-1864 years. This hypothesis is strongly rejected with a p-value of 0.008, implying that these data cannot support the causal structure of the previous model.

Note the large constant in the first relationship in (2), suggesting that Danish butter by this time enjoyed a significant premium over the Irish butter we compare it to in London. Otherwise, we cannot glean much information from the constant terms due to changing price series for the same city and/or changing qualities over longer time periods. Thus, for example, since due to transportation costs and the law of one price Danish butter must have sold for more in London than it did in Copenhagen, if we were comparing like with like the constant in the first relationship of (2) would have been negative. This issue is explored more fully in the chapter's main text.

8

Industrial and Trade Policy

We have demonstrated that discovering and refining Danish capabilities in dairy production was largely something that took place among economic elites and their administrators, aided by merchants and shipping entrepreneurs. For most of our period, these elites were also members of the ruling class, although their political influence became less salient in the second half of the eighteenth and the first half of the nineteenth centuries. The end of absolutism brought about a prolonged period of constitutional conflict whereby the liberal constitution of 1849 was replaced by a new constitution in 1866, following the loss of the duchies, which favored the rights of estate owners and large industrialists (Hvidt 1990, 150–55). This ensured that the conservative landowner-led party Højre remained in government for most of the later nineteenth century, although it was more and more under pressure from the emerging liberal-farmer coalition in the Venstre party, which eventually took office in 1901 after the majority in the lower house of parliament, the Folketinget, was finally permitted to form a government. Much of the story of modern Denmark has been written as the late nineteenth-century liberal success story of the ascent of farmers, their Grundtvigian anti-central-government movement (with its private—although state-subsidized—schools and adult education), and the cooperative movement (see chapter 2).

This story of rising liberalism fits well with the international reputation of Danish agriculture, since Denmark stands as a curious outlier in the history of late nineteenth-century globalization. After a brief flirtation with free trade inspired by the British repeal of the Corn Laws in the 1840s, many European countries returned to agricultural protection from the 1870s as a response to the inflow of cheap grain from the United States and other new producers. The United Kingdom chose to remain a free trader and saw the dramatic decline of its agricultural sector. In this story, Denmark also chose to remain open but with rather different results (O'Rourke 1997; Henriksen 2009, 117–47). After a "crisis of grain sales," Danish farmers succeeded by diversifying into high-quality meat and dairy produce and, from being a net exporter of grains, Denmark now became a net importer and used this cheap supply to feed the animals its agriculture was to become so heavily dependent on.

As we have repeatedly made clear, however, achieving this success required sacrifices on the way, for example, by landless agricultural laborers and smallholders who were dependent on wage labor on the larger family farms. First, the number of holdings increased by more than 50 percent from 1860 to 1905, while the area belonging to them measured in *hartkorn* only increased by about 10 percent (Rasmussen 1988b, 224–25). The reason for this was above all the growth in the rural population, with the fertility transition only setting in from around 1900 in Denmark. Second, the farms on which they worked were themselves hit by the "crisis of grain sales" from the late 1870s and associated protectionist measures in neighboring countries, most notably the protectionist turn of the German empire from 1878, which involved hardship and gave additional motivation to diversify and reorient production, as we have discussed earlier. Nevertheless, the resulting transformation of Danish agriculture is generally seen as an unqualified success: By "maintaining free trade, the Danes adhered to a national tradition of liberalism, a reflection of a small economy without any domestic mineral resources" (Henriksen 1993, 156). By the end of the nineteenth century, Denmark's progress in these industries stood as testament to the folly of the return to protectionism in other countries.

In previous chapters, we have already challenged one traditional fundament of the liberal paragon of Danish success by stressing the long-run roots of this process in the efforts of large landowners in developing the necessary specialization patterns and market connections. In this chapter, we aim to qualify the lack of government intervention in the process—government intervention (specifically, in response to external adversities confronting Danish agriculture) being a second piece of the liberal story of the emergence of the Danish dairy sector.

We have highlighted in chapters 2, 3, 6, and 7 that the government did help the evolution of the Danish economy and agriculture in general through various modernization efforts, including the agricultural reforms and educational reform. Also, the Royal Agricultural Society was formed to encourage improvements in agriculture and was sustained by the economic elites of the time despite not being a formal government body. The land reforms meant that holdings were large enough to be able to benefit from new technologies, and thanks to peasant emancipation the medium-sized farmer class gained new freedom to make decisions and calculate and obtain financing. Through the extended educational system, farmers enjoyed a high educational level and used their freedom of assembly to self-organize agricultural schools. There was also public support for research and research institutions, most importantly the Royal Veterinary and Agricultural College. From 1846, there were also no grain tariffs, which meant that cheap grain could be imported freely to feed the animals involved in dairy production (cf. S. P. Jensen 1988b, 348–49).

A conscientious industrial policy for the dairy sector, however, came rather late. For example, no law for cooperatives existed until 1999. A sole exception is the margarine legislation first introduced in the 1880s and briefly referred to below, which, by enabling buyers to distinguish butter from margarine, helped protect the reputation of Danish butter on international markets. But since this law came toward the end of the timeline of our story it cannot be regarded as conventional industrial policy to foster the evolution of that sector, although it surely helped in overcoming a major challenge once the industry was expanding (see chapter 9). In addition, none of these efforts would be judged inconsistent with the view of a noninterventionist government that created beneficial conditions for development but trusted the workings of the invisible hand of market forces to direct this development along the most favorable specialization path.[1]

In the following, however, we show that Danish success in dairying owed much to a prudent use of trade policy which favored dairy production through a path-dependent and probably initially unintentional distortion in the tariff structure toward cheese. Duties especially on cheese but also on other animal products remained in force after grain tariffs were much reduced and abolished in the first half of the nineteenth century. These provided incentives to Danish farmers to diversify into livestock-based products, lending a direction to the enquiries and developments analyzed in previous chapters. This rather early diversification of Danish agriculture toward animal-based products in turn meant that Danish agriculture was in a privileged position when opportunities for dairy expansion presented themselves in the second half of the nineteenth century.[2] We thus aim to modify the traditional story, which stresses much more the role of the long "crisis of grain sales" (ca. 1876 to 1894) in Denmark's productive reorientation (S. A. Hansen 1984, 184).

As we have seen in chapter 1, the shift toward animal products in reality started as early as the 1850s (see figure 1.2), a fact that is occasionally mentioned in the Danish literature (see Olesen 1977, 10–36; and Nielsen 1977, 37–64), but is often absent from the broader story, which focuses on exports on the one hand and the spectacular increase in absolute figures after 1880 on the other. In the introduction to this book we comment that this picture demonstrates a rational reorientation following the emergence of diverging trends in prices for dairy products versus grains on the British market, which in previous chapters we have attributed to the larger income elasticity of animal products combined with rising incomes in Denmark and abroad. As we have seen in chapter 7, these price signals reached Denmark first via Hamburg and then directly from the 1860s.

In the following we argue that Danish tariff policy, although liberal and nondistorting for the most part, also played a role by sheltering Danish dairy producers from competition on the market for cheese, an important low-quality by-product of high-quality butter production using traditional technologies. Trade policy made trends in relative prices of grain versus animal products more pronounced in Denmark, and a favoritism toward dairying can be observed even after a more general movement to free trade in the 1860s. Using microlevel data from individual dairies, we quantify the implied subsidy to dairy production from the tariffs and demonstrate that this in many cases ensured the profitability of individual dairies, thus ensuring their increasingly strong hold on the Danish countryside.

The Development of Trade Policy

To understand the full context, we first need to turn to Danish trade policy focused on agriculture and animal husbandry. Until 1863, Danish import duties were based on the tariff law of 1797 which, for its time, was fairly liberal and has been considered a clear break with mercantilist thinking, consistent with other reforms of the period (Scharling 1892, 276; 1905, 260; Becker-Christensen 1988, 518–20). The process of liberalization continued over the years with various reforms—with a particularly significant one in 1838—always in the direction of tariff reductions, including the elimination of tariffs for unprocessed grain in 1846 (Fode 1989). The major reform that established the tariff in force for the rest of the nineteenth century came in 1863. It seems tempting to attribute this to the influence of free-trade-oriented trade agreements in western Europe following the Anglo-French Cobden-Chevalier Treaty of 1860, but, despite attracting initial attention and even admiration, this was not particularly important for the movement toward tariff reform in Denmark, and Denmark did not conclude significant treaties with major powers in the process.

Unlike many other European countries, Denmark passed on the possibility of readjusting its tariff policy through bilateral trade agreements and the most-favored nation clause. Although four treaties were signed, all of them were pure most-favored nation agreements—that is, they stipulated nondiscrimination but did not involve the reduction of duties on any item. Maybe this was the case because none of the treaty partners was a major trading partner. In 1857, the cumulative share of Danish exports going to the four countries Denmark would conclude treaties with until the late 1870s (Belgium 1863, Italy 1864, Spain 1872, and Switzerland 1875) was below 1 percent according to Danish statistics (Lampe and Sharp 2011, 132–33), which, however, as we know from our analysis in chapter 7, were not too reliable regarding countries of origin and destination. A proposal by the main driver of the extension of the treaty network, France, for a trade treaty including actual tariff reductions was declined by the Danish government in 1867 because the concessions asked for found no political consensus in Denmark (Falbe Hansen 1880, 305–27; Scharling 1892, 278; Gerlach 1911, 156–62).[3] In fact, the Danish tariff reform seems to have had roots going rather farther back in time (Winding 1959).

The 1863 tariff law, which came into force on April 1, 1864, generally led to lower duties, although it was formulated so that government revenue would not be affected (S. A. Hansen 1984, 193). While it established the free importation of all agricultural products except cheese, the new tariff retained (modest) duties on industrial inputs such as iron, coal, and timber (Scharling 1892, 277–78). Tariffs on manufactures were defined as specific duties by weight for rather broad classes of similar goods; this implied that crude and simple products received the highest ad valorem protection. This has often been considered as somewhat irrational, since it provided incentives for industrialization focused on low-quality varieties. This would not help the development of international competitiveness of domestic manufacturing in the medium run, particularly as nominal prices declined over much of the period from the mid-1860s to the early 1890s, which meant that the incidence of this protection was increasing over time (Hyldtoft 1999, 160).

A second irrationality highlighted in the literature was that industrial protection in the 1863 tariff in part seems to have been intended to support the somewhat more industrialized areas in the duchies; with the loss of the duchies and with them two-fifths of the home market (Hyldtoft 1999, 58) the tariff became thus somewhat anachronistic.[4] However, despite being a frequent topic of debate (and occasional suggestions for amendment), there was simply not the necessary political consensus for change (Hyldtoft 1999, 183; Scharling 1905, 571–83). For example, there was not any major opposition from agriculture, despite the fact that it had a negative impact on their terms of trade (although this might be because industrial inputs were not of major importance until relatively late in the period). Thus it was not until 1908 that substantial changes were made to the structure of protection (S. A. Hansen 1984, 194).[5]

Although the 1863 tariff implied a decisive movement for free trade in dairy products, particularly butter, when assessing the support for individual industries it is the *relative* protection that mattered. The fact that agricultural goods were free of duty after 1863, but cheese remained a notable, still dutiable exception, was of course protection of the dairy industry, since its inputs (grain to feed the animals and milk) were duty-free.[6] Probably based on path dependency since at least 1820, cheese seems to have received tariff treatment like a luxury good (along with products such as tobacco and sugar with accordingly high ad valorem equivalent rates), and the fact that just one class of cheese was mentioned in the tariff led to particularly high protection for low quality, which is analogous to the argument presented above for industrial goods.[7] Thus, what was a substantial duty on high-quality imported cheeses was a prohibitive barrier to the import of low-quality cheese.

The surviving cheese duty of 1863 tied into a long, rather low-key tradition of supporting dairy production, despite the liberal reform of the tariff laws in 1797. So, for example, already in 1820 dairies benefited when the export tax on butter and cheese was abolished, and in 1825 an indirect export subsidy on butter was granted by allowing duty-free imports of one barrel of Lyneborg (Lüneburg) salt for every twenty-five barrels of butter exported (Drejer 1925–33, 204). The tariff law of 1838 reduced the tariff rate on butter slightly, left the cheese tariff unchanged, and reduced the rates on processed grains considerably. In 1846, duties were abolished on unprocessed grains, which clearly benefited animal production in relation to grain production as previously noted.

Figure 8.1 presents our calculations of ad valorem equivalents of the specific tariff rates for agricultural products valued at Danish prices. The decrease after 1821 was due to increasing prices rather than decreasing tariff rates; in fact, the nominal tariff rate on cheese was even increased by 25 percent in 1863.[8] It can be seen that the main products of Danish dairies—butter, cheese, and pork (with beef as an obviously related product)—were protected until 1864. Moreover, dairy inputs (grains) enjoyed rather low tariffs and were free of duty from 1846.

The Production of Cheese in Denmark

How important was cheese for Danish dairy producers? Cheese was, despite early attempts by the Royal Agricultural Society to drive high-quality cheese production, not of importance as an export commodity in Denmark (see

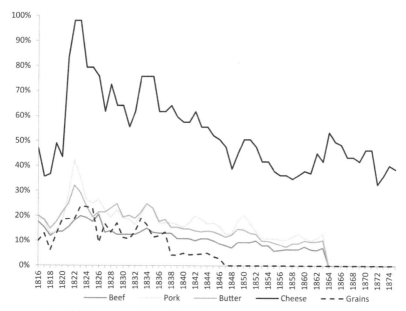

FIGURE 8.1. Ad valorem equivalents of the tariffs on butter, cheese, pork, beef, and grains, 1816–75
Source: Ad valorem tariff equivalents were calculated by dividing specific tariffs by average prices per unit. Tariff rates come from Thorbrøgger (1816, 1823), MacGregor (1850, 9–28), BPP (1850, 2), and Hübner (1866). Prices are from S. A. Hansen (1984, table 15), converted from Danish volume tons into weights following Hansen, p. 362.
Note: The "grains" line represents a weighted average of AVEs for wheat (18 percent), barley (54 percent), oats (15 percent), and rye (13 percent) using 1865 export values (calculated from data underlying Lampe and Sharp 2011) as weights.

figure 8.2), which has meant that it has been somewhat overlooked in the literature. The specific nature of the tariff of 1863 (and tariffs prior to this date) meant that cheap import cheeses faced effectively prohibitive trade barriers and caused Danish producers to specialize in low-quality cheeses. Only in the summer, when there was plenty of milk, and butter prices were thus at a low, did some dairies produce cheese with a higher fat content. Even this was mostly sold to the neighborhood (Burchardt 2005, 5). Thus Danish dairies were not structurally incapable of producing good-quality cheese; it was simply more profitable to produce butter. Although there had been some debate before 1860 as to whether the dairy industry should concentrate on butter or cheese for export (see chapter 6; Bjørn 1982a, 28), and this debate continued in later years (see, e.g., Tesdorpf 1875), it was only after 1900 that interest in cheese production increased substantially (Drejer 1925–33, 405).

The reason why Danish cheese exports were so unsuccessful is not difficult to explain. By all accounts the common Danish cheese was disgusting.

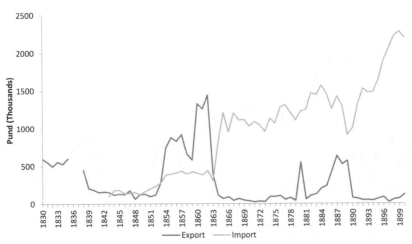

FIGURE 8.2. Imports and exports of cheese, 1830–1900
Source: Data from J. Christensen (1985, 88–89, 94–95).
Note: The peaks in the 1850s likely reflect the inclusion of the duchies of Holstein and Schleswig in the Danish trade statistics for these years (see the discussion in the previous chapter).

Following old traditions imported with the *hollænderier*, it was produced from the skimmed milk left after as much cream as possible was removed in order to make butter, and this skim-milk cheese was tellingly known as *læderost* (leather cheese[9]) (Drejer 1925–33, 214). Of these, the poorest quality, produced by peasants as late as the mid-1870s were described as "never made for sale. . . . There are only small, dry, sharp-edged cheeses hanging from a board under the roof as a great temptation to the sparrows, although even these could only cope with them for the first few days."[10] As Jenkins wrote in his report on the Danish dairy industry for the British Parliament, it does "not commend itself to the English palate" (Jenkins 1882, 29).

Nevertheless, a substantial amount of cheese was produced. Segelcke (1879), as professor of dairy husbandry at the Royal Veterinary and Agricultural College, was probably the best-informed commentator on the state of the industry. He states that the "two principal products of Dairy-Husbandry are . . . butter and skim-milk cheese," the production of which was "very considerable." It might not have been palatable, but it was an almost necessary by-product of butter production, and by virtue of the prohibitive tariff on cheese, Danes were forced to consume it (and many probably knew little else). This implied a substantial subsidy to dairy production, even *after* the tariff reform of 1864.

The importance of the tariff on cheese was understood by contemporaries. For example, there is a revealing discussion between merchants and producers recorded in *TfL* in 1876 (Tesdorpf 1876). Merchant Busck describes how, if the tariff on cheese were abolished, it would be impossible to sell the cheese Denmark produced. He believed that this would (as had happened with butter) force producers to produce better cheese. Broge disagreed, however, and suggested that the threat of abolition itself stopped producers from experimenting with cheese production. Importantly, even that great hero of liberal Denmark, Edward Tesdorpf himself, agreed that abolition would not help produce better cheese, and he cites the example of Schleswig-Holstein, where cheese production, after their separation from Denmark and its protective tariff, went into decline. He concludes that he could "in no way support a reduction of the tariff, and even less a full abolition of the cheese tariff" (Tesdorpf 1876, 576; our translation). Three years later, in their annual report on the dairy industry, *TfL* suggested that the tariff was necessary to allow cheese producers to become established before it would be possible to conquer foreign markets—a classic argument for infant industry protection (Winkel 1879, 58). In fact, in 1887 there were even suggestions that the tariff might be raised, so that experiments with better-quality cheese might be made (Bøggild 1888, 89–90).

Tariff Policy as an Implicit Subsidy to Dairying

In order to quantify the importance of the tariffs for dairying, in Henriksen, Lampe, and Sharp (2012) we made use of some of the sources introduced in chapters 5 and 6. We complemented the data provided by Tesdorpf for Orupgaard (see chapter 6) with data from the discussion of the bookkeeping and performance of individual farms in *TfL* and *UfL*:[11] data reported by Jenkins (1876, 1882) from his travels to Denmark and further records from Danish provincial archives.[12] For the years after 1876 we relied on the yearly— except for 1878—reports on the performance of Danish dairies in *TfL* (see chapter 5), which provide detailed data on a changing sample of individual dairies, including milk, butter, cheese, and pork production, farm-gate prices for these products, and the value of feedstuffs other than skim milk and whey fed to pigs.[13]

Since we have farm-gate prices for the majority of the dairies included,[14] we could calculate the gross revenue of individual dairies from butter, cheese, and pork production as well as the gross value of the milk transformed into these products. The latter is calculated by subtracting the cost of nonmilk feedstuffs in pork production from the gross revenue of butter, cheese, and pork. We could then proceed to calculate implicit subsidies from tariff protection for each of the dairies. We did this by first calculating the farm-level ad valorem equivalents (AVEs) of the three final products by dividing the specific tariff rate by the farm-gate price of each product; after 1864, this was only done for cheese since the tariffs on butter and pork were abolished. We interpreted this as the share of the farm-gate price attributable to tariff protection. From here, we calculated the implicit subsidy per farm by multiplying the average tariffs with the production values (gross revenues) for each product,[15] and sum these up across products. This sum is then divided by the total production value for butter, cheese, and pork, so that we get an implicit subsidy by dairy unit as a percentage of its total production value.

Figure 8.3 presents the consistent series for Orupgaard, and figure 8.4 compares it to a weighted average (by number of cows) of the available observations from early bookkeeping records and the *TfL* surveys.[16] Contrary to figure 8.3, figure 8.4 should not be interpreted as a time series because the number of observations changes for almost every year, and the sample is also changing with the accounts available to us. For the calculations presented in figure 8.3, one very special feature had to be taken into account: for all years before 1857 and from 1861 to 1864 the price of Orupgaard cheese was below the amount of the specific tariff, which led to AVEs of more than 100 percent (133.8 percent on average before 1857); after the increase in the cheese tariff in 1864, the Orupgaard AVE still fluctuates between 59.7 percent in 1877 and 97.2 percent in 1865, with an average of 78.7 percent. An AVE of more than

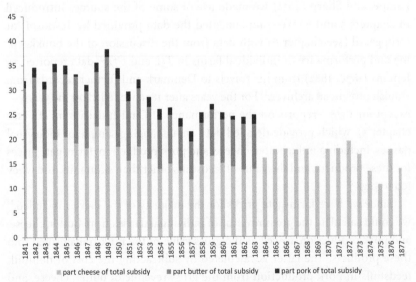

FIGURE 8.3. Percentage of total income per cow at Orupgaard attributable to the tariffs on cheese, butter, and pork, 1841–77

Source: Authors' calculations based on tariff data underlying figure 8.1 and price and income data from PA Zealand, QA-257 Orupgård Gods, Statistik over høst, mejeridrift og fårehold 1849–1904.

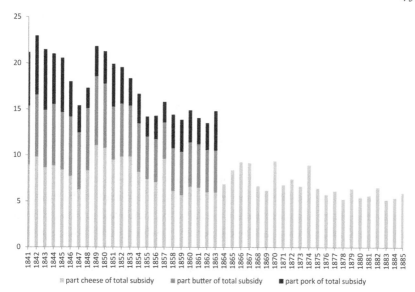

part cheese of total subsidy   part butter of total subsidy   part pork of total subsidy

FIGURE 8.4. Percentage of total income per cow for multifarm sample attributable to the tariffs on cheese, butter, and pork, 1841–85
Source: Authors' calculations based on tariff data underlying figure 8.1 and price and income data from sources specified in appendix to Henriksen, Lampe, and Sharp (2010), updated with data from sources detailed in the text.

100 percent implies for our calculations that the subsidy for cheese would exceed the revenue from the cheese. Since this might bias our calculations, we assume conservatively that in these cases the subsidy to cheese is equivalent to the revenue received from cheese (AVE = 100 percent), a reasonable idea, since such a high tariff effectively excludes any competing foreign cheese from the relevant market segment.[17]

Thanks to the relative importance of low-quality cheese in Orupgaard's dairy (16.9 percent of revenue was generated from it until 1863 and 17.7 percent afterward), it is clear why Tesdorpf supported the cheese tariff: he benefited substantially from it. For the larger sample, the picture is similar, although the subsidy following from the cheese tariff is on average somewhat lower. Before 1864, the total subsidy exceeds 10 percent for all farms and is 17.5 percent on average. Most of this subsidy clearly comes from the cheese tariff, although the actual production value of cheese is relatively small (about 13 percent of the corresponding revenue on average), given its low prices (and quality). From 1864, only the cheese tariff gives a subsidy to production, and its contribution stays at the same level as before, between 5 and 10 percent of the gross production value.[18]

The calculated value of protection per cow can be compared with the typical profit that could be expected, as revealed in a detailed and probably unique account, provided by Jenkins (1876, 26–37), of the accounts of an individual dairy (Kjærsgaard, near Horsens, Jutland). The accounts revealed gross income of £21 7s. per cow, and a profit of £1 5s. 6½d.—that is, just 6 percent of gross income.[19] The value of the subsidy from the tariffs clearly made individual dairies profitable.

We do not report data for the years after 1885, when the cooperatives became more important and our main source in the *TfL* becomes less representative (as stated by the authors of the source themselves).[20] This is a consequence of technological progress and the fast spread of the new technology, the cream separator (made available to small-scale producers by the institutional arrangement of the cooperatives, which we will discuss in the following chapter). The separator could remove nearly all the butterfat from cream instead of just two-thirds, which was the average of more traditional methods (S. P. Jensen 1988a, 247; Henriksen, Lampe, and Sharp 2011). While this led to increases in production and the price (quality) of butter—and is considered one of the reasons for the rise of cooperative dairies—it meant that cheese became difficult and therefore more expensive to make as a by-product of butter production (see also the experiments described by Fjord 1882, and Storch 1886).

Despite initial fears, however, experimentation soon proved that this skimmed milk could be used perfectly effectively for feeding pigs (Fjord 1884). Although reports in the early stage focus on the problem of poor handling of cheese (Bøggild 1891, 318–19, 323) and explain how it was not cost-effective to feed pigs rather than produce cheese (Leegaard 1878, 91), this soon changes (Winkel 1880, 37, 45). By 1881 cheese is described as being worth much less than pork (Sonne 1882, 70). Jenkins (1882, 30) describes how dairy factories with cream separators were "somewhat careless about the manufacture of skim-cheese, which was only made occasionally, and then, as it seemed to me, rather badly" and that it was necessary to add "butter-milk . . . to the skim-milk for cheese-making, as the separator so entirely denuded it of cream." He concluded that "a sufficient time has not yet elapsed to enable dairymen to find out exactly how best to treat skim-milk which is so entirely deprived of its cream as that which has passed through a well-managed separator." The dairy survey for 1882 describes the problems of using skimmed milk from a centrifuge (Sonne 1883, 56), and the following year's survey explains how this makes the concentration on butter even more pronounced (Sonne 1884, 53). There were experiments with adding cheaper fats, but these did not seem to work (Sonne 1885, 65). Instead, the skimmed milk was used more and more for feeding pigs and calves; there were even experiments with feeding children (69). The report from 1887 notes the fact that many cooperatives produced no cheese at all.[21] By 1892, reports suggest that the waste products from butter production were now "more frequently used for feeding swine and young stock" (BPP 1893, 9). Moreover, by 1897 it seems that Danish cheese, despite its protection, could no longer compete due to competition from cheap Russian cheese (Bøggild 1898, 78).

Another problem with the data is that, for some years, production of cheese exceeded demand, and this might mean that we overestimate the revenue from cheese production, although again these data originate at a late date. It seems that excess cheese production often came when pork prices were low. This was the case in 1875–76, for example (H. N. Valentiner 1876a, 317, 322), and in 1878 when cheese became "unsellable" (Winkel 1879, 54). In 1885 there were large quantities of cheese left unsold, and the author scolds producers by saying that it "doesn't make sense to keep producing a product just because of old habits" (Bøggild 1886, 64)—that is, those inherited from the Holstein system. The same was the case in 1886 (Bøggild 1887b, 52) and in 1888 (Bøggild 1889a, 81). High prices in 1890 again caused many cooperatives to begin making large quantities of cheese (Bøggild 1891, 97), and even greater price increases in 1891 exacerbated this trend. Bøggild described how cheese became difficult to get hold of, even centrifuge cheese, and that it was difficult to find workers to produce it (1892, 132). This boom inevitably led to bust in 1892: prices fell, but, since there were no large inventories, there was no overproduction "like six years previously" (Bøggild 1893, 134). Inventories are however again described as full in 1893 (122–23), and similar overproduction problems are seen in 1896, when low pork prices again caused an increase in cheese production (Bøggild 1897, 108). The problems with overproduction of cheese are attributed in the report of 1885 to the increased income of Danish workers, who had become "too prosperous to consider the simple cheese as a main source of nutrition," and "trying to change people's taste" was hopeless.[22]

However, in many cases for the individual dairy accounts, we have the actual revenue from sales of cheese, and, moreover, excess cheese could be fed to the pigs (Bøggild 1887b, 72). Furthermore, since we are principally concerned with the period prior to 1880, the changing importance of cheese in the postcentrifuge product mix need not impact our conclusions much. It is clear from figure 8.4 that the dairy industry enjoyed considerable support until the 1860s—a period during which the transformation of Danish agriculture was already under way—and enjoyed some continued support after this, despite the long-standing idea that Denmark's success came as a free-trading country.

The modern dairy system then generally gave low priority to the production of skim-milk cheese.[23] Instead skim milk was sent back to the producers, where a large part was used to feed pigs. It seems that cheese production, and thus the importance of the tariffs, died with the invention of the separator.[24] However, it is clear that in this way the great advances of the Danish dairy industry in introducing new technologies and institutions, which owed so much to the previous expansion under the tariffs, was also the source of the later great increase in pork production.

The Margarine Law

Nevertheless, with the declining importance of the cheese tariff after 1880, another regulatory measure in support of the dairy industry came to the forefront: in 1885 the Margarine Law (Loven om Fabrikation, Forhandling og Udførsel af Kunstsmør) was passed; it came into force on May 1, 1888. This, among other regulations, limited the fat in margarine and forced all retailers who sold it to put up signs in three-inch-high lettering stating *Her sælges Margarine* (Margarine is sold here; Bøggild 1889a, 95–97). This was helpful for producers within Denmark to differentiate butter from margarine, but it was far more important as a signal to export markets that what was sold as Danish butter was really butter. The Margarine Law helped to defend the top-quality reputation that Danish butter had gained, thanks to estate exports, by the early to mid-1880s.[25]

Similar laws aimed at distinguishing margarine from butter were enacted in most countries, largely due to pressure from butter producers, and margarine eventually became subject to a great deal of discriminatory legislation in many places (Van Stuyvenberg 1969), usually through a ban on adding yellow coloring and through similar warning signs in places where margarine was sold. However, in many countries, such legislation appeared rather late to avoid initial damage to the reputation of butter in the consumer's eye, which is why the fact that Denmark was a first mover in margarine legislation was of decisive importance to the international reputation of Danish dairy produce (Higgins and Mordhorst 2008). Margarine was relatively late coming to Denmark, and until 1884 it was imported (from Norway and Holland) and was known as Norwegian butter (a Frenchman had started a factory in Oslo). But in 1884 the first margarine was produced in Denmark. The threat to the reputation and price premium of Danish butter was obvious.

In an attempt to diminish this threat, Denmark passed the world's first margarine law on April 1, 1885, declaring that margarine should be clearly marked. Because it took the law to new areas, the legislation included the promise that it would be reconsidered after three years. This failed to allay fears, however, and a political debate of perhaps unprecedented proportions began, which ran through all levels of society (Higgins and Mordhorst 2008). Thus began the Butter War or Margarine War as it is sometimes known. In 1886 a commission was formed to investigate the margarine problem; it included Segelcke, two chemists, two estate owners, and a butter trader (but notably no one from the margarine industry). They reported on September 21, 1886, that margarine had indeed destroyed the Dutch butter industry through reputational damage caused by margarine production and exports from the Netherlands. Since the commission deemed that margarine was both healthy and cheap, it did not recommend a ban but rather simply new controls (Strandskov, Sørensen, and Pedersen 1998, 66–67).

The situation remained volatile, however, eventually resulting in the passage on April 1, 1888 (81), of a much tougher margarine law, which enforced the display of warning signs in stores selling margarine, forbade the mixture of margarine with more than 50 percent butterfat,[26] and included a ban on the addition of yellow coloring to margarine,[27] which was necessary to make it appear like butter, and without which exports to the United Kingdom were impossible (Strandskov, Sørensen, and Pedersen 1998, 84). Finally, the Margarine Law of 1897 restricted the amount of butterfat to be blended with margarine from 50 to 15 percent and forbade the addition of any preservatives other than salt (Drejer 1925–33, 387–88).[28] At the same time, the Danish government also supported a dairy consultant as a representative in Britain, namely the chemist Harald Faber. He became a salient defender of the reputation and the denomination of origin of Danish butter through numerous lawsuits against both butter and margarine fraudulently sold as Danish butter (Higgins and Mordhorst 2008; French and Philips 2000, 49) and thus implemented the ideas behind the Danish margarine legislation in the United Kingdom.

In conclusion, the Danish government in the long run fulfilled what modern development economists would expect from a government in favor of rural development. It was mostly focused on creating general conditions that facilitated the economic initiative of the population but occasionally directly intervened in favor of certain sectoral developments. This was surely done intentionally with the Margarine Law but was probably less intentional with the cheese tariff. However, the persistence of the latter surely suited the interests of dairy producers and would have provided extra incentives for the specialization in butter which, of course, was already well under way.

The Spread of Modern Dairying beyond the Estates: The Rise of the Cooperatives

As we have discussed, the success of Danish dairying at the end of the nineteenth century falls into a conveniently simple narrative. Cooperative creameries—butter factories owned by the suppliers of the milk—brought a tremendous expansion of butter production as well as improvements in quality. Danish butter captured more than 35 percent of the important British butter market before the First World War, up from less than 1 percent a couple of decades earlier (Henriksen, Lampe, and Sharp 2011). The medium-sized farmers who owned the cooperatives came to dominate society and politics, and eventually established themselves as a new elite, replacing those that we have argued laid the foundation for their success. At the same time, as Tesdorpf and others did before, they rewrote national history to emphasize their role in the development of the country.

Nevertheless, the rise of the cooperatives, as we highlighted in chapter 1, was truly extraordinary. That these were major capital investments—mini factories with tall chimneys, steam-powered generators, and, of course, at least one centrifuge—serves only to emphasize this point. Bjørn (1982a) provides a detailed account of their spread around Denmark, from the first in 1882 in southwestern Jutland. By 1890, which is usually considered to mark the end of the first wave of expansion, the entire country was covered, as illustrated by figure 9.1.

A central point of our argument is that the cooperatives did not emerge from nothing. Much of the framework needed to support this world-leading industry was in place before the 1880s, which helps explain how they were able to spread so rapidly. Thus, for example, the cooperatives adopted the technology and accounting systems that were already in place on the estates, and they learned about them from the educational system that had been de-

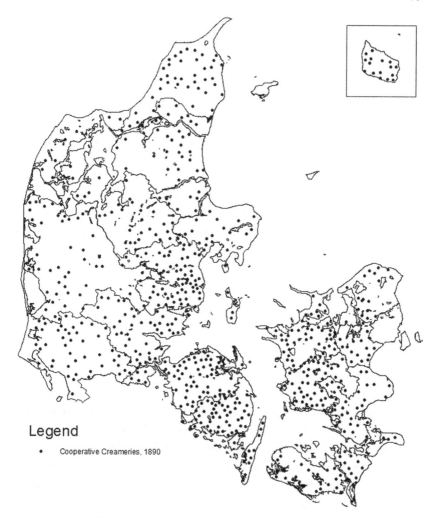

FIGURE 9.1. Location of cooperative creameries in 1890
Source: Created by the authors with the assistance of Christian Volmar Skovsgaard, based on data from Bjørn (1982a), 84.

veloped in the previous decades. Even the idea of centralizing production was ultimately taken from the *hollænderier*, and, as we demonstrated in chapter 4, the spatial distribution of the cooperatives correlates strongly with the areas where the estates had perfected the Holstein system over a century previously. Despite this, as we mentioned briefly in chapter 5 and will discuss more below, the rise of the cooperatives brought them into competition and, to a certain extent, into conflict with the existing elites on the estates and elsewhere. However, there is nothing to suggest that the estates lost economically from this, and in fact many stopped producing butter on the estate and instead supplied a cooperative, suggesting that they gained from doing so.

There were losers, however. For example, by 1880 cotters and smallholders comprised about 65 percent of the total rural population (Christiansen 1975, 8). Although those with one or two cows would gain from the cooperatives, since their milk would now fetch the same price as milk from larger producers, much of this class, not having the capital or livestock needed to join a cooperative, formed a large share of the Danish emigration before the First World War (Hvidt 1971, 215, 245, 250). Indeed, it was only in 1899 that a Law on Procurement of Plots of Land for Farmworkers put the acquisition of land within reach for more rural laborers, thus potentially giving access to resources that enabled participation in dairy production. Doubts were expressed, however, both at the time and among Danish historians today, about whether this was an economically efficient measure or a concession based on "social justice" alone (Henriksen 1993, 166–67).

At the same time, the cooperatives decisively ended the dominance of female labor in dairying, as had already happened in the brewing, baking, and clothing industries. Men increasingly looked for employment in the creameries, and the agricultural schools worked hard to attract them to give them the necessary skills. A number of reasons have been suggested for this change, including the introduction of machinery it was thought could best be worked by men, as well as new cultural norms. Whatever the case, the end result was that women's role in the countryside took on more of a service nature: they were to "clean, enjoy time with their husbands and children, provide a central focus for the family, make food, look after the garden and help with the men's work during periods of peak activity" (B. K. Hansen 2006, 285). Women lost economic status relative to men, although not all women missed the drudgery of producing butter by hand, of course.

In earlier work (Lampe and Sharp 2014a), we have suggested that apart from the movement of relative prices for grains and dairy products highlighted in earlier chapters, an important catalyst for the centralization of peasant production of butter was the invention of margarine in 1869, which we touched on in the previous chapter. Despite different ingredients and production technologies, margarine constituted a close substitute to existing low-quality varieties of butter. We demonstrated, both from historical sources and with formal econometric analysis, that this had an impact on all established producers in the market for spreads, by increasing total supply. However, the impact of the new substitute was different for different product varieties, and hence low-quality butter producers suffered much more from the price reduction resulting from the outward shift of the supply curve than makers of high-quality varieties.

In our case, Danish producers of the best variety, estate butter, who already over the preceding decades had engaged in a process of continuous quality improvements, were able to use the new challenge to their advantage. Furthermore, the knowledge of producing and marketing high-quality butter trickled down quickly to the average producer of former peasant butter. An upgrade of average-quality varieties and the disappearance of low-quality varieties from the product portfolio then became possible. We thus argued that the appearance of margarine "greased the wheels of transformation" in the sense that it provided critical incentives for the adoption of technologies, institutions, and marketing practices such as cream separators, winter dairying, and the cooperative form of production. This process also occurred in Ireland, the other main supplier of butter to the British market, but producers there did not adapt quickly enough to the joint challenge of Danish butter and cheap margarine. The reason for this is likely to be found in domestic institutions related to the organization of the production process, as we return to below. A similar explanation might be given as to why margarine was able to emerge in the Netherlands and damage the reputation of Friesland butter— the very reason for what became known as the Butter War in Denmark and the resultant strict controls on the export of margarine and the quality and content of butter.

We continue this chapter by first summarizing the traditional narrative about how the centrifuge allowed cooperatives to emerge and to dominate other organizational forms including the estates—in particular, proprietary forms of ownership which had been emerging, with support from the agricultural establishment, from the 1860s. We follow this by explaining that this in part rested on the weakness of the competition and did not necessarily reflect advantages of the cooperative form as such. Finally, we discuss some of our previous empirical work, where we provided a quantitative analysis of the relative gains from cooperation as an institution and the centrifuge as the new technology.

The Traditional Story: The Centrifuge and How the Cooperative Institutional Form Came to Dominate

Two innovations are normally considered to have been the main contributors to the big breakthrough of the dairy industry on international markets in the last two decades of the nineteenth century: one technological and one institutional. First, the invention of the automatic cream separator in 1878 allowed for butter production on a larger scale than had been possible under previous technologies. In particular, it allowed for the extraction of more cream from the (whole) milk and for the immediate separation of cream from milk which had been transported over longer distances (without first needing a period of time for the cream to separate by itself). The technology quickly replaced preexisting practice in almost all dairies after the advantages had been demonstrated by experiments on the estates as we mentioned in chapter 6. Second, the cooperative movement emerged as an efficient way to utilize this technology. By solving some of the incentive problems involved in the management of a creamery dependent on many small suppliers, cooperatives allowed for the efficient use of the technology (Henriksen 1999; Henriksen, Hviid, and Sharp 2012).

Since the technological and institutional determinants of the success of the cooperatives are clearly interdependent—the invention of the automatic cream separator led to the success of the cooperative movement, which in turn allowed for the successful use of the technology—it is difficult to know whether the productivity increases were due to better technology (a shift in the production possibility frontier) or better institutions (higher productive efficiency bringing the firm closer to this frontier) or both. Separating these is something that we examine below, but most research has in fact focused on the institutional explanation (see, e.g., Henriksen 1993 and O'Rourke 2007). Thus, it is described how the cooperatives successfully outcompeted rival institutional forms, such as the old estate dairies (by now not usually described as *hollænderier*) and private creameries (usually so-called community creameries or *fællesmejerier*).

Thus, an important part of the traditional story can be summed up by table 9.1, and emphasizes how the cooperative institution quickly dominated the proprietary organizational form. The first cooperative creamery was formed

TABLE 9.1. Number of Danish dairies by ownership

Year	Cooperatives	Private enterprises
1888	388	468
1894	907	215
1898	1013	260
1901	1067	209
1905	1087	207
1909	1163	255

Source: Henriksen (1993).

Note: "Private enterprises" excludes estate dairies.

in Hjedding in 1882, perhaps not coincidentally in Jutland, where community creameries had not become widespread. By the end of the decade, well over one thousand such cooperatives were to spring up over the whole of Denmark. These outcompeted the community creameries, which either closed or were bought up by the farmers and became cooperatives. By the close of the 1880s, new private creameries were founded only on small islands or were so-called commercial creameries (*handelsmejerier*) around Copenhagen, mostly supplying fresh milk for consumption in the city (Bjørn 1977a, 70).

Community Creameries and the Spread of Cooperatives

As we have explained, the origins of modern dairying in Denmark can be traced to developments on traditional landed estates from the late eighteenth and early nineteenth centuries when new organizational forms and practices spread from the Danish duchy of Holstein. Danish estate butter established a reputation for itself on the British market, but the majority of butter was still of poor quality, produced by peasants, largely for local consumption. As the opportunities represented by exports to the expanding and urbanizing British market became obvious, however, merchants and others saw the benefits of increasing the supply of butter for export by encouraging larger, homogeneous quantities from the largest pool of dairy producers: those outside the estate farms (Lampe and Sharp 2015b).

Thus, from the 1860s, a new type of creamery emerged, the so-called *fællesmejeri* or community creamery. The idea of processing peasant-produced milk in a central location had been around since at least the eighteenth century in the form of the Swiss *fruitieres* (Henriksen, McLaughlin, and Sharp 2015, 38), and a number of community creameries were already operating even before a meeting of Danish farmers in Odense in 1863 debated the question, "Would it be a good idea to build creameries for whole villages or a number of farms, and how should these be constructed?" (Bjørn 1977a, 66). The big takeoff was however in the 1870s, and in the second half of that decade community creameries were widely spread on the islands of Funen and Zealand, although they enjoyed less success in Jutland. Nevertheless, by 1880, community creameries were an established part of the Danish dairy industry, helped particularly by the introduction of the automatic cream separator, which processed the milk for butter production more efficiently but required a large supply (Bjørn 1977a, 67). During the early 1880s, community creameries expanded further, and societies were formed to support the industry (Bjørn 1977a, 68), but, as illustrated above, they were soon outcompeted by the cooperatives.

In order to see how the cooperatives so successfully outcompeted the community creameries in Denmark, it is first necessary to understand what exactly a community creamery was. In an address to leading farmers in 1885, the estate manager N. P. J. Buus divided community creameries into three categories:

1. Community creameries with agriculture, where individual men, who have usually run a creamery before, expand their premises and equipment and thereafter purchase milk from their neighbor, and process it together with their farm's own milk at the expense of the buyer

2. Community creameries without agriculture, where an experienced dairy-man buys a plot of land, builds a creamery, buys milk from the neighbor-hood, and processes it at his own expense

3. Public creameries without agriculture, where the owner is not a single man but a partnership consisting of many or a few participants, who at their own expense build a creamery on new soil, and process both their own milk and milk bought up from others at the expense of the partnership. (Buus 1886, 1; our translation)

The first category consisted of a small number of large estates, many small estates and medium-sized farms with twenty-five to seventy-five cows, as well as smaller farms, although these were typically very small scale. These types of creameries were spread over the whole country. The second category was on the other hand concentrated in the (by now) traditional dairying regions of Copenhagen County, the islands of Funen, Lolland, and Falster, as well as parts of northwestern Jutland. These typically processed the supply of milk from around 150 to 400 cows, and most were financed, established, and run by the same man. Only very rarely did they reach a large scale, such as when the merchants Busck in Copenhagen and Hans Jacob Schou in Slagelse opened the large creamery Slagelse Mejeri in 1875 for the production of butter in tins, which Busck's firm exported (Bjørn 1977a, 75). Many of these creameries even before the cooperatives emerged were having difficulties due to the limited supply of milk, and since the risk usually fell entirely on the dairyman, it became common for more than one person to work together in financing the initiative. Thus, there was a link between Buus's second and third categories (Bjørn 1977a, 76).

The majority were however from the first two categories, and Bjørn has stated that the Danish community creameries represent merely a "phase in the development of the Danish dairy industry," although they were an important step on the way from the tradition of dairying at home to technologically advanced, large-scale initiatives outside the estates. In fact, he argues that one factor allowing the cooperatives to spread so rapidly from the 1880s was the experience they took from earlier attempts at the centralized processing of milk (Bjørn 1977a, 74).

The dividing line between cooperatives and community creameries is somewhat blurred, and the earliest cooperatives were frequently referred to as community creameries (Bjørn 1982a, 50). The experience of Kaslunde Mejeri in western Funen serves to illustrate this. It was founded in 1875 by a young farmer, Hans Christensen. He formed a partnership with eight medium-sized farmers in the neighborhood, writing a contract which specified capital and management conditions as well as rules for how the milk was to be delivered, paid for, and so on. The contract also included the following: "§5: Any profits or losses should be shared, after all operating costs are accounted for, such that each participates in relation to the amount he has delivered." This led some to conclude that Kaslunde was the first cooperative (Bjørn 1982a, 44–45).[1]

Between 1901 and 1902 the dairy journal *Mælkeritidende* hosted a lively debate as to whether Kaslunde or the aforementioned Hjedding was the first cooperative creamery in Denmark. Bjørn (1982a, 45) quotes the following conclusion reached by the editors:

1. Kaslunde Creamery was the first in Denmark which was managed and the milk suppliers were paid according to cooperative principles.

2. Hjedding Creamery, which was founded in 1882, seven years after Kaslunde Creamery and without any knowledge at all of the latter, was the first creamery which was imitated, and the present history of the cooperative creameries starts undoubtedly on the 10th of July 1882, when Stilling Andersen established Hjedding Creamery.

Despite today not being considered the origin of the subsequent cooperative boom, Kaslunde did in its time have an impact in Funen, where the initial spread of creameries in 1883–84 were modeled on Kaslunde, rather than the cooperatives, although with the addition of a binding clause (Bjørn 1982a, 45). This further blurs the line between cooperatives and community creameries, since this rule, enforced by contracts that committed farmers to supplying their entire output of milk to the cooperative of which they were a member, has been considered a "fundamental" feature of Danish cooperation in dairying (Henriksen, Hviid, and Sharp 2012). Kaslunde was therefore another step on the way to the cooperative creameries, which would take off only from the 1880s with the spread of the automatic cream centrifuge.

As Henriksen (1993) and others have argued, and we discuss below, the cooperative form outcompeted the community creameries because they were better able to ensure quality; they enjoyed supply from a larger area,[2] allowing them to use the centrifuge more efficiently; and "funds for expansion were harder to obtain for the individual owner" (173). This latter suggests some sort of capital market imperfection, since this difficulty could have been overcome by incorporation, and this idea is in fact supported by S. A. Hansen (1972, 283), who estimates that 70 percent of total investments in Danish agriculture between 1900 and 1914 were financed out of retained profits.

In short, the incumbent dairy producers in Denmark before the first cooperative in 1882 were either traditional estates or small-scale and undercapitalized community creameries. Moreover, these latter often had much in common with the cooperative creameries for which they can be considered a sort of evolutionary precursor. Indeed, they often converted to true cooperatives once the advantages of this form became obvious. As McLaughlin and Sharp (2015) have demonstrated, this contrasted with Ireland, where several theories have been put forward for the relative failure of dairy cooperation and dairying more generally in that country, perhaps most famously by O'Rourke (2006, 2007), who emphasizes the relative cultural homogeneity of the Danes compared to the Irish, which meant that they were more able to cooperate. McLaughlin and Sharp argue, however, that a more important but related issue was the presence of existing competitors for milk supplies. As we will discuss more in chapter 11, the first cooperative creamery was opened in Ireland in 1889, the result of the work of the Irish Agricultural Organisation Society (IAOS), which explicitly sought to copy and emulate the Danish success. Their expansion was, however, checked considerably by large highly capitalized proprietary competitors such as Cleeve's (with a share capital of £350,000 in 1923 at the time of its forced nationalization after Irish independence),[3] the Newmarket Dairy Company, and the Golden Vein Dairy Company, as well as numerous smaller companies. This suggests that the competitive environment, rather than an inability to cooperate, explains much of the relative failure in Ireland. Moreover, this competition between organizational forms for milk supplies seems to have fueled existing tensions in the countryside.

It was not the case, however, that all was plain sailing for the Danish cooperatives. A year after the founding of Hjedding Cooperative Creamery in 1882, ten cooperative creameries had been established nearby; already in 1884 cooperatives had been founded in other parts of Jutland, as well as on Funen, Zealand, and Lolland (see figure 9.2 for a representative example). The agricultural establishment, which had been pushing for more community creameries, seems to have been taken by surprise. Notoriously, the chairman of the dairy committee of the United Jutland Agricultural Associations (who was also a member of the board of the Royal Agricultural Society) commissioned M. C. Pedersen, from the agricultural school Ladelundgaard, to travel

FIGURE 9.2. Fårevejle cooperative creamery shortly after 1900
Source: Courtesy of Odsherreds Local Archive, Vig, Denmark.
Note: The small building to the right of the chimney is probably one of the woodchip-covered icehouses, which became common at the end of the nineteenth century. The church is just behind the creamery.

around eighteen of the cooperatives in order to demonstrate their inferiority to the privately owned community creameries that Pedersen had previously reported on. However, comparing the results from the cooperatives and the community creameries, Pedersen ([1885] 1981) found the cooperatives markedly superior (see also Drejer 1925–33, 352). This report then spread through the professional and popular press, trumping misgivings from such towering figures as Buus and Segelcke.

The cooperatives soon established contacts with Ladelundgaard, from which many were to employ creamery managers. M. C. Pedersen and Niels Pedersen from Ladelundgaard became prominent proponents of cooperation together with the dairy consultant Sophus Hansen. By 1885 agricultural associations across the country were debating the question of home dairying versus community and cooperative creameries; at the same time cooperatives began to win prestigious prizes for butter production at agricultural shows, performing well relative to their proprietary competitors. Soon a true cooperative movement developed, with enthusiastic proponents going from farm to farm to raise support. By 1887 or 1888, with over five hundred creameries across the country, cooperatives were no longer a merely academic subject of debate but an established and soon-to-be dominant part of the agricultural economy. Although more were founded after 1890, already by then expansion had been slowing for a couple of years, so that by this point the process of transformation of Danish dairying, which had begun over one hundred years earlier with a few estate owners, was complete.

The Determinants of the Productivity Advances in Butter Making

As we described in chapter 1, butter production is essentially a three-stage process: the first concerns producing the milk; in the second cream is extracted from the milk; and in the third cream is churned to make butter. In chapter 7 we discussed the advances in the first stage, but, with the advent of cooperation and the centrifuge, rapid progress was made in the second. This in turn certainly contributed to even greater savings of all kinds of resources at the first stage: cows, milkmaids, land for pasture and fodder, labor for cultivating it, and commercial feed. So what productivity advantages did cooperation bring relative to the introduction of the centrifuge?

In Henriksen, Lampe, and Sharp (2011) we presented an econometric analysis of advances in butter production at the level of the firm, the results of which are summarized below. As we stated there, in analyses of firm-level efficiency, a division is usually made between technical and cost efficiency, but we concentrated exclusively on the former. This is not because cost efficiency is uninteresting; there are certainly reasons to believe that many of the advantages enjoyed by cooperatives owed to keeping costs down—for example, through a more efficient transportation network. However, we simply do not have the data on prices of multiple inputs that would be necessary for such an analysis.

Nevertheless, we can learn much from a simple look at the amount of butter produced per unit of milk. Contemporaries were well aware that the milk to butter ratio was one of the key indicators of a creamery's productivity, and it was standard accounting practice to report this statistic. A number of factors, however, could explain differences in this ratio—such as differing returns to scale to different technologies: different ratios of output to input at different scales of production or other efficiency differences could cause production to fall below the possibility frontier of best practice. Another important factor was time, during which the existing technologies were improved.

Considering returns to scale, we observe in our period the movement from one technology to another, so it is sensible to consider what implications this might have. The traditional system for separating cream from milk, as we discussed in chapter 7, was what in Denmark was called the *bøtte* system (see figure 9.3), in which the milk was poured into a flat container with a

FIGURE 9.3. Christian Vilhelm Mourier-Petersen (1858–1945), *Dairy Cellar at Ryomgaard*, 1892
Source: Courtesy of the Hirschsprung Collection, Copenhagen.
Note: Some estates continued to use old-style technologies, like the *bøtter* technology depicted here alongside a traditional butter churn, long after the invention of the automatic cream separator. The pictured Ryomgaard estate, situated between Aarhus and Randers in Jutland, was owned from 1854 to 1902 by the painter's uncle, Christian Helenus Mourier-Petersen.

large surface area, the *bøtte*, after which the cream would gradually rise to the surface. Although experimentation improved the system gradually, particularly through the use of cold water and ice, clearly we should expect to find decreasing returns to scale to such a technology, since the production process was not easily replicable within the confines of an existing dairy.

With the invention of the automatic cream separator, however, the water and ice dairies were very quickly replaced by those using the new technology.[4] Here the centrifuge was the bottleneck in the day-to-day running of the dairy. Time was essential for the skimmed milk to be returned to the dairy farmers in a useful state for the feeding of calves and pigs. However, a study of the most important Danish producer of centrifuges, the Burmeister & Wain machine factory, demonstrates that this bottleneck widened over time. The technical capacity of the largest centrifuges, here measured in kilograms skimmed per hour, was growing quickly over time from 240 in 1880 to 800 in 1885. At the same time, the price of a machine of a given size was declining measured in fixed prices.[5] Moreover, it is clear that early creameries made an allowance for future expansion when they were built. A contemporary account giving a sample of designs of some early centrifuge dairies of various capacities[6] demonstrates that the creameries were flexible with respect to the number of centrifuges installed (Bøggild 1896, 469–72). The earliest example, from 1887, illustrates that "room was left for an additional centrifuge." The newest ones, from 1889 and 1890, had two and four centrifuges installed, respectively.

There was, of course, an upper limit to the possibility of adding more centrifuges to the original steam engine. This limit was not necessarily hit early in the life of a modern creamery, however. Microevidence from the diary of an influential farmer, Hans Christian Sørensen,[7] involved in the first cooperative creamery on Zealand in 1884, tells us that this creamery was successful in attracting suppliers from the neighboring villages and that it had to add new machines on several occasions. It was not, however, until 1907 that it had to be "rebuilt and modernized" (S. P. Jensen 1985, 86). All in all, it might seem reasonable to expect, if not constant returns, then less diminishing returns to the new technology compared to the old.

Turning to differences in efficiency, it is first important to repeat that in some ways the institutional development of the cooperatives was inseparable from the technological development of the separator. In fact, the centrifuge at first presented a challenge to Danish agriculture, which the new organizational form helped to solve. The first steam-driven cream separators were made for the daily milk of three hundred to four hundred cows, thus exceeding by far the average Danish herd size of six to fourteen cows. Only a small fraction of Danish farmers, mostly traditional estates, could aspire to run these cream separators on their own. However, even many of these estates had herd sizes far below three hundred.[8] The new technology thus presented difficulties for the organization of the second step of production, since increasing the average herd size to optimum sizes for all farms would have required reallocation of land and farms to a degree exceeding that possible (since it would have involved many small tenants becoming dependent farm workers; see Persson and Sharp 2015, 101).

By bringing together large numbers of small producers, the community creameries and later the cooperative movement were able to take advantage of the many benefits the centrifuge offered, perhaps most importantly that cream could be instantly separated from the milk. This was even the case for milk that had been transported over long distances, which would have been completely homogenized by the process of transportation and thus would have required much longer time for separation under the old system, with higher risks of the milk spoiling. The Danish cooperative dairies, relying as they did on the transportation of milk from outlying small producers to a central creamery, depended exclusively on the centrifuge technology. Also, Morten Hviid (2006) describes how the ability to produce large quantities of a homogeneous product helped small producers realize a better price for their product. Moreover, Henriksen (1999, 61) quotes historical evidence about the new technology that suggests that it was able to produce about 25 to 30 percent more butter out of the same amount of milk, when compared to the simplest version of the *bøtter* technology as used by small herd owners. The change from the *best* traditional practice, the ice dairy, to the steam-driven separator would still improve efficiency by more than 10 percent.[9]

The community creameries used essentially the same technology as the cooperatives (Henriksen 1999, 63), but Henriksen (1999) and Henriksen and Hviid (2005) have argued that cooperative creameries were the superior institutional form for several reasons. First, they were attractive to farmers because they offered them a larger slice of the cake, since farmers as owners received not only payments for their milk as suppliers but also dividends as residual claimants. This should have reduced deadweight losses and adverse redistribution effects due to the market power of the owner of the cream separator. Second, they seem to have been the best option to avoid the problem posed by the large initial investment involved in acquiring the cream separator and the associated capital (particularly the creamery building and steam engine) which involved the risk of ex post extortion by milk suppliers (lock-in and hold-up). They achieved this by forcing their members to sign collective agreements with the aforementioned binding clause for the regular provision of all their milk (except that for own consumption in the household) to their creamery for a fixed minimum, thus ensuring that the initial investment could be recovered. Third, the cooperative institutional form was also helpful for dealing with asymmetric information on the quality (cream content) of the milk provided and could furthermore ensure year-round supply of milk by forcing their members to provide winter feeding of milch cows (see Henriksen 1999; Henriksen and Hviid 2005; Henriksen and O'Rourke 2005).

To obtain a good result the milk had to be fresh—that is, newly milked, given the technology for transport and refrigeration in the late nineteenth century. In their readings of the minutes of 215 cooperatives, Henriksen, Hviid, and Sharp find that this was an issue particularly in the (few) creameries that were closed on Sundays for religious reasons.[10] The members were supposed to find use for the Sunday milk in their own household and were, consequently, rebuked for delivering a conspicuously large amount of milk on Mondays. The milk also had to be clean—that is, free from microbes that could make the butter-making process fail. Before the introduction of better measurement methods such as the lactoscope, the creameries had to rely on being able to see or smell dirt. The manager of the creamery was authorized to reject such supplies, and the board of the cooperatives was in most cases to inspect the barns of a member suspected of neglecting cleanliness. Both old and dirty milk would lead to more waste in the production process. Equally important was the avoidance of deliberate fraud that lowered the fat percent of the milk, making it less suitable for butter production per kilo of milk. Henriksen and Hviid (2005) have shown how new technology for everyday testing of the fat percentage was, albeit somewhat slowly, adopted by the cooperatives. The resistance to pricing the milk according to the fat content came from suppliers that suspected they were going to lose in the process because the milk from their cows was naturally meagre. Henriksen, Hviid, and Sharp (2012) demonstrate how the cooperatives, before complete testing was implemented, monitored and enforced the statutes on milk adulteration, mostly resulting in hard material punishment to the perpetrators. The claim is that private contractual arrangements on hygiene and adulteration could not have accomplished the same result.

Private dairies seem therefore to have faced a problem of less-regular milk supply and potentially lower quality of the supplied milk due to hold-up problems. Additional problems for the quantity of supplied milk (although not for the quality) might come from their weaker position as regards the enforcement of winter feeding among their suppliers. A lower fat content might lead to lower quality of the butter, higher milk to butter ratios, and temporary or permanent underutilization of the capital embodied in the cream separators and the creamery (see Henriksen 1999, 68; Bjørn 1977a, 78; M. C. Pedersen 1981, 44).

For the third institutional form, the vertically integrated private estate dairies that we have argued led the way for emergence of modern dairying in Denmark, the expected result is less clear. Henriksen (1999, 71) notes that, especially on the islands of Lolland and Falster, large established estate producers that did not have to rely on external suppliers to run a cream separator led to a lower share of cows belonging to members of cooperatives, although we do actually find a large number of cooperatives being founded in that region. In earlier chapters, we highlighted in general how specialized dairy units in the estate sector advanced productivity frontiers in butter production and marketing and in establishing quality breeds, although this might not apply to all estates, and both cooperatives and community creameries could be expected to have caught up rapidly from 1882. In that respect, Henriksen and Hviid (2005, 367, 390) mention the problem of monitoring the effort of employees responsible for milking, where the last drops of milk have the highest fat content and therefore would provide the highest butter to milk ratio.[11] This problem should increase with herd size and hence might be less problematic for the average cooperative-member herd size cited above than for estates with herd sizes large enough to supply a cream separator on their own. Contemporary accounts also expressed much concern that larger herds, such as those associated with the estates, were less efficient than the smaller herds associated with the cooperatives, since owners of small herds were better able to allocate more feed to the most productive animals, thus taking advantage of each animal's productive potential (see, e.g., Bøggild 1895, 120–22).

In general, therefore, we can establish two kinds of hypotheses: first, the steam-driven cream separator was technically able to extract a higher share of the cream from milk of any fat content in a shorter period of time than the traditional system of containers and cooling, which should translate into lower milk to butter ratios for the new system compared to the traditional one. We might also expect the old technology to be subject to more sharply diminishing returns to scale. Moreover, the centrifuge technology was improving over time, thus we would expect a trend in milk to butter ratios. Second, for several reasons, we would expect—given the same technology—that cooperative creameries were able to use this technology more efficiently than private creameries. Since these reasons are mostly related to the hold-up power of suppliers, private creameries might have been also less efficient than estate dairies, which were integrated owner-suppliers. However, the latter might face principal-agent problems in milking and additionally might run cream separators below their best capacity utilization because not all of them had sufficiently large herd sizes.

Econometric Results on the Sources of Productivity Increases in Butter Making

Here we briefly present some of the results of the econometric analysis presented in Henriksen, Lampe, and Sharp (2012), the full results of which are given in the appendix to this chapter. For this, we collected from a number of sources. We used archival sources,[12] as well as data published in the Danish journals *TfL*[13] and *Mælkeritidende* and in the survey of Danish creameries compiled by Ellbrecht (1915–18). Our sample comprises twenty-seven time series for creameries using traditional technologies (primarily ice dairies), which we summarize under the heading Old Technology, while we call the use of cream separators New Technology. All of these are estates or private creameries.[14] In addition we have time series for 334 centrifuge creameries (a mixture of private, estate, and cooperative creameries). Table 9.2 gives descriptive statistics of average input-to-output ratios for the different organizational forms using the two different technologies. Note that there were no cooperatives using old technology.

Clearly, old technology gave on average worse ratios than new technology, and cooperatives were on average more efficient than private dairies, which were on average more efficient than the estates. We have, however, very few observations from private creameries.

In Henriksen, Lampe, and Sharp (2011), we performed a stochastic frontier analysis in order to quantify both the productivity advantages of the new technology as well as the efficiency advantages of the cooperatives. In table 9.3 we report the results of putting the sample mean of milk inputs into the

TABLE 9.2. Summary statistics on milk to butter ratios

	All	*Estates*	*Private*	*Cooperative*
Old technology	30.7	30.7	27.4	n/a
Period	1865–1900	1865–1900	1871–74	n/a
N	186	182	4	0
Number of dairies	27	26	1	0
New technology	26.8	28.0	27.1	26.7
Period	1882–1904	1882–1900	1882–1904	1884–1904
N	1,389	176	19	1,194
Number of dairies	329	33	4	292

Source: See text.

TABLE 9.3. Comparisons of the efficiency of different types of creameries at different scales of production

	Old technology, private creamery	New technology, private creamery	New technology, cooperative creamery
(1) Milk	4,172,026	4,172,026	4,172,026
Butter	122,705	153,485	160,960
Ratio	34.0	27.2	25.9
% of new co-op	76	95	100
(2) Milk	1,094,899	1,094,899	1,094,899
Butter	34,566	40,504	42,476
Ratio	31.7	27.0	25.8
% of new co-op	81	95	100
(3) Milk	292,990	292,990	292,990
Butter	9,918	10,898	11,429
Ratio	29.5	26.9	25.6
% of new co-op	87	95	100

Note: The trend is set to 1900; (1) using average milk input for whole sample; (2) using average milk input for private creameries; (3) using average milk input under old system; "% of new co-op" is the percentage of butter extracted from the given amount of milk as a proportion of cooperatives with the new technology.

production functions obtained from the stochastic frontier models, in terms of milk to butter ratios for the average enterprise. We calculate these for 1900 and use three kinds of assumptions about the average enterprise, given in table 9.3 together with the results, in which private creameries and estates are grouped in just one category, private creamery, which, as can be seen in table 9.2, mostly consists of estate dairies.[15]

We observe that, depending on the scale of production (the amount of milk processed) for the old technology, the new technology used between 9 and 20 percent less milk for the production of the same amount of butter for the same institutional form with—as reported above—almost identical average inefficiency. Additionally, since, for the creameries in our sample, the old technology showed decreasing returns to scale, creameries using old technologies would have been much less productive at the sort of scales the cooperatives operated at in 1900, which is in line with the fact that all cooperatives relied on cream separators only.

For the new technology, however, the amount of milk used does not have such an impact, since it has constant returns to scale. If we compare the two governance forms, we find a 5 percent differential in the milk to butter ratios. This would suggest that of the total gain of technological progress and institutional innovation of 13 to 24 percent, between 63 and 79 percent would be due to the technological innovation of the cream separator and the rest due to the greater efficiency of the cooperatives in using it. The substantively larger share of the efficiency gain that is attributable to technological innovation rather than institutional innovation is a point we will return to in chapter 11.[16]

We have argued in this chapter that the traditional story about the rise of the cooperatives requires some qualifications. Certainly the centralization of production was an important step toward enabling the medium-sized farmers to increase the quality of their products and to enter the world market for butter. We maintain, however, that the rapid spread of the cooperative form would not have been possible without, first, the preceding century of innovation, including the idea of centralizing production itself, and, second, the lack of significant competition for the supply of milk. Finally, our empirical work reveals that the cooperative institution as such was not the defining determinant of the productivity increases in butter making, which instead mostly came from the introduction of the centrifuge, although other organizational forms using the new technology only enjoyed somewhat smaller gains.

A question which is outside the scope of the present work but deserves more consideration in the literature is how the farmers secured credit to finance the considerable capital investments required for building the creamery and purchasing the necessary equipment (not least the steam-powered generator and the centrifuge). In a study by Leon Buch (1960) on this question, he finds that the total investment in new creameries (including community creameries) between 1882 and 1899 would have amounted to around 25 million kroner, at a time when net factor income for agriculture only amounted to around 250 million kroner per year. From a sample of seventy-six cooperative creameries he found that this was principally financed by the *sparekasser* (savings banks)—most importantly the *landbosparekasser* (agricultural savings banks)—to the tune of around three-quarters of the total finance (135). The first savings bank in Denmark was established in 1810, but the first agricultural savings bank, Bondestandens Sparekasse, was established in 1856, with most of the rest founded in the 1860s. Agricultural savings banks emerged due to rural disenchantment with the original savings banks, which were considered to be happy to take the peasants' savings but unwilling to lend them out to the rural population again.[17]

Unfortunately it is not possible to know where the savings banks themselves received their capital from, although it was almost certainly mainly from the farmers themselves—particularly the same circle of larger peasant farmers who also founded the cooperatives. Since deposits increased from 300 million kroner to 600 million kroner between 1883 and 1899—that is, ten times the capital required to establish the creameries—capital does not seem to have been lacking among the peasantry by the time of the emergence of the cooperatives. The ease with which they were able to attract loans was also due to the particular institutional setup of the cooperatives, including their members' joint liability (see Henriksen 1999; Henriksen, Hviid, and Sharp 2012). In fact, as early as 1860, Rainals, the British vice-consul in Copenhagen, noted that "the Danish farm labourer is generally well off and while he is without family is able to save part of his wages as is sufficiently proved by the large sums of money placed in the savings banks by this class" (Rainals 1860, 290). This perhaps surprising wealth of Denmark before the breakthrough of the cooperatives is discussed and documented more in the next chapter and serves to support the general point of our work: that the cooperatives marked a continuation of Danish agricultural success and not a turning point.

Appendix

Assessing productive inefficiency requires the estimation of a production function. For this we need data on inputs and outputs. We argue that the relevant input variable for our analysis is the amount of milk used, and the output is of course the amount of butter produced. This gives us a simple production function of the form

(1) $\ln(butter_{it}) = \beta_{0t} + \beta_{1t} \ln(milk_{it})$

where *butter* is output of butter in *pund* (500 g) and *milk* is the input of milk in *pund*. Our data is a panel, so inputs vary across both creameries (*i*) and time (*t*).

We are aware that this is a somewhat untraditional production function, since the usual factors of production (capital, labor, and so on) are not present. Nevertheless, it is a production function in the sense that it gives the production of an output based on an input. Moreover, the literature on productive efficiency usually terms these production functions, so this choice of words is also to avoid confusion. Also, this should be seen in the light of the fact that the production of butter is in reality a two-stage process, the first being the production of milk (which requires labor and capital in the form of land, cows, a dairy, and so on) and the second being the production of butter from the milk.

We concentrate on the second stage, where the role of capital and labor in the production process is of rather secondary importance[18] if we consider this to be largely a story about extracting cream from (whole) milk. By this, we effectively assess the technological efficiency of the creameries in our sample, not cost efficiency, which would imply also using data on prices.[19]

Our motivation for focusing on the second stage is that data for the first stage (numbers of cows, laborers, and so on) is lacking in almost all cases since the vast majority of the milk suppliers were small farms for which no records were preserved, if kept at all. This also implies that the two stages were conducted by two different firms for all producers except the estate dairies. Moreover, the main technological innovation concerns the second stage—that is, the movement from ice creameries to those using centrifuges. We can capture the form of the production function under the alternative technologies using this simple one-input specification although, as discussed above, the inefficiency term might be capturing inefficiencies in the first stage rather than in the second stage.

To estimate the production function, we use the stochastic frontier model with a time-varying technical efficiency term formulated by Battese and Coelli (1995) and described by Kumbhakar and Lovell (2000, 271).[20] These models have the general form

(2) $\quad y_{it} = \boldsymbol{\beta}' x_{it} + v_{it} - u_{it}$

where $u_{it} = g(z_{it})|U_i|$ where U_i is half normal, and $g(z_{it}) = \exp(\boldsymbol{\eta}' z_{it})$. Equation (2) is the general formula for a stochastic frontier model in a panel setting, where the production of y is given by a vector of inputs, x. The important contribution of these models is the separation of the error term into a standard stochastic error, v_{it}, and an inefficiency term, u_{it}. The Battese and Coelli (1995) formulation of the model allows us to explain this inefficiency term with a vector of variables z_{it}.

For our purposes, y_{it} obviously corresponds to the (log) output of butter and x_{it} to the (log) input of milk. We also introduce a trend, t, to capture for example technological progress over time. Since we have two technologies, we estimate two production functions, one for the old technology (primarily ice creameries) and one for the new (using centrifuges). For the centrifuge creameries, we wish to explain the inefficiency term with reference to their institutional status: estates, private creameries, or cooperative creameries (since no cooperatives used the old technology). These are coded through the use of the dummies ESTATE (= 1 if an estate) and PRIVATE (= 1 if private). Due to data scarcity for private creameries, we however initially introduce only one dummy, ESTPRIV (= 1 if estate or private). In addition, we control for size in the efficiency term, which we measure by the (log) input of milk.

Table 9.A1 gives the results of our estimations. Models (1) and (3) are from a standard stochastic frontier analysis for the creameries using the old and new technologies respectively. Models (4) and (5) attempt to explain the inefficiency term by institutional type, and models (2) and (6) introduce the size explanation of inefficiency.

TABLE 9.A1A. Estimation results, old technology

	(1) Old technology	(2) Old technology
Constant	−2.632***	−2.773***
log $(milk_{jt})$	0.947***	0.959***
t-value for test of constant returns to scale	−2.33	−1.65
Trend	−0.002	−0.002
"Size"	n/a	0.472
λ	1.635***	0.005
σ	0.089***	0.000
η	−0.023	n/a
Period covered	1865–1900	1865–1900
No. of cross-sections	27	27
No. of observations	186	186
Log-likelihood	253.278	255.726

Note: $\lambda = \sigma_u/\sigma_v$; $\sigma = \sqrt{\sigma_u^2 + \sigma_v^2}$; stochastic frontier, $e = v - u$; time varying $u_{it} = \exp[-\eta(t - T)]|U_i|$ (models 1 and 3) or $u_{it} = \exp(\eta z_{it})|U_i|$ (models 2, 4, 5, and 6).

*** = significant difference from 0 at 1% level.

TABLE 9.A1B. Estimation results, new technology

	(3) New technology	(4) New technology	(5) New technology	(6) New technology
Constant	−3.298***	−3.251***	−3.250***	−3.215***
log$(milk_{it})$	0.999***	0.996***	0.996***	0.993***
t-value for test of constant returns to scale	−0.34	−3.03	−3.07	−3.85
Trend	0.004***	0.004***	0.004***	0.004***
$ESTPRIV_{it}$	n/a	0.954***	n/a	0.717***
$ESTATE_{it}$	n/a	n/a	0.991***	n/a
$PRIVATE_{it}$	n/a	n/a	0.433	n/a
"Size"	n/a	n/a	n/a	−0.159**
λ	1.505***	1.088***	1.086***	11.358***
σ	0.043***	0.031***	0.031***	0.330***
η	−0.005	n/a	n/a	n/a
Period covered	1882–1904	1882–1904	1882–1904	1882–1904
No. of cross-sections	329	329	329	329
No. of observations	1,389	1,389	1,389	1,389
Log-likelihood	2,730.760	2,765.371	2,766.154	2,762.48

Note: $\lambda = \sigma_u/\sigma_v$; $\sigma = \sqrt{\sigma_u^2 + \sigma_v^2}$; stochastic frontier, $e = v - u$; time varying $u_{it} = \exp[-\eta(t - T)]|U_i|$ (models 1 and 3) or $u_{it} = \exp(\eta z_{it})|U_i|$ (models 2, 4, 5, and 6).

/* = significant difference from 0 at 5%/1% level.

The results seem intuitive and in line with our a priori expectations. For the old technology (models 1 and 2), there is no significant trend, which implies that productivity was not increasing over time using this technology, and there were diminishing returns to scale. For the new technology (models 3, 4, 5, and 6), however, we see productivity growth of 0.4 percent per year, and we now have (approximately) constant returns to scale. This growth in productivity might be due to technological progress, the breeding of cows that could produce a higher fat content in their milk, or might be due to the sort of institutional innovations (such as performance-related pay) discussed by Hviid (2006). The finding of constant returns to scale for the new technology might seem surprising at first. In reality, the production function probably demonstrated increasing returns at low volumes of milk as the centrifuge required a certain minimum level of input to function effectively. Then, after a certain level of input, there would be diminishing returns as the machine's operating capacity was exceeded. However, our finding simply reflects the fact that no machines in our sample were operating at unreasonable levels of input. For normal usage, the new technology demonstrated constant returns, which was not the case for the old.

The significance of λ indicates the presence of inefficiency in the production process (and thus justifies the use of a stochastic frontier model).[21] The average inefficiency of creameries under the old system was 6.6 percent, as calculated by taking the simple average of the inefficiency terms, u_{it}. For the new system we estimate four models. Model (3) uses the same methodology as model (1), and the fact that η is insignificant in both implies that there is no time-varying inefficiency. Thus, for models (4) and (5) we attempt to explain the inefficiency by factors other than time and compare the relative efficiency of the various systems. Since we have relatively few observations for private creameries, we group them with the estate dairies in the first estimation attempt, giving the results for model (3). The mean inefficiency for the whole sample is 3.1 percent, so significantly lower than for the old technology above. However, and as expected, model (4) reveals that estates and private dairies were significantly less productive than cooperatives: the coefficient should be interpreted as implying that they had 95.4 percent higher inefficiency. This implies that the average efficiency of estates/private creameries was $(1 - 0.031)^*0.954 = 0.924$ percent, giving an average inefficiency of 7.6 percent—rather similar to their inefficiency under the old system of 6.6 percent.

Although we have very few observations of private dairies, we attempt to differentiate between them by coding them differently in model (5). As might be expected, since we have so few observations, the coefficient for private creameries is insignificant. However, it nevertheless implies that they were in fact less inefficient than estate dairies.

Finally, in models (2) and (6) we control for size in the efficiency term. In this context it is important to distinguish between returns to scale and efficiency differences owing to size. The first relates to maximum production possibilities, while the second relates to inefficiencies at different sizes that cause production to fall short of this possible maximum. There is an insignificant positive effect for the old technology, implying that larger creameries were less efficient than smaller. A tentative interpretation might be that this reflects the gains from better monitoring and greater milking effort, since most of this sample consists of estates, so a larger amount of milk processed corresponds to larger herd sizes, which is not the case when we look at cooperatives, who source their milk from a large number of small herds. For the new technology we thus find a significant negative coefficient, so larger creameries were more efficient.[22] Thus, despite constant returns to scale, larger producers were able to achieve higher levels of output relative to input (and thus approach the production possibility frontier) by minimizing inefficiencies. The reasons for this are unclear but might have to do with more efficient organizational structures and/or a better-educated workforce in larger creameries. Interestingly the *ESTPRIV* coefficient falls but remains significant, implying that, as expected, the efficiency gains from cooperatives are less when we control for the size of the creameries.

Agriculture, Industry, and Modern
Economic Growth in Denmark

The previous chapters have demonstrated the remarkable progress made in Danish agriculture over the eighteenth and nineteenth centuries, which was part of a general story of balanced economic development, in which agriculture played an active role alongside other sectors. The combination of overall economic growth and balanced development between town and countryside makes the Danish experience a success story different from the traditional textbook case of growth—in which industry forges ahead, and agriculture donates redundant resources (as outlined in chapter 1)—and closer to recent accounts of the process and drivers of balanced economic development. How agriculture compared to and interacted with the rest of the economy is thus central to embedding our story into the wider narratives on economic development.

We start by discussing the available data on GDP and real wages, providing some context for the "success" in the late nineteenth century, in which certain groups gained more than others. This is followed by a discussion of sectoral developments at the national level, where we demonstrate that high productivity in the countryside led to a relatively balanced growth path between agriculture and industry. Finally, we summarize the debate about the role of industrialization for Danish development and how this fits in with the developments in agriculture we have described.

Economic Outcomes: Growth and Distribution

We will first describe the overall process through the lens of GDP per capita and real wages as overall indicators of development. The data on Danish GDP for the nineteenth century is, as already mentioned in chapter 2, unfortunately not considered particularly reliable, especially in the sense that the existing estimates of gross factor income given by S. A. Hansen (1984), which entered Angus Maddison's famous historical data set, are not well documented and seem to rely on questionable assumptions, such as a constant per capita consumption of grains.[1] Since, as we discussed in chapter 2, the last version of the Maddison data set of global GDP per capita comparisons (Bolt and Van Zanden 2014) gives Denmark as already one of the richest countries in Europe in 1820, growth until 1880 or 1913 appears rather moderate, although the aforementioned studies by Bairoch (1981) and Prados de la Escosura (2000) show a more rapid catch-up with the leading economies. Figure 10.1 graphs the Danish series from the Maddison data set, which shows an almost constant increase, although with some periods of stagnation. Interestingly, there is a noticeable takeoff in the 1840s, and again in the 1870s, which, consistent with our narrative, predates the famous story of Danish catch-up and development driven by the introduction of the steam-powered cream separator and cooperative creameries from 1882. The fall in GDP per capita shortly before the First World War is probably a result of the global financial crisis and banking panics of 1907 (Bordo and Landon-Lane 2010), which hit Denmark particularly hard, as well as the collapse of a speculative housing bubble (Hyldtoft 1999, 246).

Nevertheless, Denmark remained from this point and remains today one

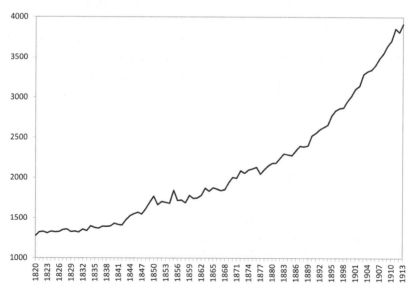

FIGURE 10.1. Danish GDP per capita, 1990 int. GK$, 1820–1913
Source: Data from Bolt and Van Zanden (2014).

of the richest countries in the world. The "little divergence" between north
and south Europe (see, e.g., De Plejt and Van Zanden 2016), when the north
overtook the historically more prosperous south, saw Denmark very much in
the northern club of countries—but dependably so only from the late nineteenth century.

Is it surprising that Denmark was so well-off? We have already seen in
chapter 9 that capital was relatively abundant among the farmer class by the
time of the cooperatives, as backed up by the quote taken from Rainals, the
British vice-consul in Copenhagen, in 1860 (Rainals 1860, 290). Other quantitative accounts of Denmark over this period point toward similar findings.
Hans Christian Johansen (1998, 2005) finds that the "consumer revolution"—
that is, the point at which there is a constant decline in the proportion of income being spent on food—probably started before 1790 in Denmark, earlier
than the other Nordic countries. He is however skeptical about the source
material.

The general findings of the GDP per capita series coincide quite well with
the new estimates of real wages for unskilled workers in town and countryside, as demonstrated in table 10.1, which continues where table 2.1 left off and
again makes use of the methodology suggested by Robert C. Allen (2009a)
to calculate prices of a "respectable" basket of goods, which is comparable to
those he and others have constructed for other countries.[2] The comparison of
urban and rural wages gives us a first possibility to assess whether the country developed the rural-urban divide in productivity and living standards so
characteristic of most countries' growth experiences.

As we discussed in chapter 2, real wages were surprisingly constant until
the early nineteenth century, with an urban laborer in Copenhagen only just
able to support his family on his own salary, but a respectable basket requiring his wife and/or children to work. This began to change from the 1840s,
however, and an almost constant improvement in living standards is reflected

TABLE 10.1. Welfare ratios (nominal wages/respectability basket), 1820–1913

	Copenhagen	Copenhagen (rural)	London	Amsterdam	Antwerp	Leipzig	Madrid	Milan	Paris
1820	0.55	0.55	1.27	1.02	1.22	0.66	...	0.35	...
1840	0.71	0.71	1.31	0.99	1.21	0.64	0.82	0.39	0.96
1860	1.19	0.64	1.55	0.85	1.12	0.89	0.90	0.31	1.12
1880	1.79	0.88	2.21	1.16	1.26	1.07	0.87	0.41	1.10
1900	2.28	1.10	2.61	1.77	1.72	1.58	0.83	0.63	1.80
1910/13	2.21	1.28	2.85	2.30	1.99	2.23	1.26	0.91	1.70

Source: R. C. Allen (2001), Khaustova and Sharp (2015).

in both wage series as well, with stagnation in urban real wages at the very end of the period reflecting the crisis also visible in the GDP per capita series. Already by 1880, an urban laborer would have been able to purchase almost twice the respectability basket for his (assumed) family of three. Thus, by 1880 urban welfare ratios for Copenhagen were second only to London. A similar catch-up spurt can, in this table, only be observed for Leipzig, which by the First World War caught up with Copenhagen, as did Antwerp. For rural wage rates, which however have been calculated with the same (urban) prices, we have less obvious points of comparison in the sample, although their increase was surely somewhat lower than those for urban areas. In nominal terms, rural wages increased 5.7-fold between 1790 and 1913, and 2.5 times between 1820 and 1880, while urban wages increased 10- and 5.5-fold, respectively.

Nevertheless, we have shown in previous chapters that Danish historians have long argued that rural laborers and part-time wage-dependent small-holders were among the losers of the development process, especially before the welfare reforms introduced in the 1890s. As we noted in the previous chapter, inequality in the countryside manifested itself especially through the fact that more than two-thirds of Danish overseas migrants between 1868 and 1900 were rural workers (Henriksen 1993, 165–66; Hvidt 1972, 9), although the overall numbers of emigrants were rather small in relation to the population, especially in comparison to neighboring Sweden and Ireland; only 165,000 Danish emigrants were registered in the United States between 1868 and 1900 (Hvidt 1972, 8; Rasmussen 1988a, 213). For the period 1880 to 1913, Timothy J. Hatton and Jeffrey G. Williamson (1994) report average gross emigration rates of 3.0 per thousand for Denmark, but 6.0 per thousand for Sweden, 7.3 per thousand for Norway, and 11.2 per thousand for Ireland; and even the Netherlands had higher gross emigration rates than Denmark at 4.7 per thousand. This indicates that Danish emigration was in part a valve for inequality in the countryside but not an indicator of overall dysfunctional rural labor markets. Of course, it could also indicate that instead of emigrating abroad there was increased rural-urban migration within Denmark, but this would depend on the capacity of urban production to absorb this workforce, something that was not necessarily the case as we will see below. Overall, the agricultural share of the workforce decreased from 52 percent in 1870 to 39 percent in 1914, with the share of the population depending on agriculture decreasing from 44 to 36 percent over the same period.[3]

Despite these developments the agricultural workforce actually increased by about 9 percent in absolute terms (from 486,000 to 529,000 between 1870 and 1911), and the number of persons dependent on agriculture increased even more, from 788,000 to 1.1 million, over the same period due to the acceleration in population growth outlined in chapters 2 and 8. Also, partially offsetting emigration from Denmark, the country actually attracted immigrants during the first era of globalization. Many unskilled seasonal workers (for example, from Poland) migrated to Denmark, in particular to work in the agricultural sector, but highly skilled immigrants also entered the country from, for example, Germany, Sweden, and the Netherlands (Willerslev 1983; Østergaard 2007). Danish labor markets must therefore have been relatively attractive, even in agriculture. Also, a significant rise in living standards can indeed be observed even in the lowest segment of the labor market despite an increasing workforce. Rising wages were possible only because of all the innovations and investments outlined in previous chapters, which increased labor productivity, and because of the rise in production, which offset the labor-saving effects of innovations and investments.

Unfortunately, data on the incomes of medium-sized farmers (not to mention the estate owners, who were however certainly even better off)—the winners from the rise of the cooperatives—are much more difficult to come by since few examples of peasant accounts have survived, and even fewer of them contain the information necessary to calculate the entrepreneurial income of farmers in a consistent way. The only existing example known from the literature is the collection of diaries and accounting books kept between 1867 and 1917/18 by Hans Christian Sørensen, who we met briefly in the previous chapter. He was a farmer in the parish of Holtug near Stevns in Præstø Amt south of Copenhagen, and in 1884, just two years after the first dairy cooperative had been founded on the opposite side of the country, he became treasurer of the first cooperative creamery on Zealand.

S. P. Jensen (1985), who uncovered this material, describes Sørensen's farm as somewhat ahead of the Danish average in terms of intensified dairying and reliance on imported feed,[4] a finding not particularly surprising given that it was located less than forty kilometers from Sofiendal, where Moltke first had introduced *Koppelwirtschaft*. Full accounts for his entrepreneurial income can only be reconstructed for the year 1905, when Jensen reports that the net receipts of his farm amounted to 2,994 kroner, of which about half would have to be credited as the usual return to his land and capital investments (at 5 percent annually), so that he and his wife would have received a net entrepreneurial income of about 1,450 kroner in 1905. This can be compared to the assumed annual income of a rural day laborer in Copenhagen County from table 10.1, which would be 345 kroner per year under Robert C. Allen's (2001) assumption of 250 workdays per year. An advanced farmer would thus make about four times the income of a day laborer in the countryside. When compared with a skilled laborer in Copenhagen with an estimated yearly income of 1,100 kroner (Khaustova and Sharp 2015), probably the most appropriate urban reference category, Sørensen still compared favorably, although a self-employed Copenhagen artisan might have made more than he.

Balanced Sectoral Growth

The Danish development story was not, however, simply one of development through agriculture, despite the leading role this sector initially played. From at least the 1870s, a modern industrial sector began to grow, from around 10 percent of gross factor income around the middle of the nineteenth century to around 20 percent before the First World War. The service sector also expanded, although less dramatically—from around 40 to 55 percent over the same period—as illustrated in figure 10.2, which gives the sectoral distribution for the gross national income estimate presented in figure 10.1.

In terms of sectoral productivity, Jonas Ljungberg and Lennart Schön (2013, 109–13) have shown that production per capita was actually higher in agriculture than in industry in Denmark in 1865, although both were outperformed by the service sector from the start. Agriculture grew somewhat less than industry over the following four and a half decades until 1910 (1.3 versus 1.6 percent per year), but still produced almost the same value added per head (3,088 versus 3,176 1990 int. GK$), although the service sector was still much more productive (4,010 1990 int. GK$ per capita, growing at 1.5 percent per year). Danish agriculture is presented in that study as far more productive

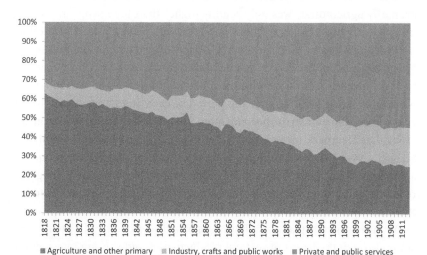

FIGURE 10.2. Shares of gross factor income (1929 prices), 1818–1913
Source: Data from S. A. Hansen (1984), 249–60.

over the whole period than in other Nordic countries. More decisively, shifts in productive activity between sectors—that is, structural change—explained relatively little of the overall Danish growth experience. Overall growth was mainly due to relatively balanced growth within each sector, in contrast to the experiences of neighboring Sweden and Norway.

These recent results connect to a long-running debate between Danish economic historians about the role of agriculture versus industry (and the connection between both), in particular, for the emergence of sustained income growth in Denmark in the nineteenth century. Sven Wunder (1987) used data presented by Nick Crafts (1985) to compare Danish development to other countries for the period 1870 to 1910. Wunder had already shown that the proportion of national income from the primary sector in Denmark was in fact consistently higher than that in Europe throughout the period looked at (and significantly so in 1910). Wunder also importantly notes that the secondary sector's (that is, manufacturing's) proportion of national income increases much more slowly than its proportion of the labor force (which, however, is also true to a lesser extent for Europe). This implies that manufacturing absorbed a larger proportion of the workforce without resulting in a proportional increase in its share of production, a finding mirrored in the almost identical value added per head estimated by Ljungberg and Schön (2013).

From the data in Wunder (1987) it is also interesting to note that, as late as 1910, the percentage of the workforce employed in industry was only 27.3 percent, as compared to 40.1 percent in the rest of Europe (Wunder 1987, 56). And, although in 1910 the primary sector labor force (which in Denmark is primarily agricultural) was only slightly higher than the European average, it was clearly higher than in those countries with a similar level of productivity as indicated by GDP per capita.[5] Also, consistent with the findings of Ljungberg and Schön (2013), its rate of decrease was far less than that in a typical European country. Indeed, employment on the land was to be significant in Denmark long after the period of early industrialization, to the extent that Henrik Christoffersen (1999, 49) argued that it was first in the 1960s that Denmark moved directly from being an agricultural country to being a service-oriented country, a process which he describes as unique in an international context, although ongoing comparative research on long-run trends in occupational structure led by Leigh Shaw-Taylor is expected to put this claim into perspective.

Wunder (1987) explains this finding of balanced growth and smooth transition through the lenses of sectoral productivities and shifting intersectoral terms of trade. By calculating the sectors' proportions of income in fixed prices, he is able to show that secondary production did indeed grow faster than agriculture, but at the same time its prices evolved unfavorably in comparison to agriculture (cf. figure 1.4). These worsening terms of trade of the secondary sector in comparison to the primary sector explain why its shares in total value added did not grow faster despite increasing output (in terms of quantities). The remainder of Wunder's explanation is, however, that the sector also did not experience above-average productivity increases, something we have also seen in Ljungberg and Schön's (2013) results above. So, Danish research confirms the relatively small productivity gap between industry and agriculture in Denmark throughout this period (Wunder 1987, 57–58).

Finally, Wunder (58–59) noted a higher consumption quota and a rather lower investment quota for Denmark compared with the rest of Europe. He concluded that due to the small productivity gap, there was little advantage to be gained by transferring resources from low to high productivity sectors. In fact, if anything, Denmark's comparative advantage seemed to lie in agriculture, with industrial expansion marked by quantitative rather than qualitative advances, although this might be put into perspective by its slightly higher per capita growth rates estimated by Ljungberg and Schön (2013) and especially by incorporating their favorable results for the service sector into the picture. In his assessment of the growth experiences of industry and agriculture, however, Wunder (1987) considered that Danish industrialization could well be partly compared to Crafts's analysis of English industrialization, and his conclusion, "That much of the industrial activity of the economy remained small-scale, little affected by the use of steam power and characterized neither by high productivity nor comparative advantage" (Crafts 1985, 69), can just as well be applied to Denmark. Denmark, like England, had a long, drawn-out industrialization. We have already seen that, at least, the part of agriculture that is at the center of the present book, dairying, did in contrast see an industrialization and the use of steam power and the discovery of comparative advantage.

Within the Danish debate on economic growth more generally, some historians have thus stressed agriculture as a leading sector, creating demand for domestic industry and services, particularly transportation, trade, and finance, while others have seen it as developing alongside the emerging urban sector. We choose to remain on the sidelines of this debate, since it concerns mostly industrialization at the time of the spread of the cooperatives, which is after our period of interest, but we would again stress that the present work demonstrates that the roots of Danish development certainly go back much further.

The traditional narrative (see, e.g., Henriksen 1993; Hyldtoft 1999; O'Rourke

2006) describes how Danish agriculture led to a demand for machinery for the dairies and slaughterhouses and thus brought about a domestic industry producing among other things centrifuges and, later, refrigerators. Moreover, increasing demand from the peasantry as they became richer stimulated the development of a market for consumption goods. Services also benefited due to, for example, the demand for trade, transportation, and financial services. Productivity growth in agriculture was similar to that in industry (S. A. Hansen 1984; Henriksen 1993), leading to a smaller gap in productivity than in other rich countries. This narrative also emphasizes that the flexibility created by an economy where yeoman farmers were backed by corporate Copenhagen led to a new and dynamic form of business in the railroad towns around the cooperatives after the First World War; this flexibility was to be of advantage in the twentieth century (Kristensen, Lotz, and Rocha 2011).

The Timing and Extent of Industrialization in Denmark

Much of the debate on the timing of economic growth in Denmark concerns when (and perhaps whether) Denmark industrialized—a debate that followed many now-less-popular themes in the international literature on the British industrial revolution (see Mokyr 1999). An important contributor to the Danish debate was Svend Aage Hansen (1970, 1984), who was inspired by W. W. Rostow (1960) to try to pinpoint the period in which Denmark experienced takeoff.

From the data he collected, Hansen concluded that there was no industrial revolution in Denmark until the 1890s, as evidenced by the fact that the industrial sector in Denmark was very small, being just 4–6 percent of Denmark's GDP at factor cost in his estimates (Hansen 1970, 13). Moreover, since he estimated that annual growth rates in total (not per capita) industrial production both before and after the 1890s were 4–5 percent, while during the 1890s they were about 7 percent, he believed that early industrialization took place during the 1890s in Denmark (13). This conclusion was strengthened by the figures he had for industrial employment. From 1855 to 1890 employment in industry rose from approximately twenty-five thousand to approximately forty-two thousand workers, but during the 1890s this figure rose by an additional thirty-six thousand. These figures revealed that it was in this decade that industry was first able to use the labor that had begun to leave agriculture (20).

The 1890s also saw the expansion of railways throughout the country, which was important for the exploitation of the domestic market, as it was fueled by the growing prosperity of agriculture (24). The efficiency of industry was also aided in the 1890s by the large number of amalgamations of individual firms (25); previously Danish industry had been very small scale. Industry also became better at absorbing innovations into the production process, which is revealed by the fact that a large proportion of industrial growth came from completely new areas—for example, electricity, cement, margarine, cable and wire, telephone, and sulfur (25–27). An organized credit market, available loans (42), and favorable monetary policies—for example, a low interest policy (62)—also did much to aid industrial growth in the 1890s.

Earlier economic historians had pointed to the 1870s as a period of industrialization due to substantial self-generated growth, the formation of joint stock companies, and the trend toward concentration. But Hansen's own figures seemed to suggest from the 1850s to 1890 there was a "thirty- or forty-year commercial expansion representing the preparatory phase for the truly vigorous industrial growth of the nineties" (16). Hansen's data itself, however, soon came to be the center of a heated debate, one that continues today.

Some fifteen years after Hansen's basic contribution, Niels Buus Kristensen (1987) took inspiration from Crafts (1985), who had reexamined the growth figures from the period around Great Britain's industrialization and found that growth rates for industrial output vary greatly depending on rather mundane statistical choices, particularly the choice of base year for deflation if relative prices between sectors change over time, something that is normally the case if one sector increases output largely because of technological advances. Kristensen set about seeing if the same methodology could be used to reappraise Hansen's national accounts figures and if this had any impact on the probable placement of industrial breakthrough. His research, however confirmed that growth in industry and services was greatest from 1890 to 1897, although overall economic growth was faster from 1882 to 1890. This was because in the subsequent period agricultural growth was weakly negative, thus affecting overall growth rates. In addition, his research revealed a so-called Gerschenkron effect[6] in the years after 1890 (and to a lesser extent between 1882 and 1890), which meant that structural changes in industry were greatest in this period, therefore reinforcing Hansen's conclusion of particularly significant industrial growth in the 1890s (Kristensen 1987, 34–35).

Further data from research undertaken by Ole Hyldtoft (1984) incorporated into Kristensen (1989) confirmed Kristensen's earlier conclusions of an incredibly smooth and uniform industrial growth performance throughout the entire period and, thus, no significant breakthrough. The new data also revealed that the idea of a breakthrough in the 1870s could be dismissed, since only in 1875 did growth exceed the average for the period as a whole. If one were to talk about a breakthrough at all, one would have to search for it in the last four years of the 1890s, when exceptional average growth rates of 9 percent per year were recorded. However, it is doubtful that such a short period can be considered a breakthrough, since this would necessarily involve large structural changes, which could not have taken place in such a short period of time. Just as importantly, this boom had no lasting impact—all the gains made were wiped out by the decline from 1901 to 1905 (Kristensen 1989, 40). These findings led Kristensen to the conclusion that industrial breakthrough embraced the entire period he examined—from 1872 to 1913.

Subsequent, more qualitative work by Danish economic historians also stresses the gradual nature of industrialization. Hyldtoft (1999) writes about strong, continuous growth from 1840 until today, broken only by short periods of recession, which he attributes to a transformation of society. New and more capital-intensive production methods began to be used, and new goods and services emerged as consumption patterns changed. Industry, trade, and the monetary system grew in importance, and towns began to grow faster than the rural population. The Danish economy also became more integrated into the international economy. Education improved and institutions changed as liberalism, capitalism, and the beginnings of democracy arrived (9–10).

Or, in other words, Denmark achieved the kind of balanced economic growth that, according to newer theories of economic development outlined in chapter 1, allows agriculture to develop within the general process of transition to modern economic growth, thus making the latter more easily sustainable through a more equal distribution of capabilities and entrepreneurship (as well as inefficiencies and backwardness) in all sectors. Hyldtoft argues in the same direction that a general transformation rather than industrialization took place. This growth he attributes mainly to growth in total factor productivity (TFP)—that is, Denmark became better at combining its inputs into outputs. This he attributes to better and cheaper capital, a more effective workforce (due to, e.g., education), better utilization of raw materials (due to, e.g., new technology), better management of production, a more mobile workforce, a better functioning financial market, fewer barriers to trade, and expansionist economic policies, among other things. Not least institutional changes are considered to be of great importance (Hyldtoft 1999, 17).

An important point made by Hyldtoft is that the main growth area during this period is not in the businesses that produced consumer and investment goods but rather in the businesses that arranged for the distribution of these goods and services, which are part of the high-value service sector highlighted by Ljungberg and Schön (2013) above. These businesses, which he calls the "transaction sector," including transportation, grew from around 10 to 15 percent in 1840 to well over 30 percent of GDP in 1910. This says much about the growth in the domestic and international distribution of goods during this period. Several factors meant that these costs were worth the extra expense. Firstly, there were absolute and comparative trade advantages to be had. Secondly, distribution became relatively cheaper. Transportation costs fell dramatically at the same time that many domestic and international barriers to trade fell away. Finally, transactions became better organized and therefore cheaper because of, among other things, a better functioning financial market, larger and more efficient companies, and a supportive legal system (Hyldtoft 1999, 21).

The most recent work on Danish industry has been highly revisionist but in a broader sense than the technical approach by Kristensen discussed above. Boje (2014, 2016) emphasizes the long-run development of the Danish economy outside agriculture and the point that, by starting their narrative in the late nineteenth century, previous generations of historians have come to focus too much on a period when agricultural interests had a very strong position politically, socially, and culturally (Boje 2016, 34). This new approach emphasizes firstly that Denmark was already relatively rich by the mid-nineteenth century, with a modern, urban, and industrialized economy based on high investments in infrastructure, education, and international contacts bringing new knowledge into the country. Second, it emphasizes that Copenhagen and other provincial cities were already modernizing by the middle of the nineteenth century as part of the international modernization process and not simply due to demand from agriculture (34). There is a stress on continuity of the business system and the development of the cities as successor organizations to the guilds introduced similar examination systems, and the cities—in particular Copenhagen—continued to expand (35). A highly efficient public administration and government support for education supported this.

Boje (2016) also emphasizes that large firms were founded before 1882, based on science and innovation, such as Carlsberg in 1847, which through its laboratory made important contributions to brewing technology, which, in turn, contributed to the later success of the Danish pharmaceutical industry. Otto Mønsted became one of the leading margarine producers in the world, and others found success in other branches—for example, certain producers of machinery such as F. L. Smith & Co. (cement), Burmeister and Wain (shipping and steam engines, as well as centrifuges), and Tietgen's Great Northern Telegraph Company (communications). Later successes in electrical engineering also had historical roots, such as the famous Ørsted, who was the first to discover electromagnetism in 1820. These were firms with a strong focus on R&D and with strong links to educational establishments as well as being open to innovations abroad. This is of course in no way in conflict with and in fact complements our narrative, which also emphasizes the triumph of Danish agriculture and the cooperatives as being the end result of a long period of modernization with roots in the eighteenth century.

That in a primarily agricultural society economic enlightenment first showed itself through agriculture is perhaps not surprising. Certainly, modern practices spread through the urban occupations as well, but it is worth noting that export of industrial goods never exceeded around 10 percent of value added before 1914, with the vast majority of exports coming from agriculture (Henriksen and Ølgaard 1960).[7] New calculations of gross factor income for Denmark presented by Hans Kryer Larsen, Søren Larsen, and Carl-Axel Nilsson (2010) emphasize (in contrast to S. A. Hansen 1984) the importance of manufacturing industry for Danish total output and export trade, although it might be noted that much of this is achieved by moving the cooperative creameries and slaughterhouses into the manufacturing sector. This is assuredly correct following modern national accounting practices, but these enterprises were nevertheless indisputably agricultural, in the sense that they were, at least since the establishment of the cooperatives, largely owned by the farmers themselves.

Much of the above work by previous generations of economic historians in Denmark reflects that they were products of their time, focused on finding evidence of a "breakthrough," "takeoff," or "industrial revolution" in Denmark. As they looked at the available evidence, it became clearer that there was a gradual expansion and development of industry, a fact that the most recent generation has taken back even further, seeing its reflection in developments in Denmark since at least the eighteenth century. Our narrative complements their work in the sense that we have also emphasized the role of knowledge institutions, the spread of technology and organizational innovations, and the importance of openness and flexibility for the success and eventual industrialization of Danish agriculture. That this was also happening in other sectors was assuredly part of the reason for the success of the Danish economy as a whole. In fact, the development of industry was complementary to the mechanization of Danish agriculture after the cooperatives.

Lessons from the Danish Agricultural Revolution for Developing Countries

In the preceding chapters, we have emphasized a number of points that made Denmark so successful during the first era of globalization prior to the First World War. We have particularly stressed pioneering efforts by an elite in terms of cultivation practices, dairy operation, empirical discourse, training, research and development, and the establishment of market connections. We have shown how these often led to unintentional improvements more generally due to the self-interest of the elites, who wanted to free themselves from administrative duties. Only with more efficient workers, skillful dairywomen, improved market contacts, and continuous supplies of high-quality butter from their neighbors could estate owners reap the benefits of collective reputation in distant markets—benefits that alone they would not have been able to achieve.

On the other hand, we have a continuous story of connections between these elites and the general agricultural population of farmers, smallholders, and, to a lesser extent, landless workers. These groups were able to employ the practices developed on leading estates once the circumstances favored their adoption. The agricultural reforms had given them full property rights over their land and labor and, thus, the possibility of benefiting from commercialization and participation in education, training programs, and even free schools and folk high schools which they themselves organized. In the cooperative movement, the elite's practices and general population's capabilities converged as the most prominent manifestation of the Danish path to economic development, marked by flexibility to adapt and founded on human capital, both at the higher end of the distribution (the elites) and in the population at large.

In this, Denmark was never the liberal paragon it has often been presented as, with early trade policy supporting the production of butter and extensive state support for education in particular. But it was open and liberal enough to take advantage of its quite favorable natural endowments such as climate and geography, which allowed ideas to flow into the country from abroad and Danish products to flow to the United Kingdom and other markets. This openness is something arguably more important than Denmark's lack of natural resources like minerals or coal.

A pertinent question, given the traditional narrative that emphasizes the role of cooperatives for Danish success, is to consider the counterfactual of how Denmark would have been had the cooperatives never emerged. Our work suggests that the foundation on which they were built was developed over the preceding century, from when Moltke introduced the Holstein system to Denmark. Clearly, the institutional innovation, the cooperative creamery, was only possible because of the technological innovation, the automatic cream separator, and the separator would perhaps have been more difficult to introduce widely in the absence of cooperation, making the true relative impact of these innovations less easy to identify. This particular form of cooperation also allowed farmers to retain control of a relatively large part of the value chain as residual claimants to profits, something that might or might not have emerged from the community creameries, although the stronger presence of merchants and local notables in them might have hampered this. Nevertheless, despite the possible organizational advantages they enjoyed (see, e.g., Henriksen 1999; Henriksen, Hviid, and Sharp 2012), we see the cooperatives as the end result of a period of modernization of Danish agriculture and not the beginning. In fact, it is quite possible that their contribution was relatively minor compared to their main rival for peasant production, the community creameries. Perhaps Denmark in 1890, given the century of developments described in this book, would have looked much the same without the cooperatives, a point that is lent support by our empirical work, as discussed in chapter 9. This suggests that the production gain from the new institution, the cooperative, was just 13–24 percent, as opposed to 63–79 percent for the new technology, the automatic cream separator.

We could also go further back in time and ask ourselves what would have happened to Denmark if the agricultural reforms had not happened. In a basic scenario, this would mean no enclosures, no updating of the rent system (and commutation of boon work), and no freehold farmers. Under this system, the estate sector would have developed probably in a similar way to what actually happened, but the peasants would not likely have been able or interested in adopting the same system. An alternative might have been that Denmark could have followed the path developed by Moltke and Völckers and ultimately superseded by enclosure, that is, the development of a communal system of *Koppelwirtschaft*. This might have meant that villages' cultivation would have been a rationalized communal version of that observed on estates and their milk might then have been received at the estate *hollænderi* and marketed through its channels, or it might have been processed in the villages by a sort of community *hollænderi*, thus spreading estate practices even faster.

Such an increase in dairy production at a much earlier stage would probably have found its limitations in the relatively small international demand; in the incentive structure of communal agriculture (particularly, the risk of overgrazing of the commons); in the boon-work obligations; and not least in the resistance of the peasants to change—although this was also initially the case with the arguably more radical enclosures. To make this alternative scenario work, the rent system would probably have had to change in a way that let peasants choose between labor obligations and money payments. And whether paternalistic community creameries would have received clean, unadulterated milk for marketing through the estate seems at least questionable. But it is possible that the system would eventually have evolved, on a different path, to a cooperative-like governance of the creamery—that is, a monetized rent payment system with inheritable tenancy. Whether it also would have led to enclosures is difficult to say. Even more complicated are the political implications and the emancipation of the peasants as a political force. All this leads us to believe that a full counterfactual is impossible to establish, that it is not necessarily the case that the agricultural reforms established the best of all possible Denmarks, but that alternative paths also might have become dead ends for a great variety of reasons related to the importance of property rights, market access, general politics, and farmers' incentives and capabilities for self-organization.

The fact that cooperatives were just one piece of the whole story matters because the historical development of Denmark has and does still today offer a tempting example to other agricultural countries: as Alan S. Milward put it almost forty years ago, it "is understandable that the extraordinary rapidity and painlessness of the transition in Denmark from peasant society to a pattern of living, a level of income, and an occupational structure typical of developed countries should have focused attention on the elements which accounted for this success" (Milward 1979, 29). Many countries have in fact tried to copy what might be termed the Danish model for growth through agricultural modernization based on land reform and cooperatives, with generally rather limited success, and we would argue that this rests on various fallacies concerning what it was that made Denmark successful in the first place.

These concern not only the importance of the cooperatives (which certainly can be a useful instrument for allowing peasants to enjoy economies of scale under particular conditions) but more importantly relate to a misunderstanding of the depth and sophistication of previous developments made over a considerable number of years. To use the old cliché, Rome was not built in a day, and cooperative Denmark was built over a century at least. Expecting the construction of a few cooperative creameries or slaughterhouses in a relatively underdeveloped country to transform agricultural fortunes is, unfortunately, likely to lead to disappointment and, in fact, often has. A few examples will suffice to make this point.

We have already touched on the example of Ireland, which had been a large traditional supplier of butter to the rest of the United Kingdom and indeed the world but suffered a relative decline compared to Denmark from the 1880s. Witnessing this, campaigners lobbied for the adoption of cooperation in dairying, explicitly modeled on Scandinavian counterparts, particularly Horace Plunkett (1854–1932) and Robert Andrew Anderson (1860–1942). In 1894, they formed the Irish Agricultural Organisation Society (IAOS). Particular emphasis was placed on introducing cooperatives in Munster, the historic heartland of the Irish dairy industry and location of the so-called Golden Vale, but efforts began early to introduce the combined innovations in the north of the island. From its establishment, the IAOS was a top-down promoter of cooperation, and the Irish experience thus contrasted greatly with that of the Danish, where cooperatives were formed by voluntary associations of farmers. Although many cooperatives were established, the majority of the Irish dairy industry remained in private hands, and the industry never again attained its dominance of the British market. Partly this failure owed to the reasons given in chapter 9—in particular, the existence of large incumbent operations, competition with which possibly exacerbated underlying sectarian tensions (McLaughlin and Sharp 2015; see also O'Rourke 2007).

Previous work has also emphasized the difficulties the Irish cooperatives suffered particularly in binding their suppliers, a problem that manifested, for example, in creameries being forced to accept poor-quality milk out of fear of losing supply (Henriksen, McLaughlin, and Sharp 2015). We might add that in part this could have reflected the lack of a tradition for such practices, which had been painstakingly introduced to Denmark, backed up with a sophisticated system of extension, over many decades. To be sure, however, comparing Ireland and Denmark purely on dairying grounds is somewhat misleading, as the agricultural structure of both countries was significantly different; a greater emphasis was placed on livestock trading in Ireland, where Irish farmers held a significant share of the livestock trade, supplying 85 percent of all British imports in the 1890s (Perren 1971). Also, Ireland's climate was different, which made grass-fed cattle raising relatively attractive, and which militated against winter dairying (Ó Gráda 1994, 2006).

Another country that attempted to imitate the Danish success in the nineteenth century was Iceland. A dependency of Denmark until 1918, after which point the two countries were joined in personal union through the monarchy until 1944, Icelanders naturally turned to Denmark for inspiration. Iceland at the end of the nineteenth century was an agricultural country, based largely on sheep rearing and fishing, with almost no manufacturing base. Thus, already in the 1870s, the Royal Agricultural Society had supported a report by the agriculturalist Peter Feilberg (1878) that concluded that Iceland's difficulties were rooted in a lack of capital and practical knowledge. Returning to the issue some years later, Feilberg emphasized cultural norms, which could in his opinion only be changed through the outside support of education and training to promote cultural change. The vast geographical differences between Denmark and Iceland meant that the import of Danish agricultural knowledge would have been of little use, and thus innovation had to be homegrown (Feilberg 1907).

In fact, greater public efforts had already been made to promote education and training, with three agricultural schools established in the 1880s, an expanding number of agricultural societies, and a government grant scheme for farm improvements. Although progress was noticeable by 1900, the improvement was slow, partly due to a shortage of capital and education, but also due to widespread tenancy and an insecurity of leases, which meant that the tenant was not guaranteed the benefits of the improvements made on the farm (Jónsson 2012, 209). In 1900 the first dairy school was established, headed by a Danish expert and supported by the Royal Agricultural Society. Then, in 1901 the first cooperative creamery was founded in Iceland to export butter for the British market. By 1913 they numbered thirty-one, supplied by 1,200 farmers. Cooperative slaughterhouses soon followed. Despite receiving substantial support from the government in the form of investment credit and export subsidies, however, the creameries were relatively small scale and suffered from having to use ewes' milk for production (212).

A more focused attempt to introduce the Danish model to Iceland came following a decline during the First World War. With broad-based backing from farmers and policymakers, the cooperative movement thus spread quickly during the 1920s, supported by massive public financing constituting 8 percent of the total government budget (215). Agricultural exports failed to take off, however, declining to a 10–15 percent share of total exports in the 1920s, compared to 20–25 percent before the First World War (217). By the time the Great Depression hit, it was clear that Iceland could not be a serious butter or meat exporter; even the established European producers were by then losing out to newcomers like Australia and New Zealand.

The examples of Ireland and Iceland serve to emphasize the importance of geography for the successful introduction of Danish practices. As we made clear in chapter 2, development through dairying requires an environment that is conducive to that activity. To highlight this point, we might present the examples of Schleswig under Prussia (and subsequently northern Schleswig under Denmark from 1921) and Scania, the formerly Danish province in the south of Sweden. There, dairying developed in parallel and in connection with Denmark, with cooperative creameries also emerging in the 1880s. The more general lesson must be that the top-down imposition of an alien institution is unlikely to work in environments and societies that are unready or are simply unsuitable.

Despite these failed attempts to copy the Danish model in the late nineteenth century and in the first half of the twentieth century, shortly after the Second World War the United Nations Food and Agriculture Organization (FAO) commissioned a study on the evolutionary changes in Danish agriculture over the previous two hundred years (Skrubbeltrang 1953), with the implication that something was to be learned for developing nations. A particular emphasis was placed on the importance of medium-sized owner-operated farms and cooperation, although, as Ingrid Henriksen has made clear, while this was certainly appropriate given the state of transportation and other technology around 1900, this was not the case after the Second World War, when larger scale operations would have been more efficient (Henriksen 1993, 175). The FAO was not alone, however, with similar points being made by Dieter Senghaas (1986), and, in prefaces to P. Manniche (1969), Jawaharlal Nehru, the former prime minister of India and champion of co-operation in that country, and Kristen Helveg Petersen, the Danish minister for technical collaboration with developing countries, again emphasized co-operation but also adult education and, in particular, folk high schools as a means of increasing efficiency in the rural economy.

India has millions of small dairy producers, and the modernization of the dairy sector has been a priority of the government since the first Five-Year Plan in 1951. Production increased substantially following the foundation of the National Dairy Development Board in 1965 and its initiative, Operation Flood, which involved organizing dairy cooperatives at the village level with the aim of supplying the large urban centers; the program received support from the World Food Program, the World Bank, and the European Economic Community (Banerjee 1994). Despite some success, Indian cooperation in dairying has nevertheless suffered from difficulties receiving adequate supplies and from inadequate rural infrastructure (see, e.g., Madan 2007). A recent study of members of the Manipur Milk Producers Cooperative Union found that farmers singled out high costs as the most serious constraint for implementing improved and scientific farming practices, particularly in the area of health care practices (Singh et al. 2012).

Inspired to a large extent by their own national story and the work of Skrubbeltrang, Danish development policy was also for a while very much geared toward exporting the Danish model to the developing world. This is examined in a somewhat lighthearted article prepared by a former Danish minister of development (Bach 2012) for a festschrift presented to a former head of the Danish panel of independent economic advisors (and economic historian), Niels Kærgård. The article describes how Danish red milch cows and agricultural equipment were sent by ship to, for example, India in order to demonstrate modern agricultural methods, where they of course faced completely unsuitable environmental conditions, leading to the ultimate failure of the project but only after many years of wasted funding. In countries such as Pakistan and Tanzania, the entire cooperative sector was controlled by governments that were not usually very supportive. Even attempts to involve private firms failed, such as when the Danish firm Atlas attempted to establish in Sudan a large slaughterhouse (with a capacity for slaughtering four hundred cows per hour) in a small town which lacked both roads and electricity and where the local nomadic population had no tradition for selling cattle or for buying meat (Danida 2012). This was of course an extreme example but represented the failing of development policies where aid was made conditional on purchases from the donor country.

These disastrous episodes led to a backlash in the 1990s against the idea of development through cooperative creameries and slaughterhouses in environments where advanced technology had no local basis for success and where, moreover, developed-world agricultural support made conditions for exports difficult. Farmers in developing countries were subject to export taxes, artificially low prices, and overvalued exchange rates (Bach 2012, 338)— all ingredients of the typical anti-agricultural development recipes of the time outlined in chapter 1. Bach concludes, however, that conditions are somewhat different today, making development through agriculture a plausible development strategy again (341), a point that has also been made, for example, by the World Bank in a series of reports (World Bank 2007, 2009; see also chapter 1). Martin Ravallion (2009) has demonstrated that the vast majority of people who have escaped from poverty in China have done so through developments in the agricultural sector.

The idea that the direct application of historical development strategies today can be counterproductive was in fact also noted by Milward. He cautioned against countries simply attempting to imitate the successful, due to the distortion of historical images (Milward 1979, 39–41). In our context we would emphasize that this was the Danish narrative of the importance of cooperation. It was not cooperation as such that led to Danish success, but rather it was the entirety of the century of developments preceding this that made it possible.

To finish off, we might consider briefly what happened to Denmark after the emergence of the cooperatives and until today. The beginning of the twentieth century until the First World War saw a continuation of the previous decades' growth, so that butter exports, which now were not so dependent on the British market, covered around 50 percent of the value of nonagricultural exports from Denmark (Bjørn 1982a, 187). Certain reforms were made during this period including the introduction of the *lurmærke* in 1906, which guaranteed certain quality requirements for exported butter. Then, after a difficult period during the First World War, during which imports of coal for the creameries, feed for the cows, and fertilizers for agriculture became difficult to source, and most exports of produce tended by necessity to go to Germany rather than to the United Kingdom, the interwar years brought little relief. Livestock herds had been heavily reduced during the war, and the productivity of the land had suffered due to the lack of artificial fertilizers. Exports to Germany almost completely ceased, leaving the United Kingdom once again by far the largest market, although until 1921 that country dictated quantities and prices (S. A. Hansen 1984, 19). The Great Depression brought predictable difficulties for Danish agriculture, which was supported by a low interest rate policy until 1935, devaluations in 1931 and 1933, subsidized loans, production quotas, and a restructuring of the tax system in favor of farmers (Johansen 1975, 69). Attempts to rationalize the industry were largely unsuccessful (Rasmussen 1982, 221–23) and were to a certain extent countered by a partitioning movement and various land acts, which sought to maintain and extend the model of small production units, which was seen as instrumental to Danish success (Skrubbeltrang 1953, 269–77). This meant that Denmark was trapped in a system ideally suited to the turn of the twentieth century but little suited to the challenges of the modern world. Low growth in agriculture from the 1950s to the 1970s followed (P. J. Pedersen 1996, 560), and a completely new competitive and regulatory regime was initiated with European Community membership in 1973. Despite these and various other challenges, however, Danish agriculture and not least dairying was progressing, with the introduction of new technologies such as electricity and milking machines after the turn of the twentieth century and important reforms to education.

It was only from the 1960s that rationalization of the industry really took off (Buksti 1982, 360–73), so that Denmark itself departed from the ideal of a small-scale, independent, democratic, and cooperative countryside. In fact, the consolidation of the industry was to continue to such an extent that by 1999 there were only fifteen small dairies and one giant monopoly cooperative dairy on the Danish market, Arla (Mordhorst 2014, 122), which had been formed by the merger of the Swedish dairy cooperative, Arla (named after the first Swedish cooperative), and Danish MD Foods in 2000.

Arla now commands 90 percent of the produced milk in Denmark, and Denmark is the eighth largest agricultural exporter in the world, with more than one-third of export income deriving from the food industry (Mordhorst 2014, 116). This success abroad has however been met with criticism in Denmark, particularly for unfair business practices, which according to Mordhorst has damaged the Danish understanding of their national story (Mordhorst 2014). The large producer of Danish pork products, Danish Crown, is no longer a cooperative.

Nevertheless, the *Economist* ran an article on January 4, 2014, titled "Bringing Home the Bacon: Tiny Denmark Is an Agricultural Superpower," appropriately illustrated with a cartoon of a pig and a red cow, emphasizing that Denmark was still at the forefront of agricultural innovation and efficiency, although it is now apparently a "land of milk and honey-roast ham" rather than a land of milk and butter. Perhaps the abolition of the European Union's restrictions on milk production in April 2015 will eventually give a boost in exports to Denmark's highly competitive dairy industry, which has however suffered for years from low prices and other challenges that the milk quotas were in part designed to mitigate.

According to the *Economist*, China has apparently "identified Denmark as a model," although mostly for quality control. We would advise caution. Denmark's success was not built in a day or even over the couple of decades during which cooperative creameries filled every corner of the little kingdom. It was a success built on education, openness, social cohesion, and many other factors, some or all of which are lacking in other countries. Moreover, as Henriksen (1993, 175) made clear some time ago, Denmark's rapid development through agriculture was only possible because of the ideological free trade stance of the United Kingdom in the late nineteenth century, which importantly in our context manifested itself in the lowering of the butter tariff in 1853 and its complete repeal in 1860. Today, developing countries wishing to develop through agriculture must, despite some progress in recent years, still contend with the protection of today's leading economies, including Denmark itself. They might, nevertheless, want to invest in the access to knowledge, markets, and technologies that would enable their rural producers to remain competitive for traditional products in their home markets or, more critically, try to find the niches of specialization that would allow for the successful diversification and long-run development of their rural and urban economies.

Notes

Chapter One

1. See Garrido (2014) on the—rather unsuccessful—orange-grower cooperatives in Valencia, Spain; see Ó Gráda (1977) for the adoption of cream separators in Irish dairying.

2. One recent example of strong growth in agriculture fueling economic development is the Green Revolution starting in the 1960s, which led to the development and diffusion of a large number of more productive varieties of traditional crops. See, e.g., Gollin, Hansen, and Wingender (2016).

3. Some of these virtues, however, might not materialize jointly, since for example productive cows are not useful for ploughing, while horses add little value in terms of direct output.

4. See Alesina, Giuliano, and Nunn (2013) for empirical evidence on the long-run effects of the introduction of the plough into arable farming for gender roles in sub-Saharan Africa. Federico and Martinelli (2015) assess the gender implications of a wider range of arable and livestock production activities. They find that in Italy cow milk production historically was biased toward male employment, probably because it required, apart from the handling of livestock by women, the male-dominated production of feed grains.

5. A similar point was made by O'Brien and Keyder (1978, 137) in their explanation of differences in agricultural productivity between Britain and France in the nineteenth century.

6. For the United States, dairy and cereals demand elasticities are similar to those given here for the United Kingdom; meat elasticities are somewhat lower than those for dairy but clearly higher than those for cereals.

7. It would be interesting to contrast these findings with the evolution of relative prices in Denmark, but consistent long-run series unfortunately are not available at this stage.

8. Refined sugar is also a highly processed agricultural product but with a much more storable raw material than milk.

9. It should be noted, however, that while the gain in purchasing power for butter in comparison to sugar was continuous since at least the 1840s, the gain against iron was mostly during the high point of the industrial revolution, between the 1810s and the 1860s, when new technologies improved the efficiency of iron production and brought down prices; some of the gains of butter versus iron prices were later reversed.

Chapter Two

1. See Østergård (2012, 47–53; 2006, 56–60).

2. The islands of St. Thomas (since 1671), St. John (since 1718), and St. Croix (since 1733), which after more than half a century of negotiations were sold in 1916 to the United States.

3. Several forts along what was called the Danish Gold Coast occupied since the 1660s and sold to the British in 1850. The main fort was Fort Christiansborg at Accra, which under the name Osu Castle is the current seat of the government of Ghana.

4. The trade bases of Trankebar (Tharangambadi in Tamil Nadu, from 1620) and Frederiksnagore (Serampore near Calcutta, from 1745), both sold to the British in 1845.

5. In the Danish West Indies, slavery was abolished only in 1848. In the duchy of Holstein, formal servitude of the German variety existed until it was abolished in 1805; the issue estranged an important part of the traditional Holstein elite from rule by the Danish king.

6. Robert C. Allen (2011, 12) argues that the subsistence basket is similar to a \$1.25 per day poverty line, since it cost about \$1.30 per day in the United States in 2010.

7. Countries for which 1830 data exists include Belgium, Canada, Denmark, France, West Germany, Italy, Japan, Netherlands, Norway, Portugal, Russia, Spain, Sweden, Switzerland, the United Kingdom, and the United States.

8. A short but more detailed overview of "deep root causes" proposed in the existing literature is given in Bhattacharyya (2011, 20–47). Our sorting of factors largely follows Dalgaard (2010).

9. See, e.g., Wright (1990) for the case of the United States. On the other hand, both Dalgaard (2010) and Svendsen and Svendsen (2010) provide (quite different) narratives of how the natural environment shaped the history, institutions, and endowments of Denmark.

10. The highest hill in Denmark, Møllehøj in central Jutland, has an altitude of less than 171 m.

11. Norway, the other large part of the composite monarchy before 1814, ranks ninth on that list.

12. The largest canal within Denmark was the canal connecting the city of Odense and its harbor to the open sea. It was 8.5 km long and opened in 1803 (Boje 2014, 87).

13. Kjærgaard (1994, 182–85) also discusses the disappearance of malaria in Denmark, which still occurred on the island of Lolland in the 1810s. There was possibly a large outbreak on the eastern islands of Denmark in 1831, but whether or not this was malaria has been questioned (see, e.g., J. Manniche 1997).

14. Kjærgaard (1994, ch. 6) provides a detailed assessment of the increased work volume and intensity of boon work in the second half of the eighteenth century, mostly at the expense of the cotter and servant class.

15. Land to labor ratios are taken from the data underlying Lampe (2011), mostly calculated from the data compilations by Mitchell (2003).

16. Árnasson and Wittrock (2012, 2), citing Uffe Østergård.

17. Although it is sometimes translated as "serfdom," *vornedskab* was not the same as eastern European bondage or serfdom since it did not restrict marriage choices or the inheritance of personal property. It also did not apply to women; neither did *stavnsbånd* (cf. Løgstrup 1984, 287; Skrubbeltrang 1978, 254–55).

18. Tithes were abolished only in 1903 and until then were an important way to finance the Church of Denmark.

19. Apart from those aspects discussed below, estate owners also acted as executors of wills and inheritances (where they enjoyed the status of preferential creditors), as trustees of inheriting minors, and as prosecutors of criminal offenses within their estates, although they exercised these powers under increasing supervision and restrictions until losing most administrative rights in the 1800s and 1810s and with the constitution of 1849. Some estate owners also had the right to appoint manorial judges, although they never acted as judges themselves, so that *some* rule of law even on the lowest level was guaranteed. See Løgstrup (1984) for details. Dombernowsky (1988, 260–61) stresses that county governors often were themselves estate owners, whose control of tenant matters might not have been too strict in practice.

20. Among them, 0.9 percent of the land belonged to the University of Copenhagen.

21. Troops trained every two weeks during peak periods of agriculture; four times per year the company met and once per year the regiment (Løgstrup 1984). Holmgaard (1986) gives further details.

22. Actually, Holmgaard (1986) mentions that already in 1731 mobility restrictions for young rural men had been authorized by the government (cf. Dombernowsky 1988, 267).

23. Churches generated incomes from the church tithe, from which in principle the local church and its activities had to be maintained.

24. On Oeder see Skrubbeltrang (1978, 325–26).

25. Struensee, however, although perceived as a German outsider, was born in the Hamburg suburb of Altona, which then belonged to Holstein and the realm.

26. There was, however, resistance to some of the measures, such as a petition of 103 Jutland estate owners, following protests in 1788–91, that disturbed Crown Prince Frederik's honeymoon. The resistance was, however, efficiently dismantled by the central government under Colbiørnsen and ended with the political humiliation and voluntary exile of the main instigator, a German-born estate owner called Lüttichau (Horstbøll and Østergård 1990, 163–66). Also, a violent strike of Copenhagen's carpenters against the suppression of some of their privileges and associations was "energetically put down" (Kjærgaard 1994, 223).

27. Actually, Denmark obtained from Sweden the island of Rügen and Swedish (western) Pommerania, which it commuted with Prussia for Lauenburg. Prussia had obtained Lauenburg from Hannover in exchange for East Frisia.

28. These were based on earlier parish councils with a certain amount of autonomy which were established by law in 1841 (H. Christensen 1991).

29. Feldbæk (1990, 186–87), referring to findings from the Great School Commission of 1789 appointed by the government, concludes, however, that "it was doubtful whether the majority of the population was literate," which suggests that an unintended side effect of the confirmation requirements was that students simply learned selected sections of the catechism off by heart.

30. Sandberg's paper certainly influenced the assessment by Landes quoted above.

31. "Patriotic" here refers to the whole realm of the Danish king, not just Denmark proper; see Engelhardt (2002, 164–65) and Østergård (2006, 6).

32. Despite his rejection of officialdom, Grundtvig was a member of the constitutional assembly in 1848/49 and a member of the parliament afterward.

33. But note that Henriksen (1999, 59–60) highlights that folk high schools helped the working of the cooperatives since their teaching and lectures facilitated the ability of farmers to listen to longer explanations, which helped when learning new methods and technologies.

Chapter Three

1. See the textbook by Jespersen (2004, 55–56) and the overview of long-run tendencies in the interpretation of 1788 by Raaschou-Nielsen (1990).

2. Central conscription, in fact, is deemed to have increased the burden of military service on young men in rural areas (Jespersen 2004, 55–56).

3. See Skrubbeltrang (1978, 135–40, 276–77) for a more detailed overview of the old system.

4. It should nevertheless be mentioned that during some periods estate owners managed to incorporate some farms or parts of their lands into the demesne (see, e.g., Dombernowsky 1988, 277–81). In some cases, especially on crown lands, demesnes were also parceled out and sold, which led to the creation of new farms. The two processes seem to have cancelled each other out, creating outstanding long-run stability in the number of farms, although not to the same degree in all regions of Denmark.

5. These numbers are rather uncertain, since apparently many peasants who owned buildings but not the land they occupied considered themselves owners as well, although many had difficulties substantiating their claims in court cases, which arose because the Danish Law of 1683 in an "extraordinary clause" had determined that labor services of owners could not exceed one fourth of those of tenants (see Munck 1977, 43).

6. This consistency probably reflected that dependent farms of equal size made tax administration easier for landlords (Jespersen 2004, 126).

7. In other villages, all cotters received lands en bloc in one part of the village, often in a remote part of the village; see the detailed account by P. G. Møller (2016).

8. See Skrubbeltrang (1978, 152, 155–59, 201–9, 214–35, 339–46) for details on both the historical evidence and the process. Cf. Løgstrup (1984, 287); and Henriksen (2003, 32–33).

9. Dombernowsky (1988, 250–57) gives an overview of the process of crown estate sales and the position of tenants in the process.

10. The decree's documentation requirement yielded important archival documentation on boon work; historians, however, tend to see the information in these documents as maxima not as actual workloads; e.g., Henriksen (2003, 25); Skrubbeltrang (1978, 364), based on Løgstrup (1974).

11. The Small Commission was dissolved in 1798; the Large Commission existed until 1816. See, e.g., Dombernowsky (1988, 298–303), for an introduction and references about the commissions.

Chapter Four

1. There was some debate between Danish agricultural historians as to the relative importance of northern German innovations vis-à-vis those from the United Kingdom, but for dairying the story seems quite clear (see D. C. Christensen 1996 for the original revisionist account and S. P. Jensen 1998 for a reply).

2. In this period, only farms located very close to larger cities might obtain external fertilizers, such as night soil or other (largely organic) waste. An alternative, to grow fodder crops (like clover or turnips, etc.) on the fallow, was not practiced in this early period, in part because several parties held legal rights to grazing on the fallow and on cultivated lands after the harvest (see Schröder-Lembke 1978, 64, and 111–20).

3. Ambrosoli (1997) also shows that the "rediscovery" of clover and alfalfa was helped by

the fact that it was continuously used in crop rotations in, for example, Muslim Spain and other parts of the Iberian Peninsula.

4. The village of Årslev depicted in figure 3.1 might serve as an example: In 1786 a communal version of *Koppelwirtschaft* was introduced in the village, with nine enclosed fields, each containing one to three broad strips per farm. The system was given up only nine years (one full rotation) later for enclosures and individual cultivation (see Feldbæk 1990, 245, 271).

5. Similarly, in the Danish literature it has been suggested that the fall and stagnation in the price of grain from the mid-1600s might have given an incentive to move into dairying (Frandsen 2005, 146).

6. Bieleman (1996) gives an account of the sophisticated dairy sector in the Lower Countries during the Dutch "Golden Age." Davids (1996) explores how the *hollænder* came to Holstein.

7. Iversen (1992, 79–83) gives information on how these charges varied across time and space in the duchies.

8. See Henriksen, Hviid, and Sharp (2012) for a description of the later importance of contracts for Danish cooperative dairying.

9. A very similar description is given by Iversen (1992, 76–77) of two contracts from northern Schleswig.

10. Von Treskow was the son of the owner of the Owinsk estate in Owińska, very close to the trading hub of Poznań/Posen in modern-day Poland.

11. At this time, however, cattle pests had done much to reduce cattle stocks.

12. From Grev Adam Moltke's *Plan for Frederik den Femtens Regering*, quoted in Porskrog Rasmussen (2010a, 9n1; our translation).

13. During the next decades, Moltke would own estates in all parts of Denmark as well as in Schleswig and Holstein and become the largest landowner in the monarchy (see the map in Porskrog Rasmussen 2010a, 14). His cultivation reforms in Denmark were centered mostly on the aforementioned estates on Zealand and the ones he bought between 1763 and 1765 on Funen (Glorup with Anhof, and Rygaard).

14. The official prices, *kapitelstakster*.

15. In the late 1760s, he and Völckers also developed a version of *Koppelwirtschaft* for the villages dependent on his estates, which respected traditional common land rights without the comprehensive institutional reforms that would come with enclosures later in the century (Porskrog Rasmussen 2010a, 30–35). This version, however, did not spread as fast and widely as its estate demesne counterpart and fell into disuse with enclosures, as evidenced by the example of Årslev in chapter 3.

16. Three hundred is almost exactly the number of cows that Johann Jürgen Bærner had envisioned in his 1770 reorganization plan based on the milk-cattle carrying capacity of Antvorskov demesne of about 888 *tønde land* in an eleven-field rotation (Linvald 1905–8, 275).

17. One exception was Thy, which was famous for its cows and its giant Thybo cheeses, which were exported to England (Drejer 1962, 20).

18. In fact, it was not until 1878 that the Danish red milch cow, which was to dominate Danish agriculture for decades, was officially designated.

19. Valentiner was born in Schwensby near Flensburg in Schleswig in 1767 and had been tenant of the Fuhrenkamp estate east of Kiel in Holstein from 1791 to 1819 before acquiring the farm of Bredeshave and Gjeddesdal estate in the 1820s. Both at Fuhrenkamp and at Bredeshave and Gjeddesdal he practiced oxen fattening. See his genealogical information online in "Skeel-Schaffalitzky, Santasilia. Stamtavler over danske adelsslægter," created by Finn Holbek, http://

finnholbek.dk/genealogy/getperson.php?personID=I51964&tree=2, last modified August 13, 2011.

20. Edward Tesdorpf was born in Hamburg to a family originating from Holstein.

21. This maximum level was maintained until about 1900 and later only slightly overtaken during the Second World War.

22. Transportation would homogenize the milk, making the traditional method of extracting the cream—waiting for it to rise to the surface—extremely slow.

23. Invariant geographical conditions are proxied by regional fixed effects, which, for example, control for the much lower number of cooperatives and hollænderier in Jutland.

24. Holck reports that two copies of the relevant publication (the very first Statistisk Aarbog or Statistical Annual) survived the fire—but in recent decades no copy could be located.

Chapter Five

1. This concept is also related to the older framework of evolutionary economics, which highlights the circular and cumulative causation leading to the gradual and self-reinforcing introduction of good accounting practice and concurrent productive specialization and professionalization.

2. Hausmann and Rodrik (2005) take this approach to a detailed case study of El Salvador.

3. Before Rosenthal, accounting historians have explored the use of accounting on slave plantations from different angles; see, e.g., Fleischman and Tyson (2004).

4. See the considerations by Olsen (1957) below.

5. There is unfortunately little direct evidence that economies of transaction density motivated individual contributors in Denmark. Nevertheless, the discussion between Thaer and the leading estate tenant Reiche in Thaer (1799, 196–97) shows that, from the late eighteenth century at least, leading estate dairy entrepreneurs in Schleswig and Holstein were not afraid of competition in limited markets but perceived that the world market was much larger than could be satisfied by local estate production.

6. See chapter 2 and Løgstrup (1984) or Kjærgaard (1994, especially ch. 8, 198–243) for an instructive overview of the relations between central government and estate owners in the centuries before 1800. Apart from survivor bias, it seems unlikely that peasants (subordinate farm tenants) had the time or incentive to implement sophisticated bookkeeping systems before 1800 or 1840. Some outliers to this pattern, so-called peasant diaries, do, however, exist (see Schousboe 1978–79).

7. The system is described in Lampe and Sharp (2017) and embedded in the wider debates regarding the usefulness of accounting for a variety of practical purposes relating to agriculture, such as decision making, monitoring, benchmarking, and land valuation.

8. Hellesen appears in the census of 1845 as a sixty-year-old civil servant on Vartpenge (which means he was a civil servant whose post had been abolished and who was receiving a salary while waiting for a similar post) living in Copenhagen. He is recorded as the translator of a number of books on diverse subjects, which might imply that his 1846 work is a translation of something published elsewhere, although this is not mentioned in the book itself, so it seems unlikely.

9. In Thaer's student list (Gräfe 2013) the following Danes appear as students at Möglin until A. D. Thaer's death in 1828, all more or less prominent in farming and agricultural husbandry: Carl Dalgas (1808/09), Carl Johann [Juel] Engelbrecht (1819–20), Peter Adolph Tutein (1819–20), Otto Arnfeld Reedtz of Palsgaard (1822–23), Gustav Michelsen (1826–27), and Hofman Bang

(1827). After Thaer's death, more Danes studied under the guidance of his son Albrecht Philipp. Friis does not appear in this list, so he was probably a visitor and not a student.

10. *UfL* is now published under the name *Jord og Viden* as the members' journal of the trade union for academic agronomists.

11. *TfL* was called *Landoeconomiske Tidender* for its first few years of publication.

12. In the 1880s a third periodical with more specialized content, the cooperatives' weekly journal *Mælkeritidende* (Dairy journal), would join them. Like *TfL* and *UfL*, it has survived to this day and is published under the same name as the periodical of the Danish association of dairy technicians.

13. His accounts can be seen in the printed version from *TfL* as well as in Sehested's original version, preserved in the Funen regional archive: Provincial Archives of Funen (hereafter PA Funen), QB-012, Stamhuset Broholm, 18/267, Diverse Mejeriregnskaber mv 1816–1887.

14. He also lists that 3,063 *kander* of the milk of his cows had been given to calves for fattening, leading to revenue of only ca. 4.7 rigsdaler per 100 *kander* milk—a much lower price for the milk.

15. This is different from the accounting schemes presented by Thaer (1806b), which introduce a separate pro forma account for manure, which is valued at a "natural cost-price" and credited as production to the cows. This reflects the different interests of Thaer and Sehested. While Thaer wanted to maximize fertilizer for grain production (see Lampe and Sharp 2017), Sehested seems much more interested in the marketable nonmanure products obtained from milking the cows.

16. Much of the information on physical outputs during the 1840s from Tesdorpf's estates, especially Orupgaard, is preserved in the regional archive for Zealand and surroundings; Provincial Archives of Zealand (hereafter PA Zealand), QA-257 Orupgård Gods, Statistik over høst, mejeridrift og fårehold 1849–1904; further accounting documents for those and other estates have been preserved in PA Zealand as well.

17. With this insight, Hofman Bang essentially provides a follow-up to a discussion that Thaer (1799, 192–93) had with one of Holstein's leading estate tenants, a Herr Reiche, who had decided to administer his dairy directly, with a female dairyist in charge, instead of leasing it to a dairy tenant. In the case of Reiche's Rundhof estate near Schleswig, net earnings per cow, as shown in Reiche's accounts for 1796, increased to more than 21 rigsdaler per cow, an increase of 80.4 percent over the estate income from renting out cows at 12 rigsdaler per cow. Reiche underlines that a dairy tenant could not have realized the same difference in profits due to a chain of incentive problems that diminished equilibrium in terms of feeding, grazing and management of the herd, partly due to incomplete contracts and partly to the limited duration of leases. Hofman Bang (1861) presents similar and additional arguments.

18. PA Zealand, QA-010, Basnæs Gods, Mejeriregnskabner 1878–1899. Since none of the anonymous data surveyed by *TfL* in this or subsequent years matches the archival information for Basnæs, we can assume that the Basnæs accounts were not standardized for *TfL*.

19. Fink (2009, 463), based on B. K. Hansen (2006, 229–36), provides another instructive example of this. All over Denmark, from the 1860s, local and regional exhibitions of dairy products were held, but while women generally displayed their products, Segelcke or other respected male scholars gave the keynote speeches.

20. Some of the materials Segelcke used to illustrate his lectures, including empty account books, have also been preserved at the library of the Royal Veterinary and Agricultural College, which is now the Frederiksberg campus of the Faculty of Natural and Health Sciences, University of Copenhagen: see Segelcke (1877).

21. A selection is *Praktisk Anviisning til Regnskabsføring for Landmænd* (*UfL* 1860[2], 57); A. P. Bromander, *Bogholderi for Landbrug og Naeringsdrivende overhovedet* (originally in Swedish; *UfL* 1861[1], 145); and then in the 1870s: A. Svendsen and C. Christensen, *Maelkeri-Regnskab* (for teaching at Tune Agricultural School; *UfL* 1875[1], 287, and 1877[2], 575); L. Friis, *Tabel for Omsætning af Hvede, Byg, Rug, Havre og Smør, beregnet fra Kroner og Øre pr. 100 to til Kroner og Øre pr. Td.* (*UfL* 1875[2], 263); T. v. d. Goltz/C. G. V. Ræder, *Den landøkonomiske Bogføring* (*UfL* 1877[1], 660); S. Hansen, *Tabeller for Mejeri-Regnskab* (*UfL* 1877[2], 109); A. Svendsen, *Regnskabsbog til Optegnelser over Køernes og Svinenes Fodring* (*UfL* 1878[1], 674).

22. Despite his general skepticism of female accounting, Segelcke published a book for accounting based on Hanne Nielsen's system, including of course a section for cheese (Segelcke 1870). On Nielsen and Segelcke see also B. K. Hansen (2006) and Fink (2009).

Chapter Six

1. S. P. Jensen (1985) shows this in more detail for a single medium-sized farm, Porsager in Holtug near Stevns in eastern Zealand.

2. See Klitmøller (2008), 20–52.

3. See Bendz (1951), Hermansen and Lobedanz (1958), Lerche (1999), and Fritzbøger (2015).

4. It should be noted that the shorthorn varieties in Denmark were—contrary to those in the United States (see Olmstead and Rhode 2008, 314–15, 339)—multipurpose varieties, which means that they were perceived as beef cattle in comparison with the main varieties used for milk production (Angler, Jutland, Funen, Danish red).

5. Of course, the PPF itself depends on the assumption that we have some estates performing on the frontier.

6. This implies that the average efficiency is 83.2 percent, ranging from 38.1 to 99.1 percent for individual observations.

7. Hence the presence of "half cows" in the data.

8. This includes all feedstuffs given to the cows as mentioned in the original records as well as an equivalent for the grass consumed during summer grazing.

9. The nine observations of estates supplying their milk to cooperatives noted above are also coded as "modern" for *system*.

10. Note in this connection that it was never the case that all cows could produce during the winter (the maximum was 87 percent), so no farm could in this way be perfectly efficient.

11. See also chapter 10 for how the model of small farm units became entrenched in Danish agriculture, with unfortunate consequences in the twentieth century; see also Henriksen (1993, 175).

12. Henriksen (1999).

13. By this, they used the same "shadow lands" or "ghost acreage" abroad to feed their cows that figure prominently in accounts of the British industrial revolution and the development of the northwestern European core of the world economy, which helped to overcome demographic constraints in the eighteenth and nineteenth centuries (see Jones 1987, 83–84; and, more specifically, Van Zanden 1991, 216, 224, 232).

14. See Henriksen, Lampe, and Sharp (2011, 489, table 3).

15. The 14.9 percent gain from cream separator and cooperatives in row 1 of table 3 in Henriksen, Lampe, and Sharp (2011, 489) is a rather conservative estimate using the average milk production of butter producers using old technologies. It does not therefore take into account the increase in the average size of production units that accompanied the spread of cream sepa-

rators, so that the 31.6 percent gain seems to be a preferable estimate for the second stage for the whole of Denmark.

16. The model = (blank), E, and T options in LIMDEP. For more on this see Greene (2009) and Kumbhakar and Lovell (2000, 72–93).

17. Although note that strictly speaking the relationships we uncover are correlations rather than causal, although we interpret them in this way in common with the vast majority of the SFA literature.

18. On the econometric problem see Greene (2009, E33–53). Its nonrelevance in our case pays tribute to the accurate record keeping of the farmers.

Chapter Seven

1. Helle Thorning-Schmidt, "Statsministerens tale ved 150-året for 1864 den 18. april 2014 i Dybbøl." Website of Statsministeriet (Ministry of the State of Denmark), http://www.stm .dk/_p_14023.html, April 18, 2014, accessed October 3, 2014.

2. See chapters 2 and 3 for a survey of the more recent literature on this complex.

3. See, most tellingly, the data presented in chapter 1 and Williamson (2011, 47, 52–53, tables 4.1–4.3), for the concentration of exports of a wide range of "peripheral" countries around 1900.

4. For a general survey of Danish trade over this period, see Thomsen and Thomas (1965).

5. For 1835–37 some trade statistics are missing; partial data appears in a periodical called *Handels- og Industri-Tidende*. The format of the available data is similar to that of the *Eksport-statistiske Tabeller*; because no important shifts in trade can be observed, we omitted these years in the tables.

6. Sweden and Norway have been combined since they are reported jointly in the trade statistics for 1844 to 1847. However, the share of Sweden in 1838–43 and 1848–52 in total exports is only marginal, on average 0.25 percent, with a maximum of 0.36 percent in 1852.

7. From 1851 to 1852, however, export volumes increase a lot, so that the absolute volume exported to Britain in 1852 is just 2.5 percent below the 1851 volume (but 29 percent below the 1850 wartime maximum).

8. Note that a fourth option—looking at Altona's trade statistics—is impossible, since comprehensive trade or shipping statistics are missing for this period. However, in previous work it has been found that Altona was something like a junior partner to Hamburg in its export activities, and it thus turned out to be a reasonable assumption that its flows more or less mimicked those of Hamburg—no customs border separated them. See Lampe (2008, 146n64) for references.

9. See the working-paper version of Lampe and Sharp (2015b) for detailed tables on British butter imports.

10. See, however, the very partial information presented below.

11. There are import statistics for 1845 to 1848 in a volume published in 1850, but these refer to seaward imports of a selected number of goods only, among which butter is not listed (but it is listed as an export item, hence the data in table 7.6).

12. Federico (2012a) provides an excellent survey of recent work by economic historians in this field; see also the section on market integration in Lampe and Sharp (2016).

13. A formal test, which consists in imposing the pre-1860 model on the post-1865 data is strongly rejected with a p-value of 0.008, implying that these data cannot support the causal structure regarding the direction of price transmission of the previous model.

14. There are substantial differences between the estimates of wage gains made by so-called

optimists (like Lindert and Williamson 1983) and pessimists (most prominently Feinstein 1998), mostly driven by the composition of the cost-of-living index and the individual price series used to deflate wages. According to Robert C. Allen's (2007) corrected Feinstein real wage index, the increase was 20.4 percent between 1770 and 1840, corresponding to 0.25 percent per year.

15. See the introduction of Lampe and Sharp (2014a).

16. See Schmidt (1870, 530) for a near-contemporary Danish account of the importance of the reductions in the British butter duties.

17. The most notable exception was apparently the production of Thybo cheese in the small town of Thy in northwestern Jutland, which was exported to England (Drejer 1962, 20–21).

18. Remember that the prices presented above are prices for Funen butter in Copenhagen.

19. However, and in line with later observations on Danish produce (see chapter 8), Kohl remarks that the cheese produced was meager, thin, and tasteless, but the pork produced from whey and buttermilk was of good quality (69–71). The British travel writer Laing (1852) records similar observations from his travels to Denmark proper and the duchies a few years later.

20. Of the "packages," 99 percent entered by train either from Kiel (74 percent) or on the Berlin-Hamburg railway (25 percent) that connected Altona to Mecklenburg and the Prussian capital.

21. In 1852, according to the data in table 7.2, Denmark exported 4,670 *tønder* of butter to Altona. The mentioned 211 *last* (as Hamburg Commerzlast) would be equivalent to 4,064 *tønder* of 112 kg after deducting 13 percent tara. This would represent 87 percent of Danish exports to Altona. The seaward imports of butter (total) in the other table, ca. 2,563 *tønder*, are clearly below that; if 84.5 percent of them were from Denmark proper, they would represent 46 percent of Danish exports to Altona. The total weight of the railway traffic to Altona in butter is difficult to determine due to the different measures, and the share of Danish butter on the Kiel-Altona railway is unknown, as is the share of Danish butter in ships or carts arriving from Schleswig or Holstein.

22. Trade to England in quantitative terms evolved from the low level of 224 *læster* in 1828 to 6,865 *læster* in 1857 (A. M. Møller 1998, 59).

23. For example, the main export point in the 1850s, Tønning in southwest Schleswig, was only connected to the railway network in 1854 (A. M. Møller 1998, 93).

24. Apparently, the steamship finished its life as a post steamer in Korsør (A. M. Møller 1998, 94).

25. He notes that the consumption of butter in Denmark is "extremely large, . . . so that greater importance is attached to quantity than to quality." Only the higher classes and foreign importers got to enjoy good-quality produce, and "the same rule applies to cattle: the worst are sent to provincial towns, the better to Copenhagen, the next best to Hamburg, and the best to England."

26. See his biography by Pedersen, Strandskov, and Sørensen (2005).

27. During the 1864 war, he was required to transport troops for the Danish government, for which he chartered steamships from Thos. Wilson and Sons in Hull (C. K. Hansen 1956, 18, 24).

28. This is thus also a rejection of the possibility of any of the series being stationary. Thus cointegration is the appropriate methodology.

29. "Test of restrictions (*p*-value)" in the table.

Chapter Eight

1. The Danish 1885 Margarine Law discussed below suggests that this noninterventionist stance of the Danish government was conditioned on the "invisible hand" not diverting the

development path toward margarine production once specialization in dairying had become sufficiently clear for politicians to protect it.

2. The importance of the early beginnings of the shift of Danish agriculture has been recognized by Danish economic historians. For example, Henriksen (1993, 159) writes: "One implication of the early reorganization of production is that the time- and capital-consuming process of building up herds of milk cows was well under way before the introduction of modern dairy technology impelled animal husbandry toward further productivity gains. It may have provided Danish farmers with an advantage over their competitors in Britain and The Netherlands, where the number of livestock per person . . . was lower in 1870." See also Henriksen (2009, 123).

3. See Lampe and Sharp (2011) for a more detailed treatment of these issues.

4. Although Hornby (1969) argues that industry protection was a(nother) liberal myth.

5. Notable exceptions were the so-called *Krigsskat* (war tax) of August 5, 1864 (Scharling 1905, 570), and the law of 1891, which reduced duties on sugar, chocolate, and crude oil (583).

6. Thomsen (1991, 37) seems to have been the only scholar to recognize this point before.

7. The official price estimates used to value Danish foreign trade tellingly illustrate the difference between imported and domestic cheese: While imports were priced at 0.25 rigsdaler (0.50 kroner) per *pund* in 1857, exports were valued at 0.10 rigsdaler (0.2 kroner). In 1875, imports were valued at 0.67 kroner per *pund*, and exports at 0.24 kroner per *pund*. Hence, Danish authorities estimated the value of the cheese imported at the high tariff rates to be 2.5 to 2.8 times the value of domestic export-quality cheese. These prices were not far from reality: at Tesdorpf's Orupgaard estate, the annual average price of cheese sold was 0.15 kroner per *pund* in 1857 and 0.17 kroner per *pund* in 1875 (0.25 for the five-year average 1873–77 since 1875 was a particularly bad year for Orupgaard's cheese prices). Taken from PA Zealand, QA-257 Orupgård Gods, Statistik over høst, mejeridrift og fårehold 1849–1904.

8. The rate changed from the equivalent of 4 to 5 shillings per *pund*, but before 1864 the unit in the tariff scheme was 50 kg.

9. German: *Lederkäse*. This cheese has recently been resurrected in Germany as a "slow food" delicacy, and it is claimed (here: Slowfood Convivium Hamburg, "Die Wiederentdeckung des Holsteiner Lederkäse," http://www.slowfood-hamburg.de/lederkaese/, accessed March 7, 2017) that the name comes from the crust that forms on the cheese rather than the texture of the cheese as a whole. Apparently it is commonly diced and added to salad, which we might very speculatively postulate gives the long-run explanation for the rise of today's extremely large Danish feta-style cheese industry.

10. Quoted by Drejer (1925–33, 318); the original source is the report on the Danish dairies by Schroll (1876, 553).

11. For *TfL*, see Sehested (1857, 1858). For *UfL*, see especially the surveys of farms on Falster by Buus (1865, 1866b), reports by Hofman Bang (1862) on his tenancies, and reports by Hasle (1858) on the Rosenlund estate. Since Buus worked for Tesdorpf, this additional data might be biased toward a similar product mix. Some data reported in idiosyncratic form could not be used, especially the reports by Ræder (1869a, 1870, 1875a) on his Dyrehavegaard farm, which sold skim milk (to be used by others, probably to make cheese and feed pigs). Some of the partial accounts by estate tenants presented in chapter 5 were also not usable for our purposes.

12. PA Funen, QB-012, Stamhuset Broholm, 18/267, Diverse Mejeriregnskaber mv 1816–1887 (1855–69); PA Funen, QB-083, Søholm Godsarkiv, Regnskabsbog vedr. Mejeriprodukter og kreaturbesætning 1865–76 (1865–75); PA Zealand, QA-010, Basnæs Gods, Mejeriregnskaber 1878–1899 (1880–87); Danish Business Archive Aarhus, 00172, Buske Spritfabrik, 1877–79 Mælkeregnskab (1877–79).

13. This section is called "Mejeribruget i Danmark" for the years 1880 (data for 1878–79) to 1887, and "Mælkeribruget i Danmark" thereafter. For 1876 and 1878 there are reports from several regions of Denmark.

14. For those where we do not have price information, we can make reasonable assumptions following the practice of the authors of the reports we used. They are explained in detail in an appendix to Henriksen, Lampe, and Sharp (2010).

15. For pork, we use the production value net of the value of nonmilk feedstuffs given to pigs in all cases.

16. Henriksen, Lampe, and Sharp (2010) contains a detailed appendix including all observations and the weighted average data per year, although we have updated this information for the early years in our sample for the present book.

17. Such adjustment was not necessary for the 312 observations underlying figure 8.4, since none of them implied AVEs higher than 100 percent of the price of cheese, butter, or pork.

18. The share of the pork subsidy until 1863 in this sample is somewhat speculative, since the vast majority of observations are interpolated here using typical values (in part based on Orupgaard observations) for the value of skim milk, buttermilk, and whey given to pigs—but for individual observations with data the picture does not look radically different. We also observe a drop in the average implicit subsidy from on average 7.7 percent in 1864–75 to 5.8 percent for 1876–85. This might be due to the higher relative importance of cheese in the farms included in the smaller early sample or to a change in relative importance in production of the different commodities over time. It is likely a mix of both, since available (archival) data for Søholm Gods, Basnæs Gods, and Hesselagergaard (the latter not used in our sample due to missing cow numbers) indicate that production of cheese became less important between the middle of the 1870s and the first half of the 1880s. Therefore, our "subsidy series" in figure 8.4 seems to reflect a general trend but might overstate it due to a possible sample selection bias before 1876/79.

19. In chapter 10 we use another unique set of information, the accounts of Porsager farm owned by H. C. Sørensen for 1905. There profits (including managerial remuneration for the farmer and his wife but excluding return on capital for the farm and the land) are 14 percent of the total gross revenues of the farm and 3.2 percent on the farm capital (on top of a normal capital rent of 5 percent). For numerous technical reasons, among them the definition of total gross and net income, results reported by and commented on by S. P. Jensen (1985, 95–99) are not comparable to those reported by Jenkins named here, which refer to dairy activities only.

20. This problem is first mentioned as a concern in the report for 1890 (Bøggild 1891, 82) but must have been the case earlier. The explanation given in the report for 1891 is that the sample is not intended to be representative but should rather illustrate dairies with different sizes, technologies, locations, and so on, and not model dairies (Bøggild 1892, 117). In 1894 many older correspondents drop out because they stop being independent (Bøggild 1895, 99), but the basic selection remains the same, inviting much criticism, with the same response again in the report for 1896 (Bøggild 1897, 88).

21. Although it also criticizes this practice for being wasteful. See Bøggild (1888, 89).

22. "Vil man endelig lave Ost, saa søg da at fremstille et Produkt, der kan afsættes. . . . Den danske Kjøbstadarbejder er for godt stillet til at betragte den simple Ost som sit Hoved-næringsmiddel. . . . At forsøge at forandre Folks Smag er i Ostespørgsmaalet i Øjeblikket haabløst" (Bøggild 1886, 66).

23. There were a few exceptions; see M. C. Pedersen ([1885] 1981, 35).

24. We document this more in detail in Henriksen, Lampe, and Sharp (2012), 784–86.

25. We have examined this more in detail in Lampe and Sharp (2014a) and will return to the general issue below.

26. As Otto Mønsted (1933), a large producer of margarine in Denmark, made clear, this provision was actually more damaging for butter producers.

27. This was somewhat ironic, since Danish winter butter, produced by cows kept in barns, was naturally paler than its summer counterpart, which was produced using cows grazed on grass, and was therefore often also colored (Strandskov, Sørensen, and Pedersen 1998, 72). Note also that the Danish Margarine Law was much less restrictive than those of some dairy states in the United States. Miller (1989, 108–10) and Dupré (1999, 355) mention state legislation in New Hampshire, West Virginia, and Vermont from the 1880s and 1890s that required margarine to be colored pink!

28. Somewhat ironically, however, Danes soon became one of the leading consumers of margarine, a point noted by Lenin (1973, 224–25), who considered it evidence of the cost to Danish peasants of capitalist agriculture: "Danish well-to-do peasants, but above all the Danish capitalists, make a good deal of money from the butter trade. And yet Denmark is the world's biggest consumer of substitute butter, margarine! What is the explanation? It is very simple. The vast majority of the Danish population, like that of any other capitalist country, consists of workers and propertyless peasants. They cannot afford real butter. Even the middle peasants in Denmark, being in need of money, sell abroad the butter they produce on their farms and buy the cheap margarine for themselves."

Chapter Nine

1. In 1885, however, the creamery was leased to a dairyman and converted to an ordinary community creamery; apparently the company had been plagued by disagreements and already in 1878 two shareholders had left.

2. Before the centrifuge, cream was separated by waiting for it to rise to the surface of the milk. Transporting the milk over long distances homogenized it, making this process extremely slow. This was not however an issue for cream separated mechanically.

3. Of 336 societies registered with the IAOS in 1920, the combined share capital was just £193,208 (IAOS Annual Report 1921).

4. See, e.g., Van der Vleuthen (1994). Drejer (1925–33, 41) reports numbers of cream separators from the journal *UfL*, according to which in 1881 there were ninety separators in Denmark. By 1887, the number had risen to about 2,200.

5. See J. Pedersen (1999, 367). Pedersen (59) also reports that both B&W and their Danish competitor, Separator, since 1886 and 1888, respectively, produced small-scale versions of the separator. "Hand-separators," where the power source was not a steam engine but the human arm, offered an additional institutional-technological choice for small-scale producers. However, according to Pedersen they were produced mainly for export to countries where the "structure of production and marketing of butter could be very different from that in Denmark." That is, they were popular in lower cow-density regions in Ireland (West Cork, see Ó Gráda 1977), Sweden, and the United States.

In correspondence with the authors Jan Pedersen has kindly pointed out that the productivity of hand-driven separators improved rather dramatically over time so that in some countries they were eventually chosen in preference to the Danish model of heavy and expensive automatic separators even in environments not too dissimilar to those in (parts of) Denmark. By this time, however, path-dependency meant that it was difficult for Danish production to shift character so radically, and these other countries thus enjoyed a classic latecomer advantage.

6. Capacity here was measured by number of cows.

7. See chapter 10 for more on Sørensen and his farm.

8. For example, Orupgaard had a herd of ca. 220 milch cows in the early 1870s (Fenger 1873). The average herd size of the twenty-seven estates covered in the dairy survey in *TfL* for 1882 was 75.5, with a maximum of 176 and a minimum of seven (Sonne 1883).

9. See Bøggild (1896, 365–66), referring to experiments carried out 1879–83, as well as modern authors on the subject (S. P. Jensen 1988b, 324).

10. This insight was obtained during the empirical work underlying Henriksen, Hviid, and Sharp (2012), but was not included in the final version of that manuscript for reasons of space.

11. See Henriksen, Hviid, and Sharp (2012, 208n24) for contemporary references on this issue.

12. The archival sources are for the estates of Broholm (1865–69) and Søholm (1865–70) and for the private creameries Visby Mejeri (1870–75) and Sjørring Sø (1894–1902), a company that drained a lake in northwest Jutland and established a rather large private dairy. The records for Broholm and Søholm can be found in the provincial archives for Funen in Odense; the records for Visby Mejeri in the Institut for Sønderjysk Lokalhistorie in Aabenraa; and those for Sjørring Sø in the Danish Business Archive in Aarhus, A/S Sjørring Sø, Regnskaber vedr. mejeriet (1867–1909).

13. This is the data set we document in chapters 6 and 8.

14. These were somewhat larger proprietary operations since records for the smaller community creameries have unfortunately not survived.

15. Since the estimates are conducted in logs, the simple antilog of these estimates is likely biased. We therefore apply the Goldberger (1968) correction by adding 0.5 times the squared standard error for every log-coefficient before taking the antilog. Since the estimates are very precise, the correction is very small.

16. However, note that we might well be underestimating the efficiency gains of the cooperatives and the centrifuge, since we are comparing them to the best practice of old-style butter making, as represented by the estates who sent accounts to the *TfL*, and not to peasants producing butter at home, for which there are no usable surviving records.

17. Credit cooperatives were not so important in Denmark (in contrast to, for example, Germany), since their role seems to have been taken by the savings banks; see Guinnane and Henriksen (1998).

18. There is an additional implication to looking at just one input: by estimating a one-factor production function we cannot capture allocative efficiency of production factors. However, Henriksen and Hviid (2005) argue based on historical evidence that in butter making the use of other inputs (especially transport services and energy) are proportional to the amount of milk processed for the relevant part of the cost/production function, which would make allocative efficiency a minor issue. In the first stage, labor input might be of importance, since through winter feeding, which was labor intensive not just during the winter but required beet cultivation before, the amount of milk produced per cow (a capital good) could be increased but not its quality (Henriksen and O'Rourke 2005). Hence the amount and regularity of milk processed in the second stage could be affected but not the quality of the latter.

19. Input prices for raw milk are not available in many cases (by definition not for the integrated estate dairies), and additionally might only be weakly informative, since effective pricing of milk supplies based on the fat content of the milk, which is the most characteristic for the

production process, was not technically feasible at the beginning of our period and introduced only slowly and incompletely during our period (see Henriksen and Hviid 2005).

20. In economic history, this method has also recently been applied by Burhop and Lübbers (2009) who look at the productive efficiency of twenty-eight German coal mines between 1881 and 1913.

21. A highly significant $\lambda = \sigma_u/\sigma_v$ implies that $\sigma_u > \sigma_v$ and thus a high degree of inefficiency.

22. This corresponds to the findings of studies of modern dairies, although these typically look at the production of milk rather than the final products, see Álvarez and Arías (2004); Bailey et al. (1989); Fan, Li, and Weersink (1996); Hallam and Machado (1995); Heshmati and Kumbhakar (1994); Kumbhakar, Biswas, and Bailey (1989); Kumbhakar, Ghosh, and McGuckin (1991); and Tauer (2001).

Chapter Ten

1. The Danish Research Council has recently funded a project at the University of Southern Denmark to rectify this situation. Their progress can be followed at the website of the Danish National Accounts Project led by Paul Sharp at https://sites.google.com/site/danishnaproject/, accessed August 23, 2017.

2. In fact, following Robert C. Allen's (2009a) arguments for the adoption of capital-intensive textile machinery during the British industrial revolution, Henriques and Sharp (2016) and Khaustova and Sharp (2015) have speculated that the increase in real wages might itself have motivated the development of highly productive agriculture from the 1880s, and that perhaps the fact that wages were high already before this, combined with cheap imports of coal from England for a country with a large coastline-to-landmass ratio and thus small domestic transportation costs, might be part of the reason why Denmark turned to such a highly capital-intensive, labor-saving technology in the first place.

3. Henriksen (1993, 163–64) reports the underlying figures based on S. A. Hansen (1972) and Wunder (1987) and stresses that both terms are concepts that are not directly comparable.

4. Before 1884, butter and cheese production were undertaken by Sørensen's wife and his mother, and exports to Copenhagen are recorded in his books.

5. Although significantly higher than the figure for Great Britain, which is given in Crafts (1985) as 20.4 percent for men in 1870.

6. Alexander Gerschenkron wrote in the 1950s and 1960s about the "advantage of backwardness." "Backward" European countries (when compared to Britain), after making political and economic changes, were quickly able to copy and utilize the institutions and technology of the more advanced country.

7. Although note that the share of net exports of agricultural products might be lower, since especially dairy production relied heavily on imported feed and coal. If one were to include services into a balance of payments statistics, service exports might also have compared rather favorably to (net) agricultural exports.

References

Abildgren, Kim. 2010. "Consumer Prices in Denmark 1502–2007." *Scandinavian Economic History Review* 58(1): 2–24.

Acemoglu, Daron, and James A. Robinson. 2012. *Why Nations Fail: The Origins of Power, Prosperity and Poverty*. New York: Crown.

Ahrens, Gerhard 1978. "Die Überwindung der hamburgischen Wirtschaftskrise von 1857 im Spannungsfeld von Privatinitiative und Staatsintervention." *Zeitschrift des Vereins für Hamburgische Geschichte* 64: 1–29.

Alesina, Alberto, Paola Giuliano, and Nathan Nunn. 2013. "On the Origins of Gender Roles: Women and the Plough." *Quarterly Journal of Economics* 128(2): 469–530.

Allen, Douglas W. 2012. *The Institutional Revolution. Measurement and the Economic Emergence of the Modern World*. Chicago: University of Chicago Press.

Allen, Robert C. 1992. *Enclosure and the Yeoman*. Oxford: Clarendon.

———. 2001. "The Great Divergence in European Wages and Prices from the Middle Ages to the First World War." *Explorations in Economic History* 38(4): 411–47.

———. 2004. "Agriculture During the Industrial Revolution." In *The Cambridge Economic History of Modern Britain*, edited by Floud Roderick and Paul Johnson, chap. 4, 96–116. Cambridge: Cambridge University Press.

———. 2007. "Pessimism Preserved: Real Wages in the British Industrial Revolution." Working Paper 314, Department of Economics, University of Oxford.

———. 2009a. *The British Industrial Revolution in Global Perspective: New approaches to economic and social history*. Cambridge: Cambridge University Press.

———. 2009b. "Engels' Pause: Technical Change, Capital Accumulation, and Inequality in the British Industrial Revolution." *Explorations in Economic History* 46(4): 418–35.

———. 2011. "Why the Industrial Revolution Was British: Commerce, Induced Invention, and the Scientific Revolution." *Economic History Review* 64(2): 357–84.

Allen, Robert C., and Cormac Ó Gráda. 1988. "On the Road Again with Arthur Young: English, Irish, and French Agriculture during the Industrial Revolution." *Journal of Economic History* 48(1): 93–116.

Álvarez, Antonio, and Carlos Arías. 2004. "Technical Efficiency and Farm Size: A Conditional Analysis." *Agricultural Economics* 30(3): 241–50.

Ambrosoli, Mauro. 1997. *The Wild and the Sown. Botany and Agriculture in Western Europe 1350–1850*. Cambridge: Cambridge University Press.

Andersen, Bent S. 1963. "Staldgård—eller hollænderi? Forsøg på status ved 1782." *Historie/Jyske Samlinger* 6(1): 379–420.

Andersen, Dan H., and Erik H. Pedersen. 2004. *A History of Prices and Wages in Denmark 1660–1800. Prices and Wages in Danish Estate Accounts*. Vol. 2. Copenhagen: Schultz.

Andersen, Thomas B., Peter S. Jensen, and Christian V. Skovsgaard. 2016. "The Heavy Plow and the Agricultural Revolution in Medieval Europe." *Journal of Development Economics* 118: 133–49.

Andresen, Carl E. 1992. *Valentinerne på Gjeddesdal 1822–1927: et kapitel af dansk landbrugs historie. Hæfte nr. 35 i series "Bidrag til Greve kommunes historie."* Greve, Denmark: Greve Lokalhistoriske Forening.

Annual Statement of the Trade and Navigation of the United Kingdom with Foreign Countries and British Possessions in the Year [1853–1897]. 1855–98. London: HMSO.

Aparicio, Gema, Vicente Pinilla, and Raúl Serrano. 2009. "Europe and the International Agricultural and Food Trade, 1870–2000." In *Agriculture and Economic Development in Europe since 1870*, edited by Pedro Lains and Vincente Pinilla, 52–75. London: Routledge.

Apostolides, Alexander, Stephen Broadberry, Bruce Campbell, Mark Overton, and Bas van Leuwen. 2008. "English Agricultural Output and Labour Productivity, 1250–1850: Some Preliminary Estimates." *Open Research Exeter*. http://hdl.handle.net/10871/13985, issued November 26, 2008.

Appel, Axel, and Niels Bredkjær. 1924–32. "Kvægets historie." In *Det danske landbrugs historie*, edited by Kristian Hansen, 241–578. Copenhagen: G. E. C. Gads.

Árnasson, Johann P., and Björn Wittrock. 2012. "Introduction." In *Nordic Paths to Modernity*, edited by Johann P. Árnasson and Björn Wittrock, 1–23. New York: Berghahn Books.

Bach, Christian F. 2012. "Fra røde danske mælkekøer til nye landbrugsmuligheder." In *Hvordan ser verden ud? 73 bidrag om økonomi, institutioner og værdier. Professor Niels Kærgård 70 år*, edited by Peder Andersen, Ingrid Henriksen, J. H. Pedersen and Henrik Zobbe, 336–43. Copenhagen: Jurist- og Økonomiforbundets.

Bailey, DeeVon, Basudeb Biswas, Subal C. Kumbhakar, and Kris B. Schulthies. 1989. "An Analysis of Technical, Allocative, and Scale Inefficiency: The Case of Ecuadorian Dairy Farms." *Western Journal of Agricultural Economics* 14(1): 30–37.

Bairoch, Paul. 1981. "Main Trends in National Economic Disparities." In *Disparities in Economic Development since the Industrial Revolution*, edited by Paul Bairoch and M. Lévy-Leboyer, 3–17. London: Macmillan.

Banerjee, A. 1994. "Dairying Systems in India." *World Animal Review* 79(2): 8–15.

Banerjee, Abhijit, and Lakshmi Iyer. 2005. "History, Institutions, and Economic Performance: The Legacy of Colonial Land Tenure System in India." *American Economic Review* 95(4): 1190–213.

Banggård, Grethe. 2004. *Befolkningsfremmende foranstaltninger og faldende børnedødelighed. Danmark, ca. 1750–1850*. Odense: Syddansk Universitetsforlag.

Bateman, Fred. 1968. "Improvement in American Dairy Farming, 1850–1910: A Quantitative Analysis." *Journal of Economic History* 28(2): 255–73.

Baten, Joerg, and Dácil Juif. 2014. "A Story of Large Landowners and Math Skills: Inequality and Human Capital Formation in Long-Run Development, 1820–2000." *Journal of Comparative Economics* 42(2): 375–401.

Battese, George E., and Timothy. J. Coelli. 1995. "A Model for Technical Inefficiency Effects in a Stochastic Frontier Function for Panel Data." *Empirical Economics* 20: 325–32.

Bech, A. W. 1865. "Sorø Amts landøkonomiske Selskab." *Ugeskrift for Landmænd* 1865(1): 161–69.

Becker, Sascha O., Francesco Cinnirella, and Ludger Woessmann. 2012. "The Effect of Investment in Children's Education on Fertility in 1816 Prussia." *Cliometrica* 6(1): 29–44.

Becker, Sascha O., and Ludger Woessmann. 2009. "Was Weber Wrong? A Human Capital Theory of Protestant Economic History." *Quarterly Journal of Economics* 124(2): 531–96.

Becker-Christensen, Henrik. 1988. *Dansk Toldhistorie II: Protektionisme og reformer 1660–1814.* Copenhagen: Toldhistorisk Selskab.

Begtrup, Gregers. 1803. *Beskrivelse over Agerdyrkningens Tilstand i Danmark.* Vols. 1–2, Sjælland and Møen. Copenhagen: A. & S. Goldins.

———. 1806. *Beskrivelse over Agerdyrkningens Tilstand i Danmark.* Vol. 3, Fyen, Langeland, and Ærø. Copenhagen: A. & S. Goldins.

———. 1808. *Beskrivelse over Agerdyrkningens Tilstand i Danmark.* Vols. 5–6, Nørre Jylland. Copenhagen: A. & S. Goldins.

———. 1810. "Ueber die Eintheilung des Ackers, die gewöhnliche Wirthschaftsmethode und Saatfolge auf Seeland und Möen." *Annalen des Ackerbaus* 12: 548–76.

Bendz, Henrik C. B. 1951. *Landbohøjskolens Oprettelse: En dagbog 1856–1858.* Edited by Ivan Katić. Frederiksberg: Veterinærhistorisk Forskning.

Bhattacharyya, Sambit. 2011. *Growth Debacles and Growth Miracles: Exploring Root Causes.* Cheltenham: Edward Elgar.

Bieleman, Jan. 1996. "Dutch Agriculture 1850–1925. Responding to Changing Markets." *Jahrbuch für Wirtschaftsgeschichte* 37(1): 11–52.

———. 2010. *Five Centuries of Farming: A Short History of Dutch Agriculture, 1500–2000.* Wageningen: Academic Publishers.

Bjørn, Claus. 1971. "Folkehøjskolen og andelsbevægelsen." *Årbog for Dansk Skolehistorie* 8: 7.

———. 1977a. "Fællesmejerierne—En fase i Dansk Mejeribrugs Udvikling." *Bol og By* 2(1): 65–80.

———. 1977b. "The Peasantry and Agricultural Reform in Denmark." *Scandinavian Economic History Review* 25(2): 117–37.

———. 1982a. "Dansk mejeribrug 1882–1914." In *Dansk mejeribrug 1882–2000*, edited by Claus Bjørn, 11–188. Odense: De danske Mejeriers Fællesorganisation.

———. 1982b. "Mejeribruget 1860—ca. 1885." *Tidsskrift for Landøkonomi* 169(3): 111–28.

———. 1988a. "1810–1860." In *Det danske landbrugs historie 1810–1914*, edited by Claus Bjørn, 7–192. Odense: Landbohistorisk Selskab.

———. 1988b. "1860–1914." In *Det danske landbrugs historie 1810–1914*, edited by Claus Bjørn, 368–81. Odense: Landbohistorisk Selskab.

Bjørnsen, Sophus. 1857. "Oversigt over Indtægten af Qvægbesætningen paa Valdemarslund fra 1. Mai 1846 til 30- April 1856." *Ugeskrift for Landmænd* 1856: 195–97.

———. 1859. "Udbyttet af Kvægbesætningen paa Valdemarslund fra 1846–1856." *Tidsskrift for Landøkonomi* 3(7): 348–53.

Bogart, Dan, Mauricio Drelichman, Oscar Gelderblom, and Jean-Laurent Rosenthal. 2010. "State and Private Institutions." In *The Cambridge Economic History of Modern Europe*, vol. 1, *1700–1870*, edited by Stephen Broadberry and Kevin H. O'Rourke, 70–95. Cambridge: Cambridge University Press.

Bøggild, Bernhard. 1886. "Mælkeribruget i Danmark 1885." *Tidsskrift for Landøkonomi* 5(5): 48–76.

———. 1887a. *Andelsmælkerier: Meddelelser, Samlede og Bearbejdede af Bernhard Bøggild*. Copenhagen: P. G. Philipsens.

———. 1887b. "Mælkeribruget i Danmark 1886." *Tidsskrift for Landøkonomi* 5(6): 52–94.

———. 1888. "Mælkeribruget i Danmark 1887." *Tidsskrift for Landøkonomi* 5(7): 67–110.

———. 1889a. "Mælkeribruget i Danmark 1888." *Tidsskrift for Landøkonomi* 5(8): 59–97.

———. 1889b. *Mælkeri—Regnskaber 1889*. Copenhagen: P. G. Philipsens.

———. 1891. "Mælkeribruget i Danmark 1890." *Tidsskrift for Landøkonomi* 5(10): 82–120.

———. 1892. "Mælkeribruget i Danmark 1891." *Tidsskrift for Landøkonomi* 5(11): 117–52.

———. 1893. "Mælkeribruget i Danmark 1892." *Tidsskrift for Landøkonomi* 5(12): 117–52.

———. 1895. "Mælkeribruget i Danmark 1894." *Tidsskrift for Landøkonomi* 5(14): 98–134.

———. 1896. *Mælkeribruget i Danmark*. Copenhagen: Det Nordiske.

———. 1897. "Mælkeribruget i Danmark 1896." *Tidsskrift for Landøkonomi* 5(16): 88–120.

———. 1898. "Mælkeribruget i Danmark 1897." *Tidsskrift for Landøkonomi* 5(17): 56–87.

———. 1899. *Mælkeri—Regnskaber*. Vol. 2. Copenhagen: Det Nordiske.

Böhme, Helmut. 1968. "Wirtschaftskrise, merchant bankers und Verfassungsreform. Zur Bedeutung der Weltwirtschaftskrise von 1857 in Hamburg (mit einem Aktenanhang)." *Zeitschrift des Vereins für Hamburgische Geschichte* 54(1968): 77–128.

Boje, Per. 1977. *Danske provinskøbmænds vareomsætning og kapitalforhold 1815–1847*. Aarhus: Universitetsforlaget.

———. 2014. *Vejen til velstand—marked, stat og utopi. Om dansk kapitalismes mange former gennem 300 år*. Vol. 1, *Tiden 1730–1850*. Odense: Syddansk Universitetsforlag.

———. 2016. "How Denmark Became Rich. On the History of the Danish Innovation System." In *Entreprenørskap: i næringsliv og politikk*, edited by Knut Sogner, Einar Lie, and Håvard Brede Aven, 29–56. Oslo: Novus.

Bokelmann, Frederik. 1877. "Mejeriberetning fra Lolland-Falster." *Tidsskrift for Landøkonomi* 4(11): 114–25.

Bolt, Jutta, and Jan L. van Zanden. 2014. "The Maddison Project: Collaborative Research on Historical National Accounts." *Economic History Review* 67(3): 627–51.

Bordo, Michael D., and John S. Landon-Lane. 2010. "The Global Financial Crisis of 2007–08: Is It Unprecedented?" NBER Working Paper 16589.

Borup, Eernst J., and Fred Nørgaard. 1939–40. *Den danske folkehøjskole gennem hundrede år*. Vol. 2. Odense: Skandinavisk bogforlag A/S.

Boserup, Ester. 1965. *The Conditions of Agricultural Growth: The Economics of Agrarian Change under Population Pressure*. London: Allen & Unwin.

Bouamra-Mechemache, Zohra, Vincent Réquillart, Claudio Soregaroli, and Aaudrey Trévisiol. 2008. "Demand for Diary Products in the EU." *Food Policy* 33: 644–56.

Boye, G. 1865. "Om Handelsforbindelsen med England og Skotland." *Ugeskrift for Landmænd* 1865(1): 257–62.

BPP (British Parliamentary Papers). 1850. *Tariffs of Foreign States, Abstract of Returns of any Alterations Made in the Tariffs of Foreign States, and in the Customs Duties of British Possessions, under the Powers of the Act 8 & 9 Vict. c. 9, in Continuation of Former Returns on the Same Subject*. London: HMSO.

———. 1854–55. *Tables Showing the Trade of the United Kingdom with Different Foreign Countries and British Possessions, in Each of the Ten Years from 1841 to 1850*. London: HMSO.

———. 1893. *Reports on Dairy Farming in Denmark, Sweden, and Germany*. London: HMSO.

———. 1897. *Customs Tariffs of the United Kingdom 1800 to 1897*. London: HMSO.

Bracht, Johannes, and Friederike Scholten. 2015. "Between Rack Rents and Paternalism: Price

Formation of Leases in Westphalian Estates 1650–1900." Paper presented at the Eurasian Rural and Agricultural History Workshop, University of Groningen, June 25–27.

Brix, Hans. 1924. *The Scandinavian Preserved Butter Company Busck Jun. & Co. A/S 1874–1924: En oversig over selskabets virksomhed gennem 50 år.* Copenhagen: J. Jørgsensen.

Broadberry, Stephen. 2013. "Accounting for the Great Divergence." Economic History Working Papers 184/13, London School of Economics.

Brugger, Hans. 1978. *Die schweizerische Landwirtschaft 1850–1914.* Frauenfeld: Huber.

Bryer, Rob A. 2000a. "The History of Accounting and the Transition to Capitalism in England— Part One: Theory." *Accounting, Organizations and Society* 25: 131–62.

———. 2000b. "The History of Accounting and the Transition to Capitalism England—Part Two: The Evidence." *Accounting, Organizations and Society* 25: 327–81.

———. 2006. "The Genesis of the Capitalist Farmer." *Critical Perspectives on Accounting* 17: 367–97.

Buch, Leon. 1960. "Investeringerne iden for mejerierne og slagterierne." *Nationaløkonomisk Tidsskrift* 98: 132–51.

Buksti, Jacob A. 1982. "Dansk mejeribrug 1955–82." In *Dansk mejeribrug 1882–2000*, edited by Claus Bjørn, 309–480. Odense: De danske Mejriers Fællesorganisation.

Burchardt, Jørgen. 2005. *Da ost blev for alle.* Odense: Egnsmuseet på Sønderskov/Forlaget Kulturbøger.

Burhop, Carsten, and Thorsten Lübbers. 2009. "Cartels, Managerial Incentives, and Productive Efficiency in German Coal Mining, 1881–1913." *Journal of Economic History* 69(2): 500–527.

Burnes, Bernard. 2009. *Managing Change: A Strategic Approach to Organisational Dynamics.* 5th ed. Harlow: Pearson Education International.

Buus, Niels P. J. 1858. "Meieri-Udbyttet paa Giedsergaard." *Ugeskrift for Landmænd* 1858: 237–41.

———. 1865. "Om Køernes Udbytte i 1864." *Ugeskrift for Landmænd* 1865(1): 179–93.

———. 1866a. "Det kgl. Landhusholdningsselskab." *Ugeskrift for Landmænd* 1866(1): 259–71.

———. 1866b. "Om Køernes Udbytte i 1865." *Ugeskrift for Landmænd* 1866(2): 202–10, 15–24.

———. 1866c. "I hvilket forhold stiller Udbyttet af Studefedningen sig i Sammenligning med Indtægt af Meieridriften?" *Tidsskrift for Landøkonomi* 3(14): 44–59.

———. 1886. *Fællesmælkerierne i Jylland.* Offprint from Landsmands-Blade ed.

Carmona, Juan. 1995. "Las estrategias económicas de la vieja aristocracia española y el cambio agrario en el siglo XIX." *Revista de Historia Económica* 13: 63–88.

Carmona, Juan, Markus Lampe, and Joan Rosés. 2017. "Housing Affordability During the Urban Transition in Spain." *Economic History Review* 70(2): 632–58.

Carruthers, Bruce G., and Wendy N. Espeland. 1991. "Accounting for Rationality: Double Entry Bookkeeping and the Rhetoric of Economic Rationality." *American Journal of Sociology* 97: 31–69.

Chaney, Thomas. 2014. "The Network Structure of International Trade." *American Economic Review* 104: 3600–3634.

Chiapello, Eve. 2007. "Accounting and the Birth of the Notion of Capitalism." *Critical Perspectives on Accounting* 18: 263–96.

Christensen, Anton. 1925–33. "Landbrugets redskaber og maskiner." In *Det danske landbrugs historie*, vol. 4, *Bygninger, Mejeri, Redskaber*, edited by Kristian Hansen. Copenhagen: G. E. C. Gads.

Christensen, C. 1886–91. *Agrarhistoriske Studier.* Vol. 2. Copenhagen: Schubothe.

Christensen, Dan Ch. 1996. *Det moderne project: Teknik & kultur i Danmark-Norge 1750–(1814)– 1850.* Copenhagen: Gyldendal.

Christensen, Harry. 1991. "De unge kommuner 1837/41–1867/68." In *Folkestyre i by og på land:*

Danske kommuner gennem 150 år, edited by Per Boje, Brigitte Dedenroth-Schou, Knud J. V. Jespersen, and Jørgen Thomasen, 13–60. Herning: Poul Kristensens.

Christensen, Jens. 1985. *Landbostatistik: Håndbog i dansk landbostatistik 1830–1900*. Copenhagen: Landbohistorisk Selskab.

Christiansen, Palle O. 1975. *Husmandsbevægelse og jordreform i Danmark*. Copenhagen: Etnologisk arbejdsgruppe for nordiske og europæiske studier.

Christoffersen, Henrik. 1999. *Danmarks økonomiske historie efter 1960*. Herning: Systime.

C. I. 1864. "Om Malkekvæg og Mælkeriregnskaber." *Ugeskrift for Landmænd* 1864: 360–61.

Cinnirella, Francesco, and Erik Hornung (2016). "Landownership Concentration and the Expansion of Education." *Journal of Development Economics* 121: 135–52.

Clark, Gregory. 2004. "The Price History of English Agriculture, 1500–1914." *Research in Economic History* 22: 41–124.

———. 2005. "The Condition of the Working Class in England, 1209–2004." *Journal of Political Economy* 113(6): 1307–40.

———. 2007. *A Farewell to Alms. A Brief Economic History of the World*. Princeton, NJ: Princeton University Press.

Cohn, Einar. 1957. *Kjøbenhavn gjennem hundrede Aar, 1857–1957*. Vol. 1, *Tietgen-Tiden*. Copenhagen: E. H. Petersen.

———. 1958. *Privatbanken i Kjøbenhavn gjennem hundrede Aar*. Vol. 2, *Efter Aar hundred skiftet*. Copenhagen: E. H. Petersen.

Crafts, Nick F. R. 1985. *British Economic Growth during the Industrial Revolution*. Oxford: Clarendon.

Dalgaard, Carl-J. 2010. "Det danske vækstmirakel." *Nationaløkonomisk tidsskrift* 148(2): 125–58.

Dalgas, Carl. 1826. *Bidrag til Kundskab om de danske Provindsers nærværende tilstand i oekonomisk henseende, foranstaltet, efter kongelig Befaling af Landhuusholdningsselskabet, 1ste Stykke. Vejle Amt*. Copenhagen: Det Kongelige Landhusholdningsselskab.

———. 1862. "En Forpagters Mejeriregnskab." *Ugeskrift for Landmænd* 1862: 266–68.

Dall, Torben S., Peter S. Jensen, and Amber Naz. 2014. "New Crops, Local Soils and Urbanization: Clover, Potatoes and the Growth of Danish Market Towns, 1672–1901." European Historical Economics Society Working Paper 65.

Danida. 2012. *Danida 50 år 1962–2012*. Edited by Danish Ministry of Foreign Affairs. Copenhagen: Danida.

Davids, Georg. 1996. "Holländer und Holländereien." In *Die Milch. Geschichte und Zukunft eines Lebensmittels*, edited by Helmut Ottenjann and Karl-Heinz Ziessow, 147–57. Cloppenburg: Museumsdorf Cloppenburg.

Degn, Ole. 2010. "Regnskabsvæsenets udvikling i Danmark—fra middelalderen til 1850." In *Regnskabshistorie: Erhvervsregnskaber som kilde i historieforskningen*, edited by Jensen Brøgger, Lone H. Liljegren, and K. Tarbensen, 67–136. Aarhus: Erhvervsarkivet.

Dell, Melissa. 2010. "The Persistent Effects of Peru's Mining Mita." *Econometrica* 78(6): 1863–903.

———. 2012. "Path Dependence in Development: Evidence from the Mexican Revolution." Working Paper, Harvard University, https://scholar.harvard.edu/dell/publications/path -dependence-development-evidence-mexican-revolution, last updated June 29, 2016.

Den Alsiske Landboforening. 1866. *Ugeskrift for Landmænd* 1866(1): 284–86.

Dennison, Tracy, and James Simpson. 2010. "Agriculture." In *The Cambridge Economic History of Modern Europe*, edited by Stephen Broadberry and Kevin H. O'Rourke, 147–63. Cambridge: Cambridge University Press.

Denzel, Markus. 2010. *Handbook of World Exchange Rates, 1590–1914*. Farnham, Surrey: Ashgate.

Depecker, Thomas, and Nathalie Joly. 2015. "Agronomists and Accounting. The Beginnings of Capitalist Rationalisation on the Farm (1800–1850)." *Historia Agraria* 65(65): 75–94.

De Plejt, Alexandra M., and Jan L. van Zanden. 2016. "Accounting for the 'Little Divergence': What Drove Economic Growth in Pre-industrial Europe, 1300–1800?" *European Review of Economic History* 20(4): 387–409.

Diamond, Jared. 1997. *Guns, Germs and Steel: The Fate of Human Societies*. New York: W. W. Norton.

Dombernowsky, Lotte. 1988. "Ca. 1720–1810." In *Det danske landbrugs historie*, edited by Claus Bjørn, 211–394. Odense: Landbohistorisk Selskab.

Doornik, Jürgen A., and David F. Hendry. 2009. *PcGive 13*. London: Timberlake Consultants Ltd.

Drejer, Aage A. 1925–33. "Mejeribruget." In *Det danske landbrugs historie*, edited by Kristian Hansen, 99–419. Copenhagen: G. E. C. Gads.

———. 1962. *Den historiske baggrund for nutidens mejeribrug og et halvt århundredes organisationsarbejde*. Copenhagen: Særtryk af "Dansk Mejeribrug."

Duflo, Esther. 2012. "Women's Empowerment and Economic Development." *Journal of Economic Literature* 50(4): 1051–79.

Dupré, Ruth. 1999. "'If It's Yellow, It Must Be Butter': Margarine Regulation in North America since 1886." *Journal of Economic History* 59(2): 353–71.

Dybdahl, Vagn. 1946–47. "Hans Broge og det jyske Landbrug." *Historie/Jyske Samlinger* 5(8): 57–134.

Ejrnæs, Mette, and Karl G. Persson. 2000. "Market Integration and Transport Costs in France 1825–1903: A Threshold Error Correction Approach to the Law of One Price." *Explorations in Economic History* 37(2): 149–73.

———. 2010. "The Gains from Improved Market Efficiency: Trade before and after the Transatlantic Telegraph." *European Review of Economic History* 14: 361–81.

Ellbrecht, Gerhard v. 1915–18. *Danske Mejerier. Illustreret haandbog for mejeribruget i Danmark*. Copenhagen: Selskabet til Udgivelse af Nationale Haandbøger.

En gammel Meierimand. 1862. "Meieriregnskaber." *Ugeskrift for Landmænd* 1862: 308.

Engelhardt, Juliane. 2002. "'Adel er arvelig, men Dyd maae erhverves'—Den patriotiske bevægelse i det danske monarki 1780–1799." *Fortid og nutid* 2002(3): 163–87.

Engerman, Stanley L., and Kenneth L. Sokoloff. 2002. "Factor Endowments, Inequality, and Paths of Development among New World Economics." *Economía* 3(1): 41–110.

Falbe Hansen, Vigand A. 1880. "De franske Told- og Skibsafgifter i Henseende til deres Forhold til Danmarks Handel og Skibsfart paa Frankrig." *Nationaløkonomisk Tidsskrift* 16(Første række): 305–27.

———. 1889. *Stavnsbaands-Løsningen og Landboreformerne set fra Nationaløkonomiens Standpunkt*. Copenhagen: G. E. C. Gads.

Fan, Yanqin, Qi Li, and Alfons Weersink. 1996. "Semiparametric Estimation of Stochastic Production Frontier Models." *Journal of Business and Economic Statistics* 14(4): 460–68.

FAO. 2012. *Livestock Sector Development for Poverty Reduction. An Economic and Policy Perspective—Livestock's Many Virtues*. Edited by J. Otte, A. Costales, J. Dijkman, T. Pica-Camarra, T. Robinson, V. Ahuja, C. Ly, and D. Roland-Holst. Rome: United Nations Food and Agriculture Organization.

Federico, Giovanni. 2005. *Feeding the World. An Economic History of Agriculture, 1800–2000*. Princeton, NJ: Princeton University Press.

———. 2008. "The First European Grain Invasion: A Study in the Integration of the European Market, 1750–1870." European University Institute HEC Working Papers 2008/01.

———. 2012a. "How Much Do We Know about Market Integration in Europe?" *Economic History Review* 65(2): 470–97.

———. 2012b. "The Corn Laws in Continental Perspective." *European Review of Economic History* 16(2): 166–87.

Federico, Giovanni, and Pablo Martinelli. 2015. "The Role of Women in Traditional Agriculture: Evidence from Italy." Centre for Economic Policy Research (CEPR) Discussion Paper 10881.

Federico, Giovanni, and Paul Sharp. 2013. "The Cost of Railroad Regulation: The Disintegration of American Agricultural Markets in the Interwar Period." *Economic History Review* 66(4): 1017–38.

Feilberg, Peter B. 1861. "En Meierigaard i det østlige Holsten." *Tidsskrift for Landøkonomi* 3(9): 321–43.

———. 1862. "Besøg paa et Par holsteenske Mejerigaarde." *Tidsskrift for Landøkonomi* 3(10): 263–75.

———. 1878. *Om Forholdene paa Island.* Copenhagen: J. Cohens Bogtrykkeri.

———. 1907. "Kulturarbejeder i Island." *Ugeskrift for Landmænd* 10: 143–45.

Feinstein, Charles H. 1998. "Pessimism Perpetuated: Real Wages and the Standard of Living in Britain during and after the Industrial Revolution." *Journal of Economic History* 58(3): 625–58.

Feldbæk, Ole. 1988. "Kongen bød—Enevælden og reformerne." In *Landboreformerne. Forskning og forløb,* edited by Claus Bjørn, 9–29. Copenhagen: Landbohistorisk Selskab.

———. 1990. *Gyldendals og Politikens Danmarkshistorie.* Vol. 9, *Den lange fred, 1700–1800.* Copenhagen: Gyldendalske Boghandel/Nordisk Forlag/Politikens Forlag.

Fenger, Hans F. 1869. "Om Kohold og Betingelserne for et normalt Agerbrug samt om Mælkeriregnskaber." *Ugeskrift for Landmænd* 1869(1): 407–11.

———. 1873. "Kan Kjødproduktionen betale sig under de nuværende forhold i Danmark?" *Tidsskrift for Landøkonomi* 4(7): 381–408.

Fernández, Eva. 2014. "Trust, Religion, and Cooperation in Western Agriculture, 1880–1930." *Economic History Review* 67(3): 678–98.

Fick, A. F. C. 1907. *Der Hamburger Buttermarkt bis 1907.* Hamburg: J. D. Hollmann.

Fink, Deborah. 2009. "'Not to Intrude': A Danish Perspective on Gender and Class in Nineteenth-Century Dairying." *Agricultural History* 83(4): 446–76.

Fjord, Niels J. 1882. "Forsøg paa Mejerivæsenets Omraade." *Tidsskrift for Landøkonomi* 5(1): 397–456.

———. 1884. "Forsøg paa Mejerivæsenets Omraade." *Tidsskrift for Landøkonomi* 5(3): 375–441.

Fleischman, Richard K., and Thomas N. Tyson. 2004. "Accounting in Service to Racism: Monetizing Slave Property in the Antebellum South." *Critical Perspectives on Accounting* 15(3): 376–99.

Fode, Henrik. 1989. *Dansk Toldhistorie III: Liberalisme og frihandel 1814–1914.* Copenhagen: Toldhistorisk Selskab.

Foley-Fisher, Nathan, and Eoin McLaughlin. 2016. "Capitalising on the Irish Land Question: Land Reform and State Banking in Ireland, 1891–1938." *Financial History Review* 23(1): 71–109.

Forpagter, En. 1868a. "Om Kohold og Mælkeriregnskaber." *Ugeskrift for Landmænd* 1868(1): 321–24.

———. 1868b. "Om Kohold og Mælkeriregnskaber." *Ugeskrift for Landmænd* 1868(1): 391–93.

———. 1875. "Om Mælkerieregns." *Ugeskrift for Landmænd* 1875(1): 392–95.

Forpagter K. 1861. "En Forpagters Mejeriregnskab." *Ugeskrift for Landmænd* 1861: 406–8.

———. 1862. "Meieriregnskaber." *Ugeskrift for Landmænd* 1862: 362–63.

Frandsen, Karl-E. 1977. "Udsæd og foldudbytte i det 17. århundrede." *Fortid og nutid* 27: 21–36.

———. 1983. *Vang og tægt. Studier over dyrkningssystemer og agrarstrukturer i Danmarks lands-byer 1682–83.* Esbjerg: Forlaget Bygd.

———. 2005. "Ager og eng." In *Herregården: Drift og landskab,* edited by John Erichsen and Mik-kel Venborg Pedersen, 25–100. Copenhagen: Dansk Bygningsarv.

French, Michael, and Jim Philips. 2000. *Cheated Not Poisoned? Food Regulation in the United Kingdom, 1875–1938.* Manchester: Manchester University Press.

Friis, Astrid, and Kristof Glamann. 1958. *A History of Prices and Wages in Denmark, 1660–1800.* Vol. 1. London: Longmans, Green.

Friis, Johannes. 1869. "Horsens Landbrugsforening og Thyrsting-Vrads Herreders Landbofor-ening." *Ugeskrift for Landmænd* 1869(1): 87–92.

Friis, Johannes, and Thomas R. Segelcke. 1866. *Mejeridagbog.* Copenhagen.

———. 1870. *Optegnelsesbøger til Meieribrug.* Copenhagen.

———. 1870–74. *Mejeritavler.* 3rd ed. Copenhagen: P. G. Philipsen.

Fritzbøger, Bo. 2015. *Mellem land og by: Landbohøjskolens historie.* Copenhagen: Copenhagen University.

Funnell, Warwick, and Jeffrey Robertson. 2011. "Capitalist Accounting in Sixteenth Century Hol-land." *Accounting, Auditing and Accountability Journal* 24(5): 560–86.

Fussell, G. E. 1936. *Robert Loder's Farm Accounts 1610–1620.* London: Royal Historical Society.

Gallup, John L., and Jeffrey D. Sachs. 2001. "The Economic Burden of Malaria." *American Journal of Tropical Medicine and Hygiene* 64(1–2): 85–96.

Gallup, John L., Jeffrey D. Sachs, and Andrew D. Mellinger. 1999. "Geography and Economic Development." *International Regional Science Review* 22(2): 179–232.

Galor, Oded, and Omer Moav. 2006. "Das Human-Kapital: A Theory of the Demise of the Class Structure." *Review of Economic Studies* 73(1): 85–117.

Galor, Oded, Omer Moav, and Dietrich Vollrath. 2009. "Inequality in Land Ownership, the Emergence of Human Capital Promoting Institutions, and Great Divergence." *Review of Economic Studies* 76(1): 143–79.

Galor, Oded, and David Weil. 2000. "Population, Technology, and Growth: From Malthusian Stagnation to the Demographic Transition and Beyond." *American Economic Review* 90(4): 806–28.

Garrido, Samuel 2014. "Plenty of Trust, Not Much Cooperation: Social Capital and Collective Action in Early Twentieth-Century Eastern Spain." *European Review of Economic History* 18(4): 413–32.

Gerhard, Hans-J., Karl H. Kaufhold, and Alexander Engel. 2001. *Preise im vor- und frühindus-triellen Deutschland: Nahrungsmittel, Getränke, Gewürze, Rohstoffe und Gewerbeprodukte.* Stuttgart: Franz Steiner.

Gerlach, Kurt A. 1911. *Dänemarks Stellung in der Weltwirtschaft. Unter besonderer Berücksichti-gung der Handelsbeziehungen zu Deutschland, England und Skandinavien (= Probleme der Weltwirtschaft 3).* Jena: Gustav Fischer.

Gerring, John. 2004. "What Is a Case Study and What Is It Good For?" *American Political Science Review* 98(2): 341–54.

Goldberger, Arthur S. 1968. "The Interpretation and Estimation of Cobb-Douglas Function." *Econometrica* 35: 464–72.

Gollin, Douglas, Casper Worm Hansen, and Asger Wingender. 2016. "Two Blades of Grass: The Impact of the Green Revolution." Centre for Economic Policy Research (CEPR) Discussion Paper 11611.

Gould, Brian W., and Hector J. Villarreal. 2006. "An Assessment of the Current Structure of Food Demand in Urban China." *Agricultural Economics* 34(1): 1–16.

Gräfe, Heike. 2013. "Die Hörer der Thaers in Möglin von 1806 bis 1861. 1. Teil: Alphabetische Zusammenstellung." *Thaer heute* 9: 111–30.

Grafe, Regina, and Oscar Gelderblom. 2010. "The Rise and Fall of Merchant Guilds: Re-thinking the Comparative Study of Commercial Institutions in Pre-modern Europe." *Journal of Interdisciplinary History* 40: 477–511.

Graugaard, Esben. 2006. *Nordvestjyske bønder som kreaturhandlere i Nordsørummet: studie i netværket omkring en regional kultur- og driftsform o. 1788–1914.* Odense: Syddansk Universitetsforlag.

Greene, W. H. 2009. *LIMDEP 10 Econometric Modeling Guide.* New York: Plainview.

Gregersen, Hans V. 1981. *Slesvig-Holsten før 1830.* Copenhagen: Politiken.

Greif, Avner. 1994. "Cultural Beliefs and the Organization of Society: A Historical and Theoretical Reflection on Collectivist and Individualist Societies." *Journal of Political Economy* 102(5): 912–50.

———. 2000. "The Fundamental Problem of Exchange: A Research Agenda in Historical Institutional Analysis." *European Review of Economic History* 4: 251–84.

Guinnane, Timothy, and Ingrid Henriksen. 1998. "Why Danish Credit Co-operatives Were So Unimportant." *Scandinavian Economic History Review* 46(2): 32–54.

Gyllembourg, Carl F. 1808. *Forsøg til et Landbrugs-Bogholderie.* 2 vols. Copenhagen: Self-published.

H—. 1869. "En fyensk Fæstebondes Mælkeriregnskab." *Ugeskrift for Landmænd* 1869(2): 89–93.

Hallam, David, and Fernando Machado. 1995. "Efficiency Analysis with Panel Data: A Study of Portuguese Dairy Farms." *European Review of Agricultural Economics* 23: 79–93.

Hansen, Bodil K. 2006. *Familie- og arbejdsliv på landet, ca. 1870–1900.* Auning, Denmark: Landbohistorisk Selskab.

Hansen, C. K. 1956. *C. K. Hansen gennem hundrede år: København, den 21. februar 1956.* C. K. Hansen.

Hansen, Hans S. 1994. *Det Sønderjyske Landbrugshistorie 1830–1993.* Aabenraa: Historisk Samfund for Sønderjylland og Fælleslandboforeningen for Nordslesvig.

———. 1996. "Das dänische Molkereiwesen als Vorbild für Nordschleswig, 1860–1914." In *Die Milch. Geschichte und Zukunft eines Lebensmittels,* edited by Helmut Ottenjann and Karl-Heinz Ziessow, 127–33. Cloppenburg: Museumsdorf Cloppenburg.

Hansen, Svend A. 1970. *Early Industrialisation in Denmark.* Copenhagen: G. E. C. Gads.

———. 1972. *Økonomisk vækst i Danmark.* Vol. 1, *1720–1914.* Copenhagen: Akademisk Forlag.

———. 1984. *Økonomisk vækst i Danmark.* Vol. 1, *1720–1914.* 3rd ed. Copenhagen: Akademisk Forlag.

Harley, C. Knick. 1971. "The Shift from Sailing Ships to Steamships 1850–1890: A Study in Technological Change and Its Diffusion." In *Essays on a Mature Economy: Britain after 1840,* edited by D. N. McCloskey, 215–31. Princeton, NJ: Princeton University Press.

Hasle, Theodor. 1858. "Meieriet paa Rosenlund." *Ugeskrift for Landmænd* 1858: 585–89.

Hatton, Timothy J., and Jeffrey G. Williamson. 1994. "What Drove Mass Migrations from Europe in the Late Nineteenth Century?" *Population and Development Review* 20(3): 1–27.

Hausmann, Ricardo, and Dani Rodrik. 2003. "Economic Development as Self-Discovery." *Journal of Development Economics* 72: 603–33.

———. 2005. "Self-Discovery in a Development Strategy for El Salvador." *Economía* (Fall 2005): 43–100.

Hayami, Yuhiro, and Keijiro Otsuka. 1993. *The Economics of Contract Choice. An Agrarian Perspective*. Oxford: Clarendon Press.

Hellesen, Hans F. 1846. *Bogholderi for Landmænd: en Anviisning til, hvorledes Landmanden paa en simpel og lidet tidsspildende Maade vil kunne faae en, saavidt mulig, fuldstændig Oversigt over Fordelen eller Tabet, ved sin Bedrivt*. Copenhagen: J. H. Schubothes Boghandel.

Henriksen, Ingrid. 1993. "The Transformation of Danish Agriculture 1870–1914." In *The Economic Development of Denmark and Norway since 1870*, edited by Karl G. Persson, 153–78. Aldershot: Edward Elgar.

———. 1999. "Avoiding Lock-In: Cooperative Creameries in Denmark, 1882–1903." *European Review of Economic History* 3(1): 57–78.

———. 2003. "Freehold Tenure in Late Eighteenth-Century Denmark." *Advances in Agricultural Economic History* 2: 21–39.

———. 2006. "An Economic History of Denmark." In *EH.Net Encyclopedia*, edited by Robert Whaples, https://eh.net/encyclopedia/an-economic-history-of-denmark/.

———. 2009. "The Contribution of Agriculture to Economic Growth in Denmark, 1870–1939." In *Agriculture and Economic Development in Europe since 1870*, edited by Pedro Lains and Vincente Pinilla, 117–47. London: Routledge.

Henriksen, Ingrid, and Morten Hviid. 2005. "Diffusion of New Technology and Complementary Best Practice: A Case Study." *European Review of Economic History* 9(3): 365–97.

Henriksen, Ingrid, Morten Hviid, and Paul Sharp. 2012. "Law and Peace: Contracts and the Success of the Danish Dairy Cooperatives." *Journal of Economic History* 72(1): 197–224.

Henriksen, Ingrid, Markus Lampe, and Paul Sharp. 2010. "The Strange Birth of Liberal Denmark: Danish Trade Protection and the Growth of the Dairy Industry since the Mid-nineteenth Century." Department of Economics University of Copenhagen Working Paper 10-04.

———. 2011. "The Role of Technology and Institutions for Growth: Danish Creameries in the Late Nineteenth Century." *European Review of Economic History* 15: 475–93.

———. 2012. "The Strange Birth of Liberal Denmark: Danish Trade Protection and the Growth of the Dairy Industry since the Mid-nineteenth Century." *Economic History Review* 65(2): 770–88.

Henriksen, Ingrid, Eoin McLaughlin, and Paul Sharp. 2015. "Contracts and Cooperation: The Relative Failure of the Irish Dairy Industry in the Late Nineteenth Century Reconsidered." *European Review of Economic History* 19: 412–31.

Henriksen, Ingrid, and Kevin H. O'Rourke. 2005. "Incentives, Technology and the Shift to Year-Round Dairying in Late Nineteenth-Century Denmark." *Economic History Review* 58(3): 520–45.

Henriksen, Ole B., and Anders Ølgaard. 1960. *Danmarks udenrigshandel 1874–1958*. Copenhagen: G. E. C. Gads.

Henriques, Sofia T., and Paul Sharp. 2016. "The Danish Agricultural Revolution in an Energy Perspective: A Case of Development with Few Domestic Energy Sources." *Economic History Review* 69(3): 844–69.

Hermansen, Niels K., and Max Lobedanz. 1958. *Den Kongelige Veterinær- og Landbohøjskole 1858–1958*. Copenhagen: Kandrup & Wunsch.

Hertel, Hans. 1889. "Busck, Gunni, f. 1840, Grosserer." In *Dansk Biografisk Lexikon, tillige omfattende Norge for Tidsrummet 1537–1814*, edited by Carl F. Bricka, 264–65. Copenhagen: Gyldendalske Boghandels Forlag (F. Hegel & Søn).

———. 1891. "Friis, Johannes." In *Dansk biografisk leksikon*, edited by Carl F. Bricka. 433–34. Copenhagen: Gyldendalske Boghandels Forlag (F. Hegel & Søn).

———. 1920. *Det kgl. Danske Landhusholdningsselskabs Historie.* Vol. 1, *Selskabets historie i tiden fra 1769–1868.* Copenhagen: August Bangs Boghandel.

Heshmati, Almas, and Subal C. Kumbhakar. 1994. "Farm Heterogeneity and Technical Efficiency: Some Results from Swedish Dairy Farms." *Journal of Productivity Analysis* 5: 45–61.

Higgins, David M., and Mads Mordhorst. 2008. "Reputation and Export Performance: Danish Butter Exports and the British Market, c.1880–c.1914." *Business History* 50(2): 185–204.

Hills, Sally, Thomas Ryland, and Nicholas Dimsdale. 2010. "The UK Recession in Context— What Do Three Centuries of Data Tell Us?" *Bank of England Quarterly Bulletin* (2010, Q4): 277–91.

Hoddinott, John, Derek Headey, and Mekdim Dereje. 2015. "Cows, Missing Milk Markets, and Nutrition in Rural Ethiopia." *Journal of Development Studies* 51(8): 958–75.

Hofman Bang, Niels E. 1861. "Om de danske Forpagtningsforhold." *Ugeskrift for Landmænd* 1862(2): 113–24.

———. 1862. "Om Meieriregnskaber og Forpagtningsforhold." *Ugeskrift for Landmænd* 1862: 213–28.

Holck, Axel. 1901. *Danmarks Statistiks Historie, 1800–1850, særlig med Hensyn til den Officielle Statistiks Udvikling.* Copenhagen: Bianco Lunos.

Hollmann, Max. 1906. "Die Entwicklung des Butterhandels und der Butternotierung in Dänemark." In *Der Butterhandel in Dänemark, Frankreich und den Niederlanden,* edited by Anton Heinrich Hollmann, Hermann Hailer, and Julius Frost, 1–13. Berlin: Deutsche Landwirtschafts-Gesellschaft/Paul Parey.

Holmgaard, Jens. 1986. "Eksercitsen bag kirken efter gudstjeneste. Var landmilitsen i stavnsbånd-stiden en ringe byrde?" *Bol og By* 1986(1): 44–64.

Hornby, Ove. 1969. "Industrialization in Denmark and the Loss of the Duchies." *Scandinavian Economic History Review* 17(1): 23–57.

Hornby, Ove, and Carl-Alex Nilsson. 1980. "The Transition from Sail to Steam in the Danish Merchant Fleet, 1865–1910." *Scandinavian Economic History Review* 28(2): 109–34.

Horstbøll, Henrik, and Uffe Østergård. 1990. "Reform and Revolution. The French Revolution and the Case of Denmark." *Scandinavian Journal of History* 15: 155–79.

Huang, Kuo S., and Fred Gale. 2009. "Food Demand in China: Income, Quality, and Nutrient Effects." *China Agricultural Economic Review* 1(4): 395–409.

Hübner, Otto. 1866. *Die Zolltarife aller Länder. Gesammelt, übersetzt, geordnet. Zweite Auflage.* Iserlohn: J. Baedeker.

Hünniger, Dominik. 2010. "Policing Epizootics." In *Healing the Herds: Disease, Livestock Economies, and the Globalization of Veterinary Medicine,* edited by K. Brown and D. Gilfoyle, 76–91. Athens: Ohio University Press.

Hvidt, Kristian. 1971. *Flugten til Amerika. Drivkræfter i masseudvandringen fra Danmark 1868–1914.* Copenhagen: Universitetsforlaget i Aarhus.

———. 1972. "Mass Emigration from Denmark to the United States 1868–1914." *American Studies in Scandinavia* 5(2): 3–30.

———. 1990. *Gyldendals og Politikens Danmarkshistorie.* Vol. 11, *Det folkelige gennembrud og dets mænd, 1850–1900.* Copenhagen: Gyldendalske Boghandel/Nordisk Forlag/Politikens Forlag.

Hviid, Morten. 2006. "Incentive Pay in the Danish Cooperative Dairies." *Advances in the Economic Analysis of Participatory and Labor-Managed Firms* 9: 149–76.

Hyldtoft, Ole. 1984. *Københavns industrialisering 1840–1914.* Herning: Systime.

———. 1999. *Danmarks økonomiske historie 1840–1910.* Aarhus: Systime.

Irish Agricultural Organization Society. 1921. *Annual Reports of the Irish Agricultural Organisation Society 1921.* Dublin: Irish Agricultural Organization Society.

Iversen, Peter Kr. 1992. "Hollænderier i Sønderjylland i 1600- og 1700-årene." *Sønderjyske Årbøger* 1992: 73–111.

Jacks, David S., Kevin H. O'Rourke, and Jeffrey G. Williamson. 2011. "Commodity Price Volatility and World Market Integration since 1700." *Review of Economics and Statistics* 93(3): 800–813.

Jacobsen, Kurt. 2003. "The Great Northern Telegraph Company and the British Empire 1869–1945." In *Britain and Denmark: Political, Economic and Cultural Relations in the 19th and 20th Centuries,* edited by Jorgen Sevaldsen, 199–229. Copenhagen: Museum Tusculanum Press.

Jakobs, Alfred, and Hans Richter. 1935. *Die Großhandelspreise in Deutschland von 1792 bis 1934.* Institut für Konjunkturforschung. Hamburg: Hanseatische Verlagsanstalt. Sonderhefte.

Jenkins, Henry M. 1876. *Report on the Agriculture of the Kingdom of Denmark with a Note on the Farming of the Duchies of Schleswig and Holstein.* London: William Clowes and Sons.

———. 1882. *Royal Commission on Agriculture. Reports of the Assistant Commissioners. Mr. Jenkins' Reports on Denmark and the North of France.* British Parliamentary Papers, Report from Her Majesty's Commissioners on Agriculture. London: HMSO.

———. 1884. *Royal Commission on Technical Instruction. Report of Agricultural Education in North Germany, France, Denmark, Belgium, Holland, and the United Kingdom.* British Parliamentary Papers, C. 3981-I.

Jensen, Einar. 1937. *Danish Agriculture Its Economic Development; A Description and Economic Analysis Centering on the Free Trade Epoch, 1870–1930.* Copenhagen: J. H. Schultz.

Jensen, Peter S., Markus Lampe, Paul Sharp, and Christian V. Skovsgaard. 2017. "A Land 'of Milk and Butter': The Role of Elites for the Economic Development of Denmark." Paper presented at the Eighth World Congress of Cliometrics, Cliometric Society, Strasbourg, France, July.

Jensen, S. P. 1982. "Den teknologiske udvikling i landbruget." *Tidsskrift for Landøkonomi* 4: 149–62.

———. 1985. "Landbrugets systemskifte 1870–1914 belyst gennem dagbøger og regnskaber fra et enkelt gård." *Bol og By. Landbohistorisk Tidsskrift* 1985(2): 56–101.

———. 1987. "Agrarøkologi og landbrugsudvikling i det 18. og 19. Århundrede." *Bol og By. Landbohistorisk Tidsskrift* 1987(2): 82–136.

———. 1988a. "Landbruget 1860–1914—production og teknologi—." In *Det danske landbrugs historie 1810–1914,* edited by Claus Bjørn, 243–49. Odense: Landbohistorisk Selskab.

———. 1988b. "Husdyrbruget 1860–1914." In *Det danske landbrugs historie 1810–1914,* edited by Claus Bjørn, 313–50. Odense: Landbohistorisk Selskab.

———. 1998. "Kobbelbrug, kløver og kulturjord." *Bol og By* 1998(1): 36–59.

———. 2007. "Væksten i dansk landbrug fra 1760 til 1860." In *Fra stilstand til vækst: Studier i dansk landbrugs udvikling fra 1682 til 1914,* 125–52. Auning: Landbohistorisk Selskab.

Jespersen, Knud J. V. 2004. *A History of Denmark.* Houndmills: Palgrave Macmillan.

Johansen, Hans C. 1975. "Krisen kommer til Danmark: Strukturændringer og krisepolitik i 1930erne." *Berlingske Leksikon Bibliotek* 98: 64–73.

———. 1998. "Food Consumption in the Pre-industrial Nordic Countries." *Scandinavian Economic History Review* 46(1): 11–23.

———. 2002. *Danish Population History, 1600–1939.* University of Southern Denmark in History and Social Sciences. Odense: University Press of Southern Denmark.

———. 2005. "The Standard of Living in Denmark in the Eighteenth and Early Nineteenth Centuries." In *Living Standards in the Past: New Perspectives on Well-Being in Asia and Europe*, edited by Robert C. Allen, Tommy Bengtsson, and Martin Dribe, 307–17. Oxford: Oxford University Press.

Johnson, D. Gale. 1993. "Role of Agriculture in Economic Development Revisited." *Agricultural Economics* 8: 421–34.

Johnston, Bruce F., and John W. Mellor. 1961. "The Role of Agriculture in Economic Development." *American Economic Review* 51(4): 566–93.

Jones, Eric L. 1987. *The European Miracle. Environments, Economies and Geopolitics in the History of Europe and Asia*. Cambridge: Cambridge University Press.

Jónsson, Gudmundur. 2012. "The Impossible Dream: Transferring the Danish Agricultural Model to Iceland." In *Alan S. Milward and a Century of European Change*, edited by Fernando Guiaro, Frances M. B. Lynch, and Sigfrido M. Ramírez Pérez, 206–20. London: Routledge.

Juselius, Katarina. 2006. *The Cointegrated VAR Model, Methodology and Applications*. Oxford: Oxford University Press.

Kærgård, Niels. 2007. "Tidsskrift for Landøkonomi og Landhusholdningsselskabet: historien kort." *Tidsskrift for Landøkonomi* 193(1): 11–22.

Kayser Nielsen, Niels. 2012. "Denmark 1740–1940. A Centralized Cultural Community." In *Nordic Paths to Modernity*, edited by Johann P. Árnasson and Björn Wittrock, 68–88. New York: Berghahn.

K. H. 1865. "Et Bondemælkeriregnskab." *Ugeskrift for Landmænd* 1865(2): 117–19.

Khaustova, Ekaterina, and Paul Sharp. 2015. "A Note on Danish Living Standards through Historical Wage Series, 1731–1913." *Journal of European Economic History* 44(3): 143–72.

Kindleberger, Charles P. 1951. "Group Behavior and International Trade." *Journal of Political Economy* 59(1): 30–46.

Kjærgaard, Thorkild. 1980. *Konjunkturer og afgifter. C. D. Reventlows betænkning af 11. februar 1788 om hoveriet*. Copenhagen: Landbohistorisk Selskab.

———. 1985. "The Farmer Interpretation of Danish history." *Scandinavian Journal of History* 10(2): 97–118.

———. 1989. "The Rise of Press and Public Opinion in Eighteenth-Century Denmark-Norway." *Scandinavian Journal of History* 14(4): 215–30.

———. 1994. *The Danish Revolution, 1500–1800 an Ecohistorical Interpretation*. Cambridge: Cambridge University Press.

Klitmøller, Linda. 2008. *Som en skorsten: Mejeribrugets udannelser i Danmark 1837–1972*. Auning: Landbohistorisk Selskab.

Klovland, Jan T., and Peter M. Solar. 2011. "New Series for Agricultural Prices in London, 1770–1914." *Economic History Review* 64: 72–87.

Kohl, Johann G. 1846. *Reisen in Dänemark und den Herzogthümern Schleswig und Holstein*. Vol. 1. Leipzig: F. A. Brockhaus.

Kopsidis, Michael. 2014. "Bäuerliche Landwirtschaft und Agarwachstum: Südosteuropa im Licht moderner Entwicklungstheorie." *Jahrbuch für Wirtschaftsgeschichte* 2014(1): 65–92.

Korsgaard, Ove. 2006. "The Danish Way to Establish the Nation in the Hearts of the People." In *National Identity and the Varieties of Capitalism: The Danish Experience*, edited by John L. Campbell, John A. Hall and Ove K. Pedersen, 133–58. Montreal: McGill-Queen's University Press.

Korsgaard, Ove, and Susanne Wiborg. 2006. "Grundtvig—The Key to Danish Education?" *Scandinavian Journal of Educational Research* 50(3): 361–82.

Kristensen, Niels B. 1987. "Indeksproblemet i Sv. Aa. Hansens væksttal, 1855–1913." In *To analyser af dansk industrialisering før 1914*, by Niels Buus Kristensen and Sven Wunder. Copenhagen: Department of Economics, University of Copenhagen Blåt Memo 161.

———. 1989. "Industrial Growth in Denmark, 1872–1913—In Relation to the Debate on an Industrial Break-Through." *Scandinavian Economic History Review* 37: 3–22.

Kristensen, Peer H., Maja Lotz, and Robson Rocha. 2011. "Denmark: Tailoring Flexicurity for Changing Roles in Global Games." In *Nordic Capitalisms and Globalization. New Forms of Economic Organization and Welfare Institutions*, edited by Peer H. Kristensen and Kari Lilja, 86–140. Oxford: Oxford University Press.

Krugman, Paul. 1993. "The Hub Effect: Or, Threeness in Interregional Trade." In *Theory, Policy and Dynamics in International Trade: Essays in Honor of Ronald W. Jones*, edited by Wilfred J. Ethier, Elhanan Helpman, and Jo P. Neary, 29–37. Cambridge: Cambridge University Press.

Krusius-Ahrenberg, Lolo. 1947. *Carl Frederik Gyllembourg-Ehrensvärd som dansk lantbruksekonom*. Svenska litteratursällskapet i Finland historiska och litteraturhistoriska studier 23. Helsinki: Helsingfors.

Kumar, Praduman, Anjani Kumar, Shinoj Parappurathu, and S. S. Raju. 2011. "Estimation of Demand Elasticity for Food Commodities in India." *Agricultural Economics Research Review* 24: 1–14.

Kumbhakar, Subal C., B. Biswas, and D. Bailey. 1989. "A Study of Economic Efficiency of Utah Dairy Farmers: A System Approach." *Review of Economics and Statistics* 71(4): 595–604.

Kumbhakar, Subal C., S. Ghosh, and J. T. McGuckin. 1991. "A Generalized Production Frontier Approach for Estimating Determinants of Inefficiency in U.S. Dairy Farms." *Journal of Business and Economic Statistics* 9(13): 279–86.

Kumbhakar, Subal C., and C. A. K. Lovell. 2000. *Stochastic Frontier Analysis*. Cambridge: Cambridge University Press.

L. 1868. "Om Kohold og Mælkeriregnskaber." *Ugeskrift for Landmænd* 1868(1): 288–93.

Ladewig Petersen, Erling. 1970. "The Danish Cattle Trade During the Sixteenth and Seventeenth Centuries." *Scandinavian Economic History Review* 18(1): 69–85.

———. 2002. *Magtstat og godsdrift det danske ressourcesystem 1630–1730*. Copenhagen: Reitzel.

Laing, Samuel. 1852. *Observations on the Social and Political State of Denmark, and the Duchies of Sleswick and Holstein in 1851: Being the Third Series of the Notes of a Traveller on the Social and Political State of the European People*. London: Longman, Brown, Green, and Longmans.

Lampe, Markus. 2008. "Bilateral Trade Flows in Europe, 1857–1875: A New Dataset." *Research in Economic History* 26: 81–155.

———. 2011. "Explaining Nineteenth-Century Bilateralism: Economic and Political Determinants of the Cobden-Chevalier Network." *Economic History Review* 64(2): 644–68.

Lampe, Markus, and Paul Sharp. 2011. "Something Rational in the State of Denmark? The Case of an Outsider in the Cobden-Chevalier Network 1860–1875." *Scandinavian Economic History Review* 59: 128–48.

———. 2014a. "Greasing the Wheels of Rural Transformation? Margarine and the Competition for the British Butter Market." *Economic History Review* 67(3): 769–92.

———. 2014b. "Tidsskrift for Landøkonomi og udvikling af modern mejeribrug i Danmark." *Tidsskrift for Landøkonomi* 200(1): 91–100.

———. 2014c. "How the Danes Discovered Britain: The International Integration of the Danish Dairy Industry before 1880." European Historical Economics Society Working Paper 66.

———. 2015a. "Just Add Milk: A Productivity Analysis of the Revolutionary Changes in Nineteenth-Century Danish Dairying." *Economic History Review* 68(4): 1132–53.

————. 2015b. "How the Danes Discovered Britain: The International Integration of the Danish Dairy Industry before 1880." *European Review of Economic History* 19(4): 432–53.

————. 2016. "Cliometric Approaches to International Trade." In *Handbook of Cliometrics*, edited by Claude Diebolt and Michael Haupert, 295–300. Heidelberg: Springer.

————. 2017. "A Quest for Useful Knowledge: The Early Development of Agricultural Accounting in Denmark and Northern Germany." *Accounting History Review* 27(1): 73–99.

Landes, David S. 1999. *The Wealth and Poverty of Nations: Why Some Are So Rich and Some So Poor*. London: Abacus.

Larsen, C. C. 1924–32. "Faaret." In *Det danske landbrugs historie*, vol. 3, *Husdyrbruget*, edited by Kristian Hansen, 579–643. Copenhagen: G. E. C. Gads.

Larsen, Hans K., Søren Larsen, and Carl-Alex Nilsson. 2010. "Landbrug og industri i Danmark 1896–1965: Nye beregninger af BFI inden for de varefremstillende sektorer." *Historisk Tidsskrift* 110(2): 358–401.

Lassen, Aksel. 1965. *Fald og fremgang. Træk af befolkningsudviklingen i Danmark 1645–1960*. Aarhus: Universitetsforlag.

Lassen, K. C. 1883. "Udviklingen af Dampskibstrafikken fra Danmark til Storbritannien." *Tidsskrift for Landøkonomi* 5(2): 384–419.

Leegaard, Johannes. 1878. "Mejeriberetning fra det nordvestlige Jylland." *Tidsskrift for Landøkonomi* 4(12): 83–95.

Lenin, Wladimir I. 1973. *Collected Works*. Vol. 18. Moscow: Progress Publishers.

Lerche, Grith. 1999. *The Royal Veterinary and Agricultural University, Its Contribution to Rural Education and Research in Denmark: An Introduction*. Frederiksberg: Royal Veterinary and Agricultural University.

Lewis, Arthur W. 1954. "Economic Development with Unlimited Supplies of Labour." *Manchester School of Economic and Social Studies* 28(2): 139–91.

Lindert, Peter H., and Jeffrey G. Williamson. 1983. "English Workers' Living Standards during the Industrial Revolution: A New Look." *Economic History Review* 36(1): 1–25.

Linvald, Axel. 1905–8. "Antvorskov og Vordingborg Krongodser 1768–1774." *Fra Arkiv og Museum* 3: 234–89.

————. 1912. "Hvem ejede Danmarks Jord omkring Midten af det 18. Aarhundrede?" *Historisk Tidsskrift* 4(8): 147–58.

Lizzeri, Alessandro, and Nicola Persico. 2004. "Why Did the Elites Extend the Suffrage? Democracy and the Scope of Government, with an Application to Britain's 'Age of Reform.'" *Quarterly Journal of Economics* 119(2): 707–65.

Ljungberg, Jonas, and Lennart Schön. 2013. "Domestic Markets and International Integration: Paths to Industrialization in the Nordic Countries." *Scandinavian Economic History Review* 61: 101–21.

Logan, Trevon D. 2006. "Food, Nutrition, and Substitution in the Late Nineteenth Century." *Explorations in Economic History* 43: 527–45.

Løgstrup, Birgit. 1974. "Markdrift og hoveri på Løvenborg, 1771–72." *Bol og By* 8: 22–57.

————. 1984. "The Landowner as Public Administrator: The Danish Model." *Scandinavian Journal of History* 9(4): 283–312.

————. 2015. *Bondens frisættelse. De danske landboreformer 1750–1810*. Copenhagen: G. E. C. Gads.

Løkke, Anne. 2007. "State and Insurance: The Long-Term Trends in Danish Health Policy from 1672 to 1973." *Hygiea Internationalis* 6: 7–24.

MacGregor, John, 1850. *Commercial Tariffs and Regulations, Resources, and Trade, of the Several*

States of Europe and America, vol. 23, *Appendices to the Commercial Reports*. London: Charles Whiting.

Madan, Gurmukh R. 2007. *Co-operative Movement in India—A Critical Appraisal*. New Delhi: Mittal Publications.

Maddison, Angus. 2006. *The World Economy: A Millennial Perspective*. Developmental Centre Studies. Paris: OECD.

Manniche, Jens Christian. 1997. "Den østdanske epidemi 1831." *Historie/Jyske Samlinger* 1997(2): 244–80.

Manniche, Peter. 1969. *Denmark: A Social Laboratory*. Oxford: Pergamon.

Marchtaler, Hildegard von. 1959. "Donner, Conrad Hinrich." *Neue Deutsche Biographie* 4: 73.

Matsuyama, Kiminori. 1992. "Agricultural Productivity, Comparative Advantage, and Economic Growth." *Journal of Economic Theory* 58(2): 317–34.

McLaughlin, Eoin. 2015. "Competing Forms of Cooperation? Land League, Land War and Co-operation in Ireland, 1879–1914." *Agricultural History Review* 63(1): 81–112.

McLaughlin, Eoin, and Paul Sharp. 2015. "Competition between Organisational Forms in Danish and Irish Dairying around the Turn of the Twentieth Century." University of St Andrews Discussion Papers in Environmental Economics 2015(16).

m-e-. 1859. "Om Mælkens Værdi efter dens Anvendelse." *Ugeskrift for Landmænd* 1859: 353–57.

———. 1862a. "Om Meieriregnskaber." *Ugeskrift for Landmænd* 1862: 157–60.

———. 1862b. "Om Udbyttet af Svineholdet." *Ugeskrift for Landmænd* 1862: 202–4.

Mellinger, Andrew D., Jeffrey D. Sachs, and John L. Gallup. 2000. "Climate, Coastal Proximity, and Development." In *The Oxford Handbook of Economic Geography*, edited by Gordon L. Clark, Maryann P. Feldman and Meric S. Gertler, 170–94. Oxford: Oxford University Press.

Menezes, Tatiane A., Carlos R. Azzoni, and Fernando G. Silveira. 2008. "Demand Elasticities for Food Products in Brazil: A Two-Stage Budgeting System." *Applied Economics* 40(19): 2557–72.

Meyer, Karl. 1916. *De forenede Bryggerier 1891–1916: bidrag til bryggeriernes historie i anledning af 25-års dagen for selskabets stiftelse*. Copenhagen: Levison.

Miller, Geoffrey P. 1989. "Public Choice at the Dawn of the Special Interest State: The Story of Butter and Margarine." *California Law Review* 77(1): 83–131.

Milward, Alan S. 1979. "Strategies for Development in Agriculture: The Nineteenth-Century European Experience." In *The Search for Wealth and Stability: Essays in Economic and Social History Presented to M. W. Flinn*, edited by Thomas C. Smout, 21–42. London: Macmillan.

Mitchell, Brian R. 2003. *International Historical Statistics—Europe 1750–2000 and the Americas 1750–2000*. 5th ed. Basingstoke: Palgrave Macmillan.

Mokyr, Joel. 1999. "Editor's Introduction: The New Economic History and the Industrial Revolution." In *The British Industrial Revolution: an Economic Perspective*, edited by Joel Mokyr, 1–127. Boulder: Westview.

———. 2002. *The Gifts of Athena: Historical Origins of the Knowledge Economy*. Princeton, NJ: Princeton University Press.

———. 2005. "Long-Term Economic Growth and the History of Technology." In *Handbook of Economic Growth*, vol. 1, part B, chapter 17, edited by Philippe Aghion and Steven N. Durlauf, 1113–80. Amsterdam: Elsevier.

———. 2009. *The Enlightened Economy: An Economic History of Britain 1700–1850*. New Haven, CT: Yale University Press.

Mokyr, Joel, and José-A. Espín-Sánchez. 2013. "The Institutional Revelation: A Comment on Douglas W. Allen's *The Institutional Revolution*." *Review of Austrian Economics* 26(4): 375–81.

Møller, A. M. 1998. *Dansk søfarts historie.* Vol. 4, *1814–1870: Med korn og kul.* Copenhagen: Gyldendal.

Møller, Per Grau. 2016. "Husmandskolonier fra udskiftningstiden." *Landbohistorisk Tidsskrift* 13: 29–72.

Montesquieu, Charles. (1748) 1989. *The Spirit of Laws.* New York: Cambridge University Press.

Mordhorst, Mads. 2014. "Arla and Danish National Identity—Business History as Cultural History." *Business History* 56(1): 116–33.

Munck, Thomas. 1977. "The Economic and Social Position of Peasant Freeholders in Late Seventeenth-Century Denmark." *Scandinavian Economic History Review* 25(1): 37–61.

Mundlak, Yair. 2000. *Agriculture and Economic Growth.* Cambridge, MA: Harvard University Press.

Nielsen, Sven B. 1977. "Landbrugseksportens varemæssige sammensætning og geografiske spredning 1850–90." *Bol og By* 2(1): 37–64.

North, Douglass C., Joseph Wallis, and Barry Weingast. 2009. *Violence and Social Orders. A Conceptual Framework for Interpreting Recorded Human History.* Cambridge: Cambridge University Press.

O'Brien, Patrick, and Calgar Keyder. 1978. *Economic Growth in Britain and France 1780–1914. Two Paths to the Twentieth Century.* London: Allen and Unwin.

Ó Gráda, Cormac. 1977. "The Beginnings of the Irish Creamery System, 1880–1914." *Economic History Review* 30: 284–305.

———. 1994. *Ireland: A New Economic History.* Oxford: Clarendon.

———. 2006. "Irish Agriculture after the Land War." In *Land Rights, Ethno-Nationality, and Sovereignty in History,* edited by Stanley L. Engerman and Jacob Metzer, 131–52. London: Routledge.

Olesen, Peter T. 1977. "Omlægningen fra vegetabilsk til animalsk production i dansk landbrug efter ca. 1850." *Bol og By* 2(1): 10–36.

Olmstead, Alan L., and P. W. Rhode. 2008. *Creating Abundance. Biological Innovation and American Agricultural Development.* Cambridge: Cambridge University Press.

Olsen, Gunnar. 1957. *Hovedgård og bondegård sudier over stordriftens udvikling i Danmark i tiden 1525–1774.* Landbohistoriske skrifter; 1. København: Rosenkilde og Bagger.

O'Rourke, Kevin H. 1997. "European Grain Invasion, 1870–1913." *Journal of Economic History* 57(4): 775–801.

———. 2006. "Late Nineteenth-Century Denmark in an Irish Mirror: Land Tenure, Homogeneity and the Roots of Danish Success." In *National Identity and the Varieties of Capitalism: The Danish Experience,* edited by John L. Campbell, John A. Hall, and Ove K. Pedersen, 159–96. Montreal: McGill-Queen's University Press.

———. 2007. "Culture, Conflict and Cooperation: Irish Dairying before the Great War." *Economic Journal* 117: 1357–79.

Østergaard, Bent. 2007. *Indvandrerne i Danmarks historie.* Odense: Syddansk Universitetsforlag.

Østergård, Uffe. 1992. "Peasants and Danes—the Danish National Identity and Political-Culture." *Comparative Studies in Society and History* 34(1): 3–27.

———. 2006. "Denmark: A Big Small State—The Peasant Roots of Danish Modernity." In *National Identity and the Varieties of Capitalism: The Danish Experience,* edited by John L. Campbell, John A. Hall, and Ove K. Pedersen, 51–98. Montreal: McGill-Queen's University Press.

———. 2012. "The Danish Path to Modernity." In *Nordic Paths to Modernity,* edited by Johann P. Árnasson and Björn Wittrock, 49–68. New York: Berghahn.

Otto Mønsted, A/S. 1933. *Margarineindustrien i Danmark 1883–1933*. Copenhagen: Egmont H. Petersens Kgl. Hofbogtrykkeri.

Parker, R. H. 1997. "Roger North: Gentleman, Accountant and Lexicographer." *Accounting History* 2(2): 31–51.

Pedersen, Jan. 1999. *Teknologisk udvikling i maskinindustrien: Burmeister & Wain 1875–1939*. Lyngby: Polyteknisk Forlag.

Pedersen, Kurt, Jesper Strandskov, and Peter Sørensen. 2005. *Philip W. Heyman*. Copenhagen: Systime Academic/Gyldendal.

Pedersen, M. C. (1885) 1981. *Beretning om Andelsmaelkerivirksomheden i Vestjylland 1884–85*. Esbjerg: Sydjysk Universitetsforlag.

Pedersen, Peder J. 1996. "Postwar Growth of the Danish Economy." In *Economic Growth in Europe since 1945*, edited by Nicolas Crafts and Gianni Toniolo, 554–74. Cambridge: Cambridge University Press.

Peet, Richard. 1972. "Influences of the British Market on Agriculture and Related Economic Development in Europe before 1860." *Transactions of the Institute of British Geographers* 56: 1–20.

Perren, Richard. 1971. "The North American Beef and Cattle Trade with Great Britain, 1870–1914." *Economic History Review* 24(3): 430–44.

Persson, Karl G., and Paul Sharp. 2015. *An Economic History of Europe: Knowledge, Institutions and Growth, 600 to the Present*. Cambridge: Cambridge University Press.

Pietrocòla-Rossetti, Teodorico. 1864. "Condizioni politiche e statistiche sulla Danimarca." *Rivista Contemporanea Nazionale Italiana* 36(12).

Pontoppidan, Erik. 1763–81. *Den Danske Atlas eller Konge-Riget Dannemark*. Copenhagen: A. H. Godiche (reprint Copenhagen: Rosenkilde & Bagger, 1968–72).

Porskrog Rasmussen, Carsten. 1987. *Det danske godssystem—udvikling og afvikling 1500–1919*. Aarhus: Forlaget Historia.

———. 2003. *Rentegods og hovedgårdsdrift: Godsstruktur og godsøkonomi i hertugdømmet Slesvig 1524–1770*. Vol. 1, *Fremstilling*. Aabenraa: Institut for grænseregionsforskning.

———. 2010a. "A. G. Moltke og det holstenske kobbelbrug." *Landbohistorisk Tidsskrift* 2: 9–48.

———. 2010b. "Innovative Feudalism: The Development of Dairy Farming and Koppelwirtschaft on Manors in Schleswig-Holstein in the Seventeenth and Eighteenth Centuries." *Agricultural History Review* 58(2): 172–90.

Poulsen, C. M. 1851a. *Behandlingen af de jydske Producter for det engelske Marked, medeelte i et Brev fra London, Decbr. 1850*. Copenhagen: Berlingske Bogtrykkeri.

———. 1851b. *Om Vigtigheden af Jyllands Handelsforbindelse med England*. Copenhagen: Berlingske Bogtrykkeri.

Prados de la Escosura, Leandro. 2000. "International Comparisons of Real Product, 1820–1990: An Alternative Data Set." *Explorations in Economic History* 37(1): 1–41.

Prange, Wolfgang. 1971. *Die Anfänge der großen Agrarreformen in Schleswig-Holstein bis um 1771*. Neumünster: Karl Wachholtz.

Prebisch, Raúl. 1950. *The Economic Development of Latin America and Its Principal Problems*. Lake Success, NY: United Nations Department of Economic Affairs.

Putnam, Robert D. 1995. "Bowling Alone: America's Declining Social Capital." *Journal of Democracy* 6(1): 65–78.

———. 2001. "Social Capital: Measurement and Consequences." *Canadian Journal of Policy Research* 2(1): 41–51.

Raaschou-Nielsen, Agnete. 1990. "Danish Agrarian Reform and Economic Theory." *Scandinavian Economic History Review* 38(3): 44–61.

Radu, Christina. 2016. "Real wages in Denmark, 1660–1800." Unpublished manuscript, University of Southern Denmark, last modified September 14, 2016.

Ræder, Carl G. W. 1868a. "Om Kohold og Mælkeriregnskabe." *Ugeskrift for Landmænd* 1868(1): 230–34.

———. 1868b. "Om Kohold og Mælkeriregnskaber." *Ugeskrift for Landmænd* 1868(1): 331–37.

———. 1869a. "Om Kohold og Mælkeriregnskaber." *Ugeskrift for Landmænd* 1869(1): 85–90.

———. 1869b. "Om Kohold og Mælkeriregnskaber." *Ugeskrift for Landmænd* 1869(1): 249–52.

———. 1870. "Om Kohold og Mælkeriregnskaber." *Ugeskrift for Landmænd* 1870(2): 495–500.

———. 1875a. "Mælkeriet paa Dyrehavegaard." *Ugeskrift for Landmænd* 1875(1): 232–37.

———. 1875b. "Landbrugs-Bogholderi." *Ugeskrift for Landmænd* 1875(1): 461–64.

Rafner, Claus. 1986. "Fæstegårdmændenes skattebyrder 1660–1802." *Fortid og nutid* 33(2): 81–94.

Rainals, H. 1860. "Report upon the Past and Present State of the Agriculture of the Danish Monarchy; Its Products, with Comparative Tables of Exports." *Journal of the Royal Agricultural Society of England* 21: 267–328.

Randsborg, Klavs. 2009. *The Anatomy of Denmark. Archaeology and History from the Ice Age to the Present.* London: Gerald Duckworth.

Rasch, Aage. 1955. *Dansk toldpolitik 1760–1797.* Aarhus: Universitetsforlag.

Rasmussen, Jørgen D. 1982. "Dansk mejeribrug 1914–55." In *Dansk mejeribrug 1882–2000*, edited by Claus Bjørn, 189–308. Odense: De danske Mejeriers Fællesorganisation.

———. 1988a. "Befolkningen." In *Det danske landbrugs historie*, edited by Claus Bjørn, 209–17. Odense: Landbrughistorisk Selskab.

———. 1988b. "Brug of besiddelse." In *Det danske landbrugs historie*, edited by Claus Bjørn, 218–42. Odense: Landbrughistorisk Selskab.

Ravallion, Martin. 2009. "Are There Lessons for Africa from China's Success against Policy?" *World Development Report* 37(2): 303–13.

Reed, Albert J., J. William Levedahl, and Charles Hallahan. 2005. "The Generalized Composite Commodity Theorem and Food Demand Estimation." *American Journal of Agricultural Economics* 87(1): 28–37.

Riis, Thomas. 2009. *Wirtschafts- und Sozialgeschichte Schleswig-Holsteins. Leben und Arbeiten in Schleswig-Holstein vor 1800.* Kiel: Ludwig.

Rixen, Claus. 1800. "Gedanken eines Schleswigers über Einführung der Stallfütterung." *Annalen der niedersächsischen Landwirtschaft* 2(2): 360.

Røge, Pernille. 2014. "Why the Danes Got There First—A Trans-Imperial Study of the Abolition of the Danish Slave Trade in 1792." *Slavery and Abolition* 35(4): 576–92.

Roholt, Pernille. 2012. "Herregårdene i landskabet og på nettet—mere end 700 herregårde lige ved hånden." *Herregårdshistorie* 7: 161–66.

Rosenberg, Nathan. 1976. *Perspectives on Technology.* Cambridge: Cambridge University Press.

Rosenberg, Nathan, and L. E. Birdzell Jr. 1986. *How the West Grew Rich: The Economic Transformation of the Industrial World.* London: I. B. Tauris.

Rosenthal, Caitlin. 2013. "From Memory to Mastery: Accounting for Control in America, 1750–1880. Dissertation Summary." *Enterprise and Society* 14: 732–48.

Rostow, Walt W. 1960. *The Stages of Economic Growth.* Cambridge: Cambridge University Press.

Rützou, Poul. 1887. "Smørmarderne i Cork og Kjøbenhavn." *Tidsskrift for Landøkonomi* 5(6): 273–300.

Sandberg, Lars G. 1979. "The Case of the Impoverished Sophisticate: Human Capital and Swedish Economic Growth before World War I." *Journal of Economic History* 39(1): 225–41.

Scharling, H. William. 1892. "Die Handelspolitik Dänemarks 1864–1891." In *Die Handelspolitik der wichtigeren Kulturstaaten in den letzten Jahrzehnten*, edited by Verein für Socialpolitik, 273–301. Leipzig: Duncker & Humblot.

———. 1905. *Handels- og Toldpolitik.* Copenhagen: G. E. C. Gads Universitetsboghandel.

Schmidt, Urban. 1870. "Nogle Bemærkninger om Smørproduktionen og Smørhandelen." *Tidsskrift for Landøkonomi* 1870: 529–36.

Schneider, Eric B. 2014. "Prices and production: Agricultural Supply Response in Fourteenth-Century England." *Economic History Review* 67(1): 66–91.

Schousboe, Karen. 1978–79. "Foldudbytte og bondeøkonomi." *Fortid og nutid* 28: 35–49.

Schröder-Lembke, Gertrud. 1978. *Studien zur Agrargeschichte.* Quellen und Forschungen zur Agrargeschichte 31. Stuttgart: Gustav Fischer.

Schroll, Henning. 1869. "Om Kohold og Mælkeriregnskaber." *Ugeskrift for Landmænd* 1869(1): 189–94.

———. 1875. "Om Mælkerieregnskaber." *Ugeskrift for Landmænd* 1875(1): 431–46.

———. 1876. "Mejeriberetning for Fyen for Sommerhalvaaret 1876." *Tidsskrift for Landøkonomi* 4(10): 546–67.

———. 1878. "Mejeriberetning fra Fyn." *Tidsskrift for Landøkonomi* 4(12): 61–82.

Schulte Beerbühl, Margrit. 2013. "Trading with the Enemy. Clandestine Networks during the Napoleonic Wars." *Quaderni storici* 143: 541–65.

Scorgie, Michael E. 1997. "Progenitors of Modern Management Accounting Concepts and Mensurations in Pre-industrial England." *Accounting, Business and Financial History* 7(1): 31–59.

Segelcke, Thomas R. 1870. *Mejeridagbog til Brug paa Havarthigaard pr. Holte Station med særlig Hensyntagen til Tilvirkning af Cheddar- og Myseost m.m.* Copenhagen: printed as manuscript.

———. 1872. *Meierilærlingen. En Veiledning til første Bind af Optegnelsesbøger til Meieribrug.* Copenhagen: P. G. Philipsen (offprint from *Ugeskrift for Landmænd*).

———. 1877. *Bilag til Forelæsninger over Landbrugsbogholderi.* Frederiksberg: Kongelige Veterinær- og Landbohøjskole.

———. 1879. *Notes of the Dairy-Husbandry of Denmark.* Copenhagen: Bianco Lunos.

———. 1891. "Forelæsninger over Landbrugsbogholderi 1891, nedskrevne af Niels Larsen [handwritten lecture notes]." Edited by Kongelige Veterinær- og Landbohøjskole. Frederiksberg.

Sehested, N. Frederik B. A. 1857. "Med Hensyn til formen af Meieriopgørelser samt Anvendelsen af Koer til Malkekøer." *Tidsskrift for Landøkonomi* 3(5): 140–52.

———. 1858. "Nærmest med Hensyn til Formen af Meieriopgjørelser." *Tidsskrift for Landøkonomi* 3(6): 125–34.

Senghaas, Dieter. 1986. *The European Experience. A Historical Critique of Development Theory.* Lemington Spa: Berg Publishers.

Simpson, James. 2004. "Selling to Reluctant Drinkers: The British Wine Market, 1860–1914." *Economic History Review* 57: 80–108.

Singer, Hans W. 1950. "The Distribution of Gains between Investing and Borrowing Countries." *American Economic Review* 40: 473–85.

Singh, Asheibam S., Khajan Singh, Rita Chakravarty, V. G. Vairagar, and Chandan Kumar. 2012. "Constraints Perceived by Members of Manipur (India) Milk Producers Cooperative Union in Practicing Improved Dairy Farming." *Journal of Dairying, Foods and Home Sciences* 31(4): 279–83.

Skrubbeltrang, Fridlev. 1941. "Hoveriindberetninger som Kilder til dansk Landbrugshistorie." *Fodit og Nutid* 14: 1–28.

———. 1952. *The Danish Folk High Schools.* Copenhagen: Det Danske Selskab.

———. 1953. *Agricultural Development and Rural Reform in Denmark.* Rome: Food and Agriculture Organization of the United Nations.

———. 1978. *Det danske Landbosamfund 1500–1800.* Copenhagen: Den Danske Historiske Forening.

Slottved, Ejvind. 2014. "Landalmuen—især til Tieneste. Det Kgl. Danske Landhusholdningsselskabs anmærkninger i almanakken i mere end 200 år." *Tidsskrift for Landøkonomi* 200(1): 31–56.

Smits, Jan-P. 2008. "Technological Change, Institutional Development and Economic Growth in Dutch Agriculture, 1870–1939." In *Agriculture and Economic Development in Europe since 1870*, edited by Pedro Lains and Vincente Pinilla, 97–116. London: Routledge.

Sombart, Werner. 1916. *Der Moderne Kapitalismus.* Leipzig: Duncker & Humblot.

Sommestad, Lena, and Sally McMurry. 1998. "Farm Daughters and Industrialization: A Comparative Analysis of Dairying in New York and Sweden, 1860–1920." *Journal of Women's History* 10(2): 137–46.

Sonne, Christian. 1882. "Mejeribruget i Danmark 1881." *Tidsskrift for Landøkonomi* 5(1): 53–79.

———. 1883. "Mejeribruget i Danmark 1882." *Tidsskrift for Landøkonomi* 5(2): 33–60.

———. 1884. "Mejeribruget i Danmark 1883." *Tidsskrift for Landøkonomi* 5(3): 27–59.

———. 1885. "Mejeribruget i Danmark 1884." *Tidsskrift for Landøkonomi* 5(4): 37–72.

Squicciarini, Mara, and Nico Voigtländer. 2015. "Human Capital and Industrialization: Evidence from the Age of Enlightenment." *Quarterly Journal of Economics* 130(4): 1825–83.

———. 2016. "Knowledge Elites and Modernization: Evidence from Revolutionary France." NBER Working Paper 22779.

Stanziani, Alessandro. 2010. "Economic Information on International Markets: French Strategies in the Italian Mirror (Nineteenth–Early Twentieth Centuries)." *Enterprise and Society* 11: 26–64.

Statistics Denmark. 1911. "Landbrugsforhold i Danmark siden Midten af det 19. Aarhundrede." In *Statistisk Tabelværk*, 5, C, 4. Copenhagen.

Statistisk Tabelværk. Danmarks vareindførsel og -udførsel [1838–1881]. 1841–82. Copenhagen: Bianco Lunos/Det Statistiske Bureau.

Storch, Vilhelm. 1886. "To Udstillingsforsøg med Ost af skummet Mælk." *Tidsskrift for Landøkonomi* 5(5): 589–641.

Strandskov, Jesper, Peter Sørensen, and Kurt Pedersen. 1998. *Pioneren Otto Mønsted—Sig navnet.* Aarhus: Forlaget Systime A/S.

Stråth, Bo. 2012. "Nordic Modernity: Origins, Trajectories, Perspectives." In *Nordic Paths to Modernity*, edited by J. P. Árnasson and B. Wittrock, 25–48. New York: Berghahn.

Svendsen, Gert T., and Lind H. Svendsen. 2010. "From Vikings to Welfare. Early State Building and Social Trust in Scandinavia." Paper presented at the International Society for New Institutional Economics Annual Conference 2010. University of Stirling (Scotland).

Tabellarische Übersichten des Hamburgischen Handels [1850–1872]. 1851–73. Hamburg: Kümpel.

Tables of the Revenue, Population, Commerce, &c. of the United Kingdom and Its Dependencies. Compiled from Official Returns [Years 1820–40, 1851–52]. 1835–43, 1854. London: HMSO.

Tauer, Loren W. 2001. "Efficiency and Competitiveness of the Small New York Dairy Farm." *Journal of Dairy Science* 84: 2573–76.

Tawney, Richard H. 1926. *Religion and the Rise of Capitalism*. London: John Murray.

Tena-Junguito, Antonio, Markus Lampe, and Felipe Tâmega. 2012. "How Much Trade Liberalization Was There in the World Before and After Cobden-Chevalier?" *Journal of Economic History* 72(03): 708–40.

Tesdorpf, Edward. 1856. "Er det rigtig at give Malkeqvæget et kraftigt Foder?" *Ugeskrift for Landmænd* 1856: 81–85.

———. 1861. "Meierierne paa Ourupgaard og Giedsergaard." *Ugeskrift for Landmænd* 1861: 207–18.

———. 1866. "Om Anvendelsen af kunstig Gjødning." *Ugeskrift for Landmænd* 1866(2): 142–48.

———. 1867. "Meddelselser om Agerbruget paa Ourupgaard, Gjedsergaard etc." *Tidsskrift for Landøkonomi* 4(1): 20–31.

———. 1868. "Mejeriregnskaberne for Aaret 1866–67 fra Ourupgaard og Gjedsergaard." *Tidsskrift for Landøkonomi* 4(2): 239–44.

———. 1871. "Hvorvidt svarer Anvendelsen af en betydelig Driftskapital Regning i danske Agerbrug." *Tidsskrift for Landøkonomi* 4(5): 90–113.

———. 1874. "Hvilke Erfaringer i Vandmejeriet har man vundet i det sidste Aar?" *Tidsskrift for Landøkonomi* 4(8): 449–73.

———. 1875. "Det sidste Aars Erfaringer angaaende de forskjellige Mejerisystemer." *Tidsskrift for Landøkonomi* 4(9): 486–506.

———. 1876. "Diskussion ved Udstillingen af Exportoste paa Landbohøjskolen den 15de Decbr. 1876." *Tidsskrift for Landøkonomi* 4(10): 568–81.

Tesdorpf, Edward, and Thomas R. Segelcke. 1862. *Mejeriregnskabsbog til ugentlige Optegnelser om Mejeridriften paa Ourupgaard, Gjedsergaard etc.* Copenhagen.

Thaer, Albrecht D. 1799. "Landwirthschaftliche Bemerkungen auf einer Reise durch Holstein und Mecklenburg (part II)." *Annalen der niedersächsischen Landwirtschaft* 1(1, 3): 102–68, 50–215.

———. 1801–4. *Einleitung zur Kenntniß der englischen Landwirtschaft*. Vol. 3. Hannover: Gebrüder Hahn.

———. 1806a. "Nachricht von einem herauskommenden dänischen Werke über landwirthschaftliche Buchführung nebst Reflexionen darüber." *Annalen des Ackerbaus* 4: 123–64.

———. 1806b. "Ueber meine Methode der landwirthschaftlichen Buchführung." *Annalen des Ackerbaus* 4: 467–624.

33. 1868. "Om Kohold og Mælkeriregnskaber." *Ugeskrift for Landmænd* 1868(1): 309–11.

Thomsen, Birgit N., and Brinley Thomas. 1965. *Dansk-engelsk samhandel: Et historisk rids 1661–1963*. Aarhus: Universitetsforlaget.

Thomsen, Niels. 1991. *Industri Stat og Samfund 1870–1939*. Odense: Odense Universitetsforlag.

Thorbrøgger, Schule T. 1816. *Tarif for Tolden i Danmark saaledes som den efter de seneste Anordninger erlægges i Rigsbankpenge rede Sølv*. Andet Oplag. Copenhagen: Schubothe.

———. 1823. *Tarif for Tolden i Danmark saaledes som den efter de seneste Anordninger erlægges i Rigsbankpenge rede Sølv. Tredie, med mange Tillæg forøgede Oplag*. Copenhagen: Schubothe.

Tilly, Charles. 1992. *Coercion, Capital, and European States AD 990–1992*. Oxford: Blackwell.

Tisserand, Eugène. 1865. *Études économiques sur le Danemark, le Holstein et le Slesvig*. Paris: Victor Masson et Fils.

Tomlinson, B. R. 2013. *The Economy of Modern India from 1860 to the Twenty-First Century*. 2nd ed. Cambridge: Cambridge University Press.

Toms, J. Steven. 2010. "Calculating Profit: A Historical Perspective on the Development of Capitalism." *Accounting, Organizations and Society* 35: 205–21.

Trampusch, Christine, and Dennis C. Spies. 2014. "Agricultural Interests and the Origins of Capitalism: A Parallel Comparative History of Germany, Denmark, New Zealand and the USA." *New Political Economy* 19(6): 918–42.

Treskow, Karl von. 1810. "Ueber Molkerei-Verpachtung." *Annalen des Ackerbaus* 12: 278–88.

Turner, Michael E., John V. Beckett, and Bethanie Afton. 2001. *Farm Production in England 1700-1914*. Oxford: Oxford University Press.

Valentiner, Adolph. 1856. "Meddelser om et Meieri." *Ugeskrift for Landmænd* 1856: 273–79.

———. 1858. "Bemærkninger ved hr. Jægermester Sehesteds Afhandlinger om Meieriregnskab." *Tidsskrift for Landøkonomi* 3(6): 349–53.

Valentiner, Heinrich N. 1876a. "Fra Sjælland." *Tidsskrift for Landøkonomi* 4(10): 314–19.

———. 1876b. "Mejeriberetninger for Sommerhalvaaret 1875–76. Fra Sjælland." *Tidsskrift for Landøkonomi* 4(10): 525–45.

Van der Vleuthen, Erik. 1994. "Smør og Damp." In *Made in Denmark. Nye studier i dansk teknologihistorie*, edited by Hans Buhl and Hanne Nielsen, 67–90. Aarhus: Klim.

Van Stuyvenberg, J. H. 1969. "Aspects of government intervention." In *Margarine: An Economic, Social, and Scientific History, 1869-1969*, edited by J. H. Van Stuyvenberg, 281–327. Liverpool: Liverpool University Press.

Van Zanden, Jan L. 1985. *De economische ontwikkeling van de Nederlandse landbouw in de negentiende eeuw, 1800-1914*. Wageningen: Brill.

———. 1988. "The First Green Revolution. The Growth of Production and Productivity in European Agriculture 1870-1914." Vrije Universiteit Amsterdam, Research memorandum 1988-42.

———. 1991. "The First Green Revolution. The Growth of Production and Productivity in European Agriculture." *Economic History Review* 44: 215–39.

Vestberg, Jens. 1933. "Koch, Cornelius Peter August, 1816–92." In *Dansk Biografisk Leksikon*, edited by P. Engelstoft, 22–23. Copenhagen: J. H. Schultz.

W. 1862. "En Forpagters Meieriregnskab." *Ugeskrift for Landmænd* 1862: 22.

Wade, William W. 1981. *Institutional Determinants of Technical Change and Agricultural Productivity Growth. Denmark, France, and Great Britain, 1870-1965*. New York: Arno Press.

Wassard, Hans M. 1864. "Om Malkekvæg og Mælkeriregnskaber." *Ugeskrift for Landmænd* 1864: 342–46.

Weber, J. Eduard. 1853. *Altona—Nicht Hamburg-Altona. Zur Würdigung der commerziellen Selbständigkeit und Bedeutung Altona's neben Hamburg*. Hamburg: Voigt.

Weber, Max. 1930. *The Protestant Ethic and the Spirit of Capitalism*. London: Allen & Unwin.

Westergaard, Harald. 1922. *Economic Development in Denmark: Before and During the World War*. Oxford: Clarendon Press.

Westring, G. F. 1866. "Kreaturudførelsen til England. 26 November 1866." *Ugeskrift for Landmænd* 1866(2): 355–56.

Willerslev, Rich. 1983. *Den glemte indvandring. Den svenske indvandring til Danmark 1850-1814*. Copenhagen: Gyldendal.

Williamson, Jeffrey G. 1994. "Coping with City Growth." In *The Economic History of Britain since 1700*, edited by Roderick Floud and Deidre N. McCloskey, 332–56. Cambridge: Cambridge University Press.

———. 2011. *Trade and Poverty. When the Third World Fell Behind*. Cambridge, MA: The MIT Press.

Wilson, John. 1867. *Report on the Agricultural Exhibitions at Vienna and Aarhuus (Denmark)*. British Parliamentary Papers, vol. 70. London: HMSO.

Winding, Kjeld. 1959. *Frihandelsproblemet i Danmark 1855–1863: En undersøgelse af 1863-tariffens tilblivelse*. Copenhagen: Dansk Videnskabs.

Winjum, James O. 1971. "Accounting and the Rise of Capitalism: An Accountant's View." *Journal of Accounting Research* 9(2): 333–50.

Winkel, Janus H. 1877. "Mejeriberetninger fra Jylland." *Tidsskrift for Landøkonomi* 4(11): 92–113.

———. 1878. "Mejeriberetninger fra Jylland (1876–77)." *Tidsskrift for Landøkonomi* 4(12): 478–87.

———. 1879. "Mejeribruget i Danmark 1878." *Tidsskrift for Landøkonomi* 4(13): 45–63.

———. 1880. "Mejeribruget i Danmark, 1878–79." *Tidsskrift for Landøkonomi* 4(14): 33–66.

Wood, Benjamin D. K., Carl H. Nelson, and Lia Nogueira. 2012. "Poverty Effects of Food Price Escalation: The Importance of Substitution Effects in Mexican Households." *Food Policy* 37(1): 77–85.

World Bank. 2007. *Agriculture for Development*. World Development Report 2008. Washington DC: World Bank.

———. 2009. "Agriculture: An Engine for Growth and Poverty Reduction. IDA at Work." International Development Association Working Paper 2009/09/01, World Bank, Washington, DC. http://documents.worldbank.org/curated/en/464451468324545355/IDA-at-work-agriculture-an-engine-for-growth-and-poverty-reduction.

Wright, Garvin. 1990. "The Origins of American Industrial Success, 1879–1940." *American Economic Review* 80(4): 651–68.

Wrigley, E. A. 2004. "British Population during the 'Long' Eighteenth Century, 1680–1840." In *The Cambridge Economic History of Modern Britain*, edited by Roderick Floud and Paul Johnson, 57–95. Cambridge: Cambridge University Press.

Wunder, Sven. 1987. "Aspekter af den danske industrialisering—en teoretisk-kvantitativ indfaldsvinkel." In *To analyser af dansk industrialisering før 1914*, by Niels Buus Kristensen and Sven Wunder. Copenhagen: Department of Economics, University of Copenhagen Blåt memo 161.

Yamey, Basil S. 1964. "Accounting and the Rise of Capitalism—Further Notes on a Theme by Sombart." *Journal of Accounting Research* 2(2): 117–36.

Zytphen-Adeler, Georg F. O. 1863. "Den daglige forretningsorden og Aflæggelsen af Regnskabet paa Hovedgaarden Adelersborg." *Tidsskrift for Landøkonomi* 3(11): 377–98.

Index

Numbers in italics refer to figures and tables.

Printed and bound by CPI Group (UK) Ltd, Croydon, CR0 4YY

16/04/2025

14658566-0001